The Protection of Foreign Investment in Times of Armed Conflict

The Protection of Foreign Investment in Times of Armed Conflict

JURE ZRILIČ

OXFORD
UNIVERSITY PRESS

OXFORD
UNIVERSITY PRESS

Great Clarendon Street, Oxford, OX2 6DP,
United Kingdom

Oxford University Press is a department of the University of Oxford.
It furthers the University's objective of excellence in research, scholarship,
and education by publishing worldwide. Oxford is a registered trade mark of
Oxford University Press in the UK and in certain other countries

First Edition published in 2019

Impression: 1

Published in the United States of America by Oxford University Press
198 Madison Avenue, New York, NY 10016, United States of America

British Library Cataloguing in Publication Data

Data available

Library of Congress Control Number: 2019941501

ISBN 978–0–19–883037–5

Printed and bound by
CPI Group (UK) Ltd, Croydon, CR0 4YY

Preface

The idea to examine investment treaties in the context of armed conflict took root against the background of a revolutionary wave that caught the Arab world at the end of 2010 and adversely affected foreign investment in the region. While investment treaties provide foreign investors with an avenue to pursue financial reparations for conflict-related losses from a host state, the practice and scholarship following 'Arab Spring' revolutions and the ongoing armed conflicts in the Middle East and Ukraine have revealed that there is lack of clarity about how effective and appropriate investment protections actually are in a conflict and post-conflict setting. This book sets out to address these questions by combining the insights from different areas of international law, including international investment law, international humanitarian law, international human rights law, the law of state responsibility, and the law of treaties. This is the first full and thorough treatment of the subject matter.

A key theme that runs throughout the book is the question of balancing competing objectives: on the one hand are investors' interests, certainty, and stability; and on the other hand, a state's sovereign right to protect its security interests and enable a smooth transition to peace. The book examines how these conflicting interests are balanced on four different levels: on the level of the application of investment treaties, on the level of the invocation of relevant treaty protections and host state defences against them, on the level of post-conflict compensation, and lastly, on the level of the resolution of conflict-related disputes. The analysis of this balancing dynamic informs the design of an analytical framework that purports to explain and evaluate how effective and appropriate is the application of the investment treaty regime in times of armed conflict.

The book offers insightful conclusions that could be of interest to practitioners, policy makers, and international law scholars. Over the past few years, international investment law has come under the severe scrutiny and ever stronger calls for its dismantlement. In my research, I show that despite the system's flaws and the need for a long-overdue reform, there is also a potential for its contribution to a better and safer world. In particular in periods of turmoil and armed conflict, the system's protections could become an important tool for inhibiting violence and arbitrariness. In view of the ongoing rise of nationalism, xenophobia, geopolitical tensions, and conflicts around the globe, this is something we ought not to forget.

Acknowledgements

The book is based on my doctoral thesis, completed in 2016 and defended in January 2017. Many people and institutions contributed to the completion of the book. My doctoral supervisor was Markus Gehring, whose aid and kindness I recall with much gratitude. I am much indebted to my examiners, Michael Waibel and Christoph Schreuer, who provided constructive and detailed comments in the *viva*, and kind encouragement later. Their support was invaluable in turning the thesis into this book. I have benefitted greatly from the stimulating intellectual environment at various institutions where parts of the book were written and revised, in particular the Hughes Hall College and the University of Cambridge, Harvard Law School, and the University of Liverpool School of Law and Social Justice. I am grateful to many colleagues who provided me with comments and advice that informed my work. I am especially thankful to Carsten Stahn, Mark Wu, Amandine Garde, Pádraig McAuliffe, Vassilis Tzevelekos, Mavluda Sattorova and Gregory Messenger. The book has benefitted from feedback received at various conferences, including the American Society of International Law Midyear Research Forum, Just Post Bellum Conference organized by Leiden University, and the Colloquium on International Investment Law & the Law of Armed Conflict organized by the European Society of International Law in Athens. Funding support, which made this project possible, came from the Arts and Humanities Research Council, and Slovene Human Resources Development and Scholarship Fund. Their aid is gratefully acknowledged. I thank the Oxford University Press, particularly, Jack McNichol, Natasha Flemming and Alison Thomas for their patience and help in the revision process, as well as the three anonymous reviewers for their insightful comments. Finally, I am immensely grateful to my friends, my partner, and my family, in particular my parents Irena and Bore. This book would not have been possible without their moral encouragement and continued support.

Table of Contents

Table of Cases

INTERNATIONAL COURTS AND TRIBUNALS

Permanent Court of International Justice (PCIJ)

International Court of Justice (ICJ)

International Tribunal for the Law of the Sea (ITLOS)

World Trade Organization Dispute Settlement Body

Iran–United States Claims Tribunal

International Criminal Tribunal for the Former Yugoslavia (ICTY)

International Criminal Tribunal for Rwanda (ICTR)

Eritrea–Ethiopia Claims Commission (EECC)

European Court of Justice (ECJ)/Court of Justice of the European Union (CJEU)

European Commission and European Court of Human Rights (ECtHR)

Inter-American Court of Human Rights (IACtHR)

Inter-State Arbitration

FRANCE–US CLAIMS COMMISSION 1880

US–CHILE CLAIMS COMMISSION 1901

FRANCE–VENEZUELA MIXED CLAIMS COMMISSION

GERMANY–VENEZUELA MIXED CLAIMS COMMISSION

ITALY–VENEZUELA MIXED CLAIMS COMMISSION

SPAIN–VENEZUELA MIXED CLAIMS COMMISSION

UK–VENEZUELA MIXED CLAIMS COMMISSION

Conciliation Commission

Mixed Arbitrations

AD HOC ARBITRATION

INTERNATIONAL CENTRE FOR THE SETTLEMENT OF INVESTMENT DISPUTES (ICSID)

INTERNATIONAL CHAMBER OF COMMERCE (ICC)

Table of Instruments and Legislation

INTERNATIONAL INSTRUMENTS

Treaties

International Investment Treaties and Free Trade Agreements

Model and Draft Treaties

OTHER DOCUMENTS

United Nations Resolutions

Preparatory Work

UNCTAD Reports

United Nations International Law Commission

Institute of International Law

Other

NATIONAL INSTRUMENTS

United Kingdom

United States

EU LEGISLATION

Directives

Select List of Abbreviations

ACHPR	African Charter on Human and People's Rights
ACHR	American Convention on Human Rights
AJIL	American Journal of International Law
AP I	First Protocol to the Geneva Conventions
AP II	Second Protocol to the Geneva Conventions
ARS	Articles on Responsibility of States for Internationally Wrongful Acts
ASIL	American Society of International Law
BIT	Bilateral Investment Treaty
BYIL	British Yearbook of International Law
COMESA	Common Market for Eastern and Southern Africa
EACT	Effects of Armed Conflicts on Treaties
ECHR	European Convention on Human Rights
EComHR	European Commission on Human Rights
ECtHR	European Court of Human Rights
EECC	Eritrea–Ethiopia Claims Commission
EFTA	European Free Trade Association
EHRR	European Human Rights Report
EJIL	European Journal of International Law
EU	European Union
FCC	Fundamental Change of Circumstances
FCN	Friendship, Commerce and Navigation
FDI	Foreign Direct Investment
FET	Fair and Equitable Treatment
FPS	Full Protection and Security
FTA	Free Trade Agreement
GDP	Gross Domestic Product
HILJ	Harvard International Law Journal
IACtHR	Inter-American Court of Human Rights
ICC	International Chamber of Commerce
ICCPR	International Covenant on Civil and Political Rights
ICESCR	International Covenant on Economic, Social and Cultural Rights
ICJ	International Court of Justice
ICLQ	International & Comparative Law Quarterly
ICLR	International Community Law Review
ICRC	International Committee of the Red Cross
ICSID	International Centre for Settlement of Investment Disputes
ICTY	International Criminal Tribunal for the Former Yugoslavia
IHL	International Humanitarian Law
ILA	International Law Association

ILC	International Law Commission
IRRC	International Review of the Red Cross
ITO	International Trade Organization
JCSL	Journal of Conflict and Security Law
JIEL	Journal of International Economic Law
JWIT	Journal of World Investment and Trade
JWT	Journal of World Trade
MAI	Multilateral Agreement on Investment
MFN	Most Favoured Nation
MJIL	Melbourne Journal of International Law
NAFTA	North American Free Trade Agreement
NGO	Non-Governmental Organization
NILR	Netherlands International Law Review
NPM	Non-Precluded Measures
NYIL	Netherlands Yearbook of International Law
OECD	Organisation for Economic Co-operation and Development
PCIJ	Permanent Court of International Justice
SIP	Supervening Impossibility to Perform
TWQ	Third World Quarterly
UDHR	Universal Declaration of Human Rights
UK	United Kingdom
UN	United Nations
UNCC	United Nations Compensation Commission
UNCTAD	United Nations Conference on Trade and Development
UNSC	United Nations Security Council
US	United States
VCLT	Vienna Convention on the Law of Treaties
VJTL	Vanderbilt Journal of Transnational Law

WTO .... World Trade Organization

1
Introduction

A. The Problem and the Questions

Mahiladittivu is a small Tamil village, surrounded by paddy fields and a lagoon, on the eastern coast of Sri Lanka. The villagers recall that there was a prawn farm that used to be the source of the local livelihood. The memory of the farm is attached to a particular event that forcefully interfered with their lives. On 28 January 1987, the Sri Lankan special task forces stormed into the village, besieging it from air, water, and land. Their target was the farm, where they rounded up the workers and the villagers who happened to be there, took them to the nearby road junction, and shot them. More than eighty Tamil civilians were killed, their bodies never to be retrieved. The farm was burnt to the ground and some of the prawns were eaten and the rest sold by the soldiers. One year later, these tragic events, as remembered by the witnesses of the massacre,[1] gave rise to an investment treaty arbitration, *AAPL v Sri Lanka*, initiated by the foreign investor who owned the farm.[2] The case perfectly encapsulates what this book is about, the situations it sets to investigate, the misconceptions it attempts to unravel, and ideas it purports to convey.

The book examines how foreign investment is protected under the investment treaty regime during times of armed conflict. There is little doubt that violent and politically volatile circumstances can adversely affect foreign investment. While investors may suffer general commercial losses as a natural consequence of political instability, they may also sustain direct injuries as a result of the actions or omissions of the host state. Political and social unrest may increase the likelihood of targeted attacks or other forms of selective interference with strategic assets by mobs, political opponents, or associated guerrillas. They may also make the investment prone to becoming a primary target of the host state's security forces if the investor's premises have been used by a party to a conflict or because of the investors' association with an enemy regime; for example, by seizing or freezing their assets in order to reduce the enemy's capacity to use force and compel its

[1] M Trawick, 'Lessons from Kokkadichcholai' (paper presented at International Conference on Tamil Nationhood and Search for Peace in Sri Lanka, 21–22 May 1999) <http://tamilnation.co/conferences/cnfCA99/trawick.html> accessed 18 December 2018; D McConnell, 'The Tamil People's Right to Self-Determination' (2008) 21(1) Cam Rev Intl Aff 59, 68; KT Rajasingham 'Sri Lanka: The Untold Story' (Online Asia Times, 30 March 2002) <http://www.atimes.com/ind-pak/DC30Df04.html> accessed 18 December 2018.

[2] *Asian Agricultural Products Ltd (AAPL) v Republic of Sri Lanka* ICSID Case no ARB/87/3, Award, 27 June 1990.

capitulation. These are not hypothetical situations; rather, they are real examples of losses that foreign investors have sustained in the past and have sought to recover through different remedial regimes.

The mistreatment of foreign investors in times of armed conflict has a long tradition. In the context of international warfare, the destruction and confiscation of enemy subjects' private property was permitted for a long time. While the English Magna Carta of 1215 stipulated that the property of enemy merchants residing in England should not be confiscated in wartime except by way of reprisals, even more enlightened views with respect to the treatment of private property emerged in the works of Hugo Grotius and French humanists after the French Revolution.[3] It was not until the eighteenth century that it became clear that states had certain obligations with respect to the treatment of alien property. The period spanning the eighteenth and nineteenth centuries was characterized by frequent internal strife in developing countries. Foreign investors who sustained losses in the midst of the violence often blamed their host state for either causing the injuries or failing to prevent them. Through the institution of diplomatic protection, they sought compensation via arbitration and before mixed claims commissions, which together built a body of jurisprudence. These precedents clarified that if a state had failed to exercise sufficient care in protecting foreign nationals, it could be held responsible for the injuries incurred by them, even if those losses were caused by non-state actors like mobs, rioters, and armed groups. The precise nature of that duty of care, however, was subject to debate, and reflected the opposing views of developing countries (who were usually the ones being sued) and developed countries (whose nationalities the foreign investors usually held). Consequently, several contemporary scholars engaged in the debate over state responsibility for injuries inflicted during times of conflict; moreover, the jurisprudence proved to be so influential that the codification of state responsibility was initially confined to the treatment of aliens alone.[4]

Since then, the legal framework governing the protection of foreign investors has gone through significant changes. In the second half of the twentieth century, countries have begun to enter into bilateral investment treaties (BITs) in which they agree to provide certain reciprocal treatment to investors who are nationals of the other contracting state. Somewhat revolutionarily, these treaties provide investors with a direct right to seek compensation for potential treaty violations from the host state via investor–state arbitration. The treaties also entail provisions that purport to protect investors from violent interferences, commonly effectuated in

[3] See Chapter 2 C.

[4] See e.g. E Huffcut, 'International Liability for Mob Injuries' (1891) 2 Ann Am Acad Pol Soc Sci 69; H Arias, 'The Non-liability of States for Damages Suffered by Foreigners in the Course of a Riot, an Insurrection or a Civil War' (1913) 7 AJIL 724; J Goebel, 'The International Responsibility of States for Injuries Sustained by Aliens on Account of Mob Violence, Insurrections and Civil Wars' (1914) 8 AJIL 802.

times of conflict, which have periodically been invoked in practice. As the number of treaties only really began to proliferate in the 1990s, until recently there had been relatively little opportunity to assess the application of treaty protections in times of armed conflict, and consequently the topic had attracted almost no attention.

However, a shift occurred in the wake of the political unrest and revolutions experienced in North African countries in 2010–11 (commonly referred to as 'Arab Spring' events)—particularly as a result of the revolution in Egypt and the civil war in Libya. Since many of these countries were (and are) parties to a number of BITs, the leading international law firms started publishing client alerts, suggesting that foreign investors could rely on BITs that afforded them effective protections and would enable them to bring lawsuits against the host states for losses sustained during the hostilities.[5] While several investment treaty claims emerged in the immediate aftermath of these conflicts,[6] the pace of claims has accelerated since 2017.[7] In parallel, the conflict in Ukraine in 2014 gave rise to another controversial cluster of conflict-related claims against Russia.[8] While the sudden increase of this type of arbitration claim clearly demonstrates the topicality of the subject matter investigated in this book, it is not a sole indicator of its relevance. Namely, in order to avoid costly litigation, the outcome of which is difficult to predict due to inconsistent interpretations of relevant investment treaty provisions, and to prevent related bad press that could deter prospective foreign investment, countries experiencing tumult may decide to settle claims instead, often on a confidential basis.

[5] See e.g. G Petrochilos and M Benedettelli, 'Investments in Libya: Potential Claims under Bilateral Investment Treaties and Political Risk Insurance Policies' (Freshfields Bruckhaus Deringer LLP, March 2011) <https://www.lexology.com/library/detail.aspx?g=c732662c-f387-45d8-bb26-03b58f9c0a9b> accessed 19 December 2018; M Levy et al, 'Civil Unrest and Sanctions: Implications for Investors in Libya' (Allen & Overy, 21 March 2011) <http://www.allenovery.com/publications/en-gb/Pages/Civil-Unrest-and-Sanctions--Implications-for-investors-in-Libya.aspx> accessed 19 December 2018; R Hill et al, 'New Business Opportunities Expected, but are Troubling Times also Ahead for Investors in Libya?' (Fulbright & Jaworsky, 6 September 2011) <https://www.lexisnexis.com/legalnewsroom/international-law/b/commentry/posts/fulbright-briefing-new-business-opportunities-expected-but-are-troubling-times-also-ahead-for-investors-in-libya> accessed 19 December 2018.

[6] See e.g. *Ampal-American Israel Corp and Others v Arab Republic of Egypt* ICSID Case no ARB/12/11 (pending); *Al Jazeera Media Network v Arab Republic of Egypt* ICSID Case no ARB/16/1 (pending); *Utsch and Others v Arab Republic of Egypt* ICSID Case no ARB/13/37 (discontinued); *Hussain Sajwani and Others v Arab Republic of Egypt* ICSID Case no ARB/11/16 (discontinued); *Yosef Maiman and Others v Arab Republic of Egypt*, UNCITRAL (not public).

[7] Over the past two years, Libya has been inundated with investment treaty claims. See L Peterson, 'As Libya Begins to See Wave of Investment Treaty Arbitrations, at Least Seven Turkish BIT Claims are Pursued at ICC' (IAReporter, 31 March 2017) <https://www.iareporter.com/articles/as-libya-begins-to-see-wave-of-investment-treaty-arbitrations-at-least-seven-turkish-bit-claims-at-icc/> accessed 19 December 2018.

[8] See e.g. *Aeroport Belbek LLC and Kolomoisky v Russian Federation* UNCITRAL, PCA Case no 2015-07 (pending); *JSC CB PrivatBank and Finilon LLC v Russian Federation* UNCITRAL, PCA Case no 2015-21 (pending); *Lugzor and Others v Russian Federation* UNCITRAL, PCA Case no 2015-29 (pending); *PJSC Ukrnafta v Russian Federation* UNCITRAL, PCA Case no 2015-34 (pending); *Stabil LLC and Others v Russian Federation* UNCITRAL, PCA Case no 2015-35 (pending); *Everest Estate LLC et al v Russian Federation* UNCITRAL, PCA Case no 2015-36, Award, 2 May 2018; *NJSC Naftogaz of Ukraine et al v Russian Federation* UNCITRAL, PCA Case no 2017-16 (pending).

For example, it was reported that Ethiopia had agreed to pay a generous amount of compensation to hundreds of foreign investors whose property was damaged in the course of riots that have afflicted the country since 2015.[9] Since the number of internal conflicts being experienced by contracting parties to BITs is on the rise (e.g. the civil war in Syria; the hostilities and insurgencies in countries like Mali, Nigeria, and Mozambique; the Yemeni civil war), and law firms continue to encourage investors to bring investment claims for conflict-related losses,[10] thereby highlighting the likelihood of being awarded damages, it is more than ever before important to re-examine the application of the investment treaty framework in the context of conflict.

There is a great deal of uncertainty as to the applicability and the scope of protections granted under the investment treaty framework in the context of armed conflict. The pre-Arab Spring investment arbitrations emerging from occasional violent strife gave rise to inconsistent, often inaccurate, and even contradictory interpretations of relevant treaty provisions, such as full protection and security and armed conflict clauses.[11] Since the doctrinal focus has been on other topics (e.g. financial crisis, environmental concerns) and treaty provisions (e.g. fair and equitable treatment, expropriation), these substantive standards have remained understudied and under-theorized. Consequently, investment law has been imbued with an unpredictability as to how effective the legal frameworks for protecting foreign investors against violence are.

In addition, the prospect of applying investment treaty protections during the tempestuous period of a conflict, when the state's control over its matters is seriously constrained, gives rise to important questions about the fairness and appropriateness of the international investment system. Some scholars have thus argued that investment treaties unfairly restrict a state's sovereignty to react to security concerns, and that other legal frameworks, notably international humanitarian law (IHL), may be more appropriate.[12] Furthermore, it has been argued that investment treaties may complicate the post-conflict transition to peace.[13] Traditionally, conflict-related claims by individuals have been dealt with via government-to-government resolution (e.g. interstate arbitration or peace treaties), thereby taking into account a number of political and strategic considerations that are normally

[9] D Gebreamanuel, 'Economic Commentary: FDI and Democracy in Ethiopia: Can FDI Push for a Well-Administered Government?' (Addis Standard, 6 July 2018) <http://addisstandard.com/economic-commentary-fdi-democracy-ethiopia-can-fdi-push-well-administered-government/#_ftnref5> accessed 12 December 2018.

[10] See e.g. H Burnett et al, 'Recent Developments: Mozambique—What Legal Options are Available to Investors in Oil, Gas and Mineral Resources?' (King & Spalding, 31 October 2013) <https://www.lexology.com/library/detail.aspx?g=390bf6e2-74c3-4a32-a5dc-a787f9f6f8d2> accessed 12 December 2018.

[11] See Chapter 4.

[12] See Chapter 6.

[13] J Zrilič, 'International Investment Law in the Context of Jus Post Bellum: Are Investment Treaties Likely to Facilitate or Hinder the Transition to Peace?' (2015) 16 JWIT 604. See Chapter 7.

prioritized in the peacemaking process. This is in contrast to investor claims which are typically not concerned with such considerations and seek to recover damages that can amount to several hundreds of millions of dollars, the payment of which may impose a heavy financial burden on an impoverished state seeking to recover and regain peace.[14]

Based on the problems outlined above, the book sets out to address two research questions. First, how effective are investment treaty protections in times of armed conflict? Second, how appropriate is the investment treaty framework for settling conflict-related disputes? For the purposes of this work, effectiveness is examined from the perspective of a foreign investor. In other words, how beneficial are investment treaties, compared to other legal frameworks, when protecting foreign investors during times of conflict and remedying conflict-related injuries? This entails a comparison of the investment treaty regime to other applicable legal frameworks, an examination of the doctrines governing the operation of international treaties in times of armed conflict, and the content of the relevant investment treaty provisions. On the other hand, the question of appropriateness is addressed from the point of view of the host state and concerns its right to pass certain measures in pursuit of its own security, and its ability to establish a stable post-conflict order.[15] This entails an analysis of the defences that host states can raise against potential investment claims, a comparison of investor–state arbitration to alternative remedial regimes, and an analysis of the negative effects of post-conflict compensation. While the emphasis in the book (as suggested by the title) is placed on the legal framework for protecting foreign investment in times of armed conflict, the effectiveness thereof cannot be examined without also addressing its appropriateness for a host state. The research questions thus reflect two sides of the same coin—stronger legal protections for foreign investors (thus a more effective legal framework) connote more limited space for a host state to react to security concerns or engage in post-conflict reconstruction (thus potentially making the investment regime less appropriate). This duality is addressed in each chapter and informs the design of the analytical framework that is articulated graphically in the concluding chapter.

So far, no scholarly work has addressed the questions raised above in a comprehensive and complete manner. While the Arab Spring events provoked some doctrinal discussions,[16] the topic has been treated from a mostly situation- or

[14] See e.g. *Mohamed Al-Kharafi & Sons Co v Libya* Ad hoc Arbitration, Award, 22 March 2013 (requiring Libya to pay exorbitant compensation).

[15] Admittedly, the question of appropriateness is broader and includes other considerations, such as the adverse impact that foreign investment can have on human rights in the context of armed conflict. While important, this aspect is outside the scope of the book.

[16] See e.g. C Schreuer, 'The Protection of Investments in Armed Conflicts' in F Baetens (ed), *Investment Law within International Law: Integrationist Perspectives* (CUP 2013) 3; G Hernández,

issue-specific perspective and in isolation from other applicable bodies of law. In contrast, this book seeks to examine the law and practices relating to the protection of foreign investment from the angle of multiple legal frameworks and their mutual interaction. While the main focus of the study is international investment law, the book ventures into other subfields of international law, such as the law of treaties, the law of state responsibility, international human rights law, and IHL. It uses historical context and draws on insights taken from other legal frameworks to inform the investment treaty practices and challenge the conventional doctrinal accounts.

The book argues that the effectiveness and appropriateness of investment treaties is ultimately a question of balancing competing objectives: on the one hand are investors' interests, certainty, and stability; and on the other hand, the state's sovereign right to protect its security interests and enable a smooth transition to peace. The study examines how these conflicting interests are balanced on different levels: on the level of the application of investment treaties, on the level of the invocation of relevant treaty protections and host state defences against them, on the level of post-conflict compensation, and lastly, on the level of the resolution of conflict-related disputes. Based on observation, it proposes a framework according to which the effectiveness and appropriateness of the investment treaty regime will depend on how the treaties are drafted and interpreted (distinguishing between investment and security paradigms) and the types of conflict and contexts that give rise to investment treaty claims. While traditionally, the investment treaty regime has tended to prioritize investment concerns over a state's security concerns, there has been a notable shift towards safeguarding states' discretion in volatile times. In particular, this reflects tribunals' interpretations of some treaty protections, the inclusion of security exceptions in new investment treaties, and post-Arab Spring scholarship. The thesis remains critical of both investment and security paradigms, acknowledging their advantages and highlighting their flaws. Rather, it advocates a new paradigm that presupposes a careful balancing of the competing interests at the different levels of treaty application, guided by the contextual circumstances of each case, most notably the type and conditions of a conflict situation.

'The Interaction between Investment Law and the Law of Armed Conflict in the Interpretation of Full Protection and Security Clauses' in F Baetens (ed), *Investment Law within International Law: Integrationist Perspectives* (CUP 2013) 21; H Bray, 'SOI–Save Our Investments! International Investment Law and International Humanitarian Law' (2013) 14(3) JWIT 578; O Mayorga, 'Arbitrating War: Military Necessity as a Defence to the Breach of Investment Treaty Obligations' (Policy Brief, August 2013) Program on Humanitarian Policy and Conflict Research Harvard University. The topic was also at the centre of the colloquium 'International Investment Law & the Law of Armed Conflict' organized on 5–6 October 2017 in Athens. The proceedings of the colloquium have not been published at the time of completing this monograph.

B. The Concept of Armed Conflict

Since the examination of investment treaty protections is contextually limited to the situation of armed conflict, it is important to clarify the scope of the study. Naturally, the question arises as to what exactly is meant by armed conflict. The concept has attracted considerable attention in legal scholarship.[17] This hardly comes as a surprise given the lack of an unequivocal definition of armed conflict and the fact that the concept bears great legal significance in the international legal system. The accurate qualification of a factual situation as an armed conflict has wide-ranging implications for different branches of international law. The presence of armed conflict triggers the application of IHL, it may affect the operation of international treaties, justify derogation from some human rights obligations, and have implications for obligations in other treaties.

1. Approaches to Conceptualizing Armed Conflict

The legally relevant definition of armed conflict has evolved over time and is by no means settled. In particular, three approaches to conceptualizing armed conflict in international law have emerged: (1) the IHL-based concept of armed conflict, (2) the autonomous concept of armed conflict, and (3) the indifferent approach to defining armed conflict.

The prevailing understanding of armed conflict has been shaped by the sources of IHL—the branch of international law that regulates situations of armed conflict and whose applicability depends on the existence of armed conflict. Depending on how the situations are legally defined, the rules applied differ from one case to the next. If a violent situation falls within the definition of armed conflict, armed parties are accorded certain belligerent powers and their conduct in hostilities is restricted by the rules of IHL. If, on the other hand, the situation of violence does not reach the threshold of armed conflict, the state's domestic policing rules continue to apply.

The concept of armed conflict in IHL is based on a double dichotomy. First, IHL distinguishes between international and non-international armed conflict.[18]

[17] A Cullen, *The Concept of Non-international Armed Conflict in International Humanitarian Law* (CUP 2010); S Vité, 'Typology of Armed Conflicts in International Humanitarian Law: Legal Concepts and Actual Situations' (2009) 91 IRRC 873; D Akande, 'Classification of Armed Conflict: Relevant Legal Concepts' in E Wilmshurst (ed), *International Law and the Classification of Conflicts* (OUP 2012); Committee on the Use of Force, 'Final Report on the Meaning of Armed Conflict in International Law' in International Law Association Report of the Seventy-Fourth Conference (The Hague 2010) (International Law Association, London 2010) 676; ME O'Connell, 'Defining Armed Conflict' (2008) 13 JCSL 393; A Duxbury, 'Drawing Lines in the Sand—Characterizing Conflicts for the Purposes of Teaching International Humanitarian Law' (2007) 8 MJIL 259; L Hill-Cawthorne, 'Humanitarian Law, Human Rights Law and the Bifurcation of Armed Conflict' (2015) 64 ICLQ 293.

[18] A critical source for international armed conflict is Common Article 2 to four Geneva Conventions 1949, while non-international conflict is introduced with a negative definition in Common Article 3. In

Second, a distinction is made between domestic violent situations that fall within the definition of non-international armed conflict and those that fall outside the scope of IHL. The decision of the International Criminal Tribunal for the Former Yugoslavia (ICTY) in the *Tadić* case has been widely relied upon as authoritative with regard to the meaning of armed conflict in both international and non-international conflicts. According to the tribunal, an armed conflict exists whenever 'there is resort to armed force between States or protracted armed violence between governmental authorities and organized armed groups or between such groups within a State....'[19] The *Tadić* tribunal emphasized two aspects of conflict: first, the intensity of the violence, and second, the organization of the parties. In this way, the tribunal aimed at distinguishing an armed conflict from situations of internal disturbance, such as riots, banditry, unorganized and short-lived insurrections, and terrorist activities, which are beyond IHL's scope.

Despite the dominant IHL understanding of the meaning of armed conflict, applying the same concept in another legal regime that pursues different objectives and purposes can be inapposite, and an autonomous definition may thus be needed. Consequently, some regimes have construed armed conflict independently from the IHL definition and set the threshold much lower. For example, the Court of Justice of the European Union rejected the reliance on IHL for the determination of armed conflict and interpreted the concept of non-international armed conflict in an EU asylum law context autonomously.[20] In this way, it has considerably lowered the threshold to include situations of great violence that may not qualify as armed conflict in IHL terms, but may nevertheless expose persons to the risk of serious human rights violations that may force them to flee their country of origin or habitual residence.

Lastly, the indifferent approach is based on the presumption that the same rules apply during times of peace or war and thus there is no need to ascertain the meaning of armed conflict. It goes a step further than the autonomous approach, which lowers the bar as to what type of situation constitutes armed conflict, by

addition, a narrower definition of non-international armed conflict was heralded in 1977 with Article 1 of the Additional Protocol II to the Geneva Conventions. See Geneva Convention (IV) Relative to the Protection of Civilian Persons in Time of War (signed 12 August 1949, entered into force 21 October 1950) 75 UNTS 287; Protocol Additional to the Geneva Conventions of 12 August 1949, and Relating to the Protection of Victims of Non-International Armed Conflicts (signed 8 June 1977, entered into force 7 December 1978) 1125 UNTS 609.

[19] *Prosecutor v Tadić* (Decision on Defence Motion for Interlocutory Appeal on Jurisdiction) IT-94-1-T (2 October 1995) para 70. This definition was followed in Article 8 of the Rome Statute that created the International Criminal Court. Rome Statute of the International Criminal Court (adopted 17 July1998, entered into force 1 July 2002) 2187 UNTS 90.

[20] See Council Directive (EC) 2004/83 of 29 April 2004 on Minimum Standards for the Qualification and Status of Third Country Nationals or Stateless Persons as Refugees or as Persons who Otherwise Need International Protection and the Content of the Protection Granted [2004] OJ L 304/12, Art 15(c). See also Case C-495/07 *Elgafaji v Staatssecretaris van Justitie* [2009] ECR-I 921; Case C-285/12 *Aboubacar Diakité v Commissaire Général aux réfugiés et aux apatrides* ILEC 033 (CJEU 2014).

disposing of any threshold. This has been particularly evident in the field of human rights. The European Court of Human Rights (ECtHR) has dealt with several cases of the violation of human rights and IHL in situations involving armed clashes, but has avoided clarifying the meaning of armed conflict.[21] This approach reflects the increasing convergence of fundamental protection rules that apply in situations of armed conflict and peace. While IHL distinguishes from among different types of armed conflicts which rules apply, in contrast, the rules espoused by the ECtHR have no thresholds but form a single body of law that covers everything from clashes between rioters and police forces to battles between insurgents and national armies.

Depending on the contexts in which investment treaty provisions are applied, all three approaches may prove relevant for the investment treaty framework. In most cases, the investment treaty practice mirrors the flexible approach adopted by the ECtHR. Like human rights treaties, investment treaties typically apply in times of peace and war. While courts and tribunals applying IHL need to first determine whether the armed conflict actually existed and then classify the situation to determine which set of IHL rules apply, investment tribunals would not typically be concerned with defining and classifying violent situations. This applies in particular to the key provision that accords investors the protection against forcible action, namely the full protection and security clause.[22] However, this does not mean that the elements that are normally considered determining factors when defining armed conflict, such as the intensity of the conflict and the organization of the armed groups, will be of no relevance. Although they will not be considered as the normative elements triggering the applicability of the provision, they will still be an important factual consideration in determining state responsibility.

On the other hand, the autonomous concept of armed conflict has emerged from armed conflict clauses that are largely harmonized in the wording used across the network of investment treaties and have a lower applicability threshold than that which was developed in IHL.[23] They encompass any violent actions related to situations of such proportion as to constitute an emergency. The departure from the IHL notion of armed conflict is best demonstrated by the example set by the Pakistan–Philippines BIT which states that the clause applies with respect to losses owing to 'war, revolution, state of emergency, revolt, insurrection, riot, *or other armed conflicts* in the territory of such Contracting Party', implying that 'armed

[21] See e.g. *Isayeva, Yusupova and Bazayeva v Russia* App nos 57947/00, 57948/00 and 57949/00, Judgment (ECtHR, 24 February 2005); *Isayeva v Russia* App no 57950/00, Judgment (ECtHR, 24 February 2005). However, recent decisions may signal a trend towards distinguishing between international and non-international armed conflicts. See *Al-Jedda v United Kingdom* App no 27021/08, Judgment (ECtHR, 7 July 2011) paras 97–110; *Hassan v United Kingdom* App no 29750/09, Judgment (ECtHR, 16 September 2014) paras 96–111.

[22] For the analysis, see Chapter 4 B.

[23] For the analysis, see Chapter 4 C.

conflict' is used as a generic term covering different situations of collective violence of varying intensity.[24] The concept of armed conflict that determines the area of operation of this treaty provision is thus broader than the IHL-based 'armed conflict', but narrower than the forcible interferences covered by the full protection and security clauses.

Although investment treaties break away from the binary understanding of armed conflict in terms of IHL, the latter can still play a limited role in situations where investment treaties interact with other legal frameworks. For example, the International Law Commission's (ILC) Draft Articles on the Effects of Armed Conflicts on Treaties[25] espouse the IHL concept of armed conflict. Thus, for the purposes of examining the effects of outbreaks of armed conflict on the operation of investment treaties, the IHL concept may become relevant. The same applies to the examination of the normative interplay between investment law and IHL.

Throughout this book, the concept of armed conflict is applied broadly and flexibly to include different types of violent situations, most notably those covered within armed conflict clauses. The narrower, IHL concept becomes important only in those chapters that discuss the application of the IHL framework and the doctrines governing the effect of armed conflict on the operation of treaties (in particular Chapters 2, 3, and 6). Beyond that, however, there appear to be no strong reasons for limiting the research to an IHL-based understanding of armed conflict. Several legal scholars have highlighted the importance of taking a broad understanding of conflict that extends beyond the traditional IHL boundaries.[26] To argue otherwise would mean unnecessarily limiting the practical relevance of this study and its findings for modern international investment law.

That said, one of the key arguments in the book is that the conditions and characteristics of a conflict situation (e.g. its international dimension, the intensity of the lethal violence, scope and scale of the conflict, its destructive impact, the level of organization, goals and motivation behind it, etc) may affect the application of investment treaty standards as well as help gauge their appropriateness. Based on these conditions, the book proposes a typology of conflicts with a view to further clarify the scope of the research and facilitate the understanding of investment law protections during violent conflicts.

[24] Pakistan–Philippines BIT (1999) Art V (emphasis added).

[25] ILC, 'Draft Articles on the Effects of Armed Conflicts on Treaties, with Commentaries' in *Yearbook of the International Law Commission, 2011, Vol II*, UN Doc A/CN.4/SER.A/2010/Add.1 (Part 2).

[26] C Bell, 'Of Jus Post Bellum and Lex Pacificatoria' in C Stahn, J Easterday, and J Iverson (eds), *Jus Post Bellum: Mapping the Normative Foundations* (OUP 2014) 197; C Stahn, 'Mapping the Discipline(s)' in C Stahn and J Kleffner (eds), *Jus Post Bellum: Towards a Law of Transition From Conflict to Peace* (TMC Asser Press 2008) 105, 233.

2. Typology of Conflicts

Drawing on the insights from the nineteenth- and early twentieth-century scholarly debates, legislative proposals, and investment jurisprudence discussed below,[27] as well as on the work of political and social scientists researching political violence,[28] the following classification of conflict situations is constructed:

- *International Armed Conflicts*
  This category, overlapping with the IHL concept of international armed conflicts, includes institutionalized forms of armed and political violence between two or more sovereign powers. It typically involves penetration of territorial borders and thus violation of state sovereignty. Examples include the South Ossetia War between Georgia and Russia in 2008, the war between Eritrea and Ethiopia (1998–2000), Persian Gulf War (1990–91), and both World Wars.
- *Internal Armed Conflicts (Including Civil Wars and Revolutions)*
  This cluster includes armed violent events that involve organized non-state groups fighting the governing regime or fighting between themselves. It crosses the rigid frontiers of armed conflict as defined by the IHL and includes borderline categories, like internal disturbances such as the Arab Spring revolutions. What is characteristic for this group is that the conflict is politically motivated, often involves intense combat, and can result in the government's loss of control over the situation or part of the territory. Apart from the revolution in Egypt and war in Libya, examples include civil wars in Syria (2011–) and Yemen (2015–), rebellions in South Sudan (2013–), Democratic Republic of Congo (2016–), and in the north border region of Nigeria (2009–).
- *Collective Protests (Including Riots and Violent Demonstrations)*
  The third category consists of violent events and clashes carried out by a large group of people that are typically precipitated by unpopular economic or social policies or motivated by xenophobic sentiments. Unlike the preceding category, this type of violent situation can usually be contained by the deployment of law enforcement agencies. Recent examples include the 'yellow vest' protests in Paris (2018), the protests and strike over the Catalonia referendum in Spain (2017), and xenophobic riots in South Africa (2015).

[27] See in particular Chapter 2 B.4.

[28] Political violence is defined as the use of force between different social groups that results in destruction, injury, and/or death. See e.g. D Hibbs, *Mass Political Violence: A Cross-National Causal Analysis* (Wiley-Interscience Publication 1973); J Vasquez, *The War Puzzle* (CUP 1993); M Marshall, *Third World War* (Rowman & Littlefield 1999); R Gurr, *Why Men Rebel* (Routledge 1970); C Tilly, *The Politics of Collective Violence* (CUP 2003); R M Ginty, 'Looting in the Context of Violent Conflict: a Conceptualisation and Typology' (2007) 25(5) TWQ 857.

- *Selective Violence (Incidents Targeting Investors)*
  The final category encompasses violent acts targeting investors either specifically or based on their nationality or some other general characteristic. Should this type of violence be a component of one of the above-stated categories or occur in their background (e.g. military attacks targeting investors, mob lootings in the context of civil wars or riots), the acts would fall within the autonomous concept of 'armed conflict' as envisioned by the investment treaty armed conflict clauses.[29] In all other cases of selective interference (e.g. isolated strikes, harassment by state organs, banditry), the threshold for the application of these armed conflict clauses is not met; however, other investment treaty protections may still be relevant.

These categories should be understood in instructive, rather than absolute and exhaustive, terms. Different situations may overlap, occur simultaneously, or metamorphose into a different conflict type, thus creating another level of complexity. However, while none of the clusters is entirely discrete, this typology is a helpful tool for exploring the interplay between the investment treaty regime and violence.[30]

C. Methodology, Limitations, and Plan of Discussion

The purpose of the book is twofold: first, to clarify the legal framework for protecting foreign investment in times of armed conflict and thereby improve its predictability; and second, to clarify the space within which states can or have to act and react in the context of armed conflict. This may help investors better appraise the risks of investing in politically volatile countries and the risk involved in conflict-related investment disputes, as well as inform the decisions of governments and state security organs, when planning and implementing their security policies and operations that may result in investment losses. In order to achieve this, the book is both descriptive and prescriptive. The descriptive part explains the state of law as it stands, compares different legal frameworks, and identifies inconsistencies in the interpretation and application thereof. On this basis, the prescriptive part critically discusses the flaws identified and sets out to propose normative and interpretative solutions. The research therefore focuses on the detailed examination of the relevant primary sources and engages with the academic commentary.

The focus of the analysis are investment treaties, in particular those provisions that are most likely to be applied in a conflict-related scenario. While a large number of treaties are examined, the project does not undertake an exhaustive

[29] See Chapter 4 C.
[30] See Chapter 8 B.

analysis of more than 3,000 treaties in existence. This inevitably means that the findings will evince a degree of generalization, and that the outcome in a particular conflict-related case will depend on the wording of the investment treaty in question. Nonetheless, the risk of generalization is minimized by the fact that the inspected provisions (e.g. full protection and security and armed conflict clauses) are often worded in a similar fashion, following the model BITs. The study is careful, however, to highlight the differing approaches in wording which may lead to different outcomes when the provisions are applied. For the purposes of identifying general trends in the drafting of treaty provisions, the project relies on existent comprehensive studies, especially those conducted by the United Nations Conference on Trade and Development (UNCTAD).

To provide a complete legal framework pertinent in times of armed conflict, the research also looks at the relevant provisions of treaties from other fields of international law, notably IHL regulations, human rights conventions, Articles on Responsibility of States for Internationally Wrongful Acts,[31] and the Vienna Convention on the Law of Treaties (VCLT),[32] as well as projects which are still at the proposal stage, like the ILC Draft Articles on the Effects of Armed Conflicts on Treaties. The meaning of the relevant treaty norms is determined in line with the rules on interpretation as envisaged in Article 31 of the VCLT, but often supported by making reference to preparatory materials, especially the reports of the ILC Special Rapporteurs, diplomatic statements voiced during treaty negotiations, and historical draft proposals of the codifications governing the treatment of aliens.

A vital part of the research is based on the analysis of arbitral awards and judicial decisions in which the observed legal frameworks were applied and interpreted. The study thus looks at all available investor–state arbitrations that have emerged from situations of conflict. The most attention is given to the *AAPL* case, since it is the first case to arise from a situation of civil war and it generated significant disagreement among the arbitrators and attracted criticism from commentators. In addition, a great number of arbitral awards not related to armed conflict are consulted when required for the analysis of the rules and principles being discussed. Since arbitral tribunals have often referred in their reasoning to the case law of the old interstate arbitrations and commissions, Chapter 2 analyses some of the precedents that have clarified the customary international law on the protection of aliens and influenced the interpretation of investment treaty standards. The study is further informed by the analysis of the conflict-related decisions of the human rights bodies, especially the ECtHR and Inter-American Court of Human Rights,

[31] ILC, 'Draft Articles on the Responsibility of States for Internationally Wrongful Acts with Commentaries' UN GAOR, 56th Sess, Supp 10, Ch 4, (2001) UN Doc A/56/10.

[32] Vienna Convention on the Law of Treaties (signed on 23 May 1969, entered into force 27 January 1980) 1155 UNTS 331.

the decisions of the Eritrea–Ethiopia Claims Commission, the Iran–United States Claims Tribunal, and the International Court of Justice (ICJ). In addition, the decisions of municipal courts are studied in areas lacking international jurisprudence, most notably with respect to the doctrine on the effects of armed conflict on treaties. Most arbitral and judicial decisions were available from online repositories or were summarized in special reports.

The choice of this methodological approach was necessary to address the research questions and tease out the analytical framework for the assessment of the investment treaty protections in times of armed conflict. The study is conducted in the frame of the typical trajectory of a conflict-related dispute, covering a wide array of issues, from the application of the investment treaties in times of armed conflict, to the analysis of the substantive protections and host state's defence mechanisms against investment claims, to the determination of post-conflict compensation. While the breadth of the study is important for providing a comprehensive and thorough overview of protections, it carries certain limitations. In particular, not all issues could be addressed in equal depth.

The study mitigates this concern by only analysing relevant norms from the perspective of their potential application in a conflict-related case. For example, the research is interested in an investment treaty security exception only as a potential defence against military and similar threats, but avoids discussing its application in the context of economic emergencies. Furthermore, issues that have attracted little scholarly attention or have not benefited from sufficient academic rigour (e.g. the application of a due diligence standard in conflict situations, full protection and security provisions, armed conflict clauses, post-conflict compensation, the relationship between investment law and IHL) are scrutinized in greater detail. This notwithstanding, the project identified several interesting and relevant topics that had to be left out from the book. For example, topics that warrant further research but have been unexplored on this occasion include the role of political risk insurance in protecting investors, the application of investment treaties in occupied and annexed territories, and the role and responsibility of foreign investors in times of armed conflict.

Following the described method, the discussion is structured in the following manner:

Chapter 2 outlines the international legal frameworks that, in parallel to investment treaties, protect foreign investors in times of armed conflict: the law of state responsibility for injuries to foreigners under customary international law, IHL, and international human rights law. Given the important role of the customary rules on the treatment of aliens in investment law, special attention is paid to the historical evolution of that framework, highlighting the scholarly and jurisprudential disagreements regarding the state's responsibility for conflict-related injuries to aliens. The chapter explains how the rules on protection of property have been interpreted and applied across different legal regimes, and discusses similarities and differences, thus setting the scene for the ensuing examination of investment treaty law.

Chapter 3 explores whether the outbreak of armed conflict could result in the termination or suspension of investment treaties. It critically inspects the ILC's codification project on the effects of armed conflicts on treaties, and, contrary to the prevailing view in the investment law scholarship, argues that certain type of conflicts could result in the suspension of certain investment treaty provisions when warranted by security concerns. In addition, it considers the VCLT doctrines of supervening impossibility to perform and fundamental change of circumstances, and argues that the former, in particular, could justify the suspension of an investment treaty provision.

Chapter 4 analyses the investment treaty provisions most likely to be invoked by investors to redress conflict-related losses, notably the full protection and security provision and the armed conflict clause. It observes that the nineteenth- and early twentieth-century ideology-fuelled disagreements as to the scope of the standard of protection against physical violence have seeped into modern arbitral jurisprudence; however, the approach that appears to be prevailing is one that combines objective (favouring the investor's rights) and subjective (favouring the state's position) views, and is reflective of approaches in the law of state responsibility for injuries to foreigners under customary international law. With respect to other treaty provisions (expropriation, and fair and equitable treatment) it is argued that despite the early inconsistent arbitral jurisprudence, investors' expectations as to their protections will be likely assessed in light of the conflict crisis.

Chapter 5 focuses on the defence mechanisms available to host states. While security exceptions in investment treaties are often touted as the strongest safeguard of the state's security interests, it is argued that their effectiveness will depend on the wording of the provision, determining their scope, the degree of autonomy given to a state in responding to a security threat, and their relationship with other treaty provisions. The chapter considers these aspects. Since most of treaties do not contain such exceptions, the defences in the general law of state responsibility, notably necessity, *force majeure*, and countermeasures, are also addressed.

Chapter 6 examines the interplay between investment treaty protections and IHL. Scholars have argued that in situations of civil war, there is a high likelihood of normative conflicts occurring between the investment treaty and IHL norms, whereby the latter should prevail. The chapter challenges these views. Using *AAPL v Sri Lanka* as a case study, it analyses different areas of normative interplay, focusing on the use of precautions and the principle of proportionality in military attacks. Specifically, it shows how the duty to exercise care in targeting operations overlaps in different legal frameworks, and thereby highlights the potential of investment tribunals for advancing more humane state conduct in hostilities. It concludes by providing a systemic overview of methods for minimizing the normative tensions.

Chapter 7 focuses on the post-conflict period and critically assesses how investment treaty claims can interfere with the transition to peace. It questions the role of investment treaties as a facilitator of peace as well as the position that investor–state arbitration is an optimal structure for remedying conflict-related losses. Based on the assumption that large compensation awards may adversely affect the host state's post-conflict transition, it examines different methods for adjusting post-conflict compensation modalities in light of the transitional circumstances. It further compares investor–state arbitration to other regimes for remedying conflict-related losses, and argues that in some cases, the re-emergence of state control in a dispute resolution process could be justified.

Chapter 8 draws upon the entire book, tying up the observations of the preceding chapters in order to present the framework for the assessment of investment treaty protections in times of armed conflict. It argues that how the competing objectives will be balanced at different stages of investment treaty claims depends on the combination of the paradigm dominating a particular treaty (investment *v* security), and the type and conditions of armed conflict giving rise to the investment claim. It uses a typology of conflicts to help explain the effectiveness and appropriateness of investment treaty claims in a particular situation. In the end, it advocates the mixed, investment-security paradigm as a desirable means for achieving the fair balancing of competing interests and thus an effective and appropriate investment treaty framework.

2

Legal Frameworks for the Protection of Foreign Investment in Times of Armed Conflict

A. Introduction

Throughout its evolution, international law has branched out into multiple fields. This is reflected in its various, and often overlapping sources, specialized legal frameworks covering different subject matters, and the variety of judicial bodies adjudicating disputes independently of each other. Not uncommonly, a particular legal or factual situation is capable of being addressed under different sources or brought before different courts and arbitral tribunals. This applies also to the treatment of foreign investors in times of armed conflict. While investment treaties constitute the most obvious and appealing legal framework for injured investors, there are other international and regional legal systems that offer similar protections to the person and property of investors against the afflictions of war and other violent situations. These frameworks are not only important in cases where investment treaties do not apply, but also because they can improve understanding of how investment treaty protections have evolved (Chapter 4), inform their interpretation (Chapter 6), and provide an alternative recourse for remedies (Chapter 7). Apart from investment treaty law, which will be examined in the subsequent chapters, three legal frameworks are relevant to investors who have sustained losses in times of conflict: the law of state responsibility for injuries to foreigners under customary international law, international humanitarian law (IHL), and international human rights law. All provide protections for property rights that traditionally fall within the definition of investments in investment treaties.

Investment treaty protections have been influenced most strongly by the customary rules on the treatment of aliens in times of conflict. These rules largely evolved in the nineteenth and early twentieth centuries, during an era rife with revolutions and wars, in the aftermath of which investors (via their home states) often brought claims against the host states for conflict-related injuries. The jurisprudence of post-conflict arbitrations and commissions helped clarify the norms and principles that applied in such volatile times and significantly contributed to the development of the law of state responsibility. In fact, in its early stages, the project of the codification of the law of state responsibility focused only on the

The Protection of Foreign Investment in Times of Armed Conflict. First Edition. Jure Zrilič.
Published 2019 by Oxford University Press.

responsibility of a state for injuries to aliens—the subject matter of the vast majority of international precedents. The cases in which state responsibility had been alleged were mainly those of responsibility for losses inflicted on foreigners in times of conflict. This chapter thus starts with a historical analysis of different theories and practices on state responsibility for conflict-related injuries to aliens, and in doing so highlights the principles that emerged in relation to the treatment thereof. It then looks into a legal regime that was specifically designed to regulate the conduct of states in time of war, namely IHL. While the jurisprudence of the same period was relevant for clarifying the state practices permitted when waging war, the codification of IHL created a two-tier system, offering a different level of protection for international and non-international armed conflicts. Finally, the chapter examines the relevance of human rights frameworks for the subject. Many human rights instruments contain provisions aiming to protect life and private property, which have been applied by human rights bodies in cases of conflict-related violations. The chapter considers the relevant cases and distils standards of protection pertinent for investors.

B. State Responsibility for Injuries to Foreigners under Customary International Law

The treatment of aliens and their property in times of conflict was part of the modern international law since its very inception. The giants of international law, Grotius, Wolff, and Vattel, all asserted that states owe certain protection and security to foreigners, even in time of war,[1] and gradually this postulation found its way into treaties of amity and commerce.[2] The content of the rules addressing the protection of the person and property of foreigners, including foreign investors, began developing in parallel with the concept of state responsibility and the use of the remedial institution of diplomatic protection in the early nineteenth century.[3] The reasons why the practical implications of the Vatellian principles on the protection of aliens were only realized in the nineteenth century are manifold. First, most of the powerful European countries had already recognized some form of group or local liability, which was considered sufficient for cases of injuries caused

[1] See H Grotius, *De jure belli ac pacis libri tres* (Clarendon Press 1925) bk III, chs 2, 4, 7; C Wolff, *Jus Gentium Methodo Scientifica Pertractatum* (1749), reprinted in *2 The Classics Of International Law 9* (Joseph H Drake tr, James Brown Scott edn, 1934) 536; E de Vattel, *The Law of Nations or the Principles of Natural Law* (1758), reprinted in *3 The Classics of International Law 145* (Charles G Fenwick tr, James Brown Scott edn, 1916) 136, 146.

[2] See e.g. Treaty of Amity and Commerce, US–Prussia (1785) Art XVIII; Treaty of Amity, Commerce and Navigation, US–Great Britain (1794) Arts II, XIV.

[3] E Borchard, *Diplomatic Protection of Citizens Abroad* (Banks Law Publishing Co 1915) 25–29, 39; C Eagleton, *The Responsibility of States in International Law* (New York University Press 1928) 3, 6, 22; C Amerasinghe, *Diplomatic Protection* (OUP 2008) 13; K Miles, *The Origin of International Investment Law: Empire, Environment and the Safeguarding of Capital* (CUP 2014) 47.

in violent situations.[4] It was not until the nineteenth century that it became clear that local remedies were not necessarily favourable to the injured aliens and the idea that foreign nationals possessed certain rights and privileges that their nations were entitled to protect began to take hold.[5] Second, these developments were advanced by the introduction of mechanical technology and industrialization, which prompted the search for natural resources in different parts of the world and the establishment of trade links.[6] Consequently, there was a large number of foreigners and foreign investors living in different capital-importing countries, which created a xenophobic environment and increased the likelihood of a conflict erupting with local residents. Third, the late nineteenth and the early twentieth centuries was a period fraught with riots, revolutions, and civil wars.[7] Decolonization movements in Latin America, and consequent struggles for power between different groups within, as well as among, individual countries, rendered the region unstable as political disorder and revolutions became commonplace.[8] Among the victims of such civil uprisings were citizens and companies from the US and Europe.

At that time, the model that governed relations between nations in the international community was strongly influenced by the values of the European powers. In the economic sphere, this was reflected in the sanctity of private property, not only in relations between private citizens, but also in its protection against government actions.[9] Ensuring such protection of private property required a certain level of order and stability which, in that period, had already been established in the old European powers but had not yet been secured in many fledgling Latin American states. This resulted in frequent accusations of unjust treatment of foreigners by the host states, and conflicting views between large and small powers as to the scope of protections that states had to accord to aliens in their territories.[10] Given the political turmoil in Latin America, most of the accusations that gave rise to claims of diplomatic protection were directed against them.

The claims of foreigners who suffered injuries in these situations were espoused by their home states who sought compensation for losses incurred via diplomatic channels or different types of adjudicative bodies, like mixed claims commissions and arbitrations.[11] The jurisprudence of this period produced a body of precedents

[4] J Goebel, 'The International Responsibility of States for Injuries Sustained by Aliens on Account of Mob Violence, Insurrections and Civil Wars' (1914) 8 AJIL 802, 808.

[5] ibid 808.

[6] Amerasinghe, *Diplomatic Protection* (n 3) 13; K Vandevelde, *Bilateral Investment Treaties: History, Policy, and Interpretation* (OUP 2010) 20. See also A Lorca, *Mestizo International Law: A Global Intellectual History 1842–1933* (CUP 2014); J Scarfi, *The Hidden History of International Law in the Americas: Empire and Legal Networks* (OUP 2017).

[7] The governments of newly independent Latin American countries were unstable, there was a civil war in the US, growing nationalist movements in Europe, and a wave of colonization in Africa.

[8] Amerasinghe, *Diplomatic Protection* (n 3) 14.

[9] ibid.

[10] ibid.

[11] Since 1839, when the first mixed claims commission between the US and Mexico was set up, there were around forty such post-conflict commissions. For a record of awards, see J Moore, *History*

that influenced the development of the law of state responsibility for injuries to aliens, and more specifically, the standard of protection afforded to aliens. Most cases from that era emerged from conflict situations and concerned the question of state responsibility for damages sustained by foreigners at the hands of non-state actors in the course of riots, insurrections, and civil wars.[12] Unsurprisingly, this narrow field of state responsibility has since undergone some important developments and inspired conflicting scholarly views. The following characteristics were particularly notable for that period: (1) there was disagreement in scholarship and diplomacy as to the scope of state responsibility for injuries caused by the third parties (e.g. mobs and revolutionary movements); (2) there was inconsistency in state practice regarding the expected protection of their nationals abroad and the treatment accorded to foreigners within their own territory; (3) the doctrinal and jurisprudential discussions often addressed the responsibility for losses emerging from civil wars alongside the state responsibility for losses related to 'lesser' violent situations, like riots and mob violence; and (4) ascertaining the principles of state responsibility was made difficult by the common practice of paying post-conflict indemnities as an expression of spontaneous liberality but without acknowledging liability.

Broadly speaking, two schools of thought developed with regard to state responsibility for injuries to aliens sustained in internal conflict. One was based on the premise that a state was generally responsible for the injuries suffered by aliens in periods of conflict, subject to certain exceptions. The other school took the opposite view by considering the non-responsibility of a host state to be the rule, while acknowledging that responsibility could apply in exceptional circumstances. Within both schools, the extreme views of absolute responsibility and non-responsibility were also advocated, but gained little support. The following sections provide an overview of the evolution of these positions, focusing on state responsibility for injuries to aliens caused by third parties in the course of conflict.

1. State Responsibility

Advocates of the theory of absolute responsibility were in the minority, and they based their arguments on different grounds. Fauchille, for example, introduced the idea of state risk (*risque étatif*), which was analogous to the legislation of some

and Digest of the International Arbitrations to Which the United States Has Been a Party (Government Printing Office 1898); J Ralston, *The Law and Procedure of International Tribunals* (Stanford University Press 1926); H Silvanie, 'Responsibility of States for Acts of Insurgent Governments' (1939) 33(1) AJIL 78; AM Stuyt, *Survey of International Arbitrations, 1794–1938* (Martinus Nijhoff 1939).

[12] See R Ago, 'First Report on State Responsibility' ILC, *Yearbook of the International Law Commission, 1969, Vol II*, UN Doc A/CN.4/SER.A/1969/Add.1126, 137; Ralston (n 11) 349.

countries, according to which the state was liable for damages resulting from the performance of certain activities from which the state drew a profit, such as public works or judicial services.[13] Fauchille argued that foreign investors brought development and money to the state in which they had invested and should therefore be protected under *risque étatif*, hence obliging the host state to assume the risk of violent events and compensate investors for any damages suffered in the course thereof.

A similar view was proposed by Emilio Brusa in his report to the Institute of International Law in 1898. According to Brusa, investors brought profit to the host state and were thus entitled to compensation whenever the state exercised its public powers, such as the power to suppress internal insurrections.[14] The state had to pay compensation regardless of the nature of its conduct, even if the latter was justified based on grounds of *force majeure*.[15] However, the Institute of International Law did not concede to Brusa's proposal and later promoted the complete opposite.[16]

Some jurists took the view that state responsibility for injuries caused in the course of internal strife was based on the obligation *ex delicto*, and the state's culpable or negligent conduct. The Peruvian lawyer Wiesse thus argued that the state is at fault in that it permits civil war to break out.[17] He rejected the *force majeure* defence by arguing that wars and revolutions could not be compared to acts of nature since the employment of violence is voluntary and there are means other than war that can be used to solve disagreements.[18]

Some scholars argued that the state was liable for injuries caused to aliens in violent outbreaks even if the state was not at fault. Goebel thus held that investors' home states were entitled to intervene to collect compensation, particularly when the violent event in question was a manifestation of xenophobic or racist sentiments, and as such was directed against residents of a particular nationality and thus against their state.[19] While he argued that the liability of a state for its own acts and the acts of its agents was absolute, he softened his view with respect to its responsibility for injuries caused by rebels and insurgents. Therefore, he held that the state might escape responsibility in certain cases, depending on the fault or imprudence of the alien, the investor's awareness of the disorder of the state into which they were entering, and the gravity and scale of the conflict.[20]

[13] P Fauchille, *Droits Et Devoirs En Cas D'insurrection* (1900) 18 Annuaire de l'IDI 234. Also cited in H Arias, 'The Non-liability of States for Damages Suffered by Foreigners in the Course of a Riot, an Insurrection or a Civil War' (1913) 7 AJIL 724, 729; Eagleton, *Responsibility of States* (n 3) 140.

[14] E Brusa, *Responsabilité des Etats á raison des dommages soufferts par des étrangers en cas d'émeute ou de guerre civile* (1898) 17 Annuaire de l'IDI 96, 108–09.

[15] ibid.

[16] FV García-Amador, L Sohn, and R Baxter, *Recent Codification of the Law of State Responsibility for Injuries to Aliens* (Brill 1974) 31.

[17] C Wiesse, Reglas de Derecho Internacional Aplicables a las Guerras Civiles (1893) cited in Eagleton, *Responsibility of States* (n 3) 140; and in Borchard, *Diplomatic Protection* (n 3) 229.

[18] ibid.

[19] Goebel, 'International Responsibility of States' (n 4) 812.

[20] ibid 817–18.

In practice, support of the theory of absolute state responsibility was exceptional.[21] Perhaps the most overt example was the settlement made in the 'Aigues-Mortes' case in 1893. In that case, a small fight that had broken out between Italian and French employees in a company operating in the French city of Aigues-Mortes quickly escalated into widespread violence, leading to the deaths and injuries of a number of Italian citizens. This massacre was related to prior hostile demonstrations against the French in some Italian cities. The French government paid the indemnity without rejecting its liability or categorizing the compensation paid as 'spontaneous liberality'.[22] What was common to cases of absolute responsibility was that the fact that the government was at fault had not been established; instead, the responsibility was tacitly acknowledged and indemnity paid merely because the violent events giving rise to the injuries occurred within the host state's territorial control. The settlements appeared to be reached on political and diplomatic, rather than legal, grounds.

In most cases, however, when a host state paid money to victims of internal violence, it did so based on the understanding that it should be deemed as a gratuity and not a lawful indemnity.[23] The practice of making a payment of indemnity as a token of goodwill can be traced to France in 1792.[24] Often, states declared that by paying money the government did not accept any responsibility for violations of their international obligations. For example, in the aftermath of the mob violence in Wyoming in 1885 against Chinese residents, the US government admitted that no adequate protection had been afforded to them and that the authorities had failed to ensure an impartial forum for adjudicating the cases related to the conflict.[25] The US president offered adequate appropriation to the injured foreigners, pointing out that 'such action is in nowise to be held as a precedent, is wholly gratuitous, and is resorted to in the spirit of pure generosity toward those who are otherwise helpless'.[26]

This case, along with many others in that period, straddled the thin line of international state responsibility and illustrates how states used diplomatic vernacular to repudiate liability and prevent creating any binding precedent for the future.

[21] See e.g. the bombardment of Antwerp in 1830 which concerned the destruction of property of foreign merchants by Dutch troops on the territory under Dutch control. However, the claims for indemnity were directed against Belgium solely on the ground that the injury was inflicted on the territory that had become part of Belgium at the time when claims were made. Reported in J Moore, *A Digest of International Law: As Embodied in Diplomatic Discussions, Treaties and Other International Agreements, International Awards, the Decisions of Municipal Law, and the Writings of Jurists*, vol VI (Government Printing Office 1906) 929, 942–48. For the summary of cases see also Goebel (n 4) 828; Eagleton, *Responsibility of States* (n 3) 126.

[22] Goebel (n 4) 827.

[23] E Huffcut, 'International Liability for Mob Injuries' (1891) 2 Ann Am Acad Pol Soc Sci 69, 75–76.

[24] Borchard, *Diplomatic Protection* (n 3) 279.

[25] Huffcut, 'International Liability' (n 23) 81; Moore, *Digest* (n 21) 834.

[26] Huffcut (n 23) 81 (citing the US president's message from 2 March 1886). For similar cases, see Moore, *Digest* (n 21) 837–41; Eagleton, *Responsibility of States* (n 3) 133.

Classifying the compensation as a liberality or bounty as opposed to an indemnity reflected the power dynamics in the international political order of the nineteenth century. The practice was beneficial to both developed and developing states. Paying compensation without acknowledging liability enabled powerful states to maintain peaceful relations with other powerful countries who paid indemnities to their citizens in similar circumstances, and served to bolster their reputation in the international legal order. On the other hand, it also enabled developing states, in particular Latin American countries, who were compelled to pay compensation (either by means of the threat of, or actual use of, force by powerful states), to do so without creating a legal custom that had to be followed in the future.[27] This practice was criticized not only for its inconsistency, but also for impeding the creation of international legal principles. Some scholars thus argued that the payment in itself was an implicit confession of liability.[28] Namely, basing the payment on a moral obligation created expectations of payment for future similar cases, and created a *de facto* legal obligation. Refusal to accept legal responsibility, when it in fact existed, only obfuscated the scope of state responsibility and slowed down the development of international law.

2. State Non-Responsibility

The theory of absolute non-responsibility was most ardently advocated by Latin American jurists.[29] It developed in response to a number of diplomatic protection claims made by powerful states with respect to the injuries that their nationals suffered in the course of violent events that took place in Latin America. In that period, diplomatic protections were often used as a justification for armed interventions.[30]

[27] C Calvo, 'De la Non-Responsibilité des États a Raison des Dommages Soufferts par des Étrangers en Cas d'Émeute ou de Guerre Civile' (1869) 1 (1d series) Revue de Droit International et de Legislation Comparee 427 (arguing that such payments did not reflect a legal obligation but rather the power of politics).

[28] Eagleton, *Responsibility of States* (n 3) 134; Goebel, 'International Responsibility of States' (n 4) 810; Huffcut, 'International Liability' (n 23).

[29] See e.g. Calvo, 'Non-Responsibilité' (n 27) 417; Arias, 'Non-liability of States' (n 13). Departing from this absolutist view, some other Latin American lawyers contemplated an exception to state non-responsibility. See e.g. L Podestá Costa, El Extranjero en la Guerra Civil (1913) 183; JG Guerrero in 'Conclusions of the Report of the Sub-Committee on State Responsibility, annexed to Questionnaire No 4 Adopted by the League of Nations Committee of Experts for the Progressive Codification of International Law' (1926) in *Yearbook of the International Law Commission, 1956, Vol II*, UN Doc A/CN.4/SER.A/1956/Add.1 222–23, Concl 8 (Guerrero Report).

[30] Towards the end of the nineteenth century, there were more than 100 military interventions by the US and European powers in capital-importing countries, mostly in Latin America (e.g. the French interventions in Mexico in 1838 and 1861; the intervention of Germany, Great Britain, and Italy in Venezuela in 1902–03; and American interventions in Santo Domingo in 1904 and in Haiti in 1915). See Amerasinghe, *Diplomatic Protection* (n 3) 15; J von Bernstorff, 'The Use of Force in International Law before World War I: On Imperial Ordering and the Ontology of the Nation-State' (2018) 29(1) EJIL 233, 248; B Simms and D Trim, Humanitarian Intervention: A History (CUP 2011). On Latin American resistance against interventionism, see Lorca (n 6) 152–58.

In order to avoid such territorial conquests, Latin American states consented to settle claims for compensation for injuries to aliens, if not by negotiation, then by submitting the claims to be heard by international arbitration. International commissions established to settle disputes were often regarded by Latin American states as prejudiced in favour of the protecting states.[31] The Argentine jurist Carlos Calvo strongly rejected the view that host states were responsible for the losses suffered by aliens during civil strife. The key ground against the presumption of liability was that a state was not bound to grant greater rights to aliens than it would to its own subjects.[32] He further buttressed his arguments with the principles of the equality of states and the inviolability of territorial sovereignty. According to Calvo, the state had the right to take all necessary lawful measures to repress civil wars and insurrections.[33] If aliens suffered injuries as a result of the host state's unlawful measures, then the state could still escape responsibility by invoking the defence of *force majeure*.[34] This view was espoused by prominent Latin American statesmen and was manifested in their diplomatic correspondence, treaties, and even their constitutions and municipal laws.[35]

Variations of such statutory acts that denied the international responsibility of a state for wrongs caused by civil unrest became common in Latin American countries and were strongly disapproved of by European states and the US. They had little practical effect and were ultimately unsuccessful.[36] On the international level, Latin American countries advanced their views by stipulating non-responsibility clauses in the international treaties that they made among themselves and with other countries.[37] Some of these clauses stipulated the absolute non-liability of the host state for losses that aliens sustained in the course of riots, revolutions, or civil

[31] F Dunn, *The Protection of Nationals: A Study in the Application of International Law* (Johns Hopkins Press 1932) 55–56.

[32] Calvo, 'Non-Responsibilité' (n 27) 417.

[33] ibid.

[34] ibid 422.

[35] For example, the Guatemalan Constitution of 1875 provided in Art 46 that 'neither Guatemalans nor foreigners shall have indemnification for damages arising out of injuries done to their persons or property by revolutionists'. See also the Salvadoran Constitution of 1886, Art 46; the Haitian Constitution of 1889, Art 185; the Honduran Constitution of 1904; and the Venezuelan Constitution of 1904, 1901, and 1891 (cited in Goebel, 'International Responsibility of States' (n 4) 833). See also MR Garcia Mora, 'The Calvo Clause in Latin American Constitutions and International Law' (1950) 33 Marqu L Rev 205.

[36] D Shea, *The Calvo Clause: A Problem of Inter-American and International Law and Diplomacy* (U Minnesota Press 1955) 21–27; Goebel, 'International Responsibility of States' (n 4) 838; Miles, *The Origin* (n 3) 51; Amerasinghe, *Diplomatic Protection* (n 3) 192.

[37] For the examples of treaties containing such non-responsibility clauses, see Arias, 'Non-liability of States' (n 13) 724; Goebel (n 4) 840; JW Garner 'Responsibility of States for Injuries Suffered by Foreigners within their Territories on Account of Mob Violence, Riots and Insurrection' (1927) 21 ASIL Proceedings 49, 59. See also Convention Relative to the Rights of Aliens Signed at the Second International Conference of American States (Mexico City, 1902) stipulating that 'the States are not responsible for damages sustained by aliens through acts of rebels or individuals, and in general . . . considering as such the acts of war . . .' in *Yearbook of the International Law Commission, 1956, Vol II*, UN Doc A/CN.4/SER.A/1956/Add.1 226.

wars, without exception.[38] The Institute of International Law at its session in 1900 expressly condemned such treaty making, and asked the states to refrain from such practices as they excused governments from the performance of their duty to protect foreigners within their territories.[39]

3. The Exception to State Non-Responsibility

Since the theories on absolute non-responsibility were considered unfairly prejudicial to aliens and their property, a more nuanced view evolved—one which acknowledged that despite the general non-responsibility of a state for injuries to foreigners in times of conflict, in exceptional cases the state could still be held responsible.

The most influential argument was put forward by scholars who asserted that the host state could be liable if it failed to exercise due diligence in protecting foreigners.[40] Fiore, for example, argued that the host state may be responsible for injurious acts of private actors if it 'could or should have prevented the injury and was voluntarily negligent of its duty in not having done so'.[41] Hall highlighted the flexible nature of due diligence and linked it to reasonableness and proportionality by stating that a state can avoid responsibility if it 'honestly gives so much care as may seem to an average intelligence to be proportional to the state of things existing at the time'.[42] The existence of the host state's responsibility was thus to be determined by establishing whether the state had complied with the international standard and exercised proper care in the prevention of injuries to aliens.

In practice, on several occasions when injury to foreigners was caused by a mob or rioters, states defended themselves by arguing that they discharged their duty of due diligence.[43] Arbitral tribunals also did not shy away from highlighting the exception to the rule of non-responsibility. For example, the theories of

[38] See e.g. the treaty between Ecuador and Salvador of 20 March, 1890, cited in Arias (n 13) 756.

[39] ibid 756; Moore, *Digest* (n 21) 323–24.

[40] For a list of authorities, see Borchard, *Diplomatic Protection* (n 3) 229, n 7; Eagleton, *Responsibility of States* (n 3) 146, 148. See Grotius, *De jure belli* (n 1) bk II ch 21, 523; Wolff, *Jus Gentium Methodo* (n 1) 317–18; de Vattel, *The Law Of Nations* (n 1) II ch VI, 162.

[41] See P Fiore, *Nouveau droit international public*, vol I (2nd edn, Pedone-Lauriel 1886) 582, cited in *Sambiaggio Case (Italy v Venezuela)* (1903) 10 RIAA 499, 511. See also J Ralston, *Venezuelan Arbitrations of 1903* (GPO 1904) 678; L Oppenheim, *International Law*, vol I: Peace (7th edn Longmans, Green & Co 1952) 757–58.

[42] W Hall, *A Treatise on International Law* (2nd edn, Clarendon Press, 1884) 196.

[43] For example, the US government argued that lynching and murder of Japanese aliens by a mob in Utah 'could not have been quelled by due diligence and energy by the Government'. Reported in Moore, *Digest* (n 21) 819. In the *Case of Bain*, which concerned the murder of the British merchant by the rioters in New Orleans in 1895, the US government denied that state authorities 'were guilty of any neglect of duty or failure to protect the commerce of the city'. Reported in Moore, ibid 850. In *Don Pacifico Case*, the liability of the Greek government for the destruction of the property of a British citizen at the hands of a mob was also alleged on the ground of 'neglect to render protection' by the authorities. Reported in Moore, ibid 852.

absolute responsibility or absolute non-responsibility were repudiated in arbitrations following the civil war of 1892 in Venezuela. The fundamental question that the Italian–Venezuelan Mixed Claims Commission faced in the oft-cited *Sambiaggio* case was whether the host state was responsible for losses inflicted on Italian nationals by unsuccessful revolutionists. The umpire, Ralston, highlighted the general rule that the government was only responsible for the acts of its agents and for the acts for which it explicitly assumed responsibility; save for exceptional circumstances, it was not responsible for the acts of revolutionists.[44] The Italian commissioner, echoing the sentiments of the US and European powers, argued that countries in which internal disorders were commonplace, and thus predictable, should show higher levels of vigilance in protecting foreigners. The Venezuelan commissioner, on the other hand, asserted that perpetual internal disorder actually reflected the state's loss of control and demonstrated its inability to extend its protection to foreigners. He also argued that foreigners had known where they were moving to and had therefore willingly assumed the risk.

Ralston adamantly rejected the binary division between more orderly and civilized states and those that were considered inferior, rife with revolution, and for whom a different presumption of state responsibility applied.[45] He did not, however, exclude the possibility that a state could breach its obligation under international law by failing to exercise due diligence to prevent injuries from being inflicted by revolutionists.[46] Such a due diligence obligation would be measured against the state's 'means at its disposal' and according to the given circumstances.[47] Since no claim of a failure to exercise due diligence was alleged or proven against Venezuela, he dismissed the case.

Ralston's incisive reasoning was not followed in all Venezuelan arbitrations. The umpire Duffield of the German–Venezuelan Commission in the factually similar *Kummerow, Otto Redler & Co, Fulda, Fischbach, and Friedericy* cases decided that Venezuela was liable for injuries to, or wrongful seizures of, alien property by revolutionists resulting from the civil war.[48] In his analysis of the general state of law, Duffield confirmed the due diligence exception but concluded that given the frequency of revolutions and ongoing disorder in the country, the Venezuelan government could not be exempt from liability.[49] Unlike Ralston, Duffield subscribed to the view that was popular with capital-exporting countries, that the continuously turbulent conditions of the host state extended the scope of the state's responsibility.

[44] *Sambiaggio* (n 41) 512.
[45] ibid 524.
[46] ibid 513.
[47] ibid 510.
[48] *Kummerow, Otto Redler and Co, Fulda, Fischbach, and Friedericy Cases* (*Germany v Venezuela*) (1903) 10 RIAA 369, 394.
[49] ibid 398.

Differentiation between Western civilized nations and the unruly periphery was advocated by influential, mostly American, legal scholars and diplomats,[50] and was more than a rhetorical device. Primarily, the Western governments used it as a legal justification for military intervention in less powerful countries when the latter failed to protect Western nationals and economic interests in the course of disorder (in US foreign policy these practices were legitimized by the Roosevelt Corollary).[51] If the host states consented to arbitration, then this differentiation was used to support the argument that they were responsible for not fulfilling the obligation of protection against physical violence. The question of how the element of chronic disorder should be considered in determining the responsibility of a host state was linked to the claim that a state bears responsibility for the failure to efficiently suppress internal disturbance regardless of the actual means at its disposal. While some tribunals held states responsible for being negligent in quashing revolutions, without taking into account their capabilities of doing so,[52] others espoused views more understanding of the impossibilities caused by such supervening events.[53]

This discrepancy is reflective of the tension between objective (what a well-organized state is expected to do) and subjective (what a particular state is able to do in given circumstances) elements of the due diligence rule. The view that a state's failure to be 'well-organized' (i.e. is riddled with perennial conflict) resulted in its responsibility, disregarded the subjective circumstances in which the obligation had to be performed. It was overly rigid and unfairly favoured the security of Western capital against predictable political risks in unstable Latin American countries.[54] The more nuanced view would consider the continuity or recurring nature of a conflict as having a twofold role: first, requiring aliens to adjust their expectations as to the level of security in such a volatile territory; and second, requiring a host state to adjust its means and capabilities to the new reality, to the extent this is possible. Ultimately, the determination of the degree of due diligence

[50] Borchard, *Diplomatic Protection* (n 3) 230–31; Eagleton, *Responsibility of States* (n 3) 144–45 (acknowledging, however, that in some cases advantage was taken of Latin American countries as 'weaker states'); E Root, 'The Real Monroe Doctrine' (1914) 8 AJIL 427, 433. For more generally on this distinction as a fundamental feature of international law of that period, see A Anghie, *Imperialism, Sovereignty and the Making of International Law* (CUP 2004); G Gong, *The Standard of Civilization in International Society* (Clarendon Press 1984); E Keene, *Beyond the Anarchical Society: Grotius, Colonialism and Order in World Politics* (CUP 2002).

[51] T Roosevelt, Annual Message to Congress (6 December 1904) <ourdocuments.gov/doc.php?flash=true&doc=56&page=transcript> accessed 18 December 2018. See also Bernstorff, 'Use of Force' (n 30) 249.

[52] See e.g. *Case of the Montijo* (*US v Colombia*) (1875) reported in Moore, *History and Digest* (n 11) 1421, 1444; *Venezuelan Steam Transportation Company Case* (*US v Venezuela*) (1892) reported in Moore, ibid 1693, 1720, 1726.

[53] See e.g. *Santa Clara Estates Case* (Supplementary Claim) (1903) 9 RIAA 455, 458; *Wenzel Case* (*Germany v Venezuela*) (1903) 10 RIAA 428, 431.

[54] Latin American countries often succumbed to the diplomatic pressures of Western powers and agreed to acknowledge their responsibility in such cases. Borchard, *Diplomatic Protection* (n 3) 232; Goebel, 'International Responsibility of States' (n 4) 831–32; Eagleton, *Responsibility of States* (n 3) 145.

that a state had to observe would require an investigation of individual instances of the alleged violation of the state's international obligation, while taking into account the unique circumstances of each case.

This approach was confirmed by the arbitrator Huber in *Spanish Zone of Morocco*.[55] The case concerned more than fifty claims made by British nationals against Spain for the losses they suffered during the riots and civil uprising that took place in the wake of the insurrection of a Berber tribe in the early 1920s. Huber held that the state was not in itself responsible for the mere fact that there was a conflict, whether a riot, rebellion, civil war, or international war; nor was it responsible for the fact that those events gave rise to damage in its territory.[56] He then emphasized that the principle of non-responsibility did not exclude the state's duty to exercise some vigilance. In particular, he held that 'if the State is not responsible for the revolutionary events themselves, it could nevertheless be responsible for what the authorities do or not do to avert, to the extent possible, the consequence'.[57] In order to establish responsibility, the conduct of the state's authorities or armed forces during the conflict had to be analysed. Huber understood due diligence as a standard that took into account the specific circumstances of the situation in which the harm was done as well as the resources available to the state.[58]

The case law shows that establishing the responsibility of the state for injuries to foreigners was inherently linked to clarifying the content of the violated rule of international law. It has become widely accepted that the obligation to act with due diligence in pursuit of the protection of foreigners is one of the elements of the international minimum standard of treatment which constituted customary international law.[59] In the context of conflict situations, the obligation required the state to exercise due diligence to protect foreign nationals from physical violence. In ascertaining the content of due diligence, commissions typically highlighted the following factors: the type, character, and intensity of conflict situation;[60] the degree of the state's control over parts of its territory;[61] the state's resources and the foreseeability of the harm;[62] and to a limited extent the importance of the interest to be protected.[63] In addition to the duty of protection, the state could be held liable

[55] *Spanish Zone of Morocco* (*Great Britain v Spain*) (1924) 2 RIAA 615, 639, 642.
[56] ibid.
[57] ibid.
[58] ibid 644.
[59] See Ago, 'First Report' (n 12) 108; E Root, 'Basis of Protection to Citizens Residing Abroad' (1910) 4 AJIL 517, 521–22; Borchard, *Diplomatic Protection* (n 3) 28; I Brownlie, *System of the Law of Nations: State Responsibility Part I* (Clarendon Press 1983) 159–79; M Paparinskis, *The International Minimum Standard and Fair and Equitable Treatment* (OUP 2013).
[60] See *Spanish Zone of Morocco* (n 55) 644–45; *GL Solis* (*US v Mexico*) (1928) 4 RIAA 358, 362.
[61] See *Sambiaggio* (n 41); *Spanish Zone of Morocco* (n 55); *Buckingham Case*, reported in G Haywood Hackworth, *Digest of International Law*, vol V (Washington 1940–1944) 480; *Wipperman Case*, reported in Moore, *History and Digest* (n 11) 3040–41.
[62] See *De Brissot Case*, reported in *Moore*, ibid 2969; *US Diplomatic and Consular Staff in Teheran (US v Iran)* [1980] ICJ Rep 3, 33 (*Hostages in Iran Case*).
[63] See *Chapman* (*US v Mexico*) (1930) 4 RIAA 632, 639; *Mallen* (*US v Mexico*) (1927) 4 RIAA 175.

through other acts of omission such as a failure to investigate and prosecute those responsible for injuries caused to foreigners.[64] The principle of due diligence has since been confirmed in policy proposals for the codification of the law of state responsibility,[65] decisions of the International Court of Justice (ICJ),[66] diplomatic practice,[67] contemporary scholarship,[68] as well as in awards of investment treaty tribunals.[69] Despite its wide recognition, the content and the scope of the standard have been continuously contested and raise several questions that will be discussed further in subsequent chapters.

4. From Mob Violence to Civil War

Despite some doctrinal proposals to classify internal conflicts into different categories for the purposes of determining state responsibility,[70] scholars and arbitrators of the nineteenth and early twentieth centuries discussed the principles of state responsibility for the losses of foreigners in civil wars together with less intense instances of internal conflict, such as revolutions, riots, and mob violence. For a long time, the rules of war referred only to armed conflicts between different nations, rather than to internal disturbances. While the legal doctrine of the late eighteenth century began to entertain the idea that the conduct of states in civil wars should be governed by the laws of war,[71] it was only in the twentieth century

[64] The dual nature of the principle was emphasized by the US–Mexico General Claims Commission established in the early 1920s. See e.g. *Janes* (*US v Mexico*) (1926) 4 RIAA 82; *Youmans* (*US v Mexico*) (1926) 4 RIAA 110; *Massey* (*US v Mexico*) (1927) 4 RIAA 155. See also Eagleton, *Responsibility of States* (n 3) 130; C Hyde, *International Law Chiefly as Interpreted and Applied by the United States* (Little Brown 1922) 517–18; A Freeman, *Responsibility of States for Unlawful Acts of their Armed Forces* (AW Sijthoff 1957) 16, 17.

[65] See e.g. Harvard Draft on the Law of Responsibility of States for Damage Done in their Territory to the Person or Property of Foreigners (1929) Arts 10–12 in ILC, *Yearbook of the International Law Commission, 1956, Vol II*, UN Doc A/CN.4/SER.A/1956/Add.1 229 (1929 Harvard Draft); Harvard Draft Convention on the International Responsibility of States for Injuries to Aliens (1961) Art 13 in ILC, *Yearbook of the International Law Commission, 1969, Vol II*, UN Doc A/CN.4/SER.A/1969/Add.1, 142, 145 (1961 Harvard Draft).

[66] See e.g. *Corfu Channel* (*UK v Albania*) [1949] ICJ Rep 4, 22; *Hostages in Iran Case* (n 62); *Armed Activities on Territory of Congo (Democratic Republic of Congo v Uganda)* (Judgment) [2005] ICJ Rep 168, 231, para 179 (*Armed Activities*); *Elettronica Sicula SPA* (*US v Italy*) (Merits) [1989] ICJ Rep 15, 65, para 108; *Application of the Convention on the Prevention and Punishment of the Crime of Genocide (Bosnia and Herzegovina v Serbia)* (Judgment) [2007] ICJ Rep 43, 221, para 430 (*Bosnian Genocide*).

[67] See diplomatic correspondence during the Cold War period, cited in R Barnidge, 'The Due Diligence Principle under International Law' (2006) 8 ICLR 81, 108–09;

[68] ibid; R Pissilo-Mazzeschi, 'The Due Diligence Rule and the Nature of the International Responsibility of States' (1992) 35 German YB Intl L 9; T Koivurova, 'Due Diligence' in Max Planck Encyclopaedia of International Law (OUP 2010).

[69] See Chapter 4.

[70] See Francis Lieber and Henry Halleck quoted by C Wiesse in *Reglas de derecho internacional aplicables a las guerras civiles* (2nd edn, Torres-Aguirre 1905) 4–8, cited in F Paddeu, 'A Genealogy of Force Majeure in International Law' (2012) 82(1) BYIL 381, 408.

[71] See e.g. de Vattel, *The Law of Nations* (n 1) bk III, ch XVIII, 644–46. De Vattel developed a concept of 'true civil war' between two independent parties within one nation who both had to comply with the laws of war in the conduct of hostilities.

that non-international armed conflicts were formally included in the same body of law as international conflicts through codification, classification as customary international law, jurisprudence, constitutive instruments of international criminal tribunals, and scholarly literature.[72] In the interim period, however, it seemed apt to address the responsibility of states for injuries to aliens in civil wars together with other types of internal strife.

This, however, did not mean that scholars and arbitrators were oblivious to the differences between the different types of internal strife. As mentioned above, arbitrators and commissioners often took into account the various characteristics of a conflict when assessing the host state's compliance with the due diligence obligation.[73] The fact that the same principle of due diligence governed the conduct of a state in times of internal conflict did not mean that the principle was applied without distinction across the spectrum of situations of different nature, scope, and magnitude. Typically, a civil war involved more intense and widespread violence and loss of control over parts of territories due to the superior organization of insurgents. Consequently, the responsibility of a state for injuries arising from civil war was easier to exempt as a result of the difficulty in proving that the state had failed to exercise due diligence in those extreme circumstances.[74] Different levels and measures of protection could be required from the host state in situations involving looting, mob violence, and rebellion, on the one hand, and full-fledged civil war employing military force, on the other.

The early codification of state responsibility for losses suffered by aliens at the hands of insurrectional movements introduced several distinctions between different types of conflict situations. According to one view, there was a difference between targeted riots and other types of internal conflict. Another approach attached different consequences to state responsibility depending on whether the insurgency amounted to a recognized belligerency, and whether the insurrectional movement was successful and resulted in a change of government.

With respect to the first view, some jurists advocated making a distinction between mob violence and riots, and revolutions and civil war, whereby the former encompassed isolated violent incidents, often based on xenophobia and directed specifically towards foreigners,[75] whereas the latter was precipitated by political motives and the goal of overthrowing the government. This distinction between targeted riots and other types of internal conflict was adopted in Guerrero Report

[72] See Section 2 C.1.

[73] *Spanish Zone of Morocco* (n 55) 644–45; *GL Solis* (n 60) 362.

[74] Eagleton, *Responsibility of States* (n 3) 150; R Ago, 'Fourth Report on State Responsibility' in ILC, *Yearbook of the International Law Commission, 1972, Vol II*, UN Doc A/CN.4/SER.A/1972/Add.1, 71, 129, para 153.

[75] Goebel, 'International Responsibility of States' (n 4) 817.

of the Sub-Committee on State Responsibility in 1926. The conclusions of the report asserted that the state was not responsible for losses that foreigners suffered in internal conflicts with the exception of riots that were 'directed against foreigners, as such, and the State failed to perform its duties of surveillance and repression'.[76] Similar views were adopted in some private codifications of state responsibility, including the Draft Code of International Law adopted by the Japanese branch of the International Law Association, and the Draft Convention on the Responsibility of States, prepared by the German International Law Association.[77]

Building on Guerrero's narrow interpretation of state responsibility, the Preparatory Committee of the Hague Conference in 1930 proposed two assumptions based on the nature of a conflict. The starting point was the principle of non-responsibility for injuries suffered by foreigners in an insurrection, riot, or mob violence, unless the state had failed to exercise its due diligence to prevent the damage or to punish the perpetrators. The opposite assumption would apply for riots or mob violence that targeted foreigners as such, or people of a particular nationality. For those losses, the state was responsible unless the government proved that 'that there was no negligence on its part or on the part of its officials'.[78] In both cases, the responsibility of the state arose only if the state had failed to act with a certain degree of vigilance. There was a difference, however, as to who bore the burden of proof. In cases of revolutions and civil wars, the claimant had to prove the government's lack of vigilance.[79] In contrast, the respondent government had to prove its due diligence if the loss to a foreigner resulted from a targeted riot or mob violence. According to Borchard, this evidentiary distinction reflected the practice of the nineteenth-century commissions.[80] The view that targeted violent events warranted different legal treatment than other types of internal conflict when considering state responsibility was not presented in the subsequent codifications and works of the International Law Commission (ILC).

Some codifications distinguished between insurgency or revolution, on the one hand, and a recognized belligerency on the other. In addition, different

[76] Guerrero Report (n 29).

[77] Draft Code of International Law, adopted by the Japanese Branch of the International Law Association and the Kokusaiho Gakkwai (1926) Art 3; Draft Convention on the Responsibility of States for Injuries Caused in their Territory to the Person or Property of Aliens, prepared by the Deutsche Gesellschaft für Volkerrecht (1930) Art 6.2 in ILC, *Yearbook of the International Law Commission, 1969, Vol II*, UN Doc A/CN.4/SER.A/1969/Add.1 141, 149.

[78] Bases of Discussion Drawn up in 1929 by the Preparatory Committee of the Conference for the Codification of International Law (The Hague, 1930) No 22(a) and No 22(d) in ILC, *Yearbook of the International Law Commission, 1956, Vol II*, UN Doc A/CN.4/SER.A/1956/Add.1 224.

[79] See e.g. *Kummerow et al Case* (n 48) 378.

[80] Borchard, *Diplomatic Protection* (n 3) 233. Brownlie was critical of this distinction, noting that the evidential burden would depend on circumstances of each case. Brownlie, *State Responsibility* (n 59) 172.

consequences were predicted for successful and unsuccessful insurrectional movements. For example, Article 13 of the 1929 Harvard Draft stated:

> a) In the event of an unsuccessful revolution, the State whose government is established thereby, is not responsible under Article 7, if an injury to an alien has resulted from a wrongful act or omission committed after their recognition as belligerents either by itself or by a State of which the alien is a national;
> b) In the event of a successful revolution, the State whose government is established thereby, is responsible under Article 7 if an injury to an alien has resulted from a wrongful act or omission committed at any time after the inception of the revolution.[81]

The latter proposition reflects the well-established principle that when an insurrectional movement replaces the old government and constitutes a new government, the new government is responsible not only for its own acts (i.e. the acts of insurgents), but also for the acts of the previous government. The losses that foreigners sustain at the hands of either insurgents fighting for power or the former government's armed forces, are attributable to the host state, which remains the only subject of international law. This view has been consistently followed in arbitral practice and applied in various codifications of state responsibility, including Articles on the Responsibility of States for Internationally Wrongful Acts (ARS).[82]

The former proposition that the responsibility of a state was dependent on the recognition of belligerency in the case of an unsuccessful revolution was more problematic. The view was advocated by some scholars who argued that the recognition of the insurrectional movement as a belligerent party could be taken as admission of inability to control the rebels,[83] and consequently exempted the state from all responsibility, even if the state breached its international obligation (e.g. failed to exercise due diligence).[84] It was brought into the codification project by the Institute of International Law in 1927, followed by the 1929 Harvard Draft cited above and the draft Convention of the German International Law Association (1930).[85] There

[81] 1929 Harvard Draft (n 65).

[82] ILC, Articles on the Responsibility of States for Internationally Wrongful Acts, *Yearbook of the International Law Commission, 2001, Vol II*, UN Doc A/CN.4/SER.A/2001/Add.1 26, Art 10. See also *French Company of Venezuelan Railroads (France v Venezuela)* (1905) 10 RIAA 285, 354; *Puerto Cabello and Valencia Railway Company (Great Britain v Venezuela)* (1903) 9 RIAA 510, 513; *Pinson (France) v United Mexican States* (1928) 5 RIAA 327, 353. For an overview, see Ago, 'Fourth Report' (n 74) paras 198–213.

[83] Eagleton, *Responsibility of States* (n 3) 147; Hyde, *International Law* (n 64) 541.

[84] See e.g. A McNair, *International Law Opinions* (CUP 1956) 245. For a reference to more authorities, see ILC, *Yearbook of the International Law Commission, 1975, Vol II*, UN Doc A/CN.4/SER.A/1975/Add.1 98.

[85] Draft on International Responsibility of States for Injuries in their Territory to the Person or Property of Foreigners, Prepared by the Institute of International Law (1927) Art VII in ILC, *Yearbook of the International Law Commission, 1956, Vol II*, UN Doc A/CN.4/SER.A/1956/Add.1 227, 228; 1929 Harvard Draft (n 65); 1930 Draft by Deutsche Gesellschaft für Völkerrecht (n 77).

seemed to be no sound legal justification for the proposal according to which a single act of recognition would have absolved the state of the responsibility for the wrongful act of failing to provide foreigners with adequate protection. The ILC was also critical, contending that:

> . . . it is difficult to see why the State, which is unquestionably responsible in the event of wrongful failure to give protection against the conduct of organs of another State, should cease to be responsible when the conduct in question is that of organs of an insurrectional movement.[86]

The proposal has since been renounced in the reports and drafts of the Special Rapporteurs on state responsibility. While the recognition of belligerency is a relic of the past, the modern interpretation of that view would attach the same consequences to the meeting of the IHL thresholds for civil war. While acknowledging the differences between types of conflicts may be relevant in other legal contexts, no distinctions should be made for the purposes of attributing responsibility to a state arising from its failure to act diligently to prevent the losses incurred by insurrectional movements.[87] According to the ILC, the illegality or the movement's lack of legitimacy is not relevant, what matters is 'the particular conduct [of the State] in question, and . . . its lawfulness'.[88] While recognition of belligerency or meeting one of the thresholds for civil war is crucial to trigger the application of the IHL rules, a state can breach its obligation of vigilance, protection, and punishment with respect to the conduct of non-state actors in all types of conflict, including civil war.[89]

The continued development of the customary principles on the treatment of aliens through the interstate arbitrations and claims commissions of the nineteenth and early twentieth centuries slowed when other remedial regimes became more popular after 1945, a development described in Chapter 7. At the same time, attempts to create a multilateral agreement on investment standards failed, while the ILC, facing difficulties reaching an agreement on substantive standards for the treatment of aliens,[90] decided to shift its focus to secondary rules on state responsibility. Thus, in the second half of the twentieth century, the treatment of foreign investors fell under the purview of investment treaties.

[86] ILC, *Yearbook 1975* (n 84) 98; Ago, 'Fourth Report' (n 74) 141, para 184, n 404. See also Brownlie, *State Responsibility* (n 59) 177 (calling this principle 'unattractively automatic and crude in its operation').

[87] Ago, 'Fourth Report' (n 74) 132, para 160; J Crawford, 'First Report on State Responsibility' in ILC, *Yearbook of the International Law Commission, 1998, Vol II*, UN Doc A/CN.4/SER.A/1998/Add.1 1, 51, 53. Art 10(3) ARS provides for this possibility.

[88] Commentary to Articles on the Responsibility of States for Internationally Wrongful Acts, Art 10, para 11 in ILC, *Yearbook of the International Law Commission, 2001, Vol II*, UN Doc A/CN.4/SER.A/2001/Add.1 51; Crawford, 'First Report' (n 87) 53, para 271.

[89] See further Section 2 C.1.b.

[90] See e.g. E Borchard, '"Responsibility of States" at the Hague Codification Conference' (1930) 24 AJIL 517.

C. Protections in International Humanitarian Law

International humanitarian law (also known as the law of armed conflict or *jus in bello*)[91] is a field of public international law that aims to regulate (and thus constrain) the conduct during armed conflict and minimize the suffering that it causes.[92] The historical evolution of the IHL rules applicable to the treatment of the private property of aliens has been addressed by prominent scholars in the past.[93] However, a brief summary aids in understanding the current legal frameworks.

In ancient times, the property of enemy aliens was considered *res nullius* and its seizure and confiscation was permitted under the law.[94] The general principle in ancient Greece, as well as in the Roman Empire, was that all the private property of enemy subjects belonged to the conqueror.[95] This practice continued in the Middle Ages when war was considered the natural means for securing property and wealth. The English Magna Carta of 1215 introduced an exception based on reciprocity, and stipulated that the property of enemy merchants residing in England should not be confiscated at the outbreak of war except by way of reprisals for the confiscation of English property in the enemy state.[96] In the late Middle Ages, some kingdoms promulgated special codes of conduct that were meant to be followed by soldiers in wartime.[97] In that period, some treaties of amity and friendship also granted foreign merchants a right to stay securely in the countries.[98]

More enlightened views developed during the Renaissance and were described in the works of Hugo Grotius, who adamantly denounced the practice of indiscriminate plunder and confiscation since he found it contrary to the natural law.[99] Grotius's ideas soon began to be reflected in practice. Eventually, the custom emerged according to which the immovable property of domiciled enemies was not interfered with, and it became uncommon to seize the moveable property of

[91] MC Bassiouni, 'The Normative Framework of International Humanitarian Law: Overlaps, Gaps and Ambiguities' (1998) 8 Trans L Contemp Probs 199, 200; H McCoubrey, *International Humanitarian Law: Modern Developments in the Limitation of Warfare* (Ashgate 1998) 1; C Greenwood, 'Historical Development and Legal Basis' in D Fleck and M Bothe (eds), *The Handbook of International Humanitarian Law* (OUP 2007) 1, 11.

[92] On how the term 'international humanitarian law' became a synonym with the 'law of armed conflict' and gradually replaced it, see A Alexander, 'A Short History of International Humanitarian Law' (2015) 26(1) EJIL 109, 114–24.

[93] N Bentwich, *The Law of Private Property in War with a Chapter on Conquest* (Sweet & Maxwell 1907); J Gathings, *International Law and American Treatment of Alien Enemy Property* (American Council of Public Affairs 1940); Oppenheim, *International Law* (n 41) 326–32; Hyde, *International Law* (2nd edn) (n 64) 1726; S Neff, *War and the Law of Nations—A General History* (CUP 2005).

[94] Oppenheim, *International Law* (n 41) 408, 413.

[95] Bentwich, *Law of Private Property* (n 93) 2; H Grotius, *De jure belli* (n 1) ch III 6, 13.

[96] Magna Carta (1215) para 41.

[97] See e.g. M Keen, *The Laws of War in the Late Middle Ages* (Keegan Paul 1965) 156–85; M Keen, *Chivalry* (Yale University Press 1984).

[98] Treaty of Amity and Friendship, and of a Free Intercourse of Trade and Merchandizes between Henry VII King of England, and Philip Archduke of Austria, Duke of Burgundy (1495); Treaty of Peace and Commerce between Francis I King of France, and Henry VIII King of England (5 April 1515) Art V.

[99] Grotius, *De jure belli* (n 1).

domiciled enemies on land or to confiscate the debts of enemy subjects.[100] If the property was confiscated, the peace treaties commonly provided for its return when the war ended.[101] Still, little regard was paid to the treatment of property in the course of military operations, and the indiscriminate ravaging and pillage had simply been replaced by systematic and organized plunder that was only marginally less oppressive.[102]

The French Revolution reintroduced the concept of natural law and asserted the rights of the individual man against the powers of government.[103] This progressive outlook was most prominently displayed in the work of Jean-Jacques Rousseau, who argued that belligerents should primarily attack state-owned property and do the least possible harm to private property.[104] The theories of the French humanists began to inform the content of the rules of war in the eighteenth century and were finally transplanted into positive law in the nineteenth century. While attempts were made to codify the law of war by introducing elements of humanism as early as the middle of the nineteenth century,[105] the true milestone in this legal development was witnessed in the Hague Peace Conferences of 1899 and 1907, when it was asserted, among others, that the rights of private property should remain intact in time of war so far as they are not disturbed by the necessities of war.

Even before the Hague Conference, however, the treatment of foreign investors by host states in armed conflict was subject to scrutiny by several arbitrations and mixed claims commissions held in the aftermath of conflicts by means of the treaties made between the respective states, which considerably contributed to clarifying the rules of war. The claims of foreigners regarding their losses resulting from international armed conflicts were usually governed by specific agreements entered into for each individual situation, and often the claims for damages inflicted by the troops of a victorious belligerent were waived by the vanquished nation in peace treaties.[106] This hampered the development of IHL. Furthermore, the content of the legal principles was obfuscated by the above-mentioned 'act of grace' payments for alleged injuries. The civil wars of the nineteenth century thus presented an opportunity in which the claims of aliens for losses suffered in wartime could be submitted to international tribunals for adjudication. Those tribunals clarified the principles applicable to the conduct in hostilities and thus contributed to the development of customary international law. The latter was

[100] Bentwich, *Law of Private Property* (n 93) 8; Oppenheim, *International Law* (n 41) 326.
[101] Vandevelde, *History* (n 6) 19.
[102] Bentwich, *Law of Private Property* (n 93) 10.
[103] ibid.
[104] ibid 11, citing Rousseau, 'The Social Contract'.
[105] Declaration Renouncing the Use, in Time of War, of Explosive Projectiles Under 400 Grammes Weight, Saint Petersburg (entered into force 11 December 1868); Geneva Convention for the Amelioration of the Condition of the Wounded in Armies in the Field (signed 22 August 1864, entered into force 22 June 1865); Instructions for the Government of Armies of the United States in the Field, prepared by Professor Francis Lieber, General Orders No 100 (24 April 1863) (Lieber Code).
[106] Freeman, *Responsibility of States* (n 64) 34; Oppenheim, *International Law* (n 41) 328–31.

then formalized in the code of conduct known as the Regulations Annexed to the Hague Convention No IV of 1907 that only concerned conflicts between states.[107] Although the Hague Regulations were largely declaratory of previous practice, they gave greater protection to private property.[108]

The general rule that was accepted in the scholarship and jurisprudence of the nineteenth century was that a state was not responsible for damages or injuries that foreigners, either enemy or neutral, sustained in the conduct of legitimate military operations in time of war.[109] The measures that could be considered legitimate military operations were clarified by the precedents of the mixed claims commissions. A belligerent state could thus be held liable, and in fact often was, for unnecessary or wanton acts of destruction, such as pillage by soldiers.[110]

On the other hand, it was continuously held that the state was not responsible for the devastation of property that occurred during the course of fighting (e.g. during hostilities) or as a consequence of a measure necessitated by war.[111] Such measures included the bombardment of military targets,[112] injuries to property in preparation to attack or defend or prevent its use by the enemy for military purposes,[113] the destruction of property to preserve the health and security of the armed forces,[114] and accidental destruction of innocent property.[115] Military necessity was the elusive standard used to determine whether the state's measure

[107] Hague Convention IV Respecting the Laws and Customs of War on Land (signed 18 October 1907, entered into force 26 January 1910) 187 Consol T S 227 (Hague Regulations).

[108] Freeman, *Responsibility of States* (n 64) 40; Borchard, *Diplomatic Protection* (n 3) 279.

[109] Freeman (n 64) 31; Borchard, *Diplomatic Protection* (n 3) 256–57; Eagleton, *Responsibility of States* (n 3) 155; Moore, *History and Digest* (n 11) 3669–70; Ralston, *Venezuelan Arbitrations* (n 41) 931.

[110] See e.g. *Joseph Chourreau v US* (French–US Claims Commission 1880); *Edward Du Bois v Chile, No 2* (US–Chilean Claims Commission 1901); *Andrew Moss v Chile, No 25* (US–Chilean Claims Commission 1901) all reported in Moore, *Digest* (n 21) 921; *Alexander Barrington v Mexico, No 365* (1868) reported in Moore, *History and Digest* (n 11) 3674. For more, see Moore, *Digest* (n 21) 905, 910, 918–22; Borchard, *Diplomatic Protection* (n 3) 261.

[111] See e.g. *Wilson's Case* (Spanish Claims Commission 1881); *Peter Bacigalupi v Chile No 42* (US–Chilean Claims Commission 1901) both reported in Moore, *Digest* (n 21) 894, 921. For more cases, see Moore, *Digest* (n 21) 883–94; Moore, *History and Digest* (n 11) 3668, 3670, 3678, 3703, 3679; Ralston, *Venezuelan Arbitrations* (n 41) 14–25, 35–36; Borchard, *Diplomatic Protection* (n 3) 256–62.

[112] See e.g. the bombardment of Greytown by the US forces, in the course of which the property of French merchants was destroyed. The US argued that there was no obligation to pay indemnity, as the property was indiscreetly placed to a custody of the enemy. Reported in Moore, *Digest* (n 21) 926–40.

[113] See e.g. *Case of Maza and Larrache (Spain v US)* (1884) (the seizure and destruction of investor's cotton by the US forces was deemed permissible as it presented a 'munition of war' that could be made use of by the insurgents), reported in Moore, *Digest*, ibid 895–901; *Claims by the Eastern Extension Telegraph Company et al against the US* (the US argued that cutting of submarine cables during the war with Spain in Cuba and Philippines was carried out in order to prevent the enemy from using it and was thus justified as a lawful operation of war. This notwithstanding, the damages were paid as an act of grace.), reported in Moore, ibid 924–26.

[114] e.g. destruction of buildings as a sanitary measure. See *Hardman Case (Great Britain v US)* (1910) 7 AJIL 897; *Jaragua Iron Co v US*, 212 US 297, 306, both reported in Borchard, *Diplomatic Protection* (n 3) 257.

[115] See e.g. the *Adams Case*, in which the US commander burnt his vessel to prevent it from falling into the hands of the British army. While the fire extended to the neighbouring warehouse, the destruction of that property was considered a 'casualty of war'. Reported in Moore, *Digest* (n 21) 893.

was legitimate or not. It was held that the assessment of whether the measure was justified according to military necessity should be left to military leaders and national authorities called upon to act in extreme circumstances.[116] The damages resulting from the seizure or destruction prompted by imperious military necessity were considered to be 'war losses', that is damages incident to combat action, and as such, no compensation could be demanded.[117] A distinction was made, however, between the damage caused to property during combat action and the seizure of property for military use. Where property was appropriated by the government to be used for military purposes, fair compensation was due.[118] Furthermore, the state was not responsible for interference with ordinary commercial and professional activities and the consequential loss of business and profit, or claims for damages.[119]

A distinction was made between two types of foreigners: neutral and enemy.[120] While the old rule was that alien nationals of a belligerent country could be expelled from the state, the treaties and practice of the late nineteenth century introduced a more humane principle: enemy aliens could continue to reside without their property being confiscated provided that they maintained a neutral position.[121] An exception was made for merchants who could only continue to reside and trade in the host state for a limited amount of time, usually for six months or one year after the outbreak of war.[122] Furthermore, the host state could sequestrate the alien's property if there was a risk that it could be used by the enemy state in the conduct of its military operations or to aid and abet the insurrection, subject to its return at the end of the war or payment of compensation.[123]

[116] *Spanish Zone of Morocco* (n 55) 645.

[117] Moore, *Digest* (n 21) 903.

[118] See e.g. *Dix Case* (*US v Venezuela*) (1903) 9 RIAA 113, 119; *William Moore Case* (*US v Nicaragua*) (1900) reported in Moore, *Digest*, ibid 914. For more, see Moore, ibid 902–15; Moore, *History and Digest* (n 11) 3720; Eagleton, *Responsibility of States* (n 3) 156; Borchard, *Diplomatic Protection* (n 3) 262–67.

[119] See e.g. *Heny Case* (*US v Venezuela*) (1903) 9 RIAA 113, 125.

[120] According to the Continental European practice, the nationality of an alien (i.e. whether they were a national of the enemy state) was decisive in determining whether or not the alien and their property had an enemy character. In contrast, according to the Anglo-American practice, the test was based on their domicile and exceptional circumstances, such as their conduct. Borchard, *Diplomatic Protection* (n 3) 253.

[121] ibid 109, 112–13.

[122] ibid 110. See also A Hamilton, *The Defence No. Xxii (Oct. 14, 1795)*, reprinted in 19 *The Papers of Alexander Hamilton* (Harold C. Syrett edn, 1973) 380, 382, 387 (arguing that enemy merchants were accorded full protection and security for six to nine months since the outbreak of war under international law). This obligation was included in many old treaties of friendship and commerce, see e.g. Treaty of Peace and Friendship between Great Britain and Spain (13 May 1667) Art XXXVI; Treaty of Peace between the Kingdom of France and the United Provinces of the Netherlands (19 August 1678) Art XV; Treaty of Amity and Commerce between the United States and France (6 February 1778) Art 22, in H Miller, *Treaties and Other International Acts of the United States of America*, vol 2 (Government Printing Office 1931) 1776.

[123] Borchard *Diplomatic Protection* (n 3) 113; Moore, *Digest Vol 7* (n 21) 289–95; Moore, *History and Digest* (n 11) 3719.

In practice, the application of these humanitarian rules was inconsistent, reflecting again the privileged position that powerful states had carved out for themselves in the world order. Thus, humanitarian standards did not apply to Western military interventions in Latin America, as they were generally considered 'measures short of war' and thus not meeting the war threshold.[124] Moreover, the Western states argued that humanitarian law did not apply with respect to colonial wars,[125] in the course of which the great powers often resorted to military strategies that involved destruction and seizure of property.[126] It took only a couple of decades for these practices to re-emerge in full force among the 'civilized' nations themselves, namely in the course of both World Wars.[127]

1. Contemporary International Humanitarian Law

The catastrophic effects of the Second World War demonstrated a collapse of the international legal regime governing warfare and led to the realization that humanitarian law had to be revised and modernized.[128] This project was taken up by the International Committee of the Red Cross (ICRC), which supervised and facilitated the revision process, eventually leading up to several documents that constitute contemporary IHL. The relevant treaty provisions aiming at protecting private property can be found in the Hague Convention No IV of 1907, the Geneva Convention of 1949 on the Protection of Civilian Persons in Time of War, and the Additional Protocols (APs) I and II of 1977.[129] The *raison d'être* of the rules is to provide the highest level of protection to civilians and their property by restraining armed violence, while taking into account war expediency and military interests (e.g. strategic and tactical considerations necessary for bringing a conflict to its optimal and quick end).[130] As explained in Chapter 1, the application of

[124] Bernstorff, *Use of Force* (n 30) 242; Neff, *War and the Law of Nations* (n 93).

[125] Bernstorff (n 30); E Colby, 'How to Fight Savage Tribes' (1927) 21 AJIL 279.

[126] Bernstorff (n 30) 246; F Mégret, 'From Savages to Unlawful Combatants: A Postcolonial Look at International Law's "Other"' in A Orford (ed), *International Law and Its Others* (CUP 2006) 265.

[127] e.g. in the aftermath of the First and Second World Wars, peace treaties determined that the private assets of enemies seized were not returned but be used for post-war reparations or claims settlements. See e.g. Treaty of Peace between the Allied and Associated Powers and Germany (28 June 1919) 225 Consol TS, 1888 (Treaty of Versailles); post-Second WW: Treaty of Peace with Italy (1947) Art 79; Treaty of Peace with Bulgaria (1947) Art 25. See Oppenheim, *International Law* (n 41) 330, 406.

[128] J Kunz, 'The Chaotic Status of the Law of War and the Urgent Necessity of Their Revision' (1951) 45(1) AJIL 37, 40–41.

[129] Geneva Convention (IV) relative to the Protection of Civilian Persons in Time of War (signed 12 August 1949, entered into force 21 October 1950) 75 UNTS 287 (GC IV); Protocol (I) Additional to the Geneva Conventions of 12 August 1949, and relating to the Protection of Victims of International Armed Conflicts (signed 12 December 1977, entered into force 7 December 1978) 1125 UNTS 3 (AP I); Protocol (II) Additional to the Geneva Conventions of 12 August 1949, and relating to the Protection of Victims of Non-International Armed Conflicts (signed 12 December 1977, entered into force 7 December 1978) 1125 UNTS 609 (AP II).

[130] See J Kunz, 'The Laws of War' (1956) 50 AJIL 313, 314; G Schwarzenberger, *International Law and Order* (Praeger 1971) 172; N Hayashi, 'Military Necessity as a Normative Indifference' (2013) 44

IHL is contingent on the existence of international or internal armed conflict. The set of rules that will apply depends on the conflict's characteristics. International conflicts (including struggles for national liberation against 'alien occupation' or 'colonial domination') are governed by the Hague Regulations, the four Geneva Conventions, and AP I. In contrast, a non-international armed conflict did not fall under IHL treaty law until 1949, and is scarcely regulated by Common Article 3 to the four Geneva Conventions (regarding less intense conflicts) and AP II (regarding high-intensity conflicts in which the armed groups are 'under responsible command' and 'exercise such control over a part of [the State's] territory as to enable them to carry out sustained and concerted military operations').[131] If the threshold for a non-international armed conflict is not met, IHL does not apply.

Civilian persons who are afforded protections are defined in Article 4 of the Geneva Convention (GC) IV, and include those with an enemy nationality living in the territory of a belligerent state and the inhabitants of the occupied territory. This definition appears to have been extended by the ICTY in the *Tadić* decision in order to encompass all victims in need of such a status during periods of armed conflict.[132] Furthermore, the rules in the AP I extend protections to all civilians, regardless of their nationality.[133] Consequently, it appears uncontroversial that IHL protections cover foreign investors as well.

Most of the rules listed in the Hague and Geneva treaties have achieved the status of customary international law.[134] This is reflected in the comprehensive study carried out by the ICRC on the customary international humanitarian law that draws on the Geneva Conventions, AP I, and state practice.[135] The IHL rules on the protection of private property in times of war would thus likely apply even if the parties to the conflict did not sign or ratify the IHL treaties.[136]

The following sections provide a brief overview of the provisions and principles that are particularly relevant for the protection of foreign investors.

Georget J Intl L 50; R Coupland, 'Humanity: What Is It and How Does It Influence International Law' (2001) 83(844) IRRC 986–87; M Newton, 'Reframing the Proportionality Principle' (2018) 51 VJTL 867, 872.

---

131 AP II, Art 1(1).

132 *Prosecutor v Tadić* (Appeal Judgment) IT-94-1-A (15 July 1999) para 168.

133 ICRC Commentary to Art 50 of AP I, para 1909. See also Y Dinstein, *The Conduct of Hostilities under the Law of International Armed Conflict* (3rd edn, CUP 2016) 142; I Henderson, *The Contemporary Law of Targeting* (Martinus Nijhoff 2009) 227–29.

134 *Legality of the Threat or Use of Nuclear Weapons* (Advisory Opinion) [1996] ICJ Rep 226, 260, para 87 (confirming that all states are bound by the rules of the AP I, that are expressions of customary international law).

135 J-M Henckaerts and L Doswald-Beck, *International Committee of the Red Cross, Customary International Humanitarian Law, vol I, Rules* (2005 CUP) (ICRC Study).

136 See e.g. *Civilian Claims: Ethiopia's Claim 5* (Partial Award of 17 December 2004) 26 RIAA 249, 262, paras 23–25; *Central Front—Ethiopia's Claim 2* (Partial Award of 28 April 2004) 26 RIAA 155, 166, paras 17–18; *Central Front—Eritrea's Claims*, 2, 4, 6, 7, 8, 22 (Partial Award of 28 April 2004) 26 RIAA 115, 127, paras 21–23.

(a) International armed conflict

Most IHL rules governing international armed conflict are extensive and specific. The general provision that stipulates that private property must be respected during wartime is laid down in Article 46 of the Hague Regulations. In addition, the provision prohibits the confiscation of private property. This prohibition, however, does not imply that no private property may ever be seized. Limited exceptions are introduced in Article 52 (the needs of the army of occupation) and Article 53 (vital property for the military effort) under the condition that seized property is compensated for immediately, in the former case, and restored or compensated for when the conflict has ended, in the latter case.

For instance, with respect to seizure, the Eritrea–Ethiopia Claims Commission (EECC) held that generally belligerent states had a right to freeze or otherwise restrict access to the assets of enemy aliens in order to deny them to the enemy state.[137] However, this had to be done 'under conditions providing for the property's protection and its eventual disposition by return to the owner or through post-war agreement'.[138] Conversely, the Commission found that Eritrea was liable for economic losses that resulted from the wrongful seizure of property by state officials and interference with the property of Ethiopian nationals (which included looting, blocked bank accounts, and forced closures of businesses followed by confiscations).[139]

Important protections of private property are also found in the GC IV. Article 33 prohibits pillage and reprisals against civilian property, and Article 53 expressly prohibits the destruction of the moveable or immoveable property of private persons except when military operations render such destruction absolutely necessary. Standards governing the treatment of enemy aliens are provided in Articles 35–46, and they include the right to depart at the outset of, or during, the conflict, unless doing so would be contrary to the national interest of the host state (Article 35). While the Geneva Conventions do not explicitly address the expulsion of nationals of the enemy state, they seem to generally accept that a belligerent state has the right to expel enemy aliens if it so chooses.[140] Another important provision is

[137] *Civilian Claims: Eritrea's Claims 15, 16, 23, 27–23* (Partial Award of 17 December 2004) 26 RIAA 195, 236–37, para 128. See also Oppenheim (n 41) 407 (making analogy with Art 53 of the Hague Regulations).

[138] *Eritrea's Civilian Claims*, ibid, 241, para 151 (referring to GC IV, Art 38); *Eritrea's Non-Residents' Claim 24* (Partial Award, 19 December 2005) 26 RIAA 429, 442, para 31; *Ethiopia's Port Claim 6* (Final Award, 19 December 2005) 26 RIAA 489, 502, para 30. During both World Wars, private enemy property was often seized (without affecting its ownership) and placed under administrative control. While custodians were not allowed to do anything confiscatory in nature, they could liquidate the property when this was necessary to prevent its waste, and hold onto the proceeds until the end of the war. The conditions under which sales of enemy property amounted to confiscation were never determined. See R Littauer, 'Confiscation of the Property of Technical Enemies' (1942–43) 52 Yale L J 739, 751.

[139] *Ethiopia's Civilian Claim 5* (n 136) 287, para 135.

[140] *Civilian Claims: Eritrea's Claims* (n 137) 225–26, paras 81, 92; Memorandum by the Secretariat, 'Expulsion of Aliens' 58th Session of ILC (2006) UN Doc A/CN.5/565, 84.

Article 38, which provides for the continuation of the protections afforded to aliens applicable in time of peace, save for exceptions authorized by GC IV. The EECC relied on this article when it held that Ethiopia, by imposing confiscatory taxes on enemy aliens, violated the minimum standards of fair and reasonable treatment.[141]

The conduct of belligerents in hostilities is governed by the cardinal principles permeating IHL rules, namely military necessity; principle of distinction; and precautionary measures and proportionality, in particular in launching military attacks. An overview of these principles follows.

(i) Military necessity

The concept of military necessity in IHL takes two forms. First, it is an animating spirit that permeates the whole legal framework governing the conduct of hostilities, and requires a balance between the need to defeat the enemy and the needs of humanity.[142] As such, military necessity is already embedded in *jus in bello* norms that present a compromise between military and humanitarian requirements.[143] In this sense, necessity aims to limit the brutality of war by, for example, outlawing certain means and methods of war that would needlessly aggravate the suffering of combatants and increase the death toll.[144]

On the other hand, the principle of military necessity can be also built into a specific IHL rule, expressly providing for an exception to the behaviour prescribed in that norm. Here, the necessity aims to provide a legal justification for the breach of the IHL norm. Instead of limiting the means and methods of warfare, it serves the opposite purpose: it legitimizes the conduct that is in conflict with humanitarian values.[145] This approach has been followed in the IHL instruments where several norms prohibiting the destruction of private property contain such escape clauses.[146] For example, Article 23(g) of the Hague Regulations prohibits the destruction or seizure of enemy property, 'unless such destruction or seizure be imperatively demanded by the necessities of war'.[147] Oppenheim cautioned that such

[141] More generally, the EECC found that Ethiopia failed to meet its duty to protect aliens' assets since the cumulative effect of the government's measures during the war substantially deprived Eritrean nationals of their property. *Eritrea's Civilian Claims*, ibid 240–41, paras 144, 151.

[142] J Gardam, *Necessity, Proportionality and the Use of Force by States* (CUP 2004) 2; M Schmitt, 'Military Necessity and Humanity in International Humanitarian Law: Preserving the Delicate Balance' (2010) 50 Va J Intl L 795; C Forrest, 'The Doctrine of Military Necessity and the Protection of Cultural Property during Armed Conflict' (2007) 37(2) Calif West Intl L J 177, 181.

[143] D Fleck (ed), *The Handbook of Humanitarian Law in Armed Conflict* (OUP 1995) 133.

[144] Declaration of St Petersburg (n 105).

[145] Forrest, *Doctrine of Military Necessity* (n 142) 191. According to the UK Manual, military necessity permits a state to use 'only that degree and kind of force, not otherwise prohibited by the law of armed conflict, that is required in order to achieve the legitimate purpose of the conflict, namely the complete or partial submission of the enemy at the earliest possible moment with the minimum expenditure of life and resources'. UK Ministry of Defence, *The Manual of the Law of Armed Conflict* (OUP 2005) (UK Manual) para 2.2.

[146] See e.g. GC IV, Art 53 and Art 147.

[147] Hague Regulations, Art 23(g).

devastation can only justified by imperative necessity when 'there is no better and less severe way' available to a belligerent.[148]

What exactly military necessity means, and how to ascertain whether it permits evading the conduct prescribed by the *jus in bello* norm, has been subject to controversy. The concern is that relying on the clause in bad faith could allow the belligerent party to circumvent the prohibition set forth in the norm. History provides plenty of examples of such abuse.[149] The ICRC Commentary thus states that the military necessity must be 'interpreted in a reasonable manner' and that a sense of proportion must be kept 'in comparing the military advantages to be gained with the damage done'.[150] Proportionality is one of the most fundamental *jus in bello* principles and the clearest manifestation of the balance between military exigency and countervailing humanitarian interests. Ruminations on how to strike the right balance have preoccupied many military trials and scholarly treatises,[151] and an in-depth analysis is beyond the scope of this chapter.[152] Suffice it to say that the principle of proportionality, as used in IHL, is guided by the vague standard of reasonableness.[153] The Nuremberg Tribunal thus stated that '[t]here must be some reasonable connection between the destruction of property and the overcoming of the enemy forces'.[154] In *Spanish Zone of Morocco*, arbitrator Huber, who later became the president of the ICRC, argued that the assessment of military necessity must be left to the military commanders and that international courts and tribunals should not interfere with this freedom.[155] Similarly, the ICTY Report on the

[148] Oppenheim, *International Law* (n 41) 416; Freeman, *Responsibility of States* (n 64) 43 (espousing a more relaxed position that the property damaged or taken must be such that, unless seized or destroyed, it presents an obstacle to military operations or jeopardizes the safety of troops).

[149] The notion 'military necessity' was used by great powers during both World Wars to justify certain actions that would be deemed unacceptable today (e.g. fire bombings of German cities and Tokyo by the US during the Second World War). See C Maier, 'Targeting the Cities: Debates and Silences about the Aerial Bombing of World War II' (2005) 87(859) IRRC 429, 434. For the examples of the use of military necessity in the First World War, see I Hull, *A Scrap of Paper: Making and Breaking International Law during the Great War* (Cornell University Press 2014) 185–94, 205.

[150] ICRC Commentary to Art 53 of GC IV, 302.

[151] For further examples of the use of military necessity, see e.g. I Detter, *The Law of War* (2nd edn, CUP 2000) 397; Forrest, *Doctrine of Military Necessity* (n 142) 195; Schmitt, 'Military Necessity' (n 142).

[152] See, however, Chapter 6 C.3. Generally, see M Wells-Greco, 'Operation "Cast Lead": Just in Bello Proportionality' (2010) NILR 397; J Gardam, 'Proportionality and Force in International Law' (1993) 87 AJIL 391; H Shamash, 'How Much is Too Much? An Examination of the Principle of Jus in Bello Proportionality' (2005–2006) 2 Israel Defense Forces L Rev 103; K Watkin, 'Assessing Proportionality: Moral Complexity and Legal Rules' (2005) 8 YIHL 4.

[153] The ambiguous language permeating some provisions of IHL conventions reflects a historical compromise between the countries arguing for more restrictive regulation of military conduct and being critical of the principle of proportionality (mostly countries of the Third World and the Eastern Bloc) and those who favoured the permissive nature of the principle of proportionality (in particular, the UK and the US). See *Official Records of the Diplomatic Conference on the Reaffirmation and Development of International Humanitarian Law Applicable in Armed Conflicts, Geneva (1974–1977)* vol 14 (1981) 61–67.

[154] *Hostage case* (*US v List et al*) (American Military Tribunal, Nuremberg, 1948) 11 NMT 1253–54.

[155] *Spanish Zone of Morocco* (n 55) 615, 645. Such assessment should be judged in view of information available to the military commander at the time of the event. See US Department of Defense, *Law of War Manual* (Office of General Counsel 2015) (US Manual) s 5.11.1.3; UK Manual, para 5.32.10 (noting

NATO bombing campaign elaborated that the proportionality between the damage done to civilian objects and the military advantage gained was determined against the standard of a 'reasonable military commander'.[156] This loose understanding of military necessity is by no means uncontested or set in stone.[157] It is feared that such interpretations, lacking more specific guidance and creating a large field of discretion for military commanders, contribute to a more permissive application of IHL and thus legitimize unrestrained conduct in armed conflict. Scholars have thus observed that despite the humanitarian rhetoric surrounding the creation of the IHL rules, their application in practice has been dictated by military demands.[158] As will be seen later on, in response to these concerns, several actors have advanced interpretation that restricts the conduct of military commanders more effectively, thus tilting the balance of military necessity and the humanity towards humanitarianism.[159]

(ii) *Principle of distinction*

The principle of distinction between the civilian population and combatants, and civilian objects and military objectives, is anchored in Article 48 of AP I, which stipulates that civilians and civilian property must be respected and protected during armed conflicts, and that military action is only allowed against combatants and military objectives. Article 51 of AP I explicitly confirms the customary rule that innocent civilians enjoy general protection against danger arising from hostilities, while Article 52 prohibits the attack of, and reprisals against, civilian objects.[160] It reiterates that attacks should be strictly directed towards military

that 'this means looking at the situation as it appeared to the individual at the time when he made this decision'). For more authorities, see Chapter 4, n 240.

[156] ICTY, 'Final Report to the Prosecutor by the Committee Established to Review the NATO Bombing Campaign against the Federal Republic of Yugoslavia' <http://www.icty.org/en/press/final-report-prosecutor-committee-established-review-nato-bombing-campaign-against-federal#IVA64d> accessed 20 April 2016. On the meaning of 'reasonable military commander' see also USAF JAG Department, Air Force Operations and the Law, A Guide for Air and Space Forces (2002) 28.

[157] e.g. the report on NATO bombing and the permissive interpretation of proportionality was met with strong criticism. See P Benvenuti, 'The ICTY Prosecutor and the Review of the NATO Bombing Campaign against the Federal Republic of Yugoslavia' (2001) 12 EJIL 503, 517; M Bothe, 'The Protection of the Civilian Population and NATO Bombing on Yugoslavia: Comments on a Report to the Prosecutor of the ICTY' (2001) 12 EJIL 531, 535; R Stone, 'Protecting Civilians During Operation Allied Force: The Enduring Importance of the Proportional Response and NATO's Use of Armed Force in Kosovo' (2001–2002) 50 Catholic Univ L Rev 501, 537.

[158] See e.g. C Jochnick and R Normand, 'The Legitimation of Violence: A Critical History of the Laws of War (1994) 35 HILJ 49; D Kennedy, *The Dark Sides of Virtue: Reassessing International Humanitarianism* (Princeton University Press 2004); L Hill-Cawthorne, 'Humanitarian Law, Human Rights Law and the Bifurcation of Armed Conflict' (2015) 64 ICLQ 293.

[159] See Section 2 D.1 and Chapter 6 C.3.

[160] For a general prohibition on reprisals, see AP I, Art 20. The ICTY in the *Kupreškić* case went a step further and suggested that the prohibition of belligerent reprisals against civilians and civilian property had become customary international law. See *Prosecutor v Kupreškić* (Trial Judgment) IT-95-16 (14 January 2000) paras 527–33.

objectives. This is important because it defines civilian objects (by using a negative definition) and military objectives, which is an issue that has attracted controversy. The definition of military objectives consists of two mandatory elements:

(a) the nature, location, purpose, or use of which makes it *an effective contribution to military action*; and
(b) the total or partial destruction, capture, or neutralization of which in the prevailing circumstances at the time *offers a definite military advantage.*[161]

According to this definition, the objects that would qualify as military targets include bridges, railroads, or other infrastructure that is of special importance for military operations in view of their location; business offices or hotels that are used to accommodate troops; installations and plants producing fuel, gas, or electricity mainly used by the military, etc.[162] It is easy to see how civilian property, including tangible assets of foreign investors, could turn into a lawful military target simply by virtue of their location, use, or purpose. While Article 52 of AP I does not expressly address the 'targetability' of objects that produce benefits to both civilians and military ('dual-use objects'), the ICRC Commentary suggests that they may be indeed subjected to lawful attacks as long as certain considerations are taken into account (time and place of attack, military advantage, and expected civilian losses).[163]

The more controversial question, which is potentially important for investors, is whether war-sustaining capabilities, such as economic objects used to generate revenue for the enemy's armed forces, can also be lawfully targeted. This would typically include facilities for production, transportation, storage, and distribution of goods such as petroleum infrastructure and electric power stations.[164] While IHL scholars overwhelmingly reject this proposition,[165] the US government has advocated the legality of such targeting decisions.[166] Although this position has

[161] AP I, Art 52(2). The distinction between military and civilian objects is customary and applies also to non-international armed conflicts. See ICRC Study, 32, 34, Rules 9 and 10; 2006 Manual on the Law of Non-International Armed Conflict, International Institute of Humanitarian Law (San Remo, 2006) (NIAC Manual) 7, para 1.1.5; *Western Front, Aerial Bombardment and Related Claims, Eritrea's Claims 1, 3, 5, 9 – 13, 14, 21, 25 & 26* (Partial Award of 19 December 2005) 26 RIAA 291, 327, para 95.

[162] ICRC Commentary to Art 52 of AP I, 632, 636, paras 2021–23.

[163] ICRC Commentary to Art 52(2) of AP I, para 2023. See also Dinstein, *Conduct of Hostilites* (n 133) 120 (noting that attacks against 'dual-use' objects, such as electric power stations distributing electricity to both the armed forces and civilians, are permitted as long as they adhere to the principle of proportionality); Henderson, *Law of Targeting* (n 133) 129–42.

[164] See US Manual, s 5.6.8.5.

[165] See e.g. Dinstein, *Conduct of Hostilities* (n 133) 109; S Oeter, 'Methods and Means of Warfare' in D Fleck (ed), *The Handbook of International Humanitarian Law* (OUP 2013) 113; W Boothby, *The Law of Targeting* (OUP 2012) 106. For a different view, see R Goodman, 'The Obama Administration and Targeting "War-Sustaining" Objects in Non-International Armed Conflict' (2016) 110 AJIL 663.

[166] See US Manual, ss 5.6.6.2, 5.17.2.3; US Department of the Air Force, *Commander's Handbook on the Law of Armed Conflict* (1980) (AFP 110–34); US Department of the Navy, Commander's Handbook on the Law of Naval Operation (1987) 2–3(a). These manuals buttress the rule by referring to the

gained some support in the jurisprudence of the EECC,[167] the more accurate view would seem to be that there must be a sufficient causal connection to military action for an object to qualify as a military objective.[168]

(iii) Precautions and proportionality

Deriving from the principle of distinction, Article 57 of AP I requires belligerents to exercise care in the conduct of military operations in order to spare civilian populations and objects. It specifies which precautions should be taken before launching an attack.[169] Among others, those who plan an attack shall 'do everything feasible' to properly identify targets, and to choose the means and methods of attack with an aim to avoid or minimize incidental civilian losses. Furthermore, they shall refrain from deciding to launch any attack that may be expected to cause incidental loss of civilian life, injury to civilians, damage to civilian objects, or a combination thereof, which would be excessive in relation to the concrete and direct military advantage anticipated (the principle of proportionality).[170] In other words, collateral casualties and damage are considered lawful under IHL as long as the principle of proportionality is adhered to in launching the attack.[171] As mentioned above, the application of proportionality in IHL has attracted much controversy. A more detailed analysis of this principle and precautions in attack, with a focus on investment law, will follow in Chapter 6.

The duty to take precautions is not incumbent only on the attacking party. According to Article 58 of AP I, a state defending itself must take certain 'necessary precautions' to protect the civilian population and civilian objects under its control against the effects of attacks by the other side.[172] Among others, a state must endeavour to remove civilians and civilian objects from the vicinity of military objectives and avoid locating military objectives within or near densely populated areas.[173] To meet this obligation, states would need to take proactive measures

nineteenth-century case law that permitted the destruction of cotton during the American Civil War because its revenues funded the purchasing of Confederate arms and ammunition. See n 113.

[167] *Aerial Bombardment, Eritrea's Claims* (n 161) 334–35, paras 120–21. President of the Commission, Hans van Houtte, expressed his disagreement on this point in a Separate Opinion. ibid 346–49.

[168] Dinstein, *Conduct of Hostilities* (n 133) 109.

[169] The obligation to take precautions in attack is customary and also applies to non-international armed conflict. See ICRC Study, 58–65, Rules 15–21; NIAC Manual, 25, para 2.1.2; *Aerial Bombardment, Eritrea's Claim* (n 161) 327, para 95.

[170] AP I, Art 57(2)(a). See also AP I, Art 51(5)(b) (prohibiting indiscriminate attacks which include those in breach of proportionality, reproducing the same wording as Art 57). Proportionality is also a customary rule. See ICRC Study, 46, Rule 14.

[171] *Aerial Bombardment, Eritrea's Claim* (n 161) 327, para 97.

[172] Boothby correctly notes that the obligations under Arts 57 and 58 AP I are complementary and equally important. The defender's failure to take precautions against the effects of attacks does not absolve the attacker in their duties to take precautions in attacks. Boothby, *Law of Targeting* (n 165) 118.

[173] AP I, Art 58(a) and (b). According to the ICRC, the rule is part of customary international law. ICRC Study, 68–79, Rules 22–24. See also *Aerial Bombardment, Eritrea's Claim* (n 161) 327, para 95.

(often already during peacetime) designed to protect civilians and civilian objects, such as building shelters, setting up systems for alarming and evacuating civilians, and for identifying high-risk areas etc.[174] Codification of the precautions against the effects of hostilities was met with criticism by some states who were concerned that the obligation could be difficult to fulfil in view of their individual circumstances.[175] The wording of the provision ('to the maximum extent feasible') abates such concerns as it implies that the fulfilment of this obligation is measured against the state's available resources and other circumstances relating to the conflict.

It should be noted that the duty to take precautions, either active (Article 57) or passive (Article 58), is one of conduct not result, and thus subject to a due diligence standard.[176] The state's obligation to take precautions and protect is qualified with phrases 'do everything feasible' (Article 57), and 'to the maximum extent feasible' and 'endeavour' (Article 58). The meaning of the 'feasibility' benchmark, discussed at length when the articles were adopted, denotes 'everything that [is] practicable or practically possible, taking into account all circumstances at the time of attack'.[177] Such circumstances comprise humanitarian and military considerations,[178] as well as means available to the state and the level of technological development (e.g. states' surveillance and networking capabilities).[179] Whether a state has met its due diligence obligation to take precautions will not only be measured on the basis of its diligent use of available means, but also on the basis of its diligence in developing relevant capabilities.[180] In this respect, the Commentary to AP I states that it is 'the duty of Parties to the conflict to have the means available to respect the rules of the Protocol'.[181] Consequently, even states with limited resources and small military budgets are obliged to exercise diligence in adapting their existing capabilities to a conflict situation, even more so if their participation in armed conflicts (or the threat thereof) has been common or continuous.[182]

More generally, the role of due diligence has been recently promoted by the ICRC who advanced a new interpretation of Common Article 1 to the Geneva

[174] J-F Queguiner, 'Precautions under the Law Governing the Conduct of Hostilities (2006) 88(864) IRRC 793, 818–9; APV Rogers, *Law on the Battlefield* (Manchester University Press1996) 74, 76; E Jensen, 'Precautions against the Effects of Attacks in Urban Areas' (2016) 98(1) IRRC 147, 169–73. For a list of such measures see Fight it Right Manual (ICRC 1999) 78.

[175] e.g. Switzerland and Austria expressed concerns about this duty as they had feared it would be particularly difficult to meet in view of their mountainous topography, cited in Queguiner (n 174) 819. See also Jensen (n 174) 176; Rogers (n 174) 76.

[176] Dinstein, *Conduct of Hostilities* (n 133) 165; Boothby, *Law of Targeting* (n 165) 122, 177; M Bothe, 'Legal Restraints on Targeting: Protection of Civilian Population and the Changing Faces of Modern Conflicts' (2001) 31 Is YHR 35, 45; K Trapp, 'Great Resources Mean Great Responsibility: a Framework of Analysis for Assessing Compliance with API Obligations in the Information Age' in D Saxon (ed), *International Humanitarian Law and the Changing Technology of War* (Martinus Nijhoff 2013) 153, 156.

[177] ICRC Commentary to Art 57(2)(a)(i) of AP I, para 2198.

[178] ICRC Study, 131, 174.

[179] Trapp, 'Great Resources' (n 176) 163–64.

[180] ibid 157.

[181] ICRC Commentary to Art 48 of AP I, para 1871.

[182] Trapp, 'Great Resources' (n 176) 159.

Conventions, which requires parties 'to do everything reasonably in their power' to ensure respect for Conventions (and more broadly the entire body of IHL) in all circumstances, and not only by its own organs but also by other state parties and non-state parties to an armed conflict.[183] In the latter case, this encompasses 'a general duty of due diligence to prevent and repress' IHL violations, whose content is contingent on particular circumstances, such as 'the foreseeability of the violations and the State's knowledge thereof, the gravity of the breach, the means reasonably available to the State and the degree of influence it exercises over the private persons'.[184]

(b) Non-international armed conflict

In contrast to the strict regulation of international armed conflict, the same cannot be said of internal armed conflict. Instead, its regulations are scarce and lack specificity. Common Article 3 of the Geneva Conventions does not regulate the conduct of hostilities at all, while AP II does so only in broad strokes.[185] However, it does not prohibit indiscriminate attacks, prescribe proportionality in attacks, or set out precautionary measures. When it comes to the protection of civilian property, AP II only prohibits the attack and destruction of objects indispensable to the survival of the civilian population (e.g. foodstuffs, agricultural areas for the production of foodstuffs, crops, livestock, drinking water installations and supplies, and irrigation works), and against works or installations containing dangerous forces, such as dams, dykes, and nuclear electrical generating stations.[186] Unlike AP I, it does not protect civilian objects in general, nor does it include any provisions on the protection of private property.

Jurists have applied different strategies to fill the gap created by the ineffective regulation of internal conflict.[187] The commonly invoked argument has been that internal conflicts are regulated by customary international law that reflects the Hague Regulations, the Geneva Conventions, and AP I.[188] This approach has become increasingly popular since 2005, as demonstrated in the ICRC study on current customary international humanitarian law. According to the study, the majority of the 161 rules of customary humanitarian law, largely analogizing the

[183] ICRC Revised Commentary (2016) to Common Article 1 of the Geneva Conventions, paras 118–19, 126.

[184] ibid paras 150, 164–73.

[185] AP II in Art 13 provides only that '[t]he civilian population and individual civilians shall enjoy general protection against the dangers arising from military operations'.

[186] AP II, Arts 14 and 15.

[187] W Abresch, 'A Human Rights Law of International Armed Conflict: The European Court of Human Rights in Chechnya' (2005) 16(4) EJIL 741, 742.

[188] ICRC Study, xxix; *Prosecutor v Tadić* (Decision on the Defence Motion for Interlocutory Appeal on Jurisdiction) IT-94-1 (2 October 1995) para 97; T Meron, *The Humanization of International Law* (Martinus Nijhoff 2006) 4; Boothby, *Law of Targeting* (n 165) 441–47 (observing that principles of distinction, proportionality and precautions in attack are applicable as customary international law in non-international armed conflicts).

treaty law of international armed conflict, are, or may be, applicable to internal armed conflicts.[189] Initially, the rules of the study were subjected to criticism and disagreement, reflecting the traditional resistance by states to apply the same degree of restraint in internal conflicts as applies in the context of international armed conflict.[190] This scepticism appears to have lessened over the years and the study is now recognized as a statement of customary humanitarian law, as demonstrated in its citations in the judgments of courts and international tribunals.[191] Of the latter, the judgments of the ICTY have particularly contributed to the clarification of the customary humanitarian law applicable to internal armed conflicts, including rules on the prohibition of attacks against civilian objects,[192] the prohibition of the wanton destruction of property,[193] the application of the principle of proportionality,[194] and the requirement that precautions be taken before launching attacks and in defence against the attack.[195]

Since Common Article 3 and AP II do not stipulate the positive obligation of the state to protect its people against armed opposition groups, some scholars contended that such an obligation existed only with respect to the prosecution and punishment of the perpetrators of the injurious acts.[196] This view mirrors the private codifications discussed above, which precluded state responsibility for losses to aliens if they had been incurred after the recognition of belligerency. The proposal is troubling since it limits a state's due diligence obligation in the context of civil wars to the post-conflict investigatory stage. It should therefore be rejected as unpersuasive. An obligation of a state to take a proactive approach in protecting civilians (including foreign nationals) in its territory against the effects of attacks has been codified with respect to situations when all belligerent parties are states,[197]

[189] ICRC Study, ibid.

[190] See e.g. the US criticism in J Bellinger III and W Haynes II, 'A US Government Response to the International Committee of the Red Cross Study Customary International Humanitarian Law' (2007) 89 IRRC 44. See also Abresch, 'Human Rights Law' (n 187) 750; T Meron, *Human Rights and Humanitarian Norms as Customary Law* (Clarendon Press 1989) 73–74; M Bothe et al, *New Rules for Victims of Armed Conflicts: Commentary on the Two 1977 Protocols Additional to the Geneva Conventions of 1949* (Martinus Nijhoff Publishers 1982) 620; Boothby (n 165) 429.

[191] S Sivakumaran, 'Re-envisaging the International Law of Internal Armed Conflict (2011) 22(1) EJIL 219, 230.

[192] See e.g. *Kupreškić* (n 160) para 521; *Prosecutor v Hadžihasanović and Kubura* (Decision on Motions for Acquittal) IT-01-42-T (27 September 2004) para 98; *Prosecutor v Strugar* (Judgment) IT-01-42-T (31 January 2005) para 225.

[193] See e.g. *Strugar*, ibid paras 227–28.

[194] ibid.

[195] *Prosecutor v Galić* (Judgment and Opinion) IT-98-29-T (5 December 2003) para 58; *Prosecutor v Galić* (Appeal Judgment) IT-98-29-A (30 November 2006) para 194; *Kupreškić* (n 160) para 524 (noting that Arts 57 and 58 of AP I constitute customary international law).

[196] L Zegveld, *Accountability and Armed Opposition Groups in International Law* (CUP 2002) 175–76 (arguing that armed opposition groups can be held responsible for the losses they caused). For a similarly cautious approach, see Boothby, *Law of Targeting* (n 165) 445.

[197] AP I, Arts 57 and 58. To reiterate, such an obligation to protect against the violence of the belligerent party will be significantly limited in those parts of the territory over which the state has lost control. The fact that this is a more typical feature of internal than international armed conflicts does not negate the existence of such an obligation to protect. See Ago, 'Fourth Report' (n 74) para 154.

and there is no reason to accept that it does not apply, as customary international law,[198] to internal armed conflicts as well. Whether the victims are able to seek remedies against the attacking party itself is irrelevant for the concept of state responsibility. Similarly, the fact that an insurrectional movement can be held liable for the damages it caused should not prevent the state from also being held responsible if the loss was due to its failure to act vigilantly, for example, by taking necessary precautions.[199] Moreover, as seen above, the pre-IHL treaties' practice is abundant and clear about a state's duty of care during internal conflicts, including civil war.[200] This has been explicitly confirmed in the revised ICRC Commentary,[201] and acknowledged by the international criminal tribunals,[202] the ICJ,[203] and the International Law Association.[204]

This notwithstanding, the focus of the conventional IHL on international conflict has subjected the regime to ongoing criticism that it failed to provide sufficient protections to victims of internal conflict.[205] Thus, the investors sustaining losses in the midst of non-international armed conflict could be faced with some degree of uncertainty as to the scope of the protections afforded to them under the IHL treaties.

D. Protections in International Human Rights Law

Human rights law traces its origins to national movements aiming to protect the individual against government abuse, which then led to the recognition and protection of civil, political, and later social rights in domestic law.[206] Although some human rights were already recognized on the international level at the end of the nineteenth century and at the beginning of the twentieth century,[207] only since the

[198] ICRC Study, 68–79, Rules 22–24.

[199] See e.g. Report of the United Nations Fact-Finding Mission on the Gaza Conflict, Human Rights Council, UN Doc. A/HRC/1 2/48, 25 September 2009, paras 496–98; Queguiner, 'Precautions' (n 174) 821.

[200] See e.g. *Spanish Zone of Morocco* (n 55); *Sambiaggio* (n 41); *Don Jacinto Gardino*, cited in Ago, 'First Report' (n 12) 108; Ago, 'Fourth Report' (n 74) paras 160–79.

[201] ICRC Revised Commentary (2016) to Common Article 1 to the Geneva Conventions, para 125.

[202] See *Prosecutor v Akayesu* (Appeal Judgment) ICTR-96-4-T (1 June 2001) paras 432–45; *Kupreškić* (Trial Judgment) (n 160) para 524; *Galić* (Judgment and Opinion) (n 195) para 58.

[203] See *Armed Activities* (n 66) 253; *Military and Paramilitary Activities in and against Nicaragua case* (*Nicaragua v US*) (Merits) [1986] ICJ Rep 14, 114, para 220.

[204] Study Group on Due Diligence in International Law, 'First Report' (International Law Association 2014) 11.

[205] L Hill-Cawthorne, 'Humanitarian Law, Human Rights Law and the Bifurcation of Armed Conflict' (2015) 64 ICLQ 293; A Duxbury, 'Drawing Lines in the Sand—Characterising Conflicts for the Purpose of Teaching International Humanitarian Law' (2007) 8 MJIL 259, 269–71.

[206] Generally on history of human rights, see PG Lauren, *The Evolution of International Human Rights* (University of Pennsylvania Press 1998); M Ishay, *The Human Rights Reader* (Routledge 1997).

[207] e.g. the prohibition of slavery and the protection of some minority rights became international standards. See D Weissbrodt and C de la Vega, *International Human Rights Law: An Introduction* (University of Pennsylvania Press 2007) 14–17; T van Banning, *The Human Right to Property* (Intersentia 2002) 34.

Second World War and the adoption of the UN Charter have these rights become a subject of international law.[208] The development of international human rights law was enhanced by the adoption of the Universal Declaration of Human Rights (UDHR) in 1948,[209] followed by a series of international (both universal and regional) conventions, such as the International Covenant on Civil and Political Rights (ICCPR);[210] the International Covenant on Economic, Social and Cultural Rights (ICESCR);[211] and the European Convention on Human Rights (ECHR), adopted in 1950;[212] the American Convention on Human Rights (ACHR) of 1969;[213] and the African Charter on Human and Peoples' Rights (ACHPR) of 1981.[214]

These instruments primarily aimed at limiting a government's abuse of its own citizens since the protection of foreign nationals was already established through international custom and reciprocal treaties regarding the treatment of citizens between different states long before the Universal Declaration was adopted. While international protection of foreign property sometimes led to the preferential treatment of aliens,[215] human rights treaties have corrected this asymmetry by establishing the same standard of protection for anyone within the jurisdiction of the state party, whether the state's own citizens or foreign nationals,[216] individuals, or companies.[217] Thus, unsurprisingly, the idea to include private property in the international human rights instruments had a strong foundation in historical developments regarding the protection of alien property, described in the preceding sections.[218]

[208] See Charter of the United Nations (UN Charter) (signed 26 June 1945, entered into force 24 October 1945) 1 UNTS xvi, Arts 1(3) and 55(c).

[209] Universal Declaration of Human Rights (adopted 10 December 1948) 217 A (III).

[210] International Covenant on Civil and Political Rights (adopted 16 December 1966, entered into force 23 March 1976) 999 UNTS 171.

[211] International Covenant on Economic, Social and Cultural Rights (adopted 16 December 1966, entered into force 3 January 1976) 993 UNTS 3.

[212] Convention for the Protection of Human Rights and Fundamental Freedoms (adopted 4 November 1950, entered into force 3 September 1953) 213 UNTS 222.

[213] American Convention on Human Rights (adopted 22 November 1969, entered into force 18 July 1978) 1144 UNTS 123.

[214] African (Banjul) Charter on Human and Peoples' Rights (adopted 27 June 1981, entered into force 21 October 1986) (1982) 21 ILM 58.

[215] e.g. the French government paid more compensation to foreigners than to nationals at the time of nationalizing the railways in 1937. Banning, *Human Right to Property* (n 207) 34.

[216] Aliens have often sought protection by using the mechanisms available to them through human rights instruments. See e.g. *AGOSI v United Kingdom* (1986) 9 EHRR 1; *Loizidou v Turkey* (1995) 23 EHRR 513; *Gasus Dosier v the Netherlands* (1995) 20 EHRR 403; *Beyeler v Italy* (2000) 33 EHRR 53.

[217] Regional bodies have confirmed that the right to private property covers interference with a company's property. See e.g. *Yarrow et al v United Kingdom* App no 9266/81, Decision (EComHR, 28 January 1983) 155, 185; ECtHR, *Tre Traktörer AB v Sweden* (1991) 13 EHRR 309; *Ivcher-Bronstein v Peru* Judgment of the IACtHR of 6 February 2001.

[218] Regarding the historical link, see T Weiler, *the Interpretation of International Investment Law* (Martinus Nijhoff 2013) 169–78 (documenting how the early proponents of international human rights used the jurisprudence of mixed claims commissions to advance their advocacy); R Lillich (ed), *International Law of State Responsibility for Injury to Aliens* (University Press of Virginia 1983) 26; Weissbrodt, *International Human Rights Law* (n 207) 16; U Kriebaum and A Reinisch, 'Property, Right

While most human rights instruments contain standards protecting private property,[219] their inclusion in the global catalogue of human rights was for a long time the subject of controversy, reflecting the sentiments of the post-war period. There was a strong disagreement between capitalist and socialist countries as to whether property rights should be protected on an international level or be left to the regulation of national legislation.[220] This notwithstanding, the UDHR included the right to property in Article 17.[221] Less successful were the attempts to reconcile the conflicting views on including property rights in the ICCPR and ICESCR which do not provide protection of the right to property as such. In contrast, all three major regional instruments on civil and political rights include a provision protecting property rights.[222] The ECHR has been particularly important in promoting the right to the peaceful enjoyment of property, mainly as a result of the large body of case law produced by the European Court of Human Rights (ECtHR).[223]

What is also common to these instruments is that they apply at all times, including in time of war, which has been confirmed by the extensive state practice, numerous UN General Assembly resolutions, and the UN investigations into violations of international human rights law in armed conflict situations, as well as the ICJ and overwhelming scholarship.[224] During public emergencies such as war, however, states are permitted to derogate from certain human rights

to, International Protection' in R Wolfrum (ed), *Max Planck Encyclopedia of Public International Law* (OUP 2009).

---

[219] J Alvarez, 'The Human Right of Property' (2018) 72 U Miami L Rev 580.

[220] ibid 584; J Sprankling, 'The Global Right to Property' (2014) 52 Colum J Trans L 464, 469–73; G Alfredsson, 'Article 17' in A Eide et al (eds), *The Universal Declaration Of Rights: A Commentary* (OUP 1992) 255, 255–56.

[221] UDHR Art 17: '(1) Everyone has the right to own property alone as well as in association with others.
(2) No one shall be arbitrarily deprived of his property.'

[222] ACHR Art 21; ACHPR Art 14. According to Art 1 of the First Additional Protocol to the ECHR:

> [e]very natural or legal person is entitled to the peaceful enjoyment of his possessions. No one shall be deprived of his possessions except in the public interest and subject to the conditions provided for by law and by the general principles of international law.

[223] According to the latest figures of the ECtHR, the third most frequently found violation has concerned the right to private property. European Court of Human Rights, *ECHR Overview 1959–2017* (March 2018).

[224] *Legal Consequences of the Construction of a Wall in the Occupied Palestinian Territory* (Advisory Opinion) [2004] ICJ Rep 136, 178; Human Rights Committee, *General Comment 29, States of Emergency (Article 4)* (2001) UN Doc. CCPR/C/21/Rev.1/Add.11 para 3; Concluding Observations of the Committee on Economic, Social and Cultural Rights: Israel (2003) UN Doc. E/C.12/1/Add.90 para 19. See also J-M Henckaerts, 'Concurrent Application of International Humanitarian Law and Human Rights Law: Victim Perspective' in R Arnold and NR Quénivet (eds), *International Humanitarian Law and Human Rights Law: Towards a New Merger in International Law* (Brill 2008) 250; L Doswald-Beck and S Vité, 'International Humanitarian Law and Human Rights Law' (1993) 293 IRRC 94; H Heintze, 'On the Relationship between Human Rights Law Protection and International Humanitarian Law' (2004) 86(856) IRRC 798.

obligations.[225] Such derogations are subject to limitations: first, derogation is only allowed if it is 'strictly required by the exigencies of the situation'; second, it has to be officially declared by the government so as to prevent arbitrary, unwarranted action; and third, some rights can never be derogated. The non-derogability of a right implies that a state would remain responsible for guaranteeing the right to all persons within its jurisdiction during a period of conflict that would otherwise precipitate derogation.[226]

None of the human rights treaties considers the right to private property fundamental enough to be included on the list of such non-derogable rights, which may suggest that the invocation of the breach of the right to private property in time of crises would likely be unsuccessful. This would be a hasty conclusion. First, the measures that a state is permitted to take in derogation of its obligation must not be 'inconsistent with its other obligations under international law', including those in the UN Charter (specifying when the use of force is lawful) and above-discussed IHL obligations.[227] Second, even if the state successfully derogated from the applicable treaty, the injured investor would still be able to seek remedy if the breached right could also qualify as non-derogable such as the right to life or the prohibition of torture.[228]

In practice, this will likely matter less as such derogations are rarely used. Although some states have proclaimed public emergencies, thus far they were reluctant to defend their measures taken in times of armed conflict by relying on derogations for policy reasons.[229] Consequently, human rights courts were presented with an opportunity to address violations that emerged in situations of conflict and in this way importantly contributed to fleshing out of obligations that states owe to individuals.[230] The following section provides an overview of the relevant decisions.

[225] e.g. ICCPR Art 4; ACHR Art 27(1); ECHR Art 15(1). The African Charter does not contain a derogation clause; however, the limitations to human rights are allowed on the basis of Art 27(2) which states that 'the rights and freedoms of each individual shall be exercised with due regard to the rights of others, collective security, morality and common interest'.

[226] Henckaerts, 'Concurrent Application' (n 224) 258.

[227] ICCPR Art 4; ACHR Art 27(1); ECHR Art 15(1). See also European Commission of Human Rights, *Travaux Préparatoires to the Convention, Preparatory Work on Article 15 of the European Convention on Human Rights* (22 May 1956) para 43. See also *Hassan v the UK* App no 29750/09, Judgment (ECtHR, 16 September 2014) para 103 (noting that 'the lack of a formal derogation under Article 15 does not prevent the Court from taking account of the context and the provisions of international humanitarian law when interpreting and applying' relevant ECHR provisions).

[228] e.g. in one case, the ECtHR found that the deliberate destruction of property at the hands of security forces amounted to inhumane and degrading treatment under Art 3 of the ECHR, which is a non-derogable right. See *Selcuk and Asker v Turkey* (1998) 26 EHRR 477, paras 72–79.

[229] e.g. Greece, Ireland, Turkey, and the UK. For more on ECHR Art 15, see P Dijn and GJH Van Hoof, *Theory and Practice of the European Convention on Human Rights* (2nd edn, Kluwer 1990) 548–60.

[230] T Meron, 'The Humanization of Humanitarian Law' (2000) 94 AJIL 239, 240.

1. Violations of Private Property in Times of Armed Conflict

Human rights instruments require a state party to guarantee, secure, or ensure the rights listed in those treaties. This entails a dual obligation: first, a duty to respect human rights, that is to refrain from actions violating them (negative obligation); and second, a duty to prevent violations of the rights by non-state actors, which calls for action by the state organs (positive obligation). Both are addressed in turn.

(a) Violations of a negative obligation to refrain

In several decisions, human rights bodies have held that the conduct of state organs in time of conflict has amounted to the violation of a state's human rights obligations, including the right to private property. The Turkish occupation of Northern Cyprus gave rise to a few cases concerning the protection of property. In *Cyprus v Turkey*, the European Commission of Human Rights found that Turkey breached Article 8 ECHR (right to respect for family life and the home) by expelling Greek Cypriots from their homes, and Article 1 of Protocol No 1 to the ECHR by looting, robbing, and depriving Greek Cypriots of their possessions.[231] While the Commission made no reference to IHL, it arrived at a conclusion that would have very likely been the same had the IHL rules been applied.[232] Similarly, in the context of anti-terrorist operations in south-eastern Anatolia, the ECtHR held that the deliberate destruction of property and the consequent eviction of the applicants from their homes by Turkish security forces breached Article I of Protocol No 1 and Article 8 ECHR.[233]

The Commission and the Court have also addressed the planning and the conduct of military operations. In particular, they have emphasized that the failure by state security forces to take the requisite precautionary measures ahead of security operations with a view to avoid or minimize the incidental losses of civilian life,[234] or the use of disproportionate means and methods in the conduct of security operations, may give rise to the responsibility of the state.[235] The same principles of proportionality, precautionary measures, and prohibition of indiscriminate attacks have also been confirmed in cases emerging from the conflict between Russia and the separatists in Chechnya, in which the ECtHR held that Russian forces did not

[231] See *Cyprus v Turkey* App nos 6780/74 and 6950/75, EComHR (1976) 4 EHRR 482, paras 208–11 and 486. Similarly, the ECtHR found that preventing refugees fleeing war from returning to their property constituted an interference with the 'peaceful enjoyment' of the said property. *Loizidou* (n 216) para 63.

[232] ibid, Dissenting Opinion by Sperduti and Trechsel on Art 15 of the Convention. See also *Cyprus v Turkey* App No 8007/77, EComHR (1983) EHRR 15, Separate Opinion by Tenekides.

[233] See e.g. *Akdivar and Others v Turkey* App No 21893/93, Judgment (ECtHR, 16 September 1996) para 88; *Mentes and Others v Turkey* (1997) 26 EHRR 595, paras 70–73; *Selcuk* (n 228) paras 86–87.

[234] *Ergi v Turkey* App No 23818/94, Judgment (ECtHR, 28 July 1998) para 79.

[235] *Güleç v Turkey* App No 21593/93 (ECtHR, 27 July 1998) paras 71, 83.

plan and execute their military operation with requisite care.[236] In view of the importance of the interest protected under the provision in question (right to life),[237] the Court applied 'strict proportionality', a more exact and compelling test requiring that the recourse to lethal force is minimized to the greatest extent possible, and in this way departed from a more deferential application of IHL proportionality by military commanders.[238] In other words, while proportionality, as often formulated in the military vernacular, permits lethal force as the first recourse against a legitimate military target provided that the harm to people and objects in the vicinity is not excessive,[239] the human rights approach prioritizes non-lethal force with a view to avoid loss of civilian lives.[240]

Another regional human rights court has dealt with these issues in a similar manner. The Inter-American Court of Human Rights (IACtHR) has found states responsible for violations of private property either at the hands of enforcement organs[241] or armed forces in various types of conflict.[242] For example, in *Santo Domingo Massacre* case, Colombia was found responsible for failing to take necessary precautions in conducting an aerial attack of a small village.[243] In contrast to the ECtHR,[244] the IACtHR did not shy away from making direct reference to IHL to support its reasoning regarding the obligation to take precautions in a military attack.

(b) Violations of a positive obligation to protect

The regional courts have confirmed that the state not only has the duty to protect human rights from violations by the state's organs, but also infringements by non-state actors in time of conflict. In *Ergi v Turkey*, the ECtHR held that Turkey had an obligation to conduct its military operations with the requisite care to protect the civilian population from attack by the Kurdistan Workers' Party.[245] The state's duty of care did not apply only to the conduct of its own forces, but also had to account for the effects of the operation of the terrorists.[246] In a similar vein, the ECtHR in

236 *Isayeva, Yusupova and Bazayeva v Russia* App Nos 57947/00, 57948/00, and 57949/00, Judgment (ECtHR, 24 February 2005) para 199 (*Isayeva I*); *Isayeva v Russia* App no 57950/00, Judgment (ECtHR, 24 February 2005) para 191 (*Isayeva II*).

237 ECHR Art 2 (using the term 'absolutely necessary' for determining the permitted use of force).

238 *Isayeva I* (n 236) paras 156, 170, 198; *Isayeva II* (n 236) para 173. See also *McCann and Others v The United Kingdom* App no 18984/91 (ECtHR, 27 September 1995) paras 149–50.

239 Dinstein, *Conduct of Hostilities* (n 133) 42.

240 N Lubell, 'Challenges in Applying Human Rights Law to Armed Conflict' (2005) 87(860) IRRC 737, 744–45. On how these seemingly different approaches converge, see Chapter 6 C.

241 See e.g. *Barrios Family v Venezuela* Judgment of the IACtHR of 24 November 2011, para 149.

242 *Massacres of El Mozote v El Salvador* Judgment of the IACtHR of 25 October 2012, para 168; *Santo Domingo Massacre v Colombia* Judgment of the IACtHR of 30 November 2012, paras 68–69, 75, 79.

243 *Santo Domingo Massacre*, ibid para 229.

244 EctHR has traditionally avoided direct use of IHL. See Lubell, 'Challenges' (n 240) 743.

245 *Ergi* (n 234) para 79.

246 ibid para 80. The Court said that '[e]ven if it might be assumed that the security forces would have responded with due care for the civilian population in returning fire against terrorists caught in the approaches to the village, it could not be assumed that the terrorists would have responded with such restraint.'

Isayeva II held that Russia was responsible for not warning and evacuating residents from the village, although it knew (or should have known) that rebels were likely to enter the village and cause damage.[247] In another case of *Albekov v Russia*, the Court found that Russia should have warned the local population of an anti-personnel minefield allegedly laid by the rebels, of which it was aware.[248] Similar reasoning has been followed by the IACtHR which found Colombia responsible for failing to prevent the murder of El Aro inhabitants along with the destruction and theft of private property at the hands of the paramilitary group.[249] The obligation to protect against the violence of private actors also applies in less intense situations of violence, such as demonstrations and riots.[250] Furthermore, the duty to protect extends beyond the prevention of physical violence to encompass the post-conflict treatment of the violations. On several occasions, the human rights bodies emphasized that a state could be held responsible if it failed to adequately investigate violations at the hands of private individuals, and to identify and penalize the perpetrators.[251]

The duty to protect individuals against the violence perpetuated by armed groups is not absolute, but is measured, like in the rules governing state responsibility for the protection of aliens and IHL, by due diligence. Human rights bodies have consistently held that a state is not required to guarantee total security for everyone in its territory, but only to undertake reasonable and appropriate measures to prevent harmful actions by private actors in the light of the availability of the state's resources, the foreseeability of the injury, and other surrounding circumstances.[252] As articulated by the IACtHR in the *Velásquez Rodríguez* case:

> [while] the State has a legal duty to take reasonable steps to prevent human rights violations and to use the means at its disposal . . . [i]t is not possible to make a detailed list of all such measures [that the State must undertake], since they vary with the law and the conditions of each State Party.[253]

In contrast to the international tribunals applying the law governing state responsibility for the protection of foreigners, human rights bodies have stressed another

[247] *Isayeva II* (n 236) para 187.

[248] See *Albekov and Others v Russia* App no 68216/01, Judgment (ECtHR, 9 October 2008) paras 84–85.

[249] *Ituango Massacres v Colombia* Judgment of the IACtHR of 1 July 2006 paras 132–35.

[250] *Plattform 'Ärzte für das Leben' v Austria* (1988) 13 EHRR 204, para 32.

[251] See *Ergi* (n 234) paras 85 and 98; *Ituango Massacres* (n 249) paras 291, 297; IACHR, 'Annual Report of the Inter-American Commission on Human Rights 1996' (17 March 1997) OEA/Ser.L/V/II.95, Doc 7, rev, para 80; UN Human Rights Committee, 'Concluding Observations on Algeria' (5 August 1998) CCPR/C/79/Add.95, para 6.

[252] See *Plattform* (n 250) para 182; *Velásquez Rodríguez v Honduras* Judgment of the IACtHR of 29 July 1988, paras 174–75; *Ergi* (n 234) paras 80–81; *Isayeva II* (n 236) para 187; *Osman v The United Kingdom* (2000) 29 EHRR 245, para 116.

[253] *Velásquez Rodríguez*, ibid.

variable for assessing due diligence and proportionality, namely the importance of the protected interest. While the old mixed commissions took that into account to the extent it concerned the difference between 'common' aliens and foreign officials (e.g. consuls and diplomats),[254] human rights case law highlighted the distinction between the property and a human life, whereby the prevention of the harm to the latter required a higher level of vigilance than what was expected for the prevention of injury to property.[255] The stricter standard of care spilled over to the protection of the property only when the property was used for 'the maintenance of basic living conditions', or when the injury to the property was intertwined with the harm to the human person, with special attention being paid to the scale and gravity of the violations.[256] The position that not all interests are equally relevant and do not merit the same level of vigilance when responding to the adverse measures in conflict situations is reflective of the IHL rules.[257] This apparent distinction from the practice on state responsibility for injury to aliens could potentially reduce the appeal of the human rights framework for foreign investors whose claims are largely based on economic losses.

E. Preliminary Conclusions

This chapter has shown how the legal protections accorded to foreign investors in times of armed conflict have a long history and have existed across different international legal frameworks. The most influential of these for modern investment law has been the law of state responsibility for injuries to foreigners, which was largely shaped along the arguments of developed and developing countries as to whether, and to what extent, host states were responsible for losses inflicted on foreigners, especially at the hands of non-state actors. The rules and principles established and clarified through jurisprudence of post-conflict arbitrations and commissions also contributed to the development of the rules on the protection of property in IHL and their inclusion into the human rights framework. While discussing the similarities between the rules across different frameworks, the chapter has also highlighted some differences in the way they have been applied and interpreted in practice. Whether these differences are irreconcilable, and what this means for modern investment law, is explored later in the book.

[254] See e.g. *Chapman* (n 63) 632, 639; *Mallen* (n 63) 175. See also Ago, 'Fourth Report' (n 74) 113, para 114; ILC, *Yearbook of the International Law Commission, 1975, Vol I, Summary of the 27th Session*, UN Doc A/CN.4/Ser.A/1975 25–26, paras 12–16.

[255] *McCann* (n 238) para 147; *Isayeva I* (n 236) para 170; *Isayeva II* (n 236) para 174; *Ergi* (n 234) para 79; *Ituango Massacres* (n 249) para 178; *El Mozote Massacres* (n 242) para 168; *Santo Domingo Massacre* (n 242) para 273.

[256] *Ituango Massacres* (n 249) para 181–82; *El Mozote* (n 242) para 180.

[257] See e.g. AP II, Arts 14 and 15.

3
The Effects of Armed Conflicts on Investment Treaties

A. Introduction

Armed conflicts disrupt peaceful relations between states, including the legal relations they establish through treaties. While some international treaties are concluded with the aim of regulating armed conflict, and their applicability does not depend on the outbreak thereof (e.g. the Geneva Conventions of 1949), the majority do not contemplate its existence. This raises the question of how such treaties are affected by a sudden deterioration in the relationship between state parties. The question is further complicated when treaties concluded between states regulate relations directly affecting individuals like private investors.[1]

The outbreak of armed conflict can bring about a number of changes. This chapter focuses on the most immediate change,[2] that is the direct effect of armed conflict on the applicability and operation of international treaties. The outbreak of armed conflict may deteriorate the relations between states so severely that a treaty is either terminated or suspended. The doctrine governing the effect of armed conflict on treaties has been acknowledged in the scholarship, state practice, and jurisprudence—most recently by the Eritrea–Ethiopia Claims Commission which decided that certain treaties between the state parties were not operative during the war since 'bitter international armed conflict [had] fundamentally changed the nature of [the parties'] relationship'.[3] History provides several other examples of wars that altered the conditions surrounding such treaties to the extent

[1] For better understanding of this chapter, a reader not familiar with investment treaty law is advised to read Chapters 4 and 5 first.

[2] Other changes can involve the occupation of a state's territory and changes of territorial borders (e.g. due to annexation). While these issues have emerged in recent Crimea cases (see Chapter 1, n 8), their analysis is beyond the scope of this chapter. See, however, D Costelloe, 'Treaty Succession in Annexed Territory' (2016) 65 ICLQ 343; R Happ and S Wuschka, 'Horror Vacui: Or Why Investment Treaties Should Apply to Illegally Annexed Territories' (2016) 33 J Intl Arb 245; O Mayorga, 'Occupants, Beware of BITs: Applicability of Investment Treaties to Occupied Territories' (2017) 19 Palestine YB Intl L 136; P Dumberry, 'Requiem for Crimea: Why Tribunals Should Have Declined Jurisdiction over the Claims of Ukrainian Investors against Russian under the Ukraine-Russia BIT' (2018) 9 JIDS 506.

[3] *Civilian Claims: Eritrea's Claims 15, 16, 23, 27–23* (Partial Award of 17 December 2004) 26 RIAA 195, 214, para 38. The Commission held that the payment of pensions to enemy nationals can be suspended for the period of hostilities. *Pensions: Eritrea's Claims 15, 19 & 23* (Final Award of 19 December 2005) 26 RIAA 471, 482, para 27.

that they were modified or terminated.[4] Predecessors of investment treaties, that is treaties of friendship, commerce, and navigation (FCN), were often terminated or suspended due to the outbreak of war. It is thus important to explore whether investment treaties or their specific provisions continue to apply in such changed circumstances. This chapter will provide a brief historical overview of how armed conflicts have affected the application of treaties in the past and critically examine the International Law Commission's (ILC) attempt to codify the subject matter in the Draft Articles on the Effects of Armed Conflicts on Treaties (Draft Articles).[5] Contrary to the prevailing view in the investment law scholarship, it will argue that the specific provisions of investment treaties can be suspended upon the outbreak of conflict either by the application of the doctrine on the 'effect of armed conflict on treaties' (EACT), or the doctrines codified in the Vienna Convention on the Law of Treaties (VCLT).

B. Applicability of the EACT Doctrine

The direct effect of armed conflict on the operation of international treaties has been one of the most controversial topics under international law. There is no shortage of alarming adjectives that scholars have used to describe it: 'problematic',[6] 'uncertain',[7] 'obscure',[8] 'unsettled'[9], 'highly controversial',[10] and 'incomplete and confused',[11] being just a few. This academic pessimism is a reflection of the differing views in the legal doctrine, the contradictory decisions of municipal courts, and divergent state practice. Consequently, there is no binding instrument that would govern the subject matter on an international level.

While the effect of armed conflict on treaties has been frequently considered by academics in the past,[12] there has been a conspicuous lack of interest in the topic in contemporary scholarship. One explanation for this paucity of research could be that armed conflict has become less formalized since resorting to force

[4] See Memorandum by the Secretariat, 'The Effect of Armed Conflict on Treaties: An Examination of Practice and Doctrine' 57th Session of ILC (2005) UN Doc A/CN.4/550 (Secretariat Memorandum).

[5] ILC, 'Draft Articles on the Effects of Armed Conflicts on Treaties, with Commentaries' in *Yearbook of the International Law Commission, 2011, Vol II*, UN Doc A/CN.4/SER.A/2010/Add.1 (Part 2).

[6] B Broms, 'Preliminary Report to the Fifth Commission: The Effects of Armed Conflict on Treaties' (1981) 59(1) Inst Intl L YB 224, 227.

[7] A Aust, *Modern Treaty Law and Practice* (2nd edn, CUP 2007) 308.

[8] D O'Connell, *International Law*, vol 1 (Stevens & Sons 1970) 268; I Brownlie, *Principles of International Law* (7th edn, OUP 2008) 620.

[9] L Oppenheim, *International Law* (7th edn, Longmans 1952) 303; *Techt v Hughes*, 229 NY 222 (1920) para 240.

[10] H Krieger, 'Article 65' in O Dörr and K Schmalenbach (eds), *Vienna Convention on the Law of Treaties: A Commentary* (Springer 2012) 1256.

[11] C Chinkin, 'Crisis and the Performance of International Agreements: The Outbreak of War in Perspective' (1981) 7 Yale J World Pub Ord 194.

[12] For a complete literature review, see Secretariat Memorandum, paras 7–8.

was declared unlawful in Article 2(4) of the United Nations Charter. Consequently, states began to engage in conflicts 'under the guise of police actions, limited acts of self-defence or humanitarian intervention', abandoned the practice of official treaty denunciations, and less commonly concluded peace agreements from which the effect of armed conflicts on treaties had often been inferred.[13] As noted by the ILC, '[t]he informal, lower-magnitude conflicts of the modern era have proved far less likely to generate commentary from courts and political departments than the wars of the past'.[14] With few primary and political sources to be scrutinized, scholars' attention shifted to other topics.

In the past, however, three main schools of thought developed. The traditional view that was prevalent in nineteenth-century scholarship and jurisprudence maintained that all legal relations between belligerents ceased to exist with war, and thus all treaties between contracting state parties were automatically terminated upon the outbreak of armed conflict.[15] While this rule provided clarity, it ignored the needs of the international community for legal stability in relations between states. At the beginning of the twentieth century, the opposite view gained traction, namely that all treaties continued to exist despite the outbreak of hostilities, subject to some exceptions.[16] The first two attempts to codify the topic, one by the Institute of International Law in 1912,[17] and the other by the Harvard Research on Law of Treaties in 1935,[18] both reflected the 'continuity' approach.[19] However, since after the First World War inconsistent practice of states rendered this approach unsatisfactory, a third school of thought emerged advocating a moderate view according to which armed conflict could lead to the termination or suspension of some treaties, while the operation of others would remain intact.[20]

What the criteria are for ascertaining which treaties are affected by armed conflict has been the subject of disagreement, however. Some scholars have advocated for the use of a test based on either the intention of the parties (subjective criterion),[21] or the compatibility of the treaty with national policy during armed

[13] ibid para 4.

[14] ibid.

[15] ibid para 14; C Hurst, 'The Effect of War on Treaties' (1921) 2 BYIL 37, 39; J Delbrück, 'War, Effect on Treaties' in R Bernhardt (ed), *Encyclopedia of Public International Law:* Vol IV (Amsterdam Elsevier 1982) 311.

[16] Secretariat Memorandum, para 15.

[17] Institute of International Law, 'Effects of War upon Treaties and International Conventions: A Project Adopted by the Institute of International Law at its Session in Christiania, in August 1912' (1913) 7 AJIL 149.

[18] Research in International Law under the Auspices of the Faculty of the Harvard Law School, Drafts of Conventions Prepared for the Codification of International Law, 'Article 35, Effect of War' (1935) 29 AJIL Supplement: Research in International Law 1183–204.

[19] Secretariat Memorandum, para 15; Chinkin, 'Crisis and Performance' (n 11) 192–93.

[20] Delbrück, 'War, Effect on Treaties' (n 15) 311.

[21] See e.g. R Rank, 'Modern War and the Validity of Treaties' (1952) 38(3) Corn L Q 321, 325; Secretariat Memorandum, para 10.

conflict (objective criterion).[22] The subjective approach is interested in whether the state parties intended the treaty to remain binding during times of armed conflict. Since treaties rarely contain express provisions on parties' intentions, or they are difficult to discern, the objective test emerged in the jurisprudence of American courts.[23] Accordingly, a treaty was terminated or suspended if it was deemed incompatible with the conduct of the war. The modern EACT doctrine seems to combine both criteria to distinguish between different types of treaties (classification approach).[24] The two latest attempts to codify the rules on the effect of armed conflict on treaties, one by the Institute of International Law in 1985,[25] and the most recent by the ILC (which resulted in the Draft Articles in 2011), both reflect this approach. The following sections seek to provide a more complete critical assessment of the Draft Articles in the light of their relevance to investment treaties.

1. Draft Articles on the Effects of Armed Conflicts on Treaties

In 2004, the ILC decided to start working on the topic of EACT by placing it on its long-term agenda. Special Rapporteur Ian Brownlie undertook an extensive analysis of state practice and doctrine and submitted four reports before he resigned in 2009. The next Rapporteur, Lucius Caflisch, brought the work to conclusion with the ILC adopting the Draft Articles in 2011. While the articles are supposed to reflect the current state of law, they do not have a binding effect; instead, they merely serve as guidance. The ILC recommended the General Assembly adopt the articles in the form of an international convention. While the General Assembly decided in resolution 66/99 of 9 December 2011 to discuss the potential binding nature of the Draft Articles in 2014,[26] this has not yet happened. Thus, it seems unlikely that the Draft Articles will take the form of a convention anytime soon.

The Draft Articles define armed conflict as a 'situation in which there is resort to armed force between States or protracted resort to armed force between governmental authorities and organized armed groups'.[27] This reflects the concept of armed conflict that was developed by the International Criminal Tribunal for

[22] See e.g. Aust, *Modern Treaty Law* (n 7) 309; M Prescott, 'How War Affects Treaties between Belligerents: A Case Study of the Gulf War' (1993) 7(1) Emory Intl L Rev 197, 222; Secretariat Memorandum, paras 11–12.

[23] See e.g. *Techt* (n 9); *Clark v Allen*, 331 US 503 (1947) 513; *Brownell v San Francisco*, 271 F.2d 974 (1954).

[24] Secretariat Memorandum, part III; A McNair, *The Law of Treaties* (OUP 1961) 697–728; J Starke, *An Introduction to International Law* (5th edn, Butterworths 1963) 409–10.

[25] Institute of International Law, 'Resolution on The Effects of Armed Conflicts on Treaties' (1986) 61(2) Annuaire de l'IDI 200 (1985 Resolution).

[26] See UNGA Res 66/99 (2011) paras 3–4.

[27] Draft Articles, Art 2(b).

the Former Yugoslavia in the *Tadić* decision,[28] with the exception that the Draft Articles do not cover violent situations between organized armed groups within a state.

Article 3 of the Draft Articles stipulates the overarching principle that armed conflict does not, *ipso facto*, cause the termination or suspension of a treaty. The article reflects the underlying aspiration of the ILC's project, which is to foster the legal stability and continuity of treaty relations.[29] In its formulation, the ILC was careful to dispel assumptions of discontinuity, rather than establish principles of continuity, as has sometimes been suggested.[30] Articles 4–7 provide further guidance in ascertaining whether a treaty ceases to operate upon the outbreak of armed conflict. First, the intent of the parties is given priority: if the treaty contains provisions on its operation in situations of armed conflict, then those provisions shall apply (Article 4). The Draft Articles articulate the factors that indicate whether a treaty is susceptible to termination or suspension. They are divided into two groups. The first group of factors relates to the nature of the treaty, in particular its subject matter, its object and purpose, its content, and the number of parties to it (traditionally, armed conflicts have had greater effects on bilateral treaties than on multilateral treaties). The second group entails the characteristics of the armed conflict, such as its territorial extent, its scale and intensity, its duration, and, in cases of non-international conflict, the degree of outside involvement as well (Article 6).[31] This shows that the ILC decided to take a contextual approach to responding to political crises. Not all armed conflicts are equally detrimental to treaty relations. Conflicts vary in their seriousness and duration, and an appropriate reaction to them should be determined according to the level of intensity and coercion involved.

Lastly, the Annex to the Draft Articles provides for an indicative list of treaties the subject matter of which involves an implication that they continue in operation, in whole or in part, during armed conflict.[32] While the classification approach ensures greater clarity, it is also problematic because it creates artificial categories based on one feature of a treaty.[33] This can lead to inaccurate assumptions as to the

[28] See Chapter 1 B. See also L Caflisch, 'First Report on the Effects of Armed Conflicts on Treaties' in *Yearbook of the International Law Commission, 2010, Vol II*, UN Doc A/CN.4/SER.A/2010/Add.1 (Part 1) 95, para 21.

[29] Commentary to Draft Articles, Art 3, para 1.

[30] cf J Ostřanský, 'The Termination and Suspension of Bilateral Investment Treaties due to an Armed Conflict' (2015) 6 JIDS 136, 141.

[31] Caflisch, 'First Report' (n 28) paras 51, 81.

[32] The list is not exclusive but rather creates a rebuttable presumption. See, I Brownlie, 'Third Report on the Effects of Armed Conflicts on Treaties' ILC 59th Session, 2007, UN Doc A/CN.4/579/Corr.1, para 54; ILC, 'Report of the International Law Commission' ILC 60th Session, 2008, UN Doc A/63/10, 98; Caflisch, 'First Report' (n 28) paras 53, 65, 70.

[33] Several states voiced criticism against this approach. See e.g. the statements of India in the Official Records of the General Assembly, 60th Session, Sixth Committee, 18th meeting, UN Doc A/C.6/60/SR.18, para 64; Poland, ibid, 19th meeting, UN Doc A/C.6/60/SR.19, para 19; the UK, ibid, 20th meeting UN Doc A/C.6/60/SR.20, para 1. See also, Brownlie, 'Third Report' (n 32) paras 34–38; Chinkin, 'Crisis and Performance' (n 11) 192.

treaty's applicability in times of conflict. Since the Commentary to Draft Articles notes that bilateral investment treaties (BITs) are covered by the list,[34] the next section turns to investigate this claim.

2. The Application of EACT to Investment Treaties

Since investment treaties are a relatively recent phenomenon and their rising prominence on the international stage coincides with the 'deformalisation' of armed conflict, it is not surprising that there has been almost no detailed analysis of their fate in times of armed conflict. Scholarly contributions in the aftermath of the 'Arab Spring' briefly addressed this topic by uncritically referring to the ILC's Draft Articles as the authoritative statement of law.[35] Consequently, the dominant view has been that investment treaties continue to apply in times of armed conflict. One scholar, for example, asserted that investment treaties or treaty provisions 'must be presumed to remain in force even when an armed conflict commences between the Home and Host States'.[36] This conclusion seems to be hastily drawn. The result of an outbreak of conflict may not necessarily be the continued operation or non-operation of a treaty in either extreme; in fact, a middle-ground outcome is also possible. Namely, the Draft Articles allow for only certain parts of a treaty to survive the conflict, while the other parts can be suspended or terminated under specific conditions (principle of separability).[37]

The importance of the separability doctrine was emphasized as early as 1920 by Judge Cardozo in the celebrated *Techt v Hughes* case. The judge noted that the incompatibility of some of the treaty provisions with the emergence of war did not mean that the other parts of the treaty were also suspended or abrogated:

> The treaty does not fall in its entirety unless it has the character of an indivisible act . . . . To determine whether it has this character, it is not enough to consider its name or label. No general formula suffices. We must consult in each case the *nature and purpose of the specific articles involved*.[38]

[34] Commentary to Draft Articles, Annex, paras 48 and 69.

[35] C Schreuer, 'The Protection of Investments in Armed Conflicts' in F Baetens (ed), *Investment Law Within International Law: Integrationist Perspectives* (CUP 2011) 3; G Hernández, 'The Interaction between Investment Law and the Law of Armed Conflict in the Interpretation of Full Protection and Security Clauses' in F Baetens (ed), *Investment Law Within International Law: Integrationist Perspectives* (CUP 2013) 29; T Cole, *The Structure of Investment Arbitration* (Routledge 2013); H Bray, 'SOI–Save Our Investments! International Investment Law and International Humanitarian Law' (2013) 14(3) JWIT 578; J Bonnitcha, 'Investment Treaties and Transition from Authoritarian Rule' (2014) 15 JWIT 965. For more cautious view which permits the application of EACT in limited circumstances, see Ostřanský, 'Termination and Suspension' (n 30) 136.

[36] Cole (n 35) 78.

[37] Draft Articles, Art 11.

[38] *Techt* (n 9) para 244 (emphasis added).

The principle of separability enables a more nuanced assessment of the operation of treaties and their specific provisions in armed conflict. The application of the principle of separability to investment treaties has been confirmed in investment law jurisprudence.[39]

Some scholars have further argued that the fact that investment treaties contain specific provisions addressing armed conflicts implies the application of the principle of continuity.[40] Indeed, when such provisions exist, the parties should adhere to them in accordance with Article 4 of the Draft Articles. First, some treaties contain provisions directly prescribing their continuity in times of armed conflict. An example of such a provision is Article 11 of the Germany–Papua New Guinea BIT:

> The present Treaty shall remain in force also in the event of a conflict arising between the Contracting Parties, without prejudice to the right to such temporary measures as are permitted under the general rules of international law. Such measures shall be repealed not later than on the date of the actual termination of the conflict, irrespective of whether or not diplomatic relations exist.[41]

The provision clearly asserts the continuity of the BIT as a whole in times of conflict, while noting that this does not preclude states in conflict from taking certain temporary measures that may be necessary for the duration of the conflict. The clause applies to all treaty provisions and it explicitly prioritizes suspension over termination as an effect of a conflict. Such specific provisions are rare in investment treaties and bear resemblance to provisions found in some economic development agreements.[42]

More commonplace are security exceptions included in non-precluded measures clauses which allow states to take certain measures necessary for the protection of their national security, or for the protection of international peace and security.[43] Sometimes, the exceptions specifically address situations of armed conflict.[44] According to the ILC, this type of derogation clause commonly found in human rights instruments provides evidence that an outbreak of hostilities as such may not affect the continuation of a treaty as a whole and that the treaty itself regulates its operation in times of armed conflict.[45] One should, however, keep in mind

[39] The tribunal in *Plama* applied the principle to dispute resolution clause. *Plama Consortium Ltd v Republic of Bulgaria* ICSID Case no ARB/03/24, Decision on Jurisdiction, 8 February 2005, para 212.

[40] See e.g. Schreuer, 'Protection of Investments' (n 35) 5; Hernández, 'The Interaction' (n 35) 31.

[41] Germany–Papua New Guinea BIT (1980) Art 11.

[42] See e.g. Art 9 of the Agreement between India and USSR (28 September 1959) providing for financial assistance to India, cited in G Delaume, 'Excuse for Non-Performances and Force Majeure in Economic Development Agreements' (1971) 10 Columb J Trans L 242, 249.

[43] See Chapter 5 B.

[44] Energy Charter Treaty (1994) Art 24(3)(a)(ii).

[45] Commentary to Draft Articles, Annex, para 50.

that such clauses do not necessarily derogate from all treaty provisions, and that most BITs still do not contain them.

Another investment treaty provision that addresses armed conflict explicitly is an armed conflict clause.[46] In its basic form, the clause provides for non-discriminatory treatment with respect to the payment of indemnities for losses related to armed conflict. Since this type of clause regulates a situation in the aftermath of a conflict, the inclusion of the provision in the treaty is unlikely to be interpreted as a rejection of the EACT doctrine. This may be different for advanced armed conflict clauses which impose on state parties a substantive obligation to pay compensation for losses inflicted by a host state's armed forces, and which likely continue to apply in times of conflict. Nevertheless, to conclude that the mere inclusion of an advanced armed conflict clause in an investment treaty implies that all other treaty provisions continue to apply as well would be an imprecise assertion.

Commentators have further relied on Article 7 of the Draft Articles to reinforce the continuity of investment treaties. The provision creates a link to the Annex that contains an indicative list of categories of treaties, therefore implying that they continue to operate in whole or in part during periods of armed conflict. Since the list includes 'treaties of friendship, commerce and navigation (FCN) and agreements concerning private rights', commentators have taken this as an indication that investment treaties, fitting in this category, could not be terminated or suspended.[47] The ILC has indeed confirmed that BITs are meant to be included in the category of treaties of FCN and analogous agreements concerning private rights.[48] What is more problematic, however, is that these treaties do not indicate there is a trend in favour of their continued applicability in times of conflict, as the ILC has suggested in the Commentary.[49] On the contrary, the case law surveyed by the ILC is conflicting, and with respect to some types of treaty provisions even points towards a trend in favour of suspension.

In addition, the Secretariat Memorandum places FCN and similar treaties in the group of treaties that exhibit a varied and controversial likelihood of applying in times of conflict.[50] It is thus not surprising that some state delegates proposed the elimination of the FCN treaties and analogous agreements concerning private rights from the list of the Draft Articles.[51] The Special Rapporteurs rejected

[46] See Chapter 4 C.

[47] See e.g. Schreuer, 'Protection of Investments' (n 35) 4; Aust, *Modern Treaty Law* (n 7) 310; Krieger, 'Article 65' (n 10) 1261.

[48] Commentary to Draft Articles, Annex, paras 48 and 69; I Brownlie, 'First Report on the Effects of Armed Conflicts on Treaties' ILC 57th Session, 2005, UN Doc A/CN.4/552, para 83.

[49] Several state delegations stressed that certain categories included in the list did not find support in practice. See e.g. statements of the Republic of Korea in Official Records of the General Assembly, 60th Session, Sixth Committee, 18th meeting, UN Doc A/C.6/60/SR.18, para. 36; Jordan, ibid, 18th meeting, UN Doc A/C.6/61/SR.18, para 89; Chile, ibid, 61st Session, Sixth Committee, 19th meeting, UN Doc A/C.6/61/SR.19, para. 7; Malaysia, ibid, 19th meeting, UN Doc A/C.6/61/SR.19, para 54.

[50] Secretariat Memorandum, 2, 14–47.

[51] See Brownlie, 'Third Report' (n 32) para 34; Caflisch, 'First Report' (n 28) para 231.

the concerns, stating that the list was only suggestive, and that, while it was true that treaties from this category did not always survive in their entirety, the Draft Articles provided for the possibility of the separability of individual provisions.[52] The inclusion of the list of categories in the Draft Articles, despite inconclusive state practice, divergent case law, and lack of consensus among state delegates, reflects the ILC's attempt to progressively develop the law rather than rely on customary international law. However, it brings with it disadvantages related to rigidity and overgeneralization, and risks forgetting that not all treaty provisions are affected by hostilities in the same way.

3. Analogies with FCN Treaties and Agreements Concerning Private Rights

FCN treaties are often considered the predecessors of BITs, thus the analogies with respect to their applicability in times of armed conflict are apt. The treaties aimed to determine the legal status that each state granted to nationals of the other contracting party in its territory.[53] They covered a variety of issues ranging from trade, investment protection, shipping, taxation, human rights, and migration, to inheritance and workers' compensation. Although states no longer enter into the FCN treaties, they still provide valid insight into the interpretation of the more specialized treaties that have replaced them, such as BITs. This is particularly true for treaties involving the rights and benefits of individuals, since the case law focusing on the effects of war on their operation was more common in the aftermath of the two World Wars. Most of the available case law consists of the decisions of municipal courts, which are characterized by their diverging views and, arguably, their deference to the policies of their governments.[54] Nevertheless, that case law illustrates the state practice at the time and as such was inspected by the ILC in preparation of the Draft Articles. The municipal decisions regarding the operability of FCN treaties upon the outbreak of conflict can thus still be used as a guide or a source of inspiration for a modern adjudicator or policy maker dealing with the same question in an analogous legal and factual setting.

The US and UK courts departed from the traditional view that all treaties are abrogated upon the outbreak of conflict quite early. In 1823, the US Supreme

[52] Brownlie, ibid para 54; Caflisch, ibid para 232.

[53] See e.g. J Coyle, 'The Treaty of Friendship, Commerce and Navigation in the Modern Era' (2012) 51 Columb J Trans L 302, 304.

[54] Chinkin, 'Crisis and Performance' (n 11) 190. See, however, the ICJ's decisions suggesting that FCN treaties are not automatically suspended or terminated. *Military and Paramilitary Activities in and against Nicaragua (Nicaragua v US)* (Merits) [1998] ICJ Rep 14, paras 219, 270, 282; *Oil Platforms (Iran v US)* [2003] ICJ Rep 161, para 41.

Court, when considering whether a provision on the acquisition of real property applied in wartime, famously wrote that 'treaties stipulating for permanent rights and general arrangements, and professing to aim at perpetuity, and to deal with the case of war as well as the case of peace, do not cease on the occurrence of war, but are, at most, only suspended while it lasts'.[55] Seven years later, the UK High Court of Chancery reached a similar conclusion in *Sutton v Sutton*, a well-known case concerning Article 9 of the Jay Treaty made between the US and the UK, allowing for the reciprocal rights of nationals of each of the contracting parties to hold, sell, pass on, and acquire titles to land. The Court held that the outbreak of war between the UK and the US in 1812 had no effect on the treaty provision and based its reasoning on the perceived intention of the parties that the treaty should be permanent and its operation unimpeded by war.[56]

The most articulate pronouncement on the issue was made by Judge Cardozo in the landmark case *Techt v Hughes*. This case concerned a reciprocal inheritance provision in the 1848 Treaty of Commerce and Navigation between the US and Austria–Hungary. The Court of Appeals of the State of New York decided that the provision survived the outbreak of the war as it was compatible with the policy of the government, with the safety of the nation, and with the maintenance of the war in the enforcement of a mutual inheritance treaty.[57] Judge Cardozo rejected the relevance of the Trading with the Enemy Act, pointing out the difference between the ability of an alien with respect to the ownership of land and the privileges of trade.[58] He acknowledged that the question of the effect of war on treaties was as yet unsettled, and that, save for some categories of treaties for which there was a general consensus about their (dis)continuation in wartime, international law dealt with the problem 'pragmatically, preserving or annulling [treaties] as the necessities of war exacts'.[59] This decision was important because it promoted a policy-based test focusing on the compatibility of specific treaty provisions with a state's security interests during wartime. It thus presented an adjustment to the rigidities of the classification test, and clarified the distinction between EACT and other grounds for terminating or suspending treaties. In general, the courts in subsequent cases followed this pragmatic approach.[60] The following sections discuss how the doctrine was applied with respect to different types of FCN treaty provisions, commonly found in modern investment treaties.

[55] *Society for Propagation of the Gospel v Town of New Haven* (1823) 21 US 8, 464. See also McNair, *Law of Treaties* (n 24) 699–700; Commentary to Draft Articles, Annex, para 28.
[56] *Sutton v Sutton*, Court of Chancery, 29 July 1830, BILC, vol 4, 367–68.
[57] *Techt* (n 9) para 244.
[58] ibid para 237.
[59] ibid para 241.
[60] See e.g. *Clark v Allen* (n 23).

(a) Border-crossing provisions

Foreign investors often need to travel between their country of national origin and the country where their investment is located. Moreover, the proper functioning of their investment may depend on the presence of expatriate personnel in the host state for an extended period of time. The early FCN treaties commonly entailed provisions granting the nationals of one contracting party a right to enter and reside in the territory of another contracting party, without exceptions.[61] Did such provisions survive the outbreak of war between the parties? In the *Karnuth* case (1929), the US Supreme Court addressed EACT with respect to the border-crossing provision entailed in the Treaty of FCN between the US and the UK.[62] The Court decided that the provision allowing for the reciprocal crossing of the US–Canadian border was terminated by the War of 1812. The Court made a distinction between reciprocal inheritance provisions that had the smallest effect on national policy in times of war, and treaties guaranteeing the private right to cross an international border that affected national policy and security the most, and thus were abrogated.[63] The same reasoning became entrenched in subsequent cross-border cases that were handled by American and Canadian courts.[64]

The post-war FCNs and modern BITs espoused a stricter approach in drafting cross-border provisions, aligning them with state immigration policies. Thus, as long as such provisions are drafted in hortatory language and do not impose a legally binding obligation on the contracting parties to permit the entry of the investors or investment-related personnel,[65] or condition such an obligation on their domestic immigration policy,[66] it is unlikely that the question of the effect of armed conflict on them would become relevant.

On the other hand, more uncertain would be the fate of BIT provisions that provide for an absolute obligation for the contracting parties to abstain from imposing quotas or numerical restrictions when granting entry into their state to the nationals of the contracting party.[67] If, in the event of an armed conflict occurring between states who are parties to a BIT containing such a provision, one state decides to limit the entry of the nationals of the other state, including foreign investors or

[61] K Vandevelde, *Bilateral Investment Treaties: History, Policy, and Interpretation* (OUP 2010) 52.

[62] *Karnuth v US* (1929) 279 US 231.

[63] ibid para 239. See also Secretariat Memorandum, 41, para 67. Suspension of such provisions was believed to prevent treasonable intercourse.

[64] See e.g. *In re Francis v The Queen* 1955 ILR 591, 603, 4 DLR 760 (1955). For an overview, see S McIntyre, *Legal Effects of World War II on Treaties of the United States* (Martinus Nijhoff 1958) 48–50; Secretariat Memorandum, nn 239–40.

[65] See e.g. Bolivia–Republic of Korea BIT (1996) Art 2; France–Mexico BIT (1998) Art 4. See also UNCTAD, 'Bilateral Investment Treaties 1995–2006: Trends in Investment Rule Making' (UN 2007) Doc UNCTAD/ITE/IIT/2006/5, 69.

[66] See e.g. Nicaragua–US BIT (1995) Art VII(1)(a); Australia–India BIT (1999) Art 5; Japan–Republic of Korea BIT (2002) Art 8.

[67] See e.g. Nicaragua–US BIT (1995) Art VII(2) and other BITs concluded by the US in the 1990s; Japan–Republic of Korea BIT (2002) Art 8(2). Such provisions purport to limit the discretion of immigration organs when issuing permits for entry and sojourn to foreign investors.

their personnel,[68] such a measure could constitute grounds for a claim for losses inflicted thereby. The tribunal would then be faced with the question of whether it needs to assess if there was a breach of the BIT, or simply disallow the case on the basis that the relevant provision was not operational during armed conflict. Should one follow the reasoning of *Karnuth* and subsequent 'cross-border' cases, the answer is likely to be that the 'entry of foreign nationals' provision would be suspended. While those cases are not binding on arbitral tribunals, they present persuasive guidance to investment tribunals when deciding analogous cases. To minimize the risk of uncertainty, however, states that have tightened or plan to tighten their immigration laws due to security concerns would be advised not to include provisions imposing absolute obligations in their BITs.[69]

(b) Protection and security provisions

The case that could serve as the closest analogy to an investment treaty is *Ex parte Zenzo Arakawa* (1947).[70] In this case, a US district court considered whether Article I of the Treaty of Commerce and Navigation concluded between the US and Japan, which provided for the constant protection and security of the citizens of each party while in the territory of the other, applied during the war between the US and Japan. The 'constant protection and security' provision was a predecessor of similarly worded 'protection and security' clauses in BITs, analysed in the next chapter. The *Arakawa* case was brought to the court by the Japanese aliens who were detained in various locations in the US during the war with Japan following an order made by the US president. The petitioners argued that their detention and deportation constituted a breach of the 'most constant protection and security' clause. The judge rejected their claim by asserting that the treaties of commerce and navigation should be either suspended or completely abrogated 'because the carrying out of their terms would be incompatible with the existence of a state of war',[71] but he failed to explain what exactly this incompatibility was.

Consequently, the argument appeared to be flawed. Even in the absence of the treaty, the concept of 'constant protection and security' is still provided in customary international law as part of the international minimum standard. The standard is not suspended upon the outbreak of conflict—on the contrary, as discussed in Chapter 2, it was commonly applied and its content evolved in the context of conflict in particular. Many courts and tribunals held that if the

[68] For example, in November 2018, Ukraine introduced a ban prohibiting the entry into the country for Russian men with an aim to prevent Russian land invasion by means of formation of 'private armies' on Ukrainian soil. See A Roth, 'Ukraine Bans Entry to Russian Men "To Prevent Armies Forming"' *The Guardian* (30 November 2018) <https://www.theguardian.com/world/2018/nov/30/ukraine-bans-russian-men-from-entering-the-country> accessed 12 December 2018.

[69] e.g. the 2004 US Model BIT excluded a specific provision concerning the issue of the entry of foreign investors and personnel. See UNCTAD Report (n 65) 71.

[70] *Arakawa v Clark* (1947) 79 F Supp 468.

[71] ibid 472.

necessity of war required the state to take certain measures that violated the standard, the state could be absolved of its responsibility. However, this is only possible after the facts have been carefully assessed—in the case in question, it was only upon the examination of whether the detained aliens presented a real danger to the public peace and safety of the US that the order was made for their deportation. The US court took a shortcut by deciding that it was 'apparent' that the treaty 'was totally abrogated, or at least suspended, when Japan struck at Pearl Harbor'.[72]

Such a conclusion is troubling as it stripped aliens of protections that may have been compatible with the national policy of the state during armed conflict. The distinction between the aliens for whom the treaty protection continued to apply and those for whom the protections were suspended could only be made on the basis of a factual assessment and an analysis of the scope of the relevant treaty provision. Furthermore, the court ignored the temporal dimension of the provision: namely, the wording 'the most constant protection' arguably implied its continuous application in wartime. This decision is especially problematic because the final outcome would have likely been different had the court applied the provision in an accurate manner. The reasoning applied in *Arakawa* should thus be disregarded in the context of analogous BIT cases. It is unlikely that a full protection and security clause would be terminated or suspended as a consequence of an outbreak of armed conflict since the purpose of the provision is precisely to provide investors with protection against physical interference, including during times of conflict.[73]

(c) Procedural provisions

The national jurisprudence with respect to procedural provisions of treaties regulating private interests seems to be even more incoherent. While the ILC attempted to show in the Commentary that there is a trend towards holding that the 'procedural rights' of individuals protected by treaties subsist, the case law is inconsistent.[74] The ILC suggested that 'as a matter of principle and sound policy, the principle of survival would seem to extend to obligations arising under multilateral conventions concerning arbitration and the enforcement of awards'.[75] The view is supported by the decision of the Scottish Court of Session in *Masinimport v Scottish Mechanical Light Industries Ltd*, where such treaties, namely the Protocol

[72] ibid.

[73] The support for this view can be found in the historical materials leading to the 1985 Resolution, which stipulated that the existence of armed conflict did not authorize the suspension or termination of treaty provisions relating to the protection of the human person. 1985 Resolution (n 25) Art 4. See also the intervention of Mr McDougal at 11th plenary session of Institute of International Law (1986) 61(2) Annuaire de l'IDI 221.

[74] Commentary to Draft Articles, Annex, para 39.

[75] ibid para 44.

on Arbitration Clauses of 1923 and the Convention on the Execution of Foreign Arbitral Awards of 1927, were held to survive the Second World War.[76]

These legal instruments preceded contemporary conventions regulating arbitral proceedings and the enforcement of arbitral awards, such as the New York Convention on the Recognition and Enforcement of Foreign Arbitral Awards of 1958 (New York Convention),[77] or Convention on the Settlement of Investment Disputes between States and Nationals of Other States (ICSID Convention).[78] Such treaties can be classified as multilateral law-making treaties according to the Draft Articles, and they likely survive the outbreak of armed conflict, inasmuch they are of a non-political and technical nature.[79] While investment treaties primarily provide for certain substantive standards beneficial to individuals and are thus to be distinguished from these treaties, they also contain procedural provisions, most notably dispute resolution clauses, for which separability from the rest of the treaty could be established. Do the procedural provisions of BITs, notably investor–state arbitration clauses, continue to apply in times of armed conflict?

The ILC has discussed this type of provision as part of the procedural provisions of 'FCN treaties and agreements concerning private rights', and concluded that despite the incoherence of the case law, there was a clear trend that such provisions subsisted.[80] This conclusion appears to be oversimplified and unsubstantiated. Although the case law is scarce, the courts generally held that dispute resolution clauses did not apply in time of war. The Secretariat Memorandum notes that during the Second World War, treaties or treaty provisions providing the right of access to the courts by non-resident enemy aliens were suspended.[81] For example, the Supreme Court of Nebraska held in *Meier v Schmidt* that a treaty provision providing for reciprocal access to the courts to nationals of the US and Germany was suspended by the Second World War.[82] The Court found that the treaty provision in question was incompatible with the Trading with the Enemy Act and US national policy, thus an enemy alien was barred from pursuing an action in the

[76] *Masinimport v Scottish Mechanical Light Industries Ltd*, 30 January 1976, ILR, vol 74, 559, cited in Commentary to Draft Articles, Annex, para 44.

[77] 1958 Convention on the Recognition and Enforcement of Foreign Arbitral Awards (adopted on 10 June 1958, entered into force on 7 June 1959) 330 UNTS 3.

[78] Convention on the Settlement of Investment Disputes between States and Nationals of Other States ICSID Convention (adopted on 18 March 1965, entered into force on 14 October 1966) 575 UNTS 159.

[79] Commentary to Draft Articles, Annex, paras 15, 17–19; McIntyre, *Legal Effects* (n 64) 328; McNair, *Law of Treaties* (n 24) 723; G Fitzmaurice, 'The Juridical Clauses of the Peace Treaties' (1948) 73 Recueil Des Cours 260.

[80] Although Art 7 of the Draft Articles includes the category of 'treaties relating to dispute settlement', the ILC was clear that this group does not comprise 'treaty mechanisms of peaceful settlement for the disputes arising in the context of private investment abroad'. Commentary to Draft Articles, Annex, para 69.

[81] Secretariat Memorandum, 49, para 80. See also McIntyre, *Legal Effects* (n 64) 198, 203.

[82] *Meier v Schmidt* (1948) 150 Neb 383, 34 N.W.2d 400.

state's courts, even though the proceedings were instituted before hostilities commenced.[83] The decision reflected an old rule according to which an enemy subject was prevented from taking proceedings in the courts upon the outbreak of war.[84]

Could the same principle apply to arbitration clauses? In one reported case, the arbitral tribunal held that the hostilities between India and Pakistan in the Rann of Kutch Desert in 1965 did not affect the validity of the arbitration agreement between the countries. The tribunal came to this conclusion by drawing inferences from the countries' conduct (i.e. the appointment of arbitrators) which implied that the governments of both countries believed that the arbitration clause in the treaty they concluded continued to be in operation.[85] The tribunal also found, however, that the fact that the arbitration agreement had not been abrogated was evidence that there was no war between the two countries, thus suggesting that if there had been, the fate of the agreement could have been different.[86]

Should one follow the principle outlined in *Meier v Schmidt*, investor–state arbitration clauses could be suspended for the duration of armed conflict with respect to investors coming from enemy countries. This is unlikely, however, as it is difficult to imagine how instituting arbitration proceedings could contradict a state's security policy in wartime. That said, a country in the midst of hostilities, which is compelled to invest its resources into ensuring its survival and the protection of its people, may find it cumbersome and practically impossible to engage in procedures to resolve commercial and economic disputes, with respect to which the gathering of evidence may present a further practical obstacle. In that case, the arbitration clause is not untenable for policy reasons, but rather the provision is temporarily impossible to enforce for practical reasons. These two sources of suspension, while recognized in state practice, have often been conflated in court decisions and policy declarations.[87] The distinction was noted in one reported case by a Dutch court that held that '[t]here could only be a question of suspension [of a procedural provision] in so far and for so long as the provisions . . . should have become untenable'.[88] Since that was not the case there, the court concluded that the issue was 'one of temporary impossibility of performance rather than one of the effects of armed conflict of treaties'.[89] Whether the grounds for suspension are rooted

[83] The Court held that the treaty provisions might 'be disregarded only to the extent and for the time required by the necessities of war, or when they conflict with policies established by the Chief Executive or the Congress'. ibid 387.

[84] Oppenheim, *International Law* (n 9) 309–12 (noting that the rule survived in the UK and US judicial practice).

[85] Reported in Secretariat Memorandum, 56, para 95, citing S P Sharma, *The Indo-Pakistan Maritime Conflict, 1965* (Academic Books 1970) 107–23.

[86] Reported in Secretariat Memorandum, 56, para 95.

[87] e.g. after the Second World War, the US position was that the existence of armed conflict does not automatically terminate the treaties 'although . . . as a practical matter, certain of the provisions might have been inoperative'. cited in Rank, 'Modern War' (n 21) 334–44.

[88] *In re Utermöhlen* (1948) AD 1949, No 129, 381, cited in Commentary to Draft Articles, Annex, para 41.

[89] ibid.

in the VCLT doctrine of supervening impossibility to perform or in the EACT doctrine may not always be clear. Thus, the next section looks into the applicability of the VCLT doctrines in situations of armed conflict.

C. Applicability of the VCLT Doctrines

Treaties are governed by the VCLT which entered into force on 27 January 1980 and has been ratified by 116 states as of September 2018. While the VCLT is binding upon its state parties, it is also relevant for non-signatory countries as some of its provisions express rules of customary international law. The basic principle of treaty law is codified in Article 26 of the VCLT, under the heading 'Pacta sunt servanda': 'Every treaty in force is binding upon the parties to it and must be performed by them in good faith.' In some cases, however, treaties or their provisions may cease to apply. Part V, Section 3 of the VCLT contains provisions on the termination and suspension of the operation of treaties. While the primary rule is that treaties are terminated or suspended in conformity with their provisions or by consent of all the parties (Articles 54 and 57), provisions that may become relevant at the outbreak of conflict are Article 61 on 'Supervening impossibility to perform' (SIP) and Article 62 on 'Fundamental change of circumstances' (FCC). The International Court of Justice (ICJ) held that both articles reflect customary international law.[90] While these doctrines are not necessarily triggered by armed conflict, the outbreak thereof may create factual circumstances leading to their applicability. This raises the question of what is the relationship between the VCLT doctrines regulating suspension and termination of treaties and the EACT doctrine?

Article 18 of the Draft Articles addresses this issue by stating that 'the present draft articles are without prejudice to the termination, withdrawal or suspension of treaties as a consequence of, inter alia . . . (b) supervening impossibility of performance; or (c) fundamental change of circumstances'.[91] The ILC elaborates in the commentary that the article aims to preserve the possibility to terminate, withdraw, or suspend a treaty on grounds that can be found in other rules of international law, in particular the SIP and FCC doctrines.[92] The commentary goes on to explain that the article intends to avoid the possible implication that the outbreak of an armed conflict gives rise to a *lex specialis* precluding the operation of other grounds of termination, withdrawal, or suspension.[93]

[90] *Case Concerning the Gabčíkovo-Nagymaros Project (Hungary/Slovakia)* (Merits) [1997] ICJ Rep 1, 62, para 99 (*Gabčíkovo*); *Fisheries Jurisdiction Case (Federal Republic of Germany v Ireland)* (Jurisdiction) [1973] ICJ Rep 1, 18, para 36 (*Fisheries Jurisdiction*).

[91] Draft Articles, Art 18.

[92] Commentary to Draft Articles, Art 18, para 1.

[93] ibid.

Thus, the grounds exist in parallel: they do not interfere with each other and do not trump each other on the basis that of one of them is a more special law. Does this mean that the SIP and FCC doctrines do not cover the situation of armed conflict, but may still be invoked for some other, unrelated reason, for example a natural disaster that may occur at the time of an armed conflict? According to this interpretation, Article 18 of the Draft Articles aims to preserve the VCLT grounds for the suspension or termination of treaties for this purpose only and not as standards for determining the effects of armed conflict.[94] At first glance, this view appears to be supported by Article 73 VCLT, according to which the VCLT provisions 'shall not prejudge any question that may arise in regard to a treaty from the outbreak of hostilities between States'.[95] Therefore, some scholars have concluded that the VCLT does not regulate the consequences of armed conflict.[96] More pointedly, the ILC stated in its commentary on draft Article 69 VCLT (the predecessor of Article 73), that the VCLT did not 'purport to regulate the consequences of an outbreak of hostilities.'[97]

Yet, in the present author's view, nothing in Article 73 VCLT suggests that the VCLT does not address the consequences of armed conflict. Rather, the Article implies that armed conflict may create legal repercussions not covered by the VCLT, which are unaffected by the potential applicability of the SIP and FCC doctrines. This interpretation is preferable, in particular when Article 73 VCLT is read together with Article 18 of the EACT Draft Articles. The fact that the ILC found it necessary to include an explicit explanation in later drafts of the Commentary to the Draft Articles that the Draft Articles do not reflect a *lex specialis*, vis-à-vis VCLT, implies that both SIP and FCC can be just as to the point and effective in regulating the suspension or termination of treaties in times of armed conflict as the EACT Draft Articles themselves. Upon the outbreak of armed conflict, all these doctrines exist on the same level of speciality, and all of them may affect the operation of a treaty, although it may be difficult to differentiate them, as stressed by the ILC itself.[98] The support for this view is reflected in the preparatory work leading to the Draft Articles,[99] as well as in the opinions of the First Rapporteur to the

[94] B Peng, 'The International Law Commission's Draft Articles on the Effects of Armed Conflicts on Treaties: Evaluating the Applicability of Impossibility of Performance and Fundamental Change' (2013) 3 Asian J Intl L 51, 58.

[95] VCLT Art 73.

[96] Chinkin, 'Crisis and the Performance' (n 11) 187; T Giegerich, 'Article 61' in Dörr and Schmalenbach (n 10) 1059, 1081.

[97] ILC, 'Draft Articles on the Law of Treaties with Commentaries' in *Yearbook of the International Law Commission, 1966, Vol II*, UN Doc A/6309/Rev 1, Commentary to Article 69 (which became Article 73), 267–68.

[98] ILC, Report of the International Law Commission, 60th Session, 2008, UN Doc A/63/10, 98.

[99] See e.g. ILC, Report of the International Law Commission, 62nd Session, 2010, Supplement No 10, UN Doc A/65/10, para 2020 (noting that several member states proposed the express acknowledgment that SIP and FCC grounds can be applied in armed conflict). The 1985 Resolution, which influenced the EACT Draft Articles, also insisted on the parallel application of the VCLT doctrines. See Institute of International Law, Deliberations (1982) 59(2) Annuaire de l'IDI 217. See also R Provost, 'Article 73' in O

Draft Articles, who in his international law textbook remarked that war could lead to an impossibility of performance or fundamental change of circumstances.[100] Furthermore, this position has received the support of scholars,[101] governments,[102] and courts.[103] Even if one subscribes to the view that Article 73 excludes the outbreak of armed conflict from the scope of the VCLT, it will do so only with respect to international conflicts since the Article expressly refers to outbreak of hostilities between states. In other words, Articles 61 and 62 VCLT could still be potentially invoked as a consequence of factual circumstances emerging from internal conflicts. Lastly, regardless of how one interprets Article 73, the effect of hostilities can be still governed by the doctrines as encapsulated in customary international law.[104]

In order to comprehend the differences between the grounds for terminating or suspending treaties, as provided for in the EACT Draft Articles and VCLT doctrines, the latter are first briefly discussed.

1. Supervening Impossibility to Perform

The SIP is codified in Article 61 VCLT which in its first paragraph states that:

> A party may invoke the impossibility of performing a treaty as a ground for terminating or withdrawing from it if the impossibility results from the permanent disappearance or destruction of an object indispensable for the execution

Corten and P Klein (eds), *The Vienna Conventions on the Law of Treaties, The Commentary* (OUP 2011) 1656–57.

[100] Brownlie, *Principles* (n 8) 620.

[101] See B Conforti and A Labella, 'Invalidity and Termination of Treaties: The Role of National Courts' (1990) 1 EJIL 44, 58; R Sonnenfeld, 'Succession and Continuation, A Study on Treaty Practice in Post-War Germany' (1976) 7 Nl Ybk of Intl L 91; McIntyre, *Legal Effects* (n 64) 25; Peng, 'Draft Articles' (n 94) 60.

[102] Some state delegations raised the relevance of FCC and SIP for determining the application of treaties in armed conflict. See the views of Belarus in the Official Records of the General Assembly, 63rd Session, Sixth Committee, 16th Meeting, UN Doc A/C.6/63/SR.16 (2008), para 40; and Ukraine in Official Records, ibid, 65th Session, 25th meeting, UN Doc A/C.6/65/SR.25 (2008), para 30. See also the US views expressed in the Restatement of the Law Third, Foreign Relations Law of the United States (1987) American Law Institute, s 336(e), giving support to the application of the FCC doctrine in case of 'major hostilities'. See also Secretariat Memorandum, 69, para 122 (listing examples when FCC doctrine was invoked by states). For more examples, see n 109 and n 135.

[103] See e.g. *Lanificio Branditex v Soceita Azais e Vidal* (1971) Court of Cassation, Joint Session, No 3147, reported in 1 Italian Ybk of Intl L (1975) 232–33; Case 162/96 *Racke v Hauptzollamt Mainz* [1998] ECR I-3655. For other judicial decisions, see the sections below.

[104] VCLT Art 73 does not reflect customary international law. It merely bears 'innocuous, if cautionary, function'. See *Appeal Relating to the Jurisdiction of the ICAO Council (India v Pakistan)* (Judgment) [1972] ICJ Rep 46, Separate Opinion of Judge Dillard 109; *Racke* (n 103) para 53. See also US Restatement of the Law, Third (n 102) Reporter's note 4; H Krieger, 'Article 73' in Dörr and Schmalenbach (n 10) 1331–32.

of the treaty. If the impossibility is temporary, it may be invoked only as a ground for suspending the operation of the treaty.

The notion pervading this provision is that a party cannot be expected to execute its treaty obligations when exceptional circumstances render it impossible,[105] and such impossibility is not due to a breach by that party either of an obligation under the treaty or of any other international obligation owed to any other party to the treaty.[106] This provision was perceived to reflect 'common sense' and thus generated almost no debate.[107] Although the practical examples of the treaty termination based on SIP have been very rare,[108] there were instances when the doctrine was invoked due to an armed conflict.[109]

Could the SIP grounds be invoked in the context of investment treaties? Some commentators argued that the SIP is not applicable to the investment treaty regime because Article 61 refers exclusively to physical impossibility, that is the impossibility that occurs due to natural events that result in the 'permanent disappearance or destruction of an object indispensable for the execution of the treaty'.[110] According to this view, the scope of the Article is limited to situations of physical disappearance such as submergence of an island and rivers drying up or changing course.[111] This restrictive interpretation is not accepted unanimously. Some have argued that an 'object' may be read more broadly to include non-physical objects and consequently SIP would extend to the disappearance of a treaty field of action or legal situations necessary for the execution of treaty obligations (so-called juridical impossibility).[112] While the uncertainty as to the scope of the term 'object' under Article 61 was also noted, but left unaddressed, by the ICJ in the *Gabčíkovo* case,[113] the ILC appeared to favour a broader reading that extends the scope to

[105] For more on the doctrine, see I Sinclair, *The Vienna Convention on the Laws of Treaties* (2nd edn, MUP 1984) 190–92; P Bodeau-Livinec and J Morgan-Foster, 'Article 61' in Corten and Klein (n 99) 1383–1410; Giegerich, 'Article 61' (n 96) 1051–65.

[106] VCLT Art 61(2).

[107] Bodeau-Livinec and Morgan-Foster, 'Article 61' (n 105) 1386.

[108] ILC, Commentary to Article 58 (which became Article 61 VCLT) 256; H Waldock, 'Second Report on the Law of Treaties' in ILC, *Yearbook of the International Law Commission, 1963, Vol II*, UN Doc A/CN.4/156/Add.1–3, 79, para 5.

[109] See McIntyre, *Legal Effects* (n 64) 134 (observing that labour treaties and the payment obligations arising from treaties governing intergovernmental debt, in particular, were impossible to perform during the period of the Second World War).

[110] Ostřanský, 'Termination and Suspension' (n 30) 139.

[111] ILC, Commentary to Article 58 (which became Article 61 VCLT) 256, para 2; M Villiger, *Commentary on the 1969 Vienna Convention on the Law of Treaties* (Martinus Nijhoff 2009) 755.

[112] See G Fitzmaurice, 'Second Report on the Law of Treaties' in *Yearbook of the International Law Commission, 1957, Vol II*, UN Doc A/CN.4/107, 50–51, paras 99, 101. See also the argument put forward by Hungary in the *Gabčíkovo* case. *Gabčíkovo* (n 90) Memorial of the Republic of Hungary–Vol I, 2 May 1994, para 10.49. For scholarly support, see Bodeau-Livinec and Morgan-Foster (n 105) 1389–90; Sinclair, *Vienna Convention* (n 105) 191–92; Giegerich, 'Article 61' (n 96) 1056.

[113] The ICJ refrained from making any pronouncement on the matter, and found that the doctrine did not apply on the ground of Art 61(2), i.e. the state contributed to the impossibility. *Gabčíkovo* (n 90) para 103.

non-physical impossibilities.[114] This interpretation is indeed more persuasive and at least more easily accepted when considering if the treaty or treaty provisions should be suspended rather than terminated.[115]

In armed conflicts, states' resources that are necessary for the execution of their treaty obligations are often under severe strain, which may lead to the state's temporary inability to fulfil its obligations. Although one cannot speak of the 'destruction' of a physical object in this case, the situation of armed conflict still causes the kind of deprivation in a state's means that can paralyse its legal and economic infrastructure and render it temporarily incapacitated and unable to meet its obligations. This reading is in line with Article 61 VCLT, which ascribes 'permanent disappearance or destruction' alone as a criterion necessary for the withdrawal or termination of a treaty. The temporary impossibility to perform as a ground for suspension is set out in a separate sentence, and is independent from the preceding formulation of irrecoverable impossibility due to the 'permanent disappearance or destruction of an object'. According to the Oxford Dictionary, the words 'destroy' and 'disappear', as used in the first sentence of Article 61(1) VCLT, denote the end or cessation of the existence of something.[116] An object cannot cease to exist temporarily; it may, however, become incapable of being used for a certain duration (i.e. the legal situation is still remediable), thus resulting in the suspension of the operation of the treaty.[117]

A state could thus invoke the ground for the suspension of a treaty not only for reasons associated with the physical destruction of the object of a treaty, but due to any other circumstance which makes it temporarily impossible for it to perform its obligation. As mentioned above, some courts have recognized armed conflict as a circumstance that justifies a state's invocation of SIP and suspension of a treaty. For instance, the Italian Court of Cassation held that armed conflict could lead to SIP and the suspension of treaties pending cessation of the hostilities and the resumption of normal international relations.[118] In the *Utermöhlen* case cited above, a Dutch court similarly concluded that the exercise of the rights deriving from the Hague Convention on the Conflict of Law in Matters of Marriage was suspended, but not as a result of the effect of armed conflict, rather due to the temporary impossibility of performance.[119] Similarly, governments have held in the past that as

[114] The ILC deleted the word 'physical' from the final version of the provision, extending the meaning of the object to 'legal situation' indispensable for execution of a treaty, and confirming the permissibility of juridical impossibility. Fitzmaurice, 'Second Report' (n 112) 51, para 101; Giegerich, 'Article 61' (n 96) 1056. See also ILC, 'Draft Articles on the Law of Treaties between States and International Organizations or Between International Organizations'in *Yearbook of the International Law Commission, 1982, Vol II*, UN Doc A/CN.4/SER.A/1982/Add.1 (Part 2) 59, para 3.

[115] Fitzmaurice, 'Second Report' (n 112) 50, para 99.

[116] Oxford Dictionary <http://www.oxforddictionaries.com/> accessed 10 May 2018.

[117] *Gabčíkovo* (n 90) para 103; Giegerich, 'Article 61' (n 96) 1059; Bodeau-Livinec and Morgan-Foster (n 105) 1403 (noting that there is a preference for suspension unless the impossibility is clearly permanent).

[118] *Lanificio Branditex* (n 103).

[119] *In re Utermöhlen* (n 88) para 381.

a practical consequence of armed conflict, certain treaty provisions might become inoperative.[120] The Second Rapporteur on the Law of Treaties, Fitzmaurice, also noted that certain situations of juridical impossibility (e.g. a country entering into conflicting military alliances) could result in suspension.[121]

This would suggest that the SIP doctrine could also be utilized to suspend some of the provisions of investment treaties. For example, the circumstances resulting from armed conflict may prevent a state from fulfilling its obligation to freely transfer payments, which is commonly required in BITs.[122] The host state's financial system may be severely impaired by widespread armed conflict. Consequently, banks can be prevented from carrying out certain financial transactions, which could render the transfer of profits, dividends, compensations, and other due payments impossible. The view that such an action amounts to the breach of a BIT is simplistic, and tribunals would need to closely examine whether the conditions of a political and military crisis were such that the transfer of funds would be rendered temporarily impossible, in which case the respective treaty provision could be suspended. It should be stressed that such impossibility would need to be absolute rather than merely relative (i.e. the fulfilment of the obligation would be still possible but would create excessive costs or jeopardize the existence of the state). While in the latter case the SIP would not be available, the state could invoke *force majeure* to preclude the wrongfulness of non-performance of the obligation.[123]

Could a state invoke SIP to suspend dispute settlement provisions? The general rule for the arbitration clauses would seem to be that they continue to apply in the period of the conflict provided that they are not incompatible with national policy. Depending on the conditions of armed conflict, however, it may become technically impossible for a state to deal with the organizational, procedural (e.g. evidence-collecting), and financial arrangements around arbitration claims during hostilities, in which case the provision could be suspended. Suspension would not

[120] For example, after the Second World War, the US State Department's view was that the existence of war did not abrogate non-political multilateral treaties, however, as a 'practical matter, certain of the provisions might have been inoperative'. Cited in Rank, 'Modern War' (n 21) 343–45.

[121] Fitzmaurice, 'Second Report' (n 112) 50, para 99.

[122] See e.g. Russia–Ukraine BIT (1998) Art 17.

[123] *Force majeure* is similar to SIP in that it deals with impossibility of performing an international obligation, however, the threshold of impossibility is arguably higher for SIP than *force majeure*. There are other differences between the two principles, the most important being that SIP is a primary rule enabling states to terminate or suspend a treaty, whereas *force majeure*, as a secondary rule of the law of state responsibility, merely excludes the wrongfulness of a state's conduct otherwise contrary to an international obligation. See J Crawford, 'Second Report on State Responsibility' in *Yearbook of the International Law Commission, 1999*, UN Doc A/CN.4/498/Add.1–4, 59, 66, paras 224–28, 259; *Gabčíkovo* (n 90) 63, para 102; Bodeau-Livinec and Morgan-Foster (n 105) 1394–99, 1405–07; Giegerich, 'Article 61' (n 96) 1057, 1065. The material distinction between the impossibility under the doctrines is, however, blurred if the impossibility is temporary and leads to suspension, in which case SIP appears to be a preferred option to *force majeure* if the impossibility is continuing and concerns a recurring obligation. See Waldock, 'Second Report' (n 108) 79, para 7; ILC, 'Commentary to Article 58 (which became Article 61 VCLT) 256, para 3. For more on *force majeure*, see Chapter 5 C.2

occur due to untenableness of the clause for policy reasons, but due to a state's temporary impossibility to perform it.[124]

Some scholars have opposed the view that specific treaty provisions could be suspended by the application of Article 61 VCLT. Paddeu and Szurek thus held that the rule was only relevant with respect to the treaty as a whole, and that Article 44(3) VCLT, which regulates separability, did not apply to the SIP doctrine.[125] This view does not reflect the drafting history of Article 61 VCLT which in its earliest incarnation contained a separate paragraph on the termination and suspension of specific treaty provisions due to impossibility. Although the paragraph was later removed as the question of the separability of treaty provisions was relegated to Article 44 VCLT, Special Rapporteur Waldock confirmed in his second report that separability applied to questions of termination and suspension.[126]

Commentators pointed to the practical difficulties of reconciling the requirement for the application of SIP, that is that the object must be 'indispensable to the execution of the treaty', and the condition of Article 44(3) that the separable provision must not be an 'essential basis' of the parties' consent.[127] This concern is based on the rigid interpretation of Article 61(1) VCLT according to which the suspension of a specific treaty provision would only be possible in the event of the destruction or disappearance of an object indispensable to the execution of the treaty as a whole, rather than an object indispensable to the execution of the treaty provision being suspended. According to this approach, for instance, the suspension of the 'transfer of payments' investment treaty provision would not be possible despite the complete incapacitation of the host state's banking system (which is necessary for meeting the provision's objective) because the general object indispensable for the investment treaty as a whole,[128] did not disappear. A more persuasive view is that if the termination or suspension of a treaty is linked to the existence of the object of the treaty, then, *ad maiore ad minus*, the termination or suspension of a treaty provision should depend on the fate of the object of that specific treaty provision. The treaty provision may not necessarily be an essential basis of the consent of the parties and can thus be severed from the rest of the treaty. This interpretation,

[124] In practice, this would seem to matter less since compensation claims are usually filed once the hostilities have ceased and when it is agreed that dispute resolution clauses continue to apply.

[125] See F Paddeu, 'A Genealogy of Force Majeure in International Law' (2012) 82(1) BYIL 381, 472–73. Paddeu also refers to S Szurek, La force majeure en droit international (PhD thesis, Université Paris II Panthéon-Assas 1996) vol 1, 28, 236.

[126] Waldock, 'Second Report' (n 108) 93.

[127] Paddeu, citing Szurek (n 125).

[128] Ostřanský, 'Termination and Suspension' (n 30) 139; A Newcombe and L Paradell, *Law and Practice of Investment Treaties* (Kluwer 2009) 551, n 141. These authors have held that SIP cannot be applied to investment treaties since their object (i.e. foreign investment) is too general. This is not entirely correct; the object of investment treaties is that investors from either state parties will enjoy certain rights and protections in each other's territories. Consequently, the 'indispensable object' includes the elements (e.g. juridical situation) that are essential for the execution of the object (protection of foreign investment). See also Bodeau-Livinec and Morgan-Foster, 'Article 61' (n 105) 1388.

which gives meaning and effect to separability in the context of SIP, is in line with the internationally recognized interpretive principle of effectiveness,[129] and makes SIP practically relevant for determining the operation of investment treaty provisions in the context of armed conflict.

2. Fundamental Change of Circumstances

FCC or, as it is known outside the scope of the VCLT, *rebus sic stantibus*,[130] is a contested concept,[131] often described as the *enfant terrible* of international law.[132] As put by the ILC, it can be invoked by states to escape from obligations when a treaty or a treaty provision places an 'undue burden on one of the parties as a result of the fundamental change of circumstances'.[133]

Many commentators in the past have held that the effect of armed conflict is very similar to *rebus sic stantibus* and that major armed conflicts present 'changed circumstances', thus providing a basis for the suspension or termination of treaties.[134] The ILC found a few instances where states invoked the *rebus sic stantibus* doctrine in the context of armed conflict in order to either terminate or suspend a treaty,[135]

[129] The principle of effectiveness means that in treaty interpretation all treaty terms must be given meaning, and interpretation that would make a treaty provision devoid of purpose or effect must be avoided. See e.g. *Corfu Channel Case* (*UK v Albania*) (Merits) [1949] ICJ Rep 4, 24; *United States—Standards for Reformulated and Conventional Gasoline* Appellate Body Report (29 April 1996) WT/DS2/AB/R, para 621. See also G Fitzmaurice, 'The Law and Procedure of the International Court of Justice: Treaty Interpretation and Certain Other Treaty Points' (1951) 28 BYIL 1, 8; H Lauterpacht, 'Restrictive Interpretation and the Principle of Effectiveness in the Interpretation of Treaties' (1949) 26 BYIL 48 ; R Gardiner, *Treaty Interpretation* (OUP 2008) 159–61.

[130] The principle and its various variations can be found in many domestic private law systems. See H Lauterpacht, *The Function of Law in the International Community* (The Clarendon Press 1933) 272–76; A Vamvoukos, *Termination of Treaties in International Law: the Doctrine of Rebus Sic Stantibus and Desuetude* (OUP 1985) 32–59.

[131] Fitzmaurice described it as one of the most controversial questions of treaty law. Fitzmaurice, 'Second Report' (n 112) 56–57, paras 141, 144. For a detailed discussion of the doctrine, see Vamvoukos (n 130); OJ Lissitzyn, 'Treaties and Changed Circumstances (Rebus sic Stantibus)' (1967) 61 AJIL 895; McNair, *Law of Treaties* (n 24) 681–91; R Mullerson, 'The ABM Treaty: Changed Circumstances, Extraordinary Events, Supreme Interests and International Law' (2001) 50 ICLQ 509; M Fitzmaurice and O Elias, *Contemporary Issues in the Law of Treaties* (Eleven 2005) 173–200; M Shaw and C Fournet, 'Article 62' in Corten and Klein (n 99) 1412–33; Giegerich, 'Article 62' in Dörr and Schmalenbach (n 10) 1143–81.

[132] See *Racke* (n 103) para 85.

[133] ILC, Commentary to Article 59 (which became Article 62 VCLT) 258.

[134] See Secretariat Memorandum, para 121; Conforti and Labella, 'Invalidity and Termination' (n 101) 58; Brownlie, *Principles* (n 8) 592; McIntyre, *Legal Effects* (n 64) 25; Vamvoukos, *Termination of Treaties* (n 130).

[135] For examples of state practice, see Secretariat Memorandum, 69, paras 122–23; Vamvoukos (n 130) 21–27, 61–126; Lissitzyn, Treaties and Changed Circumstances' (n 131) 908; Mullerson, 'ABM Treaty' (n 131) 524–31. For example, Franklin Roosevelt declared the Second World War as FCC to suspend the US obligations under the International Load Line Convention. See Secretariat Memorandum, para 123. In 1982 the Netherlands suspended all of its bilateral treaties with Surinam by invoking *rebus sic stantibus* due to civil strife that took place in Surinam. See RCR Siekmann, 'Netherlands State Practice for the Parliamentary Year 1982–1983' (1984) 15 NYIL 321. The US withdrew from the Treaty on the Limitation of Anti-Ballistic Missile Systems in the aftermath of 11 September 2001, by relying

however it also noted that courts, both domestic and international, were reluctant to apply it.[136] The concern was that the doctrine would open up room for abuse of *pacta sunt servanda* and could be used to frame ideological or political motifs for abandoning treaty obligations as justifiable 'changed circumstances'.[137] To prevent this, the VCLT prescribed stringent conditions for its application.

The first paragraph of Article 62 VCLT codifies *rebus sic stantibus* as:

> A fundamental change of circumstances which has occurred with regard to those existing at the time of the conclusion of a treaty, and which was not foreseen by the parties, may not be invoked as a ground for terminating or withdrawing from the treaty unless:
> a) The existence of those circumstances constituted an essential basis of the consent of the parties to be bound by the treaty; and
> b) the effect of the change is radically to transform the extent of the obligations still to be performed under the treaty.

As with Article 61,[138] the existence of an armed conflict does not, by itself, meet the rigorous threshold of Article 62—certain cumulative conditions must be met that are narrower for the invocation of FCC than SIP.[139] This can be explained by the broader scope of the FCC, which is not limited to situations of actual impossibility and is more susceptible to subjective appreciation of circumstances and potential abuse.[140] Consequently, the successful invocation of armed conflict as FCC in modern jurisprudence has been very rare.

In one case, *Questech v Iran*, the Iran–US Claims Tribunal held that unilateral termination of a military contract by the Iranian Ministry of Defence was justified due to 'fundamental changes in the political conditions as a consequence of the Revolution in Iran'.[141] The tribunal paid attention to the fact that the contract in

on the FCC reflected in military-strategic changes and the 'emergence of new security threats'. See the White House statement at <http:/state.gov/t/ac/rls/fs/2001/6848.htm> accessed 5 November 2018.

[136] Fitzmaurice, 'Second Report' (n 112) 56, para 141; ILC, Commentary to Article 59 (which became Article 62 VCLT) 257–58, paras 2–4. See e.g. *Free Zones of Upper Savoy and the District of Gex (France v Switzerland)* (Order) [1929] PCIJ Rep Series C No 17/1, 283–84; *Fisheries Jurisdiction* (n 90) 20; *Gabčíkovo* (n 90) 65, para 104. For the overview of the relevant decisions of municipal courts, see Vamvoukos, *Termination of Treaties* (n 130) 152–185.

[137] Fitzmaurice, 'Second Report' (n 112) para 142; ILC, 'Report of the International Law Commission on the Work of the Second Part of its Seventeenth Session' 1966, Vol II, UN Doc A/6309/Rev.1 258, para 7.

[138] There is a close connection between the SIP and FCC doctrines, since the situation giving rise to impossibility of performance can result in a fundamental change of circumstances. See Waldock, 'Second Report' (n 108) 82.

[139] For an analysis of the conditions, see Shaw and Fournet, 'Article 62' (n 131) 1424–32; Giegerich, 'Article 62' (n 131) 1079–89; Fitzmaurice and Elias, *Contemporary Issues* (n 131) 187–95.

[140] Fitzmaurice, 'Second Report' (n 112) 59, para 150.

[141] *Questech Inc. v Iran* (1985) 9 Iran–USCTR 107, para 123.

question was based on military cooperation (it concerned Iranian defence interests and policy) and was consequently more prone to be affected by the negative shifts in political relationship between the states.[142] While the tribunal invoked VCLT Article 62 in its general discussion of FCC, the legal basis for the application of the doctrine was the applicable (Iranian) law and the contractual provision which mandated the tribunal to 'take into account . . . changed circumstances' when applying the law.[143] This, coupled with the private nature of the contract, renders the case of little importance for the application of FCC to investment treaties. It does, however, show how foreign investors in sensitive military domains are expected to foresee that such changes (e.g. a conflict between their home state and a host state) can affect the fate of investment contracts, and potentially preclude contractual claims.

More relevant for the treaty context was the application of FCC by the European Court of Justice in the *Racke* case.[144] The Court considered the application of the doctrine to the trade cooperation agreement concluded between the European Economic Community and the Socialist Federal Republic of Yugoslavia (SFRY). In that case, the European Economic Community unilaterally suspended the Cooperation Agreement because the 1991 war in SFRY constituted 'radical changes in the conditions' under which the agreement was concluded.[145] One of the questions that the Court had to answer in the preliminary ruling proceeding was whether the hostilities in Yugoslavia justified taking recourse to *rebus sic stantibus*. The Court answered in the affirmative. It first clarified that Article 62 VCLT reflected customary international law. It then went on to examine whether the conditions set out in Article 62(1) had been met.

With respect to the first condition, it noted that given the wide-ranging objectives of the agreement,[146] the existence of peace was a prerequisite to initiate and pursue the cooperation envisaged by the Cooperation Agreement.[147] As for the second condition, it held that the hostilities indeed radically transformed the extent of the Community's obligations towards SFRY and that there was no point in continuing to perform treaty obligations with a view to stimulate economic cooperation in circumstances in which SFRY was splitting into new political entities.[148] The Court emphasized the seriousness of the situation that had caused the fundamental change by referring to the use of armed forces, the presence of bloodshed and destruction caused by the conflict, the disintegration of the internal

[142] *Questech*, ibid para 121.
[143] ibid paras 122–23.
[144] *Racke* (n 103).
[145] *Racke*, AG Opinion (n 103) para 9.
[146] See the Preamble and Art 1 of the Cooperation Agreement, stating that the object of the agreement is the promotion of cooperation between the parties with a view to contribute to the economic and social development of Yugoslavia.
[147] *Racke*, Judgment (n 103) para 55; *Racke*, AG Opinion, para 92.
[148] *Racke*, Judgment, para 57. See also *Racke*, AG Opinion, paras 51, 62, 63, 92, 93.

order and organization of the state, and the Security Council's characterization of the situation as a threat to international peace and security.[149]

Could the FCC doctrine be relevant in the context of investment treaties? There are certain elements of the *Racke* case that could invite analogies to be drawn between it and a potential situation involving an investment treaty. The Cooperation Agreement between the Community and SFRY was primarily an economic agreement which had conferred certain rights and benefits on individuals and whose preamble resembled the preamble of a typical BIT, aiming to facilitate economic cooperation between state parties. However, there are also important differences that would make the invocation of FCC much more difficult in the investment law context. First, the Cooperation Agreement was broader in scope and its object and purpose much wider than an investment treaty: it contained provisions on financial cooperation and social provisions, and it instituted privileged political relations between the Community and the Member States and SFRY. By contrast, the object and purpose of investment treaties is confined to the promotion and protection of foreign investment, and through that, contribution to the economic development of state parties. Second, the threshold for the second condition of Article 62 VCLT (that the hostilities radically transform the extent of the obligation) is very difficult to meet. A likely explanation for why the European Commission was successful in the *Racke* case was that armed conflict was accompanied by the dissolution of SFRY. Third, the negative definition of the FCC in Article 62 dictates a narrow interpretation that reflects the intention of the drafters of the VCLT,[150] and was confirmed by the ICJ in the *Gabčíkovo* case.[151]

In view of the above, it is difficult to envision a situation in which a plea of FCC due to a conflict situation could result in the suspension or termination of an investment treaty. If, for example, a political relationship between two states deteriorates and even escalates to a war, and a host state finds the BIT obligations owed to investors with the nationality of the enemy state burdensome, this would merely reflect the disappearance of the initial motif for entering into a BIT, which in itself does not justify the operation of the doctrine.[152] Moreover, the fact that in many of their provisions an increasing number of investment treaties contemplate conflict situations in express terms,[153] precludes the operation of the principle on the

[149] *Racke*, AG Opinion, paras 51, 61. The commentators agreed that the application of FCC in that case could be explained by the severity of the factual circumstances. See J Klabbers, 'Re-inventing the Law of Treaties: The Contribution of the EC Courts' (1999) 30 NYIL 45, 57–59; O Elias, 'General International Law in the European Court of Justice: From Hypothesis to Reality' (2000) 31 NYIL 3, 17–22.

[150] ILC, 'Report on the Seventeenth Session' (n 137) 259; Shaw and Fournet, 'Article 62' (n 131) 1411.

[151] The ICJ held that 'the negative and conditional wording of Article 62 of the Vienna Convention on the Law of Treaties is a clear indication moreover that the stability of treaty relations requires that the plea of fundamental change of circumstances be applied only in exceptional cases'. *Gabčíkovo* (n 90) para 104.

[152] *Fisheries Jurisdiction* (n 90) para 34.

[153] See Chapters 4 and 5.

ground of the non-foreseeability criterion.[154] Potentially, the principle could be applied if the state parties to a BIT would expel each other's foreign investors and ban future investment flows. Changes of such magnitude could indeed frustrate the object and purpose of the treaty, destroy its *raison d'etre*,[155] radically transform the parties' obligations, and thus possibly provide justification for termination on the ground of FCC (although it would not preclude claims of investors based on grounds that existed when a treaty was still in operation). Beyond such extraordinary situations, however, FCC is unlikely to play a role in affecting the operation of investment treaties.

D. The Relationship between the EACT and VCLT Doctrines

Having argued that the VCLT doctrines, in particular SIP, can provide a basis (although very limited) for the suspension of an investment treaty provision in the event of hostilities, the subject addressed next is the relationship between the doctrines. Notably, there seem to be a few differences between them.

First, and most obviously, the SIP and FCC are not only binding through the VCLT but apply beyond its scope given their status of customary international law. In contrast, EACT is not regulated in a binding instrument and does not fall under a clear customary law regime due to inconsistent and changing state practice.[156] The EACT Draft Articles merely function as interpretive guidance.

Second, armed conflict is a normative factor under the EACT Draft Articles, but only a factual circumstance under the VCLT doctrines. Consequently, the conflict situation would need to meet a formal threshold of armed conflict for the effect to take place (as said, the ILC adheres to the *Tadić* definition of armed conflict), whereas no such threshold needs to be satisfied for the application of SIP and FCC.

Third, there is a difference in the grounds for suspending a treaty, which also leads to different rationales behind the respective rules. Under EACT, suspension is justified by a distorted political relationship, the loss of mutual trust and confidence between the parties to the treaty,[157] and by the incompatibility of the treaty or a particular treaty provision with the state's security policy in times of armed conflict.[158] In contrast, Article 61 VCLT does not concern itself with considerations

[154] *Fisheries Jurisdiction* (n 90) para 43; *Gabčíkovo* (n 90) para 104.

[155] Fitzmaurice, 'Second Report' (n 112) 56–57, para 142.

[156] Aust, *Modern Treaty Law* (n 7) 307–08; McNair, *Law of Treaties* (n 24) 693; Delbrück 'War, Effect on Treaties' (n 15) 312; Krieger, 'Article 73' (n 104) 1256.

[157] See Peng, 'Draft Articles' (n 94) 67. The substantive overlap in policy motivation for termination or suspension is more apparent with FCC than with the SIP doctrine.

[158] I Brownlie, 'Fourth Report on the Effects of Armed Conflict on Treaties: Procedure for Suspension and Termination' ILC, 59th Session, 2007, UN Doc A/CN.4/589, 87, para 29; Y Ronen, 'Treaties and Armed Conflict' in C Tams, A Tzanakopoulos, and A Zimmermann (eds), *Research Handbook on the Law of Treaties* (Edward Elgar 2013) 541, 551.

of mutual trust between state parties, but refers to changes that affect only a state's ability to perform its obligation. This change is triggered by the impossibility in executing the treaty or treaty provision and not by policy considerations or a strained relationship with other states. This would suggest that the doctrines are not mutually exclusive—they are triggered by different causes that could result in the same outcome: the temporary inapplicability of the treaty or treaty provision. The situation of armed conflict could amount to both a practical impossibility to perform as well as a loss of trust between the state parties, which could give the state the ability to choose from among the different grounds for suspension.

This brings us to the fourth distinction, which is the manner in which the grounds can be invoked. The procedural difference between the EACT and the VCLT doctrines appears to be that the EACT could potentially emerge automatically, while the VCLT ground must be invoked. The Secretariat Memorandum notes that if that difference indeed exists, then it bears great legal significance.[159] Regretfully, the question has attracted almost no attention in the scholarship.

In order to suspend the operation of a treaty or a treaty provision under the SIP ground, a state needs to follow a complicated and lengthy notification procedure set out in Articles 65–67 VCLT. The drafters were not completely insensitive to the practical difficulties that a state may encounter in trying to suspend a treaty. Article 65(2) thus provides that in cases of special urgency, the minimum waiting period of three months, during which time the other state party may raise its objections to the invocation of termination or suspension, can be disregarded. Arguably, an armed conflict situation would constitute such a case of special urgency. Along these lines, in the above-mentioned *Racke* case, the European Court of Justice held that it was permissible to proceed with the suspension of the Cooperation Agreement with no prior notification or waiting period.[160]

Whether EACT operates automatically or must be invoked by the state remains an open question.[161] While in the past, some states have considered the effects of armed conflict to be automatic, this practice has been criticized as obsolete.[162] Similarly, both Rapporteurs considered that automatic effect is inconsistent with the modern position that armed conflicts do not *ipso facto* affect the operation of treaties, and undermines the principle of stability.[163] Consequently,

[159] Secretariat Memorandum, 77, para 139.

[160] *Racke*, Judgment (n 103) para 58; *Racke*, AG Opinion (n 103) para 98. The Court noted that the formal procedural requirements laid down in Art 65 VCLT did not form customary international law. For the argument against strict notification procedures during wartime, see also Opinion of Acting Attorney General Francis Biddle on Suspension of the International Load Line Convention, 40 Official Opinions of the Attorneys General of the United States Advising the President and Heads of Departments in Relation to their Official Duties 119–24 (John T Fowler, ed, 1949) para 123, cited in Secretariat Memorandum, n 447. See also Krieger, 'Article 73' (n 104) 1359 (noting that the obligation to notify in case of armed conflict is not clearly established in customary international law).

[161] Secretariat Memorandum, 77, para 139.

[162] Peng, 'Draft Articles' (n 94) 66.

[163] Brownlie, 'Fourth Report' (n 158) 88, para 33; Caflisch, 'First Report' (n 28) 105, para 89.

the Draft Articles prescribe a notification procedure that is modelled on that of Article 65 VCLT, but streamlined and adjusted to reflect the urgency of armed conflict. Specifically, there is no time framework for a formulation of objections to a notification and no requirement for additional recourse to the third-party adjudication.[164]

The inclusion of the notification procedure in the Draft Articles was subject to a heated discussion, and the first Special Rapporteur acknowledged the relevance of the argument that in view of the realities of an armed conflict, it might be reasonable for the effect on treaties to operate automatically.[165] Many states' delegations highlighted the practical difficulties associated with giving notice to opposing state parties in times of hostilities and admonished the notification requirements for being too strict.[166] It was recommended that the provision be drafted in a sufficiently flexible manner to allow for the possibility that in certain cases notification would not be necessary.[167]

The second Special Rapporteur confirmed in his concluding remarks on the ILC report that this concern could be 'taken care of through appropriate drafting',[168] although the extent to which this has happened is questionable. One thing that could indicate more flexibility in the interpretation of the state's duty to notify is the use of the word 'shall' instead of 'must'. While Article 65 VCLT requires that a state 'must notify the other party of its claim', Article 9 of the Draft Articles makes a small change by using the 'shall notify' formulation. According to the Oxford Dictionary, 'shall' can express both an obligation and an instruction.[169] Although lawyers often use 'must' and 'shall' interchangeably, oftentimes 'shall' is interpreted as 'may'.[170] Since Article 9 of the Draft Articles was expressly modelled on Article 65 VCLT, this glaring departure from 'must' could be taken as an indication that the ILC wanted to imbue the provision with more flexibility.

Finally, in state practice, the notification procedure was not typically considered a prerequisite for relying on EACT.[171] Since the ILC aspired for the Draft Articles to reflect state practice as much as possible, it is surprising that it adopted the opposite approach with notification as a condition for termination or suspension. While such a mandatory duty promotes legal stability and the continuity of treaty relations, it is detached from the reality of armed conflict when a state has other priorities, namely fighting for its survival. It may often be impossible for a state in the

164 Caflisch, ibid; Commentary to Draft Articles, Art 9, para 1.

165 Brownlie, 'Fourth Report' (n 158) 88, para 30.

166 See the statements of the Netherlands in Official Records of the General Assembly, 'Summary Record of the 24th Meeting' 65th Session, 2010, UN Doc A/C.6/65/SR.23, para 43; Greece, ibid, UN Doc A/C.6/65/SR.24, para 40; Sri Lanka, ibid, UN Doc A/C.6/65/SR.26, para 41.

167 ibid.

168 ILC Report on its 62nd Session, UN Doc A/65/0 (2010), para 251.

169 Oxford Dictionary <http://www.oxforddictionaries.com/> accessed 10 May 2014.

170 For a discussion of 'shall' and 'must', see B Garner, *A Dictionary of Modern Legal Usage* (2nd edn, OUP 1995) 939–42.

171 Secretariat Memorandum, 83.

midst of hostilities to deliver proper notice about the termination or suspension of a treaty or a treaty provision, or to engage in the subsequent objection procedure with the opposing party. This argument gains additional weight when a state fighting an armed conflict must notify a third state that is not a party to the conflict.

The situation is further complicated if the number of states involved is high, and the notification only concerns a treaty provision, as could be the case with investment treaties. The better approach would thus seem to be to encourage the notification procedure but allow for suspension to take place even in the absence thereof, when in light of the circumstances, such a notification could not reasonably be made. Such a flexible approach does not reinstate the old 'abrogation doctrine' but accommodates the particularities of different conflict situations. This approach equally makes sense for the VCLT doctrines when the grounds for their invocation are related to armed conflict, but since the ILC did not intend the VCLT to cover armed conflict situations primarily, the objections against the mandatory notification procedure were not raised as vocally as they were in the process of negotiating the EACT Draft Articles. Consequently, there exists an important procedural difference between the VCLT doctrines and EACT, which, at least in theory, makes the suspension of a treaty provision under the latter doctrine easier.[172]

In sum, a state facing hostilities would likely be able to choose between two legal frameworks to suspend an investment treaty provision: SIP under the VCLT, and EACT as codified in the Draft Articles. While the former concerns practical obstacles in the execution of treaty obligations and requires engaging in a notification procedure, the latter addresses incompatibility with the state's security policy, and likely does not entail a mandatory duty to notify the other state party about a suspension in advance. Despite the uncertainty regarding the legal consequences of a state's failure to adhere to the procedural requirements, the notification procedure in the context of armed conflict should be more relaxed, as suggested by case law, state practice, the 'urgency situation' clause in the VCLT, and the drafting history of the Draft Articles. It is nonetheless recommended that states, to the extent that it is possible, consult the concerned parties in keeping with the principle of good faith, and make public declarations as to their actions.[173]

E. Preliminary Conclusions

This chapter has examined the effect of armed conflicts on the continued operation of investment treaties. It established that certain provisions of some investment

[172] In practice, however, these differences may be less important because states invoking the VCLT grounds for termination, withdrawal, or suspension rarely follow the procedure set out in Art 65. See Vamvoukos, *Termination of Treaties* (n 130) 61–126; M Prost, 'Article 65' in Corten and Klein (n 99) 1489.

[173] Chinkin, 'Crisis and Performance' (n 11) 186, 206.

treaties could be suspended on the basis of either the EACT doctrine, if their continued operation poses a serious threat to a state's security; or the VCLT doctrines, in particular SIP, when armed conflict renders the fulfilment of treaty obligations impossible. It has been argued, however, that such disruptions to treaty operation will be rare, since the invocation of the doctrines is limited to the most serious armed conflicts of the highest magnitude. In most cases, the investment treaties will thus continue to apply and their fate in a given situation will depend on specific treaty protections and state defences embedded in treaties. This is the focus of the next two chapters.

4

Investment Treaty Protections against Conflict-Related Injuries

A. Introduction

Historically, the international investment regime was primarily based on the law of state responsibility for injuries to foreigners under customary international law and treaties of friendship, commerce, and navigation (FCN). The advent of modern international investment law traces its roots to the second half of the twentieth century; in particular, the 1990s when states increasingly began to conclude bilateral and multilateral investment treaties, the number of which has now surpassed 3,000. Investment treaties are entered into between two or more states who undertake to provide certain reciprocal treatment to investors holding the nationality of the other contracting state(s). The main objective of the treaties is to promote foreign investment by enhancing the protections thereof and enabling foreign investors to seek remedies when treaty provisions have been breached.

Investment treaties contain several provisions that foreign investors can use to claim damages for losses sustained in the course of armed conflict. Broadly speaking, conflict-related claims can be divided in two groups: first, claims for losses that investors have suffered as a direct consequence of a forcible action in the conflict, either by the host state's organs or by non-state actors (e.g. destruction or seizure of the investment facility). Second, claims for losses sustained by investors indirectly during a conflict or in its immediate aftermath (e.g. as a result of the ensuing economic and political measures). Accordingly, relevant investment treaty provisions can also be divided in two sometimes overlapping groups: those that provide remedies for injuries that are a direct consequence of actions taken in conflict, such as physical damage and destruction of property (full protection and security and armed conflict clause), and those that cover losses that are a consequence of measures indirectly related to conflict (fair and equitable treatment and prohibition of expropriation).

The application of investment treaty provisions in times of armed conflict has been mostly ignored in investment law scholarship.[1] The provisions most relevant

[1] For the first relevant contribution on this topic, see C Schreuer, 'The Protection of Investments in Armed Conflict' in F Baetens (ed), *Investment Law Within International Law: Integrationist Perspectives* (CUP 2011) 3.

The Protection of Foreign Investment in Times of Armed Conflict. First Edition. Jure Zrilič. © Jure Zrilič 2019.
Published 2019 by Oxford University Press.

for the context of conflict, namely the standard of full protection and security and the armed conflict clause, have been under-theorized despite the great deal of inconsistencies and controversies their application has generated in practice. This chapter sets out to fill this doctrinal gap by examining the scope and the content of these provisions, focusing in particular on their problematic aspects, and analyse the relationship between them. In addition, it also looks into the application of provisions on expropriation, and fair and equitable treatment (FET) in a conflict and post-conflict setting.

B. Full Protection and Security

The provision most commonly invoked by investors who sustain injury due to a violent interference is the full protection and security (FPS) clause. The treaty standard has its origin in the rule of customary international law aiming at protecting the property of aliens through claims of state responsibility and the invocation of diplomatic protection.[2] Similar clauses imposing an obligation to protect aliens and their property existed already in the seventeenth- and eighteenth-century peace treaties entered into by Great Britain,[3] and in early US commercial treaties,[4] where it was made clear that they encompassed protection against a range of threats, in particular from attacks during revolutions and war, and from government confiscations. The clause became a common element of FCN treaties of the nineteenth and early twentieth centuries and it usually provided for 'the most complete',[5] or 'the fullest measure of'[6] protection and security. During that volatile time, and in the interwar period, the standard was often invoked before post-conflict claims tribunals that helped flesh out its content.[7] A variation of the standard also featured in the US FCN treaties concluded after the Second World War,[8] which led to its adoption in different attempts to regulate the protection of foreign property in a multilateral international treaty, notably, in the influential

[2] See Chapter 2. For a historical overview, see G Foster, 'Recovering "Protection and Security": The Treaty Standard's Obscure Origins, Forgotten Meaning, and Key Current Significance' (2012) 45 VJTL 1095, 1116; T Weiler, *The Interpretation of International Investment Law* (Martinus Nijhoff 2013) 59–127.

[3] See e.g. Treaty of Peace between France and Great Britain, 13 November 1655, Art I, reproduced in F Davenport (ed), *Two European Treaties Bearing on the History of the United States and Its Dependencies, 1650–1697* (Washington Carnegie 1929) 40, 46; Treaty between Great Britain and Tunis, 5 October 1662, renewed by Treaty of 1751, Art VII, 1 Hertslet's Commercial Treaties 157.

[4] See e.g. Treaty of Amity and Commerce, US–Prussia (1785) Art XVIII; Treaty of Amity, Commerce and Navigation, US–Great Britain (1794) Arts II, XIV.

[5] See e.g. Treaty of Amity, Commerce and Navigation, US–Mexico (1931) Art III; Treaty of Commerce and Navigation, US–Japan (1894) Art I; Treaty of Friendship, Commerce and Navigation, US–Argentine (1853) Arts II, VIII.

[6] See e.g. Italy–Venezuela FCN, in *Sambiaggio Case* (*Italy v Venezuela*) (1903) 10 RIAA 499.

[7] See Chapter 2 B.

[8] K Vandevelde, *Bilateral Investment Treaties: History, Policy, and Interpretation* (OUP 2010) 244.

1959 Abs-Shawcross Convention on Investments Abroad, and in the 1967 OECD Draft Convention on the Protection of Foreign Property.[9]

In view of the above, it comes as no surprise that provisions granting protection and security for foreign investment have become an integral part of most investment treaties and vary little in their wording.[10] Article 4 of the German–Mali bilateral investment treaty (BIT) is representative of this: 'Investments by nationals or companies of either Contracting Party shall enjoy full protection and security in the territory of the other Contracting Party'.[11] Other formulations range from 'most constant protection and security',[12] and 'the complete and unconditional legal protection',[13] to a rather more vaguely worded phrase 'adequate protection and security',[14] or simply 'protection and security'.[15] While these differences seem unremarkable, they can in fact prove important when interpreting the scope of protection afforded under the clause.

Arbitral tribunals considered the application of the FPS clause in a variety of situations where investors suffered harm due to physical violence. The clause has been most frequently invoked in situations of physical violence of low intensity and limited scale, including the forceful seizure of a hotel by employees,[16] the seizure or usurpation of investment by a third party with the help of government forces,[17] social demonstrations and violent disturbances at the investor's premises,[18] demonstrations by employees,[19] and harassment, seizure, or other action by government authorities.[20] Less frequent has been the application of the clause in situations of collective violence of high intensity and wider scope. In two cases, investors sustained losses in the midst of widespread riots and lootings,[21] while in a few cases

[9] 'Abs-Shawcross Draft Convention on Investments Abroad' (1960) 9 J Public L 116, Art I (Abs-Shawcross Convention); 'OECD Draft Convention on the Protection of Foreign Property' (1968) 7 ILM 117, Art 1(a) (1967 OECD Convention).

[10] According to UNCTAD, the FPS provision has been included in 84 per cent of 2,571 mapped investment treaties. UNCTAD, International Investment Agreements Navigator <https://investmentpolicyhub.unctad.org/IIA/mappedContent> accessed 18 December 2018.

[11] Germany–Mali BIT (1977) Art 4.

[12] Energy Charter Treaty (1994) Art 10; Thailand–Vietnam BIT (1991) Art 3(2); Japan–Turkey BIT (1992) Art 5.

[13] Russia–Ukraine BIT (1998) Art 2.

[14] Indonesia–Yemen BIT (1998) Art 2(2); Indonesia–Algeria BIT (2000) Art 2(2).

[15] US–Zaire BIT (1984) Art II(4). Some use 'protection' only, e.g. China–Syria BIT (1996) Art 3.

[16] *Wena Hotels Ltd v Arab Republic of Egypt* ICSID Case no ARB/98/4, Award, 8 December 2000, para 84.

[17] *Amco Asia Corp and Others v The Republic of Indonesia* Award, 20 November 1984, 1 ICSID Rep 413; *Tatneft v Ukraine* UNCITRAL, Award, 29 July 2014, para 428; *Joseph Houben v Republic of Burundi* ICSID Case no ARB/13/17, Award, 20 May 2013, paras 167, 178; *Bernhard von Pezold and Others v Zimbabwe* ICSID Case no ARB/10/15, Award, 28 July 2015, paras 585, 597.

[18] *Tecnicas Medioambientales Tecmed SA v The United Mexican States* ICSID Case no ARB(AF)/00/2, Award, 29 May 2003, paras 175–77; *Copper Mesa Mining v Republic of Ecuador*, PCA no 2012-2, Award, 15 March 2016, paras 6.80–84.

[19] *Noble Ventures Inc v Romania* ICSID Case no ARB/01/11, Award, 12 October 2005, para 16.

[20] *Eureko BV v Poland* Ad hoc Arbitration, Partial Award, 19 August 2005, para 236.

[21] *American Manufacturing & Trading, Inc (AMT) v Republic of Zaire* ICSID Case no ARB/93/1, Award, 21 February 1997, para 6.08; *Pantechniki SA Contractors & Engineers v The Republic of Albania* ICSID Case no ARB/07/21, Award, 30 July 2009, para 82.

claims were filed for losses incurred during a security crisis amounting to a revolution.[22] The application of the FPS in a situation of insurgency and civil war was addressed prominently in *AAPL v Sri Lanka*,[23] although more instances of invocation have been reported in pending cases emerging from the civil war in Libya and the conflict in Crimea.[24]

While the provision has not attracted as much scholarly attention as other investment treaty provisions,[25] it has given rise to many controversies. Questions that have yielded conflicting views in scholarship and jurisprudence, and are particularly relevant to the application of the rule in conflict situations, concern the scope of the provision and the standard of care required thereunder. Both are analysed in the next two sections.

1. Scope of the Protection

With respect to the scope of FPS, two aspects are relevant for the present discussion. The first, which has spawned divisive opinions, concerns the delimitation between physical and legal protection. The second, overlooked by scholars but no less controversial, concerns the limits of the FPS obligation with regard to conduct of state organs.

(a) Physical v legal protection

Tribunals have adopted conflicting views as to the scope of the protection and security obligation. While some have limited the standard to physical protection only,[26] others have held that the standard extended to legal security (in particular with respect to quality of the legal system and functioning of the judicial mechanisms).[27] When a treaty provision is specific enough that it provides only for

[22] *Ampal v Arab Republic of Egypt* ICSID Case no ARB/12/11, Decision on Liability and Heads of Loss, 21 February 2017, para 240; *LESI SpA and ASTALDI SpA v People's Democratic Republic of Algeria* ICSID Case no ARB/05/3, Award, 12 November 2008, para 181.

[23] *Asian Agricultural Products Ltd (AAPL) v Republic of Sri Lanka* ICSID Case no ARB/87/3, Award, 27 June 1990, para 85(b).

[24] See Chapter 1, nn 6–8.

[25] See Foster, 'Recovering Protection and Security' (n 2); C Schreuer, 'Full Protection and Security' (2010) 1(2) JIDS 6; G Cordero Moss, 'Full Protection and Security' in A Reinisch (ed), *Standards of Investment Protection* (OUP 2008) 131; H Zeitler, 'Full Protection and Security' in S Schill (ed), *International Investment Law and Comparable Public Law* (OUP 2010) 184.

[26] See e.g. *Suez v Argentine Republic* ICSID Case no ARB/03/17, Decision on Liability, 30 July 2010, para 173; *Saluka Invs BV v Czech Republic* UNCITRAL, Partial Award, 17 March 2006, paras 483–84; *BG Group plc v Republic of Argentina* UNCITRAL, Final Award, 24 December 2007, paras 324–26; *Rumeli Telekom v Kazakhstan* ICSID Case no ARB/05/16, Award, 29 July 2008, paras 662–68; *Oxus Gold v Uzbekistan* UNCITRAL, Award, 17 December 2015, paras 830–32; *von Pezold* (n 17) para 596.

[27] See e.g. *AES Summit Generation Ltd v Republic of Hungary* ICSID Case no ARB/07/22, Award, 2 September 2010, para 13.3.2; *CME Czech Republic BV v Czech Republic* UNCITRAL, Partial Award, 13 September 2001, paras 159–60, 613; *Lauder v Czech Republic* UNCITRAL, Final Award, 3 September 2001, para 314; *Biwater Gauff Ltd v United Republic of Tanzania* ICSID Case no ARB/05/22, Award, 24 July 2008, para 729; *Azurix Corp v the Argentine Republic* ICSID Case no ARB/01/12, Award, 14 July

physical protection,[28] or when it explicitly extends beyond it,[29] determining the scope is straightforward. However, even when the provision is drafted in vague terms (e.g. using qualifiers 'full' or 'constant', or simply 'protection and security'), the practical implications of deciding whether legal security is covered therein may be less important when there is the possibility of relying on the FET provision, which is included in most investment treaties and covers the legal aspects of security.[30] Unsurprisingly, many recent tribunals avoided discussing whether the FPS extends beyond physical safety by deciding allegations pertaining to legal security under the FET heading only.[31]

While commentators appear similarly divided on the issue,[32] a few have argued that FPS require a wider reading.[33] The argument that this follows from the application of interpretive tools codified in the Vienna Convention on the Law of Treaties (VCLT) is not convincing.[34] First, interpretation in line with the ordinary meaning of the terms as found in a dictionary, and object and purpose of the treaty is of little assistance, as it renders the meaning so broad and general that FPS easily replaces all other investment treaty substantive obligations and becomes an omnipotent standard embodying the general spirit of a treaty.[35] Contextual interpretation brings more clarity, especially the fact that FPS commonly appears in the same article as a FET standard that primarily includes elements of legal security. A reading according to which there is a significant substantive overlap between two distinct standards included in the same provision betrays textual logic, renders the

2006, para 406; *Compañía de Aguas del Aconquija SA and Vivendi Universal SA v Argentine Republic* ICSID Case no ARB/97/3, Award, 20 August 2007, para 7.4.15.

---

[28] See e.g. Netherlands–Vietnam BIT (1995) Art 3(2); Albania–Netherlands BIT (1995) Art 3(2).

[29] See e.g. Macedonia–Ukraine BIT (1998) Art 3(1); Croatia–Libya BIT (2002) Art 2(5).

[30] The tribunal in *Suez* distinguished between fair and equitable treatment, which covers stability and legal security, and full protection and security, which covers physical protection only. *Suez* (n 26) paras 171–72.

[31] See e.g. *PSEG Global v Turkey* ICSID Case no ARB/02/5, Award, 19 January 2007, paras 257–59; *Copper Mesa* (n 18) paras 6.80–82; *Tatneft* (n 17) para 429. Some tribunals decided that claims regarding legal safety were not justified and thus it was not necessary to discuss the scope of the FPS provision. See e.g. *Rusoro Mining Ltd v Bolivarian Republic of Venezuela* ICSID Case no ARB(AF)/12/5, Award, 22 August 2016, para 547; *Peter Allard v Barbados* PCA Case no 2012-06, Award, 27 June 2016, paras 531–52.

[32] For views critical of extensive interpretation, see e.g. C McLachlan, L Shore, and M Weiniger, *International Arbitration: Substantive Principles* (2nd edn, OUP 2017) 335; J Salacuse, *The Law of Investment Treaties* (2nd edn, OUP 2015) 236–38; M Sornarajah, *The International Law on Foreign Investment* (4th edn, CUP 2017) 427; Zeitler, 'Full Protection and Security' (n 25) 190.

[33] Weiler, *Interpretation* (n 2) 104–05; Foster, 'Recovering Protection and Security' (n 2); Schreuer, 'Full Protection and Security' (n 25) 10; A Newcombe and L Paradell, *Law and Practice of Investment Treaties* (Kluwer 2009) 314.

[34] cf Foster (n 2) 1150 (referring to VCLT Arts 31 and 32).

[35] Oxford Dictionary defines 'to protect' as 'to keep safe from harm or injury', which, taking into account the commonly understood object and purpose of investment treaties (encouragement of investment by providing adequate protections), could be construed as protection against any action or omission that could harm investors. Oxford Dictionary < http://www.oxforddictionaries.com/> accessed 10 May 2018.

inclusion of both standards futile (in contradiction to *effet utile* interpretation),[36] and, as seen above, tends to lead to resolution of relevant claims under only one of the standards (notably FET).

Some commentators have further argued that the meaning of FPS in modern investment treaties should be informed by customary international law according to which protection and security obliges states not only to act with due diligence in protecting aliens and their property, but also to 'make available an adequate legal system, featuring such protections as appropriate remedial mechanisms, due process, and a right to compensation for expropriation.'[37] They buttressed their understanding of the customary duty by referring to historical writings, arbitral practice, and early FCN treaties where notions of 'protection' and 'security' were sometimes used broadly and all-encompassing, reflecting the international minimum standard of treatment.[38] This view is oblivious to the temporal element of interpretation and the fact that the linguistic usage of a term 'protection' during that era differed from its usage in post-Second World War FCN treaties and modern investment treaties in which new legal standards (such as FET) became commonplace.[39] Using that obsolete understanding to determine the meaning of modern FPS provisions would be contrary to interpretation in good faith.[40] Moreover, it has become widely accepted in international jurisprudence and treaty practice that FPS and FET both derive from customary international minimum standards, whereby the former covers physical protection only, while the latter concerns certain elements of legal protection (including denial of justice).[41]

Since injuries to investors in volatile times are often caused by the use of force, the application of the standard in the context of conflict will normally not be controversial. In fact, a few tribunals have held that FPS is meant to cover exactly the

[36] McLachlan et al, *Substantive Principles* (n 32) 335.

[37] Foster, 'Recovering Protection and Security' (n 2) 1130; Weiler, *Interpretation* (n 2) 61.

[38] Foster (n 2) 1116–49; Weiler (n 2) 127.

[39] The FET concept was introduced to the US FCN treaties after the Second World War. See K Vandevelde, *The First Bilateral Investment Treaties: U.S. Postwar Friendship, Commerce, and Navigation Treaties* (OUP 2017) 399.

[40] VCLT Art 31(1). Regarding temporal interpretation, see *Dispute Regarding Navigational and Related Rights* (*Costa Rica v Nicaragua*) (Judgment) [2009] ICJ Rep 213, 242–43, paras 63–66 (noting that when the parties used generic terms in a treaty, they 'must be presumed, as a general rule, to have intended those terms to have an evolving meaning', especially when a treaty has been entered into for a long period). See also H Waldock, 'Sixth Report on the Law of Treaties' in ILC, *Yearbook of the International Law Commission, Vol II, 1966*, UN Doc A/CN.4/186/Add.1–7, 96, para 7.

[41] See e.g. *Saluka* (n 26) para 484; *BG Group* (n 26) para 324; *Enron Corp v Argentine Republic* ICSID Case no ARB/01/3, Award, 22 May 2007, para 286. See also 2012 US Model BIT, Art 5(2); North American Free Trade Agreement (1994) Art 1105 (NAFTA). A number of most recently concluded investment treaties have expressly limited FPS to police protection as reflected by customary international law, see Canada–EU Comprehensive Economic and Trade Agreement (2016) Art 8.10(5); Canada–Republic of Guinea BIT (2015) Art 6; Rwanda–Morocco (2016) Art 2(2); Israel–Japan BIT (2017) Art 4; Rwanda–United Arab Emirates BIT (2017) Art 4(3); ASEAN–Hong Kong, China SAR Investment Agreement (2017) Art 5; Republic of Korea–Republics of Central America FTA (2018) Art 9.5.

kinds of losses that foreign investors may suffer during violent conflict situations.[42] Thus, the tribunal in *Saluka v Czech Republic* stated that 'the standard applies essentially when the foreign investment has been affected by civil strife and physical violence'.[43] Similarly, the tribunal in *Eastern Sugar v Czech Republic* held that the standard provides protection against 'mobs, insurgents, rented thugs and others engaged in physical violence'.[44]

When the scope of FPS provisions is not expressly extended to legal safety, it may become important to define what constitutes physical interference. The tribunal in *Siemens v Argentina* pointed to this issue by raising a question of 'how the physical security of an intangible asset would be achieved', if FPS was interpreted restrictively.[45] The tribunal concluded that the only answer was to interpret FPS broadly in order to encompass legal security also.[46] For the reasons described above, this solution is not satisfying. Importantly, the question requires interpretive re-orientation: what matters is not whether FPS provides legal security, but rather the scope of physical protection. The *Siemens* tribunal appears to have held that only tangible assets could be accorded physical protection, necessitating a broader reading of FPS.[47] According to this view, physical protection denotes protection against forceful interference that may cause physical damage to the person or property of an investor. This interpretation can leave an important category of investment unprotected, since consequences of interference with intangible assets do not necessarily manifest in physical damage. The problem was further raised in *Saluka* case, where the tribunal accepted that the guarantee of physical protection would apply with respect to police searches of an investor's premises and seizure of documents, but left open the question as to whether the scope of the guarantee would also extend to a national authority's suspension of the trading of shares or a police order prohibiting the transfer of shares.[48] Since the freezing of assets of enemy aliens is common in situations of conflict, the question of whether they constitute a breach of the FPS standard could likely be raised in conflict-related cases.

Another topical example is harm caused by cyber-attacks. Does the FPS clause offer protection in case of attacks against investors' computer networks and digital infrastructure? If a cyber-attack causes physical damage (e.g. by creating hammering in oil pipelines which causes them to break),[49] the answer would appear a straightforward yes. However, many cyber-attacks do not produce physical

[42] *Saluka* (n 26) para 483; *Rumeli* (n 26) para 668; *Eastern Sugar v Czech Republic* SCC Case no 088/2004, Partial Award, 27 March 2007, para 203; *PSEG* (n 31) paras 258–259; *Suez* (n 26) para 179.

[43] *Saluka* (n 26) para 483.

[44] *Eastern Sugar* (n 42) para 203.

[45] *Siemens AG v Argentine Republic* ICSID Case no ARB/02/8, Award, 17 January 2007, para 303.

[46] ibid para 308.

[47] Similarly, *Azurix* (n 27) para 408; *Vivendi* (n 27) para 7.4.15.

[48] *Saluka* (n 26) paras 486–93.

[49] For example, see recent cyber-attacks against US gas pipelines. P Muncaster, 'US Gas Pipelines Hit by Cyber-Attack' (*Info-Security Magazine*, 4 April 2018) <https://www.infosecurity-magazine.com/news/us-gas-pipelines-hit-by-cyberattack/> accessed 10 December 2018.

damage (e.g. causing the computer websites to crash or manipulating important information located on computer servers), thus the question of whether they are captured under the guarantee of physical protection could become vital. The more convincing position would seem to be that the protection is not limited only to traditional threats of violence capable of generating physical harm. What should be determinative is not the nature of the outcome of the breach but rather the nature of the conduct constituting it. Such an interpretation is sufficiently flexible so as to cover all categories of investment and adaptable to new forms of threat such as computer network attacks, while still excluding the breaches typically associated with legal security (concerning quality of the legal and judicial system). Following this view, FPS clauses would provide protection against any forceful intervention with the ability to generate damage, including interferences that are coercive in nature and do not result in physical damage but rather impair the functionality of investment.[50] Whether the threshold of application has been reached could only be determined on a case-by-case analysis of the nature and degree of interference, its severity, and consequences.

(b) Protection against interference of state organs

Under the FPS standard, the host state is obliged to provide protection and security against the actions of both its own organs and third parties.[51] In the latter case, which is discussed in detail in the next section, the provision imposes an obligation to protect investors against harmful activities carried out by third persons, that is private actors as well as international subjects such as other states or insurrectional movements. The duty to protect encompasses the obligation to prevent violent acts of non-state actors as well as the obligation to apprehend and punish those responsible for the harm.[52] In these situations, state

[50] This interpretation is in line with recent developments in the field of cyber warfare, which reflect a preference for a flexible definition of 'damage' caused by cyber-attacks, thus enabling application of the *jus in bello* framework. See 'Tallinn Manual on the International Law Applicable to Cyber Warfare: Prepared by the International Group of Experts at the Invitation of the NATO Cooperative Cyber Defence Centre of Excellence' (CUP 2013) Rule 5, comment 5 (noting that the cyber operation does not need to result in physical damage to objects or injuries to individuals; it is enough that it produces a 'negative effect'); ICRC, 'Cyber Warfare and International Humanitarian Law: The ICRC's Position' 2 <https://www.icrc.org/en/doc/assets/files/2013/130621-cyber-warfare-q-and-a-eng.pdf> accessed 18 December 2018; M Schmitt, 'Computer Network Attack and the Use of Force in International Law: Thoughts on a Normative Framework' (1999) 37(3) Colum J Trans L 885; T Morth, 'Considering Our Position: Viewing Information Warfare as a Use of Force Prohibited by Article 2(4) of the U.N. Charter' (1998) 30(2/3) Case W Res J Intl L 567.

[51] Schreuer, 'Full Protection and Security' (n 25) 2–5; Vandevelde, *History* (n 8) 243. For divergent views among arbitral tribunals, see nn 206–07.

[52] See *Wena* (n 16) paras 82, 84; *Frontier Petroleum Services v Czech Republic* UNCITRAL, Award, 12 November 2010, para 423; *Parkerings-Compagniet AS v Republic of Lithuania*, ICSID Case no ARB/05/8, Award, 11 September 2007, para 355. Pissilo-Mazzeschi argued that, once the harmful event has occurred, the FPS covers only the duty to investigate such an event, and pursue and apprehend those responsible for harm. Further administrative and judicial steps (trial and execution of sentence) fall within the 'denial of justice' and are not measured by the state's due diligence. See R Pissilo-Mazzeschi,

liability can emerge from the failure to exercise due diligence in protecting investors.[53]

In contrast, when it comes to actions of its own organs, the impairment to the investor is caused directly by state organs or through their contribution.[54] The responsibility emerges from the breach of the obligation to refrain from such wrongful interference and is attached to the host state through the attribution of the acts of its organs.[55] Despite the seemingly clear-cut distinction between private violence and the violence of state organs, two questions in particular have yielded unsatisfactory responses in doctrine and arbitral jurisprudence. The first concerns the use of the due diligence rule in situations when harm has been caused by state organs. The second deals with the limitation of the FPS provision in regard to a state's failure to refrain from interference.

(i) Due diligence in lieu of attribution

With respect to the first question, scholars have overwhelmingly argued that the duty of due diligence never applies in situations when harm was caused by state organs themselves.[56] According to this view, the conduct of state organs does not need to be measured against the due diligence standard since it is already directly attributed to the state. While this may be true in most cases, there appears to be an exception to this rule, highlighted in the *AAPL* case, in which the tribunal found Sri Lanka liable for failing to take precautions in the planning of its military operation.[57] Following this position, the host state has a due diligence duty to protect investors from the harm that might result from the actions of its own organs, when the latter are not *prima facie* wrongful and involve a heightened risk for incidental injuries. This would be the case if the state undertook a harmful or inherently risky but justifiable activity that included diligent planning and measures to avert or minimize the harm, for example, military targeting. While there is no general obligation to abstain from legitimate targeting operations, diligence is required in the

'The Due Diligence Rule and the Nature of the International Responsibility of States' (1992) 35 German YB Intl L 9, 29–30. See *Sewell Case (US v Mexico)* (1930) 4 RIAA 626, 632; *Chase Case (US v Mexico)* (1928) 4 RIAA 337, 339; *Massey Case (US v Mexico)* (1927) 4 RIAA 155, 162; *Kennedy Case (US v Mexico)* (1927) 4 RIAA 194, 196–97; *Way Case (US v Mexico)* (1928) 4 RIAA 391; *Minnie East Case (US v Mexico)* (1930) 4 RIAA 646; *Morton Case (US v Mexico)* (1929) 4 RIAA 428.

[53] Zeitler, 'Full Protection and Security' (n 25) 187. See also *US Diplomatic and Consular Staff in Teheran (US v Iran)* [1980] ICJ Rep 3.

[54] See e.g. *Biwater* (n 27) para 730; *Frontier* (n 52) para 261; *Parkerings* (n 52) para 355.

[55] See the general rules on attribution in Articles on Responsibility of States for Internationally Wrongful Acts, Arts 4–11.

[56] Pissilo-Mazzeschi, 'Due Diligence' (n 52) 23–25; Zeitler, 'Full Protection and Security' (n 25) 191; E De Brabandere, 'Host States' Due Diligence Obligations in International Investment Law' (2015) 42(2) Syracuse J Intl & Com 320, 333–34, 337; R Dolzer and C Schreuer, *Principles of International Investment Law* (2nd edn, OUP 2012) 162.

[57] *AAPL* (n 23). For a discussion of this aspect of due diligence, see Section 4 C.4.b and, in particular, Chapter 6 C.2.

planning and execution thereof with the view to avoid or minimize the damage. Finding the state responsible would thus depend on the assessment of whether the state organs were diligent or not, that is on whether they adequately evaluated the risks and took necessary measures for minimizing thereof to the extent possible. Moreover, as will be discussed in Chapter 6,[58] a higher degree of care is required from a state in carrying out such hazardous activities than in providing protection against harmful activities of non-state actors.

The risk-based approach that uses due diligence rather than attribution of an immediately harmful act for ascertaining state responsibility can be justified on practical, policy, and legal grounds. First, the attribution of losses emerging from hazardous or harmful operations, such as military attacks, can be challenging due to inherent difficulties in collecting evidence and establishing causality. Due diligence fills this vacuum by shifting the responsibility to the party that was more in control of the risk and was thus in a position to take certain precautions. Second, such interpretation incentivizes parties to engage better in *ex ante* risk assessments with regard to potential incidental losses, and in this way facilitates prudence. Third, it also enables tribunals to avoid making potentially controversial pronouncements on the legitimacy and legality of state actions while still finding it liable on a different, less contentious, ground.

Legal support for this understanding of the FPS can be found in some historical cases, in which it was held that state responsibility could be generated by the lack of due diligence in the execution of the lawful measures by state organs,[59] as well as in the 1967 OECD Convention, which in its comments stipulated that 'most constant protection and security' includes the obligation 'to exercise due diligence as regards actions of public authorities', rather than just private actors.[60] Lastly, such interpretation is in line with the application of due diligence in international humanitarian law,[61] international human rights law,[62] international environmental

[58] Chapter 6 C.

[59] See e.g. *In re Rizzo* (1955) 22 ILR 317, 322; *Ousset* (1945) 22 ILR 312, 314, cited in J Crawford, *Brownlie's Principles of International Law* (8th edn, OUP 2012) 559.

[60] 1967 OECD Convention, Notes and Comments to Article 1 (n 9) 9.

[61] See Additional Protocol I to Geneva Conventions, Art 57, and Chapter 2 C.1.a. More generally, the 2016 ICRC Commentary appears to confirm that a state must exercise due diligence with respect to its own organs (soldiers). ICRC Commentary to Geneva Convention I (2016) Art 12, paras 1360–61 (specifying that the obligation to protect wounded and sick requires the exercise of due diligence in preventing harm caused by, among others, party's own soldiers). See also Commentary to Geneva Convention I (2016) Art 15, para 1499; Commentary to Geneva Convention II (2017) Art 12, para 1407; Hague Convention VIII relative to Laying of Automatic Submarine Contact Mines (1907) Arts 3 and 4. See also *Armed Activities on the Territory of Congo* (*DRC v Uganda*) [2005] ICJ Rep 252 (para 246), 253 (para 250) (finding Uganda responsible for breaching the due diligence duty with respect to actions of its own military forces).

[62] See Study Group on Due Diligence in International Law, 'First Report' (International Law Association, London 2014) 22. However, as shown in Chapter 2, human rights courts have discussed the state's duty to take precautions and exercise requisite care in forceful operations not as part of a positive obligation of due diligence, but rather as part of the proportionality analysis in the assessment of a negative obligation to refrain (an approach discussed in the next section).

law,[63] the developments in the regulation of cyberspace,[64] as well as the emerging scholarship on risk in international law.[65]

(ii) The limits of obligation to refrain

In all other instances of harm caused directly by state organs, the due diligence rule does not play any role. The question, largely ignored in investment treaty jurisprudence and scholarship alike, is what then are the limits of the FPS with respect to acts of state organs interfering with foreign investment? Does any failure to abstain from physical interference constitute a breach of FPS? If not, what are the limitations and how can they be legally conceptualized? As will be shown in the following sections, some investment treaties expressly provide that a physical interference with an investment can be justified on the ground of security reasons or due to necessity inherent in situations of armed conflict.[66] Furthermore, some investment treaties specifically limit a host state's obligation under FPS with a reference to its domestic laws.[67] Even in the absence of such exceptions and limitations, however, states still have discretion to exercise certain powers with the view to protect their public order and security interests. This has been confirmed in arbitral jurisprudence.

In *Saluka v Czech Republic*, the tribunal held that the suspension of trading with investor shares was reasonable and justifiable by the state's legitimate concerns relating to securities markets and consequently no breach of FPS could be found.[68] In *Biwater v Tanzania*, the tribunal found that the removal of investor management from the offices, their subsequent deportation from the country, and seizure of premises amounted to breach of the FPS clause.[69] In its defence, the government, among others, argued that no more force had been used than lawful and necessary for carrying out orders of domestic organs, and that the measures were motivated by legitimate concerns about the safety of the water and sewerage system.[70] While

[63] See e.g. *Certain Activities Carried Out By Nicaragua in the Border Area (Costa Rica v Nicaragua)* and *Construction of a Road in Costa Rica Along the San Juan River (Nicaragua v Costa Rica)* (Judgment) [2015] ICJ Rep 665, 706 (para 104), 720–21 (paras 153–57); *Pulp Mills on the River Uruguay (Argentina v Uruguay)* (Judgment) [2010] ICJ Rep 14, 79 (para 197), 83 (para 204); *Responsibilities and Obligations of States Sponsoring Persons and Entities with Respect to Activities in the Area*, ITLOS Case no 17 (Advisory Opinion, 1 February 2011) para 131.

[64] Tallinn Manual (n 50) Rule 5, comments 1, 3; M Schmitt, 'In Defense of Due Diligence in Cyberspace' (2015) 125 Yale LJ Forum 68, 70; K Bannelier-Christakis, 'Cyber Diligence: A Low-Intensity Due Diligence Principle for Low-Intensity Cyber Operations? (2014) 14 Baltic YB Intl L 1, 4, 8.

[65] See e.g. S Townley 'The Rise of Risk in International Law' (2016) 18(2) Chicago J Intl L 594; M Ambrus et al (eds), *Risk and the Regulation of Uncertainty in International Law* (OUP 2017).

[66] For analysis of advanced armed conflict clauses and security exceptions, see Section 4 C.3. and Chapter 5 B, respectively.

[67] See e.g. Australia–Egypt BIT (2001) Art 3(3); Ethiopia–Sweden BIT (2004) Art 2(4). According to UNCTAD Navigator, such references have been found in less than 7 per cent of investment treaties. UNCTAD Navigator (n 10).

[68] *Saluka* (n 26) paras 490, 505.

[69] *Biwater* (n 27) para 731.

[70] ibid para 721.

the tribunal failed to address these arguments in any meaningful way, its ultimate description of the contested state measures as 'unnecessary and abusive' implies that a different outcome not resulting in a breach of FPS would have been possible, had the factual circumstances been different.[71] More pertinent to the context of armed conflict, in *AAPL v Sri Lanka*, it was uncontested that a state had a sovereign right to use force to prevent or suppress resurrection and regain control over its territory, and that such use of force could negatively affect foreign investors without giving rise to state responsibility.[72]

While the reasoning of these awards leaves much to be desired, what is common to them is that they recognize that in certain circumstances states have a right to physically interfere with foreign investment without violating the FPS clause. To argue otherwise would mean that one of the state's most important sovereign prerogatives, that is, its monopoly on the use of force, would be significantly constrained. While the tribunals have failed to legally conceptualize this limitation to FPS in a clear manner, two approaches can be discerned. According to the first approach, which seemed to be followed by the *Saluka* and *Biwater* tribunals, a state can interfere with the investment without violating FPS as long as its conduct is reasonable. In other words, a state will not be liable if there is a reasonable connection between a state's actions (e.g. suspension of shares, removal of management) and a legitimate public concern pursued by those actions. The use of reasonableness to justify the departure from a state's obligation to refrain from interfering with investment must be distinguished from the duty to exercise reasonable care (i.e. due diligence) in protecting investors, which is discussed in the next section. In the latter case, reasonableness is used to bring some flexibility when measuring a state's effort to protect investment. In contrast, the obligation to refrain from interfering is not an obligation of effort—reasonableness merely establishes a connection between a state's act and a state's legitimate interest, thus creating a bar against 'unnecessary and abusive' actions. The downside of this approach lies in the vague nature of the principle of reasonableness, which plays an important part in loosening of the due diligence obligation, but provides little guidance in the context of the state's interference with investment.

The second approach, which is echoed (but not expressly endorsed) in the reasoning of the *AAPL* award, seeks legal justification for such interference in the doctrine of police powers. The police powers doctrine concerns the exercise of a state's sovereign right to constrain certain individual rights and economic interests (e.g. right to property) with the view to protect and promote public policy objectives such as public safety, security, and health.[73] While originating from US

[71] ibid para 731.

[72] *AAPL*, Award (n 23) para 85B; *AAPL*, Dissenting Opinion (n 23) 592.

[73] See the definition in the *Black's Law Dictionary* (6th edn, West Publishing Co 1990) which articulates the state's police powers as the 'power of the State to place restraints on the personal freedom and property rights of persons for the protection of the public safety, health, and morals or the promotion of the public convenience and general prosperity'.

jurisprudence and legal doctrine,[74] the concept gradually found its way into international law through the draft codifications of the international responsibility of states,[75] and has become increasingly acknowledged in modern investment case law,[76] scholarship,[77] and even some investment treaties,[78] often as a reflection of customary international law.[79] Since the doctrine has been mostly analysed with respect to indirect expropriation as a justification for governments' non-discriminatory regulatory measures, the view has emerged that it cannot be applied as a defence in regard to other investment treaty standards, such as FPS, or as a justification for measures targeting a specific investor (rather than general regulatory measures).[80]

This position is not legally persuasive. First, many investment tribunals had no problem referencing or applying 'police powers' with respect to measures targeting individual investors as long as they were not discriminatory.[81] Second, there appears to be no compelling reason to limit the doctrine only to indirect expropriation, in particular if one accepts the view that it reflects customary international law.[82] This is supported by historical cases in which the doctrine was applied to justify destruction of property in emergency situations.[83] More controversially, at the turn of the twentieth century, an 'internationalized' version of police power was

[74] *Brown v Maryland*, 25 U.S. (12 Wheat) 419, 442–43 (1827). See S Legarre, 'The Historical Background of the Police Power' (2007) 9 U Pa J Const L 745.

[75] FV Garcia Amador, 'Fourth Report on State Responsibility' in *Yearbook of the International Law Commission, 1959, Vol II*, UN Doc A/CN.4/SER.A/1959/Add.1, 11–12, paras 43, 46, 133; Harvard Draft Convention on the International Responsibility of States for Injuries to Aliens (1961) Art 10(5) in ILC, *Yearbook of the International Law Commission, 1969, Vol II*, UN Doc A/CN.4/SER.A/1969/Add.1, 142 (1961 Harvard Draft); American Law Institute, Restatement (Second) of the Law of Foreign Relations of the United States, 1965, s 197(1)(a); American Law Institute, Restatement (Third) of the Law of Foreign Relations of the United States, 1986, s 712.

[76] The doctrine has been heeded by several investment tribunals, e.g. *Marvin Feldman v Mexico* ICSID Case no ARB(AF)/99/1, Award, 16 December 2002, para 103; *Saluka* (n 26) para 255; *Lauder* (n 27) para 198; *Tecmed* (n 18) para 115; *Chemtura Corp v Canada*, UNCITRAL, Award, 2 August 2010, para 266; *Quiborax SA and Non Metallic Minerals v Bolivia* ICSID Case no ARB/06/2, Award, 16 September 2015, para 202; *Renée Rose Levy de Levi v Peru* ICSID Case no ARB/10/17, Award, 26 February 2014, para 476; *Philip Morris et al v Uruguay* ICSID Case no ARB/10/7, Award, 8 July 2016, para 295.

[77] See e.g. Newcombe and Paradell L, *Law and Practice* (n 33) 358; A Pellet, 'Police Powers or the State's Right to Regulate' in M Kinnear et al (eds), *Building International Investment Law—The First 50 Years of ICSID* (Kluwer Law International 2016) 449, 451; J Viñuales, 'Sovereignty in Foreign Investment Law' in Z Douglas et al (eds), *Foundations of International Investment Law* (OUP 2014) 329, 344; C Titi, 'Police Powers Doctrine and International Investment Law' in A Gattini et al (eds), *General Principles of Law and International Investment Arbitration* (Brill 2018) 323.

[78] See e.g. COMESA Common Investment Area Agreement (2007) Art 20(08).

[79] *Saluka* (n 26) para 262; *Philip Morris* (n 76) para 301. See also Newcombe and Paradell, *Law and Practice* (n 33) 358; Pellet, 'Police Powers' (n 77) 449; Viñuales, 'Sovereignty' (n 77) 329, 344.

[80] See *Suez* (n 26) para 148. See also Titi, 'Police Powers' (n 77); Pellet, 'Police Powers' (n 77) 457.

[81] Viñuales, 'Sovereignty' (n 77) 333–35 (explaining how tribunals in *Tecmed, Chemtura*, and *Saluka* recognized that the doctrine could be applied to targeted measures).

[82] Viñuales, ibid 332–34, 344.

[83] See e.g. *Dickson Car Wheel Co* (*United States v Mexico*) (1931) 4 RIAA 669, 681–82; *Bischoff Case* (1903) 10 RIAA 420. For more authorities, see M Paparinskis, *The International Minimum Standard and FET* (OUP 2013) 224, n 50.

used by the US to safeguard America's safety and protect US investment abroad by means of military interventions in Latin America.[84] Thus in 1904, Theodore Roosevelt famously asserted that the US may have to resort 'to the exercise of an international police power' and thus intervene in a state that fails to maintain order and pay its obligations.[85] While today such invocation would undoubtedly constitute abuse of the police powers doctrine, these examples show how historically it was interlinked with the notions of security and safety. Furthermore, in US constitutional practice as well as modern investment treaty practice, police power has been associated with the right to take measures for protecting public order against riots, insurrections, and other types of conflict.[86]

Support for the application of police powers to FPS can be also found in soft-law documents which investment tribunals typically cite when applying the concept.[87] For example, the 1961 Harvard Draft states that 'deliberate destruction of or damage to the property of an alien' and 'uncompensated taking of property of an alien or a deprivation of the use or enjoyment of property of an alien which results from ... [the State's action] in the maintenance of public order ... or from the valid exercise of belligerent rights ...' is not wrongful.[88] Accordingly, the doctrine applies beyond indirect expropriation as to encompass other measures, general or specific, that may deprive the investor of its property (including by means of confiscation or destruction thereof). The express reference to maintenance of public order and exercise of belligerents' rights leaves no doubt as to the appropriateness of applying the doctrine in the context of different types of conflict.

Finally, several investment tribunals have evaluated the exercise of state's police powers by using a proportionality analysis.[89] While 'police powers' create a zone within which a state can pursue certain actions, proportionality sets the borders of this zone. This is evocative of the international humanitarian law (IHL) framework, in which military necessity in a similar manner permits belligerents the

[84] J von Bernstorff, 'The Use of Force in International Law before World War I: On Imperial Ordering and the Ontology of the Nation-State' (2018) 29(1) EJIL 233, 250.

[85] T Roosevelt, *Annual Message to Congress* (6 December 1904) <ourdocuments.gov/doc.php?flash=true&doc=56&page=transcript> accessed 18 December 2018.

[86] Some US BITs state that public order covers 'measures taken pursuant to a Party's police power to ensure public health and safety'. See letters of submittal of the US–Jamaica BIT; US–Lithuania BIT; US–Mongolia BIT. See also K Gudgeon, 'United States Bilateral Investment Treaties: Comments on Their Origin, Purposes, and General Treatment Standards' (1986) 4(1) Berkeley J Intl L 105, 121.

[87] See n 75.

[88] 1961 Harvard Draft, Arts 9 and 10(5).

[89] As will be argued in Chapter 6 C.3, the *AAPL* award reflects such application of proportionality as part of the assessment of a state's forceful conduct. Generally, see *Azurix* (n 27) paras 311–12; *Tecmed* (n 18) para 122; *Burlington Resources Inc v Ecuador* ICSID Case no ARB/08/5, Decision on Liability, 14 December 2012, para 504; *Philip Morris* (n 76) paras 295, 305; *Bear Creek Mining Corp v Peru* ICSID Case no ARB/14/21, Award, 30 November 2017, paras 453, 458 (and other decisions cited in n 604 in the *Bear Creek* award). See also C Henckels, *Proportionality and Deference in Investor-State Arbitration: Balancing Investment Protection and Regulatory Autonomy* (CUP 2015) 83–171; G Bücheler, *Proportionality in Investor-State Arbitration* (OUP 2015) 129.

exercise of certain rights, the limits of which are determined by proportionality.[90] Thus, in both legal systems, proportionality has been used as a legal constraint to state conduct otherwise permitted in certain exceptional circumstances.

As a rule of customary international law, the application of 'police powers' does not necessarily depend on its express inclusion in an investment treaty.[91] It can be applied either directly or as a principle guiding the interpretation of the investment treaty standard.[92] Despite the lack of express reference to 'police powers' in connection with the application of FPS in investment treaties and modern case law, it is safe to conclude that FPS does not impose an absolute obligation to refrain from interference with foreign investment. Which of the above-described approaches will prevail in practice, however, is yet to be seen.

2. The Standard of Due Diligence

There is a general consensus in modern arbitral jurisprudence that the guarantee of FPS does not create strict or absolute liability for harm caused by private persons, but rather provides a general obligation for the host state to exercise due diligence in the protection of foreign investment.[93] In other words, measures that states take to protect investors against non-state actors are not evaluated based on whether the investment was effectively protected in the end, but rather on the basis of the state's conduct,[94] that is that the host state acted diligently and took the measures of vigilance necessary in order to protect investors from forcible interference. This understanding reflects the customary rule discussed above and has been confirmed by the International Court of Justice (ICJ).[95] This does not mean that the application of the standard is unproblematic. The tension in the perspectives between developed and developing countries at the end of the nineteenth century as to the degree of liability of a host state has subsisted and spilled over into a debate on what exactly is the content of due diligence in the FPS clause. The central question is whether the diligent conduct should be measured against an objective standard or against the background of the local conditions of the host state.

[90] See Chapter 2 C.1.a.

[91] However, for the avoidance of doubt, it would be advisable to include a reference to 'police powers' in future investment treaties (without limiting its application to indirect expropriation).

[92] *Saluka* (n 26) paras 62, 82, 136, 270–76; *Too v Greater Modesto Insurance Associates* Award, 29 December 1989, 23 IUSCT Rep 378; *Philip Morris* (n 76) paras 287–350.

[93] See e.g. *AAPL* (n 23) paras 53, 85B; *Saluka* (n 26) para 484; *Tecmed* (n 18) para 177; *Frontier* (n 52) para 270; *Lauder* (n 27) para 308; *Wena* (n 16) para 84; *El Paso Energy v Argentina* ICSID Case no ARB/03/15, Award, 31 October 2011, para 523; *Allard* (n 31) paras 543–44; *Houben* (n 17) para 161; *von Pezold* (n 17) para 596; *Copper Mesa* (n 18) para 6.81; *Ampal* (n 22) para 241.

[94] C Economides, 'Content of the Obligation: Obligations of Means and Obligations of Result' in J Crawford et al (eds), *The Law of International Responsibility* (OUP 2010) 371, 378 (arguing that the obligation to protect foreigners is an obligation of conduct).

[95] *Elettronica Sicula SPA* (*US v Italy*) (Merits) [1989] ICJ Rep 15, 65, para 108.

A number of commentators have observed that a due diligence rule reflected a sliding scale of state liability, ranging from subjective to objective standards.[96] If due diligence is seen as a subjective standard, the state's conduct is measured solely on the basis of its existing capabilities and expectations in a given situation. The standard reflects the outdated theory of the absolute non-responsibility of states for losses incurred by aliens in situations of conflict, and has not been espoused by modern investment tribunals.

On the other hand, according to the objective standard, whether the host state fulfilled its due diligence obligation is tested against the conduct of a modern, reasonably organized government under similar circumstances.[97] All states have to adhere to the same standard, regardless of their individual circumstances. This is the approach followed by the *AMT* tribunal that explicitly recognized the standard of vigilance as an 'objective obligation' and did not take Zaire's situation into account when considering whether it had failed to protect the investor.[98] Similarly, some other arbitrators leaned towards the objective nature of due diligence by linking it to the 'parameters inherent in a democratic state',[99] 'the canons of good governance', and a 'reasonably well-organized modern State'.[100] Some have suggested that the tribunal in *AAPL v Sri Lanka* also heeded this approach.[101] The more accurate view, however, appears to be that the *AAPL* tribunal departed from the pure objective standard by limiting the host state's duty to prevent the harm to what could 'be reasonably expected' in a given situation.[102] Reasonableness brings an element of subjectivity to the due diligence standard as its content will vary depending on the local situation of the host state.

Similar references to what is 'reasonable under the circumstances' when assessing the host state's due diligence obligation have been made in some other recent cases.[103] While reasonableness is a vague term and its content will depend on the context of each individual case, it arguably provides certain leeway to accommodate a state's conditions in the assessment equation. These cases thus mark a shift towards a more tempered approach, combining subjective and objective

[96] I Brownlie, *State Responsibility* (Clarendon Press 1983) 162, 168; Newcombe and Paradell, *Law and Practice* (n 33) 310; H Bray, 'SOI–Save Our Investments! International Investment Law and International Humanitarian Law' (2013) 14(3) JWIT 578; De Brabandere, 'Due Diligence' (n 56) 353. See also *AAPL* (n 23) para 77.

[97] See A Freeman, *Responsibility of States for Unlawful Acts of their Armed Forces* (AW Sijthoff 1957) 277–78 (stating that due diligence 'is nothing more nor less than the reasonable measures of prevention which a well-administered government could be expected to exercise under similar circumstances'); Dolzer and Schreuer, *Principles* (n 56) 162 (remarking that 'lack of resources to take appropriate action will not serve as an excuse for the host state').

[98] *AMT* (n 21) paras 6.05–6.06, 6.11, 6.14. According to the tribunal, the government's duty was to take 'every measure necessary to protect' the investor, rather than what would be 'reasonably' expected.

[99] *Tecmed* (n 18) para 177.

[100] *Suez*, Separate Opinion of Pedro Nikken (n 26) para 20.

[101] De Brabandere, 'Due Diligence' (n 56) 356; Bray, 'SOI' (n 96) 591; ILA, First Report (n 62) 10.

[102] *AAPL* (n 23) para 85B.

[103] See e.g. *Lauder* (n 27) para 308; *CME* (n 27) para 353; *El Paso* (n 93) para 523.

standards. The so-called modified objective approach acknowledges that the host state is 'required to exercise an objective minimum standard of due diligence', however, the state's conduct is assessed against what could reasonably be expected of the state in the given circumstances and in the light of its resources.[104] The standard of vigilance required from the state thus depends on a number of factors, such as the intensity of the violence and the resources that can be diverted for the purposes of protection.[105] The importance of the standard in conflict situations was highlighted in *Pantechniki v Albania* in a celebrated paragraph:

> A failure of protection and security is to the contrary likely to arise in an unpredictable instance of civic disorder which could have been readily controlled by a powerful state but which overwhelms the limited capacities of one which is poor and fragile . . . it seems difficult to maintain that a government incurs international responsibility for failure to plan for unprecedented trouble of unprecedented magnitude in unprecedented places.[106]

In a similar vein, the tribunal in *LESI v Algeria* rejected the FPS claim because the government had taken reasonable and proportionate security measures during the revolution. The tribunal stressed that the duty of due diligence is an obligation of means and that its assessment depends on the circumstances such as the security situation in a host state and the specificity of a region where the investment is located and which may affect the ability to provide adequate protection.[107]

The reasoning in these cases implies that the more intense the conflict and the poorer and more fragile the host state, the more likely it is that the state will not be found liable for losses incurred by non-state actors. As articulated by Newcombe and Paradell: 'An investor investing in an area with endemic civil strife and poor governance cannot have the same expectation of physical security as one investing in London, New York or Tokyo.'[108] One could thus observe that the content of due diligence has evolved and is imbued with more flexibility which accommodates states' political and economic realities. The standard which takes into account the situation of the host state (including the character and the extent of the conflict) and the means available to it, has received support by commentators,[109] and

[104] See Newcombe and Paradell, *Law and Practice* (n 33) 310; I Brownlie, *Principles of Public International Law* (6th edn, OUP 2003) 504.

[105] *Pantechniki* (n 21) para 82.

[106] ibid para 77.

[107] *LESI* (n 22) para 181. It should be noted that the tribunal applied a basic armed conflict clause as *lex specialis* to exclude the application of FPS, which is criticized below. Effectively, however, the tribunal was analysing the government's due diligence. See Section 4 C.4.a.

[108] Newcombe and Paradell, *Law and Practice* (n 33) 310.

[109] ibid; Brownlie, *Principles* (n 104); McLachlan et al, *Substantive Principles* (n 32) 331; De Brabandere, 'Due Diligence' (n 56); N Gallus, 'The Influence of the Host State's Level of Development on International Investment Treaty Standard of Protection' (2005) 6 JWIT 711; Sornarajah, *International Law* (n 32) 162.

mirrors the application of due diligence in the law of state responsibility for injury to foreigners under customary international law discussed in Chapter 2.

The flexible nature of the due diligence standard does not imply that a state facing poverty along with a severe security crisis can never be found liable for the breach of an FPS provision. Each case and every episode of an alleged failure to protect investment must be assessed on their own facts, and it is entirely possible that even in the midst of a prolonged armed conflict, the circumstances and the available resources are such to permit state forces to prevent or mitigate losses.[110] For example, in *Ampal v Egypt*, the tribunal found that Egypt failed to protect the investor's pipeline system from terrorist attacks in the course of the Arab Spring revolution.[111] The award has been criticized by some commentators for embracing an absolute, uniform due diligence standard and disregarding Egypt's extraordinary circumstances at the time of attacks.[112] The close reading of the award suggests that the claims by the commentators are exaggerated. Namely, the tribunal, by referencing the *Pantechniki* award, expressly acknowledged the relative nature of due diligence under the FPS provision and stated that the standard 'must be assessed according to the particular circumstances in which the damage occurs'.[113]

By inspecting each violent incident separately, the tribunal paid respect to different types of circumstances that inform the assessment of whether a due diligence duty was met. Thus, it held that the government had not incurred responsibility for the losses emanating from the first four terrorist attacks as they could not have been prevented due to the unprecedented nature of violent events (foreseeability and magnitude).[114] It noted, however, that they should have served as a warning to the government 'that further attacks might be carried out if security measures were not taken and implemented'.[115] It further took into account that, in particular as of the date of attack number five, the well-resourced Egyptian armed forces were present in high numbers in the area of the pipeline (availability of resources and state's capacity), and that the attacks did not include mob violence or the use of heavy arms (degree of violence).[116] While it acknowledged the it could be burdensome to secure an almost 200 km long pipeline (topographical circumstances), it

[110] See e.g. *Houben* (n 17) paras 160–64 (the tribunal paid due regard to the state's individual circumstances, while still finding the state responsible for not utilizing the available resources to remove the squatters from the investor's premises).

[111] *Ampal* (n 22) para 290.

[112] See e.g. A Yacoub, 'The Case of Ampal v Egypt: What Are the Parameters of the Due Diligence Standard?' (*Cambridge International Law Journal*, 16 November 2018) <http://cilj.co.uk/2018/11/16/the-case-of-ampal-v-egypt-what-are-the-parameters-of-the-due-diligence-standard/> accessed 18 December 2018; I Ryk-Lakhman, 'Foreign Investments as Non-Human Targets' in B Baade et al (eds), *International Humanitarian Law in Areas of Limited Statehood—Adaptable and Legitimate or Rigid and Unreasonable?* (Nomos 2018) 171.

[113] *Ampal* (n 22) paras 241, 244, 284.

[114] ibid paras 285, 289.

[115] ibid para 289.

[116] ibid paras 808–09.

also observed that attacks concentrated on the same closely located segments of the pipeline,[117] and that there was no evidence that the authorities took any 'concrete steps' to protect the investment in reaction to terrorist activities.[118] Moreover, in one instance, the security forces were called to help stop the saboteurs from laying explosives on the pipeline, but refused to do so despite their availability, proximity of their location to the pipeline, and sufficient time for an adequate action.[119]

While one may disagree with the tribunal's assessment of the evidence in the *Ampal* case, it clearly follows from the award's reasoning that there was no deviation from the relative nature of the due diligence standard. Despite inconsistent application of the FPS provision in the early investment treaty practice, and continuing criticism in scholarship, the more persuasive view is that a state's exercise of due diligence in providing physical security against non-state actors is guided according to the relative standard that takes into account the relevant state's circumstances.

C. Armed Conflict Clause

The provision that can be found in most investment treaties and refers directly to situations of conflict has been known in investment scholarship as the 'war clause'.[120] This term appears to be a misnomer, particularly because such provisions, as a rule, refer not only to war but also to other situations of violence, such as insurrections, revolutions, riots, civil disturbances, or similar events. A more precise term would thus be an armed conflict clause, whereby 'armed conflict' is used as an overarching term encompassing the situations enumerated in the respective clause. As mentioned in Chapter 1, some BITs have explicitly embraced this approach and use 'armed conflict' as a generic term covering all situations of conflict listed in the clause.[121]

Armed conflict clauses are among the least examined provisions of investment treaties.[122] This is perhaps unsurprising given the fact that tribunals mostly rejected the application of the clause. The provision was invoked in cases involving

[117] ibid paras 793–99.

[118] ibid para 290.

[119] ibid para 288.

[120] Schreuer, 'Protection of Investments' (n 1) 12; Newcombe and Paradell, *Law and Practice* (n 33) 499; O Mayorga, 'Arbitrating War: Military Necessity as a Defence to the Breach of Investment Treaty Obligations' (Policy Brief, August 2013) Program on Humanitarian Policy and Conflict Research Harvard University.

[121] Philippines–Pakistan BIT (1999) Art V; Philippines–Myanmar BIT (1998) Art V. Some investment treaties use the term 'hostilities' to cover different type of situations, from revolution to insurrections. See e.g. Japan–Republic of Korea BIT (2002) Art 11.

[122] For a limited discussion, see Schreuer, 'Protection of Investments' (n 1) 12–16; F Perez-Aznar, 'Investment Protection in Exceptional Situations: Compensation-for-Losses Clauses in IIAs' (2017) 32(3) ICSID Rev 696.

armed conflict,[123] invasion and seizure of commercial farms,[124] economic crisis,[125] and extreme weather conditions.[126] Since they specifically address the situation of conflict and their analysis by tribunals has been inconsistent and often inaccurate, they merit deeper analysis.

The provision provides foreign investors with certain guarantees with respect to the payment of compensation for losses suffered in times of conflict. The scope of these guarantees is twofold: basic and advanced. The basic clause provides for a non-discriminatory treatment as to the payment of post-conflict indemnities, while the advanced clause creates a ground for remedying losses inflicted by government forces, and introduces exceptions to state responsibility. Before describing the content of these two types of a clause, its scope will be first outlined.

1. Scope of the Clause

The wording of armed conflict clauses across different investment treaties is similar, while demonstrating some variation as to the situations they cover. For example, some treaties entail a more detailed list of violent situations (e.g. the Libya–Portugal BIT adds 'disobedience' or 'disturbances'[127] and the 2008 UK Model BIT adds 'revolt' and 'riots'[128]), some are shorter and use more general terms (e.g. the 2012 US Model BIT is streamlined to cover 'armed conflict and civil strife'[129]), and some extend the scope of the clause to situations that are not necessarily related to violence (e.g. the 2010 Austria Model BIT also covers 'acts of God or force majeure',[130] while the 2004 Canada Model BIT adds 'natural disasters'[131] to the list).

[123] *AAPL* (n 23) paras 65–70; *AMT* (n 21) para 6.12; *LESI* (n 22).

[124] *Bernardus Funnekotter and Others v Republic of Zimbabwe* ICSID Case no ARB/05/6, Award, 22 April 2009, para 104; *von Pezold* (n 17) para 592.

[125] *CMS Gas Transmission Company v Argentine Republic* ICSID Case no ARB/01/8, Award, 12 May 2005, para 375; *LG&E Energy Corp v Argentine Republic* ICSID Case no ARB/02/1, Decision on Liability, 3 October 2006, para 243; *Enron* (n 41) para 320; *Sempra Energy International v Argentine Republic* ICSID Case no ARB/02/16, Award, 28 September 2007, para 362; *National Grid plc v Argentine Republic* UNCITRAL, Award, 3 November 2008, para 253; *El Paso* (n 93) para 559; *BG Group* (n 26) para 382; *Total SA v Argentine Republic* ICSID Case no ARB/04/1, Decision on Liability, 27 December 2010, para 230; *Impregilo SpA v Argentine Republic* ICSID Case no ARB/07/17, Award, 21 June 2011, para 341; *Suez* (n 26) para 271; *AWG Group Ltd v Argentine Republic* UNCITRAL, Decision on Liability, 30 July 2010, para 271; *EDF International SA and Others v Argentine Republic* ICSID Case no ARB/03/23, Award, 11 June 2012, paras 1157, 1162.

[126] *Consortium RFCC v Morocco v Kingdom of Morocco* ICSID Case no ARB/00/6, Award, 22 December 2003.

[127] Libya–Portugal BIT (2003) Art 7.

[128] 2008 UK Model BIT Art 4.

[129] 2012 US Model BIT Art 5(4). Similarly, NAFTA Art 1105(2).

[130] 2010 Austria Model BIT Art 8(1).

[131] 2004 Canada Model BIT Art 12(1). It would seem that the absence of the express reference to natural disasters would preclude the application of a clause to such situations. For example, *Consortium RFCC* tribunal rejected the application of the clause, which was confined to situations of conflict, to extreme weather conditions, noting that they do not constitute an event analogous to armed conflict. *Consortium RFCC* (n 126) para 80.

These differences in terminology are mostly not material. What matters is that the provision establishes a certain threshold for a conflict situation that needs to be met for the provision to apply. The concept of conflict that determines the area of operation of the clause is broader than the IHL-based 'armed conflict', but narrower than forcible interferences covered by the FPS clause. Thus, armed conflict clauses do not apply to isolated incidents specifically targeting investors, like private harassment and occupations of investors' premises. Instead, they are designed to address losses arising directly out of forcible actions related to situations of such proportion as to constitute an emergency. Given the breadth of the situations envisaged in such clauses, it should not be too problematic for a tribunal to assess *prima facie* if the clause applies. However, in some situations this may not be straightforward.

For example, does the clause cover losses arising out of acts of looting, vandalism, and mere banditry? The answer would likely depend on whether such an act was situated within the context of a wider situation of disorder covered by the clause.[132] Riots typically involve vandalism and the destruction of private and public property. Acts of vandalism and theft not carried out during times of such civil disorder would, however, be unlikely to trigger the applicability of the clause. In *AMT v Zaire*, the investor was subjected to two separate occasions of looting by the soldiers of the Zairean armed forces. The destruction and theft of the investor's property was part of the widespread looting experienced by Zaire in September 1991 and January 1993. The tribunal held that the armed conflict clause was applicable as the situation in question was covered by the wording 'riot or act of violence'.[133] Even when the clauses are worded more economically (e.g. 'armed conflict and civil strife'),[134] such acts of looting are covered therein. The same should apply to strikes—if general, appearing on a massive scale, driven by broader discontent with a social and economic situation in the state and resulting in widespread violence, they should fall under the scope of the clause. On the other hand, isolated strikes and protests of a smaller scale would probably not reach the applicability threshold.

Another question is whether armed conflict clauses also apply to terrorist acts. Many clauses are non-exhaustive in listing the violent situations, stating instead that they apply to any similar events (e.g. the US–Ukraine BIT). Would a terrorist act be interpreted as such an event? At first glance, there is a notable difference, namely situations usually listed in the clauses are forms of collective violence and mass incidents, whereas a terrorist attack can be planned and executed by a small group of people or even an individual. The number of people involved should not

[132] The government in Zimbabwe unsuccessfully relied on the armed conflict clause as a defence, arguing that its application was triggered by the state of emergency resulting from invasion by settlers and war veterans of foreign investors' farms. See *Funnekotter* (n 124) para 104; *von Pezold* (n 17) para 592.

[133] *AMT* (n 21) para 6.12.

[134] 2012 US Model BIT Art 5(4).

be a determinative factor, however. What matters more is the potential for mass impact that such an attack can have and the emergency situation to which it amounts. In fact, terrorist acts are frequently included as a type of civil emergency in national governments' strategies and on national risk registers.[135] If armed conflict clauses list a 'state of emergency' as one of the violent situations they cover, terrorist attacks may likely be covered as well. The same could apply to the scarcely worded clauses. This broad interpretation was supported by Scott Gudgeon, a key negotiator of US BITs, who explained in the commentary of the US Model BIT that even the wording 'war or civil disturbance' should be understood to include terrorism.[136] To avoid any doubt as to the broad scope of the clause, a specific reference to an 'act of terrorism' has been included in some of the early US BITs.[137]

2. Basic Armed Conflict Clause

Most investment treaties contain a basic armed conflict clause that imposes on a host state a specific non-discrimination obligation, typically with respect to the payment of indemnities for losses sustained by investors in a situation of conflict.[138] Unlike the FPS provision, the basic armed conflict clause was not featured in the FCN treaties or in drafts of multilateral investment treaties. The exceptions are the provisions in the Resolution of the Institute of International Law (1927) and the Basis of Discussion drawn by the Preparatory Committee of the Hague Conference for the Codification of International Law (1929) which provided for a national treatment as to the payment of post-conflict indemnities.[139]

The clause was first introduced in German investment treaties after the Second World War as a reaction to losses the German investors sustained abroad.[140] It was probably devised by Hermann Abs, who played a pivotal role in the design of post-war German economic policy and was part of the delegation negotiating reparations for the German assets confiscated in the US during the war.[141] The

[135] See e.g. UK National Risk Register of Civil Emergencies (11 July 2013).

[136] Gudgeon, 'United States Bilateral Investment Treaties' (n 86) 127.

[137] See e.g. US–Cameroon (1989) Art IV; US–Senegal (1990) Art IV; US–Panama (1991) Art V; US–Bangladesh (1989) Art IV.

[138] According to UNCTAD, 90 per cent of mapped investment treaties contain such clauses. UNCTAD Navigator (n 10).

[139] Draft on International Responsibility of States for Injuries in their Territory to the Person or Property of Foreigners, Prepared by the Institute of International Law (1927) Art VII in ILC, *Yearbook of the International Law Commission, 1956, Vol II*, UN Doc A/CN.4/SER.A/1956/Add.1, 227; Bases of Discussion Drawn up in 1929 by the Preparatory Committee of the Conference for the Codification of International Law (The Hague, 1930) No 21(4) and No 22(b) in ILC, *Yearbook of the International Law Commission, 1956, Vol II*, UN Doc A/CN.4/SER.A/1956/Add.1, 222 (Bases of Discussion).

[140] It is included in the first BIT between Germany and Pakistan (1959) Art 3(3). See also Vandevelde, *History* (n 8) 311.

[141] 'Abs, Hermann Josef' (Declassified and Released by Central Intelligence Agency, Nazi War Crimes Disclosure Act, 2001). <https://www.cia.gov/library/readingroom/docs/ABS%2C%20HERMANN%20J._0051.pdf> accessed 18 December 2018. Interestingly, the Abs-Shawcross Convention, drafted

only partial success in obtaining the settlement could explain the motivation behind this treaty innovation. The language from German BITs was soon adopted in Italian BITs, followed by France, the UK, and the US shortly thereafter, eventually becoming a common provision in most investment treaties.[142]

The basic clauses guarantee foreign investors that the host state will provide them with national treatment, most favoured nation (MFN) treatment, or both with respect to measures such as restitution, indemnification, or compensation for losses occurring in situations of armed conflict. For example, Article 3(3) of the US–Ukraine BIT provides:

> Nationals or companies of either Party whose investments suffer losses in the territory of the other Party owing to war or other armed conflict, revolution, state of national emergency, insurrection, civil disturbance or other similar events shall be accorded treatment by such other Party no less favorable than that accorded to its own nationals or companies or to nationals or companies of any third country, whichever is the most favorable treatment, as regards any measures it adopts in relation to such losses.

The prevailing view among commentators is that basic clauses do not create substantive rights to restitution or compensation, that is they do not oblige a host state to compensate an investor for a covered loss.[143] This view was confirmed in several arbitral awards resulting from the Argentine economic crisis and was articulated clearly by the tribunal in *CMS v Argentina* who stated that the provision is meant:

> . . . to provide a floor treatment for the investor in the context of the measures adopted in respect of losses suffered in the emergency, not different from that applied to national or other foreign investors. [It] does not derogate from the Treaty rights but rather ensures that any measures directed at offsetting or minimizing losses will be applied in a non-discriminatory manner.[144]

Some BITs explicitly limit such measures to 'restitution, indemnification, compensation or other valuable consideration'.[145] In other words, if the state does not

in the same period, did not include the armed conflict clause. The reason for this could be that Abs and Shawcross wanted to keep the draft simple and avoid any specific, politically sensitive provisions (especially in the aftermath of war) that could complicate obtaining a multilateral consensus.

[142] Only a minority of BITs do not contain the provision, e.g. the Argentina–Mexico BIT (1996).

[143] C Brown, *Commentaries on Selected Model Investment Treaties* (OUP 2013) 164; Newcombe and Paradell, *Law and Practice* (n 33) 315, 500; Gudgeon, 'United States Bilateral Investment Treaties' (n 86) 129, Schreuer, 'Protection of Investments' (n 1) 12; Salacuse, *Law of Investment Treaties* (n 32) 369; K Vandevelde, *United States Investment Treaties: Policy and Practice* (Kluwer 1992) 212; UNCTAD Report, 'Bilateral Investment Treaties 1995–2006: Trends in Investment Rule Making' (2006) 55.

[144] *CMS Gas* (n 125) para 375. For other cases, see n 125.

[145] See e.g. Germany–Syria BIT (1980) Art 4(3); Greece–Syria BIT (2003) Art 6(1).

compensate either its national investors or investors from third countries for losses covered by such clauses, foreign investors have no right to compensation under the title of this provision.[146] On the other hand, if the host state decides, as a matter of domestic law or policy (e.g. as an act of grace) to provide payment to its own or third-country investors, it should do the same, and on equal terms, for foreign investors protected under the investment treaty.

This view has been contested in the case law.[147] The tribunal in *AAPL v Sri Lanka* interpreted the clause broadly and held that it contained a *renvoi* to the entire body of customary international law.[148] It considered that the national and MFN treatment did not refer only to matters of compensation, but also to the determination of a host state's liability. In other words, it construed the provision as to impose a substantive obligation on the host state to pay compensation to investors for conflict-related losses. This enabled the tribunal to incorporate the customary rule of due diligence into the investment treaty and on that basis found the host state liable. This interpretation is problematic for several reasons and has been rightly criticized by the dissenting arbitrator as 'fundamentally erroneous'.[149] First, the provision in question was titled 'Compensation for losses' and, second, it explicitly referred to 'restitution, indemnification, compensation or other settlement'.[150] Extending the treatment beyond these measures was not in line with the wording of the provision and contradicted its purpose. Even when the clause uses a more general wording, as in the above-cited US–Ukraine BIT, and refers to 'any measures [the host State] adopts in relation to such losses', this does not provide national or MFN treatment as to the question of liability. Namely, the clause refers to measures that are adopted only after the losses have been incurred, that is after the point at which the liability arose. Such measures are beneficial to those who have already sustained losses since they purport to mitigate or repair them.[151] Thus, the basic clause arguably excludes the question of liability even in cases when it is not explicitly limited to the question of compensation.

The clause covers situations where the liability is not established but the host state nonetheless decides to implement measures, such as payments according to its own national policies. This interpretation reflects the historical practice of

[146] An odd exception to this rule seems to be created, intentionally or through hasty drafting, in some of the Italian BITs which impose a duty on a host state to offer an adequate compensation for conflict-related losses, regardless of who caused them. See e.g. Syria–Italy BIT (2003) Art 4; Armenia–Italy BIT (2003) Art 4; Morocco–Italy (2000) Art 4; Bangladesh–Italy (1994) Art 4. See also *Consortium RFCC* case, in which the tribunal acknowledged that Art 4(1) of the Morocco–Italy BIT established a strict, objective liability. *Consortium RFCC* (n 126) para 56.

[147] See e.g. *AAPL* (n 23); *AMT* (n 21) para 6.14; *LESI* (n 22) para 175. See Section 4 C.4.a.

[148] *AAPL* (n 23) paras 65–70.

[149] ibid, Dissenting Opinion, 586.

[150] UK–Sri Lanka BIT (1980) Art 4(1).

[151] The clause applies only with respect to state's corrective or compensatory measures taken in reaction to already incurred losses. See *Impregilo* (n 125) paras 341–43; *El Paso* (n 93) para 559; *BG Group* (n 26) para 382; *Total* (n 125) para 229; *Enron* (n 41) para 320.

paying voluntary awards of indemnities for conflict-related losses, for which no legal liability was incurred. While it was sometimes argued that host states were responsible for indemnifying foreigners if they had indemnified their own nationals,[152] often states arbitrarily limited the classes of the beneficiaries, which sometimes excluded foreigners from being paid voluntary indemnities.[153] Since those national compensation programmes were discretionary and no international custom emerged that would provide a national or MFN treatment with respect to such payments,[154] the investment treaty regime went further and created a binding obligation upon a host state to provide such non-discriminatory treatment. Arguably, this obligation is not covered by the general national or MFN treatment clauses that refer to establishment and treatment of foreign investment, and the activities associated with it.[155] Payment of compensation falls outside that scope which explains the rationale for including basic armed conflict clauses in investment treaties.[156]

3. Advanced Armed Conflict Clause

Much less common are advanced armed conflict clauses,[157] which cover the same situations, but go a step further. They elevate the protection of foreign investors by granting them a substantive right to restitution or compensation for losses incurred by the host state's forces or authorities through requisitioning or unnecessary destruction of an investor's property. The origin of the provision can be traced to the late eighteenth-century treaties of amity and commerce and early

[152] See e.g. the claims against Belgium after the battle of Antwerp in 1830. While the Belgian government compensated its own citizens for the losses suffered during the battle, no such measures were adopted with respect to foreign nationals. In the end, the claims were settled on an equitable basis. Reported in Study by the Secretariat, '"Force majeure" and "Fortuitous event" as Circumstances Precluding Wrongfulness: Survey of State Practice, International Judicial Decisions and Doctrine' in ILC, *Yearbook of the International Law Commission, 1978, Vol II*, UN Doc A/CN.4/SER.A/1978/Add.1, 61, 106. See also C Eagleton, *The Responsibility of States in International Law* (New York University Press 1928) 152; J Moore, *A Digest of International Law* (Vol 6, Washington GPO 1906) 892 (reporting that the US government urged the Brazilian government to pay indemnities for injuries sustained by the American investor in the course of insurrection of 1893 merely on the basis that the payment for similar losses had been made to Brazilian companies).

[153] E Borchard, *Diplomatic Protection of Citizens Abroad* (Banks Law Publishing 1915) 279, 280.

[154] For a different view, see Perez-Aznar, 'Compensation-for-Losses Clauses' (n 122) 714 (arguing that the basic armed conflict clause reflects customary international law).

[155] See *Aroa Mines Case* (*Great Britain v Venezuela*) (1903) 9 RIAA 402, 407.

[156] Newcombe and Paradell have argued that such measures qualified as 'aid', and unless the distinction between similarly situated investors was arbitrary, it was not prohibited under the customary international law. Newcombe and Paradell, *Law and Practice* (n 33) 225. A similar view was held by arbitrator Huber in *Spanish Zone of Morocco* (*Great Britain v Spain*) (1924) 2 RIAA 615, 625. On the other hand, Salacuse has argued that the clause adds no new protection to treaties already containing a national treatment or MFN clause. Salacuse, *Law of Investment Treaties* (n 32) 369–70.

[157] According to UNCTAD, they appear in around 33 per cent of investment treaties. UNCTAD Navigator (n 10).

nineteenth-century FCN treaties which sometimes required that the property seized during wartime is restored to the owner,[158] or compensated.[159] A version of the clause appeared also in the Basis of Discussion No 21 drafted by the Preparatory Committee of the Hague Conference.[160] However, it was not incorporated in other drafts addressing state responsibility for injuries to foreign property and it was not included in the US post-Second World War FCN treaties.

The clause was introduced to modern investment treaties by the UK.[161] One can but suspect that Lord Shawcross, whose familiarity with the laws of war was well established (he was a British prosecutor at the Nuremberg War Crimes tribunal), played some part in this through his role as a director of Shell which at the time actively participated in consultation with the British government in drafting the UK model investment treaty.[162] The provision has since become part of the majority of UK BITs, and also features in some other investment treaties, including the 2012 US Model BIT and the Energy Charter Treaty.[163] An example is found in Article 5(2) of the UK–Ukraine BIT:

> Without prejudice to paragraph (1) [basic clause] of this Article, investors of one Contracting Party who in any of the situations referred to in that paragraph suffer losses in the territory of the other Contracting Party resulting from
> a) requisitioning of their property by its forces or authorities, or
> b) destruction of their property by its forces or authorities which was not caused in combat action or was not required by the necessity of the situation,
> shall be accorded restitution or adequate compensation. Resulting payment shall be freely transferable.

The advanced standard mirrors the principles of the law of war on the protection of private property. As discussed in Chapter 2, the rule that compensation is due when armed forces seize an alien's private property, or when the destruction thereof was not incidental to combat action and not required by military necessity, developed in the practice and jurisprudence of the nineteenth century and was later codified in the Hague and Geneva Conventions. Some scholars have thus argued that the clause is superfluous since investors are already protected under the laws of war.[164] This assumption seems to be inaccurate as there are benefits

[158] Treaty of Friendship, Commerce and Navigation, Mexico–United Kingdom (1826) Art XII; Treaty of Friendship, Commerce and Navigation, Colombia–US (1824) Art 24.

[159] Treaty of Amity and Commerce, US– France (1778) Art 22; Treaty of Amity, US– Prussia (1799) Art XXIII.

[160] Bases of Discussion (n 139).

[161] The first BIT to introduce the clause was the UK–Egypt BIT in 1975 in Art 4(2).

[162] J Bonnitcha, L Poulsen, and M Waibel, *The Political Economy of the Investment Treaty Regime* (OUP 2017) 188.

[163] See e.g. UK–China (1986) Art 4(2); UK–Bolivia BIT (1988) Art 4(2); UK–Sri Lanka BIT, Art 4(2).

[164] See Gudgeon, 'United States Bilateral Investment Treaties' (n 86) 128.

that investors could derive from the advanced clause that are not available to them under the IHL framework.

First, although historically the customary law of armed conflict prohibited the seizure of private property without payment of compensation or its return,[165] practice during the two World Wars deviated from this rule. Thus, during the First World War, the Allied powers allowed their nationals to confiscate the private investments of enemy nationals for their own use.[166] The Treaty of Versailles did not penalize these illegal practices, but instead authorized the Allies 'to retain and liquidate all the property and interests of German subjects or companies under their control in their territory', pending Germany's payment of war reparations.[167] The confiscations of the private assets of German nationals and companies resumed in the Second World War with the aim of securing the payment of reparations and preventing Germany from becoming a global superpower.[168] In the light of these practices, the controversial view emerged that international law no longer prohibited the confiscation of private enemy property during times of war.[169] By expressly prescribing the payment of compensation for the requisition of investment property or its restitution, advanced armed conflict clauses in investment treaties could be thus seen as clarifying and re-establishing the customary protections of private property that had existed prior to the First World War. Indeed, this was the intention of the British government in drafting the first clause,[170] and is confirmed in some investment treaties in express terms.[171]

Second, and as discussed in Chapter 2, Additional Protocol II to the Geneva Conventions (AP II), which regulates non-international armed conflicts, contains no provision on the protection of private property, which makes it less clear to what extent foreign investors are protected against requisition and destruction taking place during civil wars. What is clear, however, is that IHL rules do not protect investors in internal disturbances that fall below the threshold of armed conflict. In contrast, advanced armed conflict clauses extend protections to 'lesser' types of

[165] See e.g. the *Upton Case* (*US v Venezuela*) (1903–1905) 9 RIAA 235–36.

[166] See Borchard's 'Introduction' in J Gathings, *International Law and American Treatment of Alien Enemy Property* (American Council on Public Affairs 1940) v–vi. See also *Civilian Claims: Eritrea's Claims 15, 16, 23, 27–23* (Partial Award of 17 December 2004) (2004) 26 RIAA 195, 236, para 128.

[167] Treaty of Versailles (1919) Art 297(b) and (e).

[168] See e.g. Paris Reparation Agreement (15 March 1946) 555 UNTS 69, Part I, Art 6(A). See also M McDougal and F Feliciano, 'International Coercion and World Public Order: The General Principles of the Law of War' (1958) 67 Yale L J 771; H Van Houtte et al, *Post-War Restoration of Property Rights under International Law* (CUP 2008) 275–82.

[169] See e.g. *Contra Prince Salm-Salm v The State of the Netherlands and the Nederlands Beheers-Instituut* District Court of The Hague, 28 June 1954; Court of Appeal of The Hague, 8 November 1956 and Supreme Court, 21 June 1957 (1957) 24 ILR 893, 895; Van Houtte (n 168).

[170] E Denza and S Brooks, 'Investment Protection: United Kingdom Experience' (1987) 36 ICLQ 908, 911–12.

[171] See e.g. Armenia–Austria BIT (2001) Art 6(2) (noting that the provision reflects 'common international law').

conflict, such as revolts and revolutions. Third, the investment treaty framework provides investors with the right to seek remedy directly from the host state, a privilege that is not available under IHL.

While the clause clarifies the substantive protection to investors, it also brings important benefits for a host state by specifying situations in which a state is exempt from liability for destruction of an investor's property, namely when the loss was caused in 'combat action' or due to 'necessity of the situation'.[172] While this specific exception is reflective of IHL practice, caution should be exercised in the interpretation of these concepts in the investment law context. The following two sections will explain how they were addressed by the *AAPL* tribunal, elucidating their meaning and highlight their problematic aspects.

(a) Combat action

The case *AAPL v Sri Lanka* concerned a Sri Lankan counter-insurgency operation against the Liberation Fighters of Tamil Elaam (the 'Tamil Tigers'). In January 1987, a Sri Lankan Special Task Force launched a forceful attack on the Serendib Shrimp Farm, co-owned by a Hong Kong company called AAPL. According to the official accounts, the intense combat action resulted in the death of more than twenty AAPL employees and the destruction of the farm's property, which led to the termination of the farm's operations.[173] The claimant alleged that the Sri Lankan government was liable for the destruction of the investment because it breached the advanced armed conflict clause in Article 4 of the applicable UK–Sri Lanka BIT. The clause provides that the host state has to pay adequate compensation in cases of:

> . . . war or other armed conflict, revolution, a state of national emergency, revolt, insurrection or riot [causing foreign investors to] suffer losses resulting from
> a) requisitioning of their property by [the host State's] forces or authorities, or
> b) destruction of their property by [the host State's] forces or authorities which was not caused in combat action or was not required by the necessity of the situation.

More specifically, the claimant argued that the loss was 'not caused in combat action', but amounted to 'the wanton destruction of AAPL's property and the cold-blooded killing of the farm manager and the permanent staff members' which was 'clearly not planned pursuant to any combat action'.[174] Since the invoked provision excludes from its scope property destruction caused by the government forces in

[172] In some BITs, the clause does not refer to 'combat action'. See e.g. Austria–Armenia BIT (2001) Art 6(2); Sweden–Kazakhstan (2004) Art 5(2); Energy Charter Treaty (1994) Art 12(2); Australia–Korea FTA (2014) Art 11.6.

[173] Decades later, the testimonies of witnesses provided for a different, more devastating, account. See Chapter 1, n 1.

[174] *AAPL* (n 23) para 28.

'combat action', the tribunal, presided by Professor Berthold Goldman, had to determine, first, what is meant by 'combat action', and second, whether the violent action in question could be classified as such.

The tribunal decided to interpret the term progressively, 'according to its natural and fair meaning as commonly used under prevailing circumstances, ie, within the context of guerrilla warfare which characterizes the modern civil wars conducted by insurgents'.[175] It accurately noted that the civil wars in recent history have rarely featured the classical military confrontation 'between two opposing armed groups on a battle field where the adversaries engage simultaneously in fighting each other on the spot'.[176] More commonly, they take the form of sporadic attacks by armed groups and governmental counter-insurgency actions that can take place in vast inhabited areas. This led the tribunal to conclude that the military operations on the AAPL farm qualified as 'combat action' and therefore the losses incurred as a result were not covered by the provision.

Regrettably, the tribunal's analysis was brief and left much to be desired. In particular, it would have been useful if the tribunal had clarified the criteria for distinguishing combat action from other forms of violent measures. Are there any spatial and temporal requirements for the conduct to qualify as combat action? Does the action have to involve direct confrontation between adversaries, or can it qualify as such even in the absence of the resistance of an armed opposition group? Does it matter what type of weaponry is used in the action? Does it have to be undertaken against the backdrop of a civil war, or does it also include law enforcement operations in less intense internal conflicts?

The text of the armed conflict clause implies that this exception to a state's liability applies to all types of conflict listed in the basic armed conflict clause (including riots and revolts), and to the conduct of both a state's armed forces as well as its police authorities. This makes the assessment of the contours of 'combat action' even more important. In particular, as a consequence of a broad interpretation of 'combat action', the host state could benefit from the exemption even in cases of isolated anti-terrorist measures that take place outside of the context of armed conflict, or even police action against demonstrators and rioters. It thus seems apposite to inspect how the term has been interpreted in other legal contexts.

IHL, whose principles have likely influenced the content of advanced armed conflict clauses, is limited to the regulation of belligerent parties' conduct in armed conflict as defined in its treaties and jurisprudence, excluding law enforcement measures in peacetime. Within that context, however, combat action is broadly perceived, encompassing different styles of fighting, including guerrilla actions.[177] IHL rules equate 'combat action' with the term 'attack', which is given a broad

[175] ibid para 61.
[176] ibid.
[177] Additional Protocol I to the Geneva Conventions (AP I) Art 44(3).

definition in Article 49 of AP I as 'acts of violence against the adversary, whether in offence or in defence'.[178] Military attacks must be distinguished from 'military operations', which is an even broader concept 'understood to mean any movements, manoeuvers and other activities whatsoever carried out by the armed forces with a view to combat', and typically before the actual combat.[179] While belligerents are bound by a general duty of constant care in the conduct of military operations with a view to spare the civilian population and civilian objects,[180] more specific obligations are attached to the planning and carrying out of actual attacks, in the course of which collateral casualties are tolerated as long as they are not excessive in relation to the concrete and direct military advantage anticipated.[181]

Since IHL treaties do not provide much guidance as to what constitutes 'combat action' outside the scope of IHL-defined armed conflict, other frameworks are worth investigating. As mentioned above, international human rights instruments do not formally distinguish between military operations and law enforcement actions. This notwithstanding, it would appear that the distinction between a law enforcement operation and a real combat action was taken into consideration by the ECtHR when assessing whether or not the use of force on the part of the respondent state had been lawful.[182]

A more concrete analogy can be found in domestic torts laws that exempt states from civil liability for losses incurred in combat actions. A few such cases emerged in the aftermath of the Second World War. For example, in *Adams v Naylor*, the House of Lords opted for a broad interpretation of 'combat' which included not only the actual fighting between belligerent parties, but also other measures undertaken to defeat the enemy, such as laying down a minefield.[183] *In Johnson v US*, the

[178] ICRC Commentary to AP I, Art 49(1), 602, para 1880.

[179] ICRC Commentary to AP I, Art 57(1), 680, para 2191. See also ICRC Commentary to Art 51(1), para 1936, which defines military operations as 'all the movements and activities carried out by armed forces related to hostilities'. See also J-F Queguiner, 'Precautions under the Law Governing the Conduct of Hostilities (2006) 88(864) IRRC 793, 797.

[180] AP I, Art 57(1).

[181] AP I, Art 57(2). At the time of ratification of AP I, several states clarified that in determining the anticipated military advantage, attacks are considered as a whole, rather than isolated and particular parts thereof. See e.g. 'UK Reservation Re Article 51 and 57 of Additional Protocol I' (2 July 2002) <https://ihl-databases.icrc.org/ihl/NORM/0A9E03F0F2EE757CC1256402003FB6D2?OpenDocument> accessed 18 December 2018.

[182] See *Ahmet Özkan and Others v Turkey* App no 21689/93, Judgment (ECtHR, 6 April 2004) paras 305–06; *Isayeva v Russia* App no 57950/00, Judgment (ECtHR, 24 February 2005) paras 180–81 (*Isayeva II*); *Ergi v Turkey* App no 23818/94, Judgment (ECtHR, 28 July 1998); *Güleç v Turkey* App no 21593/93 (ECtHR, 27 July 1998). See also A Gioia, 'The Role of the European Court of Human Rights in Monitoring Compliance with Humanitarian Law in Armed Conflict' in O Ben-Naftali (ed), *International Human Rights and International Humanitarian Law* (OUP 2011) 226.

[183] [1946] 2 All ER 241, [1946] AC 543. The case concerned the death of a child killed by a mine that was placed on the beach by the UK military authorities during the Second World War. The House of Lords unanimously held that the death resulted from the use of the mine for combat activities and thus the state was not responsible for the death. The question of whether laying down the mines constitutes an attack (i.e. combat action) has been raised by the ICRC, which appears to support the view that there is an attack in as much as a person is 'directly endangered by a mine laid'. ICRC Commentary to AP I, Art 49(1), para 1881.

Court of Appeal interpreted the expression 'combatant activities' to 'include not only physical violence, but activities both necessary to and in direct connection with actual hostilities'.[184]

In the context of modern combat action, the relatively recent case of the Israeli District Court is interesting. The case of *Ploni v The State of Israel* concerned an innocent bystander who was injured as a result of the targeted killing operation conducted by the Israeli Defence Forces against an active member of the Islamic Jihad terrorist organization.[185] Since the Israeli Civil Torts Act provides that the state is exempt from liability for losses incurred in combat action, the Court had to determine whether targeted killing operations qualified as such. The Court emphasized the following criteria in its assessment: the context in which the anti-terrorist operation had been executed (the conflict between Israel and terrorist organizations in Gaza), the urgency to protect Israel's security interests (the action was based on intelligence which indicated that the targeted terrorist was planning a suicide terrorist attack), and the nature of the operation (an aerial attack, a typical warfare method). The Court held that the 'combat action' did not require that the action had to be taken against the armed forces of another state, and concluded that the anti-terrorist operation in question fell within the scope of the exception. Since then, the 'combat action' definition in the Israeli Civil Torts Act has been extended to encompass actions designed to combat and prevent terrorism or hostile acts.[186]

Based on the wording of advanced armed conflict clauses, it appears that the 'combat action' exception extends beyond the scope of IHL, providing the host state with a wider space for the protection of its security interests. While it initially emerged from the principles governing hostilities in wartime, the clause typically refers to situations other than war, including riots and even terrorist threats. The rationale behind the exception is clear: to ensure that a state's efforts to combat threats to its national security are not unnecessarily curtailed. However, the broad interpretation according to which the exception includes measures such as police actions against demonstrators, or raiding an investor's property in an attempt to apprehend terrorists, could easily give rise to abuse. Thus, the preferred interpretative approach entails a careful weighing of different circumstances, including the backdrop against which the operation was taken, the temporal and spatial nexus between the state's action and the broader conflict, the methods and means deployed in the action, and the nature of the organs who undertook the operation, to name but a few. Such an interpretation is more in line with the ordinary meaning

[184] *Johnson v United States*, 170 F.2d (9th Cir, 1948) 767, 770. See also *US v Marks*, 187 F.2nd (9th Cir, 1951) 724, 727, 728; *Skeels v US*, 72 F Supp (W D La, 1947) 372, 374.

[185] CA [Civil Action] *1081/04 Ploni v the State of Israel*, cited in Y Shany and I Rosenzweig, 'Terrorism and Democracy' (Issue No 4, April 2009) <http://en.idi.org.il/analysis/terrorism-and-democracy/issue-no-4/targeted-killing-constitutes-combat-action-ca-[civil-action]-108104-ploni-v-the-State-of-israel/-> accessed 5 April 2016.

[186] ibid.

of the phrase 'combat action', as well as with the object and purpose of investment treaties.

(b) Necessity of the situation

The second exception to the host state's liability for the destruction of an investor's property under the armed conflict clause is the 'necessity of the situation'. Disappointingly, the *AAPL* tribunal avoided any analysis of the condition by concluding that there was not enough evidence to determine whether the destruction on the Serendib farm could be attributed to the necessity of the situation. The tribunal, however, indicated that the standard of necessity in question was the same as the one established in the jurisprudence of the old arbitrations and mixed commissions which refused to hold host states responsible for losses incurred during hostilities when such losses 'were compelled by the imperious necessity of war'.[187] In other words, the tribunal held that the necessity exception in the advanced armed conflict clause reflected military necessity, an IHL principle described in Chapter 2.[188]

The 'necessity of the situation' clause provides a justification for a state's conduct in specifically outlined exceptional situations. The exception is built into a substantive standard and thus purports to define permissible state actions in conflict situations.[189] It legitimizes the conduct that is otherwise inconsistent with investment treaty values. In other words, it is a more specific manifestation of a state's police powers, creating a zone within which state organs are allowed to take certain measures with an aim to protect security (not exclusively military) interests.

While commentators, in line with the *AAPL* award, suggested that the exception in advanced armed conflict clauses is a codification of the IHL principle of military necessity,[190] this view appears imprecise. This follows from the ordinary meaning of the investment treaty exception, which refers to the 'necessity of the situation' rather than the *jus in bello* expression 'necessity of war'. It is in line with the broader scope of the armed conflict clause that conceptualizes the category of conflict in wider terms than IHL. By using the word 'situation' instead of 'war', the treaty drafters made the conscious decision that the necessity of the armed conflict clause transverses the necessity of humanitarian law. It would be unfair to justify the destruction of an investor's property in any situation of internal strife by invoking a standard of military necessity that bestows a higher degree of discretion on a military commander than a police officer. While a certain forceful measure may be considered necessary for achieving a military goal in the context of severe

[187] *AAPL* (n 23) para 63.

[188] See Chapter 2 C.1.a.

[189] For the comparison and different interpretations of the legal effect of 'general' security exceptions, see Chapter 5 B.3.

[190] Mayorga, 'Arbitrating War' (n 120); Vandevelde, *History* (n 8) 310; Newcombe and Paradell, *Law and Practice* (n 33) 498.

hostilities, the same measure could be completely disproportionate and unnecessary in a different, less intense context of a law enforcement operation. A more appropriate view thus seems to be that necessity in armed conflict clauses is a graded standard that accommodates different types of conflicts.

An analogy can be made with the approach taken by the European Court of Human Rights (ECtHR) in applying necessity and proportionality in conflict-related cases. While an important part of both legal regimes, the principles of necessity and proportionality are believed to operate differently in international human rights law and IHL. The ECtHR has assessed the lawfulness of military and counter-terrorist measures pursuant to human rights standards by refusing to afford the state's armed forces a high degree of discretion in applying the necessity and proportionality standards.[191] The case law seems to suggest, however, that the means necessary for suppressing an insurrection may not be the same as those that are considered acceptable for apprehending a terrorist[192] or suppressing a riot.[193] Thus, it would appear that the Court applied the more liberal IHL standard when the situation in question was one of armed conflict that could qualify as such under the IHL framework.[194]

Like the international human rights regime, the investment regime primarily aims at protecting the individual vis-à-vis the state. While neither of the two regimes formally distinguishes between different types of conflict, at least not as a legal category, both consider them relevant factual circumstances when applying legal standards, including necessity. Necessity in the armed conflict clause should thus be used flexibly, moving on a sliding scale of different types of conflict situations. Only when the situation amounts to armed conflict under IHL would the standard converge with military necessity. Even then, however, necessity should be used restrictively to advance the protection of civilians against the effects of attacks during wartime.[195]

4. The Relationship between the Armed Conflict Clause and FPS

Having analysed the content of two provisions most pertinent for investors who sustained losses in armed conflict, the issue addressed next, and whose treatment

[191] Y Shany, 'Human Rights and Humanitarian Law as Competing Legal Paradigms for Fighting Terror' in O Ben-Naftali (ed), *International Human Rights and International Humanitarian Law* (OUP 2011) 28–29. See also Chapter 2 D.1.a.

[192] *Hamiyet Kaplan and Others v Turkey* App no 36749/97 (ECtHR, Judgment, 13 September 2005) paras 51–52.

[193] *Güleç* (n 182) paras 70–71.

[194] *Isayeva II* (n 182) paras 178–218. Even in those cases, however, the conduct of the armed forces was subjected to the strict proportionality test. See Chapters 2 and 6 for the discussion on proportionality.

[195] See Chapter 6 C.3.

in investment jurisprudence has been inconsistent and largely unsatisfactory, concerns the relationship between the FPS provision and armed conflict clauses.

(a) Basic armed conflict clause v FPS

The relationship between the FPS provision and the basic armed conflict clause is unproblematic as they pursue different objectives: the former creates a ground for state liability, while the latter only ensures that investors are not discriminated against when it comes to the payment of conflict-related compensation or indemnities, regardless of state responsibility. This understanding has been confirmed by a number of arbitral tribunals.[196] The provisions thus co-exist without any particular interaction.

Some tribunals, however, held different positions—none very persuasive with their reasoning. The way the *AAPL* tribunal construed the clause as a *renvoi* to the international minimum standard of treatment has been already critiqued above. The tribunal in *AMT v Zaire* similarly treated the clause as an additional ground for finding of the host state's liability. According to the tribunal, the purpose of the clause was merely to reinforce the FPS clause.[197] It is puzzling how the tribunal arrived at this conclusion, in view of the fact that the interpreted treaty provision expressly referred to the non-discriminatory treatment as regards making of restitution and payment of compensation.

A different but no less confusing interpretation was given to a clause in another conflict-related case, *LESI v Algeria*. Here, the tribunal held that the situation of revolution triggered the application of the basic armed conflict clause which, as *lex specialis*, excluded the application of a more general FPS provision.[198] In the tribunal's view, the state was consequently only obliged to provide investors with a national or MFN treatment rather than a 'superior' FPS.[199] It is easy to see how the tribunal's interpretation was led by the peculiar wording of Article 4.5 of the Algeria–Italy BIT which, unlike standard basic armed conflict clauses, does not expressly link the non-discriminatory treatment to the payment of compensation.[200] However, the tribunal failed to interpret the clause in its context; namely the preceding paragraph of the same provision, to which the armed conflict clause refers ('bénéficient, de la part de ce dernier'), concerns payment of compensation. It

[196] See n 125.
[197] *AMT* (n 21) para 6.14.
[198] *LESI* (n 22) para 177.
[199] ibid paras 174–75.
[200] The tribunal cited Art 4.5 of the Algeria–Italy BIT:

> Les nationaux ou personnes morales de l'un des Etats contractants dont les investissements auront subi des pertes dues à la guerre ou à tout autre conflit armé, révolution, état d'urgence national ou révolte survenus sur le territoire de l'autre Etat contractant, bénéficient, de la part de ce dernier, d'un traitement non moins favorable que celui accordé à ses propres nationaux ou personnes morales ou à ceux de la nation la plus favorisée.

ibid, para 173. In Italian version, the provision appears under paragraph 6.

follows from this that the basic armed conflict clause in question, despite its quirky wording common to early Italian BITs,[201] limits the non-discriminatory treatment to the payment of conflict-related compensation and does not establish a ground for finding a state's liability for those losses.

(b) Advanced armed conflict clause v FPS

Less certain is the added value of the advanced clause when compared to FPS. Both standards provide protection against physical violence in times of conflict. In contrast to FPS provisions, the application of advanced armed conflict clauses is limited to cases in which investment losses are caused by a host state's 'forces or authorities'. This condition may complicate the successful application of the clause, as it is often unclear during hostilities whether damage was caused by state or non-state actors,[202] or it may be difficult to prove that acts of members of a state organ are actually attributable to a host state. The latter challenge was presented to the tribunal in *AMT v Zaire*, which had to decide if looting and destruction of the investor's property by unpaid Zairean soldiers were the acts committed by the state forces or authorities within Article IV(2) of the Zaire–US BIT.[203] While the tribunal refused to apply the advanced clause and ultimately decided the claim on other legal grounds, it was inclined to conclude that the acts of soldiers were not attributable to the government since they 'acted individually without any one being able to show either that they were organized or that they were under order'.[204] A more detailed and persuasive analysis was offered in a Separate Opinion, in which the arbitrator Golsong argued that according to the rules of attribution under the law of state responsibility, acts of soldiers who were wearing official uniforms, using army weapons and vehicles in the course of lootings, and brought the stolen goods back to the army premises, should indeed be treated as those of the state, and hence the armed conflict clause ought to have been applied.[205]

If one subscribes to the view that FPS provisions only cover injuries caused by non-state actors, the advanced clause would fill the gap and provide an additional protection against the physical interference of a host state's forces. Although some tribunals supported this narrow interpretation of the FPS,[206] the prevailing and

[201] See n 146.
[202] *AAPL* (n 23).
[203] *AMT* (n 21) paras 6.15–19.
[204] ibid para 7.08.
[205] ibid, Statement of Individual Opinion of Heribert Golsong, para 15. This view reflects *ultra vires* acts regulated under Art 7 of the ARS. Golsong supported his arguments with several authorities, e.g. the *Caire Case* in which the French–Mexican Claims Commission found that a murder of an alien by members of Mexican forces was attributable to Mexico, despite the fact that the perpetrators exceeded the limits of their competences. The Commission stressed that what was relevant in considering attribution was that the perpetrators in the course of their acting at least appeared as state officials, or they used 'powers or measures appropriate for their official character'. See *Caire Case* (*France v Mexico*) (1929) 5 UNRIAA 516, 531; *Velásquez Rodríguez v Honduras* Judgment of the IACtHR of 29 July 1988 para 170.
[206] See e.g. *El Paso* (n 93) para 524; *Ulysseas v Ecuador* UNCITRAL, Final Award, 12 June 2012, para 272; *Eastern Sugar* (n 42) paras 203–07.

more convincing view is that the standard provides protection against both non-state and state actors.[207] This substantive overlap calls for a clarification of the relationship between the two provisions when included in the same investment treaty.

The *AAPL* tribunal treated the FPS provision as a more general law vis-à-vis the armed conflict clause. The tribunal appears to have agreed with the view of the dissenting arbitrator, who held that the FPS provision had been displaced by the armed conflict clause that was specifically meant to regulate conflict situations.[208] Arbitrator Asante argued that the advanced armed conflict clause as *lex specialis* 'must prevail as the definitive and exhaustive source of liability in respect of the conduct of the armed forces of the host State'.[209] In other words, if the investor sustained losses due to the host state's interference in the context of conflict, this provision would be the only source for the determination of liability. This interpretation is accurate only in part. It is hard to object to the view that an advanced armed conflict clause is a more special norm given the different levels of specialty permeating it. The specialty of the provision is reflected in five elements: (1) the type of situations in which the provision is applicable (only in defined violent situations); (2) the type of subject that can be the perpetrator of the injury (only the host state's forces); (3) the type of injuries for which the provision can be invoked (requisition and destruction of private property); (4) defined situations from which a state can escape liability (destruction of property in combat action or when required by necessity); and (5) the standard of compensation (different standard and methods of payment of compensation).

This is in stark contrast to a very succinct and broad wording of a FPS provision. The specificity of the clause indicates that the parties to the treaty wanted the provision to primarily regulate the situations enclosed therein. This is understandable due to the politically sensitive nature of the clause as it defines the limits of the host state's freedom in protecting its most vital interests. The added value of the provision for the host state is that, unlike the FPS provision, it expressly provides for exceptions to the liability for the conduct of the state's forces in the course of conflict. It would thus appear safe to conclude that when conflict-related injuries to the investor are incurred by the host state's forces, the primary recourse for remedy would be the advanced armed conflict clause.

However, contrary to Asante's argument, it is submitted that the FPS provision is not made redundant by the armed conflict clause. As a general rule, it continues to provide protection in cases not encompassed in the advanced armed conflict clause, in particular in situations when damage has been caused by non-state actors. More importantly, the advanced armed conflict clause does not exhaust the

[207] See e.g. *Biwater* (n 27) para 730; *Frontier* (n 52) para 261; *Parkerings* (n 52) para 355.
[208] *AAPL*, Dissenting Opinion (n 23) 584.
[209] ibid 585. A similar argument was advocated by arbitrator Golsong in *AMT* case. See Statement of Individual Opinion (n 21) para 6.

obligation of the host state to exercise due diligence in protecting investors with respect to its own organs. The fact that the investor's property was destroyed in a combat action or due to the necessity of the situation precludes the finding of liability under the advanced armed conflict clause. However, this should not mean that the state cannot be held liable for failing to protect investors under the FPS clause. The due diligence obligation is not limited by the exceptions defined in armed conflict clauses. It is a broader concept, which, as explained above, also entails an obligation to undertake certain precautionary measures against potential losses that may emerge in a combat action or out of necessity.[210] This can apply also, or particularly, in situations when it is impossible to ascertain who caused the injury, but is clear that the damage could have been prevented or minimized had the state exercised its duty of care, for example by issuing warnings to investors before launching the forceful operation. While such were the facts in the *AAPL* case, the majority did not feel comfortable rejecting Asante's view that the armed conflict clause completely displaced the FPS provision. The tribunal's indecision led to the legally inaccurate reliance on the basic armed conflict clause to arrive at the customary international law standard of due diligence, while the same could have been achieved by the straightforward application of the FPS provision.

D. Other Relevant Protections

While FPS provisions and armed conflict clauses are specifically designed to address losses sustained due to forcible interference, other treaty provisions may also provide investors with a remedy, in particular the prohibition of expropriation without compensation and the FET standard.[211] The following sections provide a brief analysis of these provisions in the light of their relevance in the context of conflict-related injuries.

1. Expropriation

The general rule of customary international law that has evolved over time and is encapsulated in most treaties allows expropriation under the condition that it is accompanied by compensation, is non-discriminatory, pursues a public purpose, and is in accordance with due process.[212] Expropriation can be either direct

[210] See Section 4 B.1.b. and Chapter 6 C.2.

[211] In pending cases emerging from conflicts in Egypt and Ukraine, these provisions have been reportedly invoked by investors. See Chapter 1, nn 6–8.

[212] For an overview, see J Cox, *Expropriation in Investment Treaty Arbitration* (OUP 2019); Newcombe and Paradell, *Law and Practice* (n 33) 321–98; Dolzer and Schreuer, *Principles* (n 56) 98–126; McLachlan et al, *Substantive Principles* (n 32) 359–412; Salacuse, *Law of Investment Treaties* (n 32) 313–57. See e.g. 2012 US Model BIT Art 6; Canada–Benin BIT (2013) Art 11.

(a host state openly seizes the property and transfers title to the private property to itself) or indirect (a host state's measures have as their effect the deprivation of an investor's property or its benefits). The taking of foreign, in particular enemy, investors' assets, has been a frequent measure to which states have resorted in conflict and post-conflict periods. Direct expropriation, which takes place during an armed conflict, is often described as confiscation. During the post-conflict period, which often sees a new regime assume power, expropriations may take the form of nationalizations, encompassing entire industries of the economy.[213]

Indirect expropriation must be distinguished from governmental regulatory or targeted measures not requiring compensation. In the context of conflict, a state may take a variety of measures that could prevent investors from using or enjoying their property on the grounds of maintaining public order or protecting national security. For example, it may sequestrate an investor's property to prevent its use by an enemy state, it may physically block access to an investor's premises, freeze the investor's assets, deny visas required for technical staff, or introduce war taxes. Do such measures amount to indirect expropriation?

As a general rule, the protection against expropriation applies to governmental measures that deprive investors of their ownership or control of, or substantial benefits from investment, regardless of the form of expropriation (including nationalization, confiscation, sequestration, seizure, attachment, or any other measure producing similar effects).[214] Arbitral tribunals have attempted to draw the line between indirect expropriation and non-compensable measures in a number of cases, often reaching different conclusions.[215] Some have focussed solely on the impact that the measure had on the investment ('sole effect' doctrine),[216] while others held that the state's intent and public purpose of the measure should be taken into account,[217] sometimes relying on proportionality as a technique to balance the opposing positions.[218] The last two approaches provide a fair room for

[213] Newcombe and Paradell (n 33) 324. A recent example is the nationalization programme in Egypt, in which the national courts ordered the post-revolution government to nationalize the investments that had been privatized by the overthrown regime. See M Fick, 'Egypt Drags Its Feet in Privatisation Tussle' (*Reuters*, 29 May 2013) <http:// in.reuters.com/article/2013/05/29/egypt-renationalisation-idINL6N0DX07420130529> accessed 21 March 2015.

[214] On the scope of expropriation see e.g. ACP-CEE 2172/92 of the Council of the European Communities, 'Community Position on Investment Protection Principles in the African, Caribbean and Pacific States' (Brussels, 3 November 1992) which was drafted to provide advice for the negotiation of bilateral treaties, cited in *Patrick Mitchell v Democratic Republic of Congo* ICSID Case no ARB/99/7, Annulment Decision, 1 November 2006, para 52, n 22.

[215] To minimize the unpredictability, some investment treaties stipulate the criteria for indirect expropriation, see e.g. 2012 US Model BIT, Annex B, para 4; 2004 Canada Model BIT, Annex B.13(1).

[216] See e.g. *Southern Pacific Properties Ltd v Arab Republic of Egypt* ICSID Case no ARB/84/3, Award, 20 May 1992, para 227; *Compañia del Desarrollo de Santa Elena, SA v. Costa Rica* ICSID Case no ARB/96/1, Final Award, 17 February 2000, para 72; *Metalclad Corp v Mexico* ICSID Case no ARB(AF)/97/1, Award, 30 August 2000, para 103; *Vivendi* (n 27) para 7.5.21; *Patrick Mitchell v Democratic Republic of Congo* ICSID Case no ARB/99/7, Award, 9 February 2004, para 72.

[217] *Methanex Corp v United States of America* UNCITRAL, Award, 3 August 2005, Part IV, Chapter D, para 15; *Saluka* (n 26) paras 254–65, 275–76; *Chemtura* (n 76) para 266.

[218] See n 89.

exemption of a state's measures taken for security reasons from the obligation to pay compensation. They are in line with another avenue of defence, namely the police powers doctrine. As explained above,[219] the doctrine according to which the non-discriminatory measures taken within the state's general regulatory or administrative powers with an aim to protect legitimate public objectives do not qualify as indirect expropriation, has found wide support in investment jurisprudence, [220] often as a reflection of customary international law. Measures that states take in order to maintain public order and safety have been typically found to fall within the police powers exception.

In several historical cases, host states that imposed restrictions on foreign investment in times of conflict were considered to have been merely exercising their sovereign police powers and thus no compensation was ordered.[221] For example, the Iran–US Claims Tribunal decided that setting a limitation on the type of cargo that investors could unload was a reasonable and legitimate measure during a time of civil unrest.[222] The temporary transfer of enemy-owned investments under the administration of the government-appointed custodian on security or safety grounds could be similarly justified under the doctrine. Here, an important consideration will be the duration of the measure. As emphasized by the Iran–US Claims Tribunal, an appointment of temporary management by a host state will amount to expropriation unless such 'deprivation is not merely ephemeral'.[223] What is 'ephemeral' will depend on the facts of each case.[224] For example, in *Wena v Egypt*, a forceful seizure and possession of the investor's hotels for nearly a year was considered 'more than an ephemeral interference in the use of that property or with the enjoyment of its benefits' and thus compensation was due.[225] Similarly, in *Mitchell v Congo*, the tribunal held that the sealing of the investor's premises, seizure of its documents, and the imprisonment of two employees for more than eight months, which resulted in the loss of the investor's clients, could not 'be qualified as being of an exclusively transitory nature' and was thus deemed a measure equivalent to expropriation.[226] In considering the temporariness of the measure, rigid interpretation that is oblivious to the purpose of the measure and the context in which it was

[219] See Section 4 B.1.b.

[220] See e.g. *Marvin Feldman* (n 76) para 103; *Saluka* (n 26) para 255; *Lauder* (n 27) para 198; *Tecmed* (n 18) para 115; *Chemtura* (n 76) para 266; *Quiborax* (n 76) para 202; *Les Laboratoires Servier, SAS Biofarma, SAS, Arts et Techniques du Progrès SAS v Poland* PCA, UNCITRAL, Final Award, 14 February 2012, para 276; *Renée Rose* (n 76) para 476; *Philip Morris* (n 76) para 295.

[221] See e.g. *Poggioli Case (Italy v Venezuela)* (1903) 10 RIAA 669, 691; *Parsons Case (Great Britain v US)* (1925) 6 RIAA 165, 166.

[222] *Sea-Land Service Inc v Iran* (1984) 6 Iran–USCTR 149.

[223] *Phelps Dodge v Iran (1986)* 10 Iran–USCTR 130, para 22; *Tippetts, Abbett, McCarthym Stratton v TAMS-AFFA* (1984) 6 Iran–USCTR 219, 225–26.

[224] *Azurix* (n 27) para 313; *Tecmed* (n 18) para 116; *SD Myers v Canada* UNCITRAL Arbitration, First Partial Award, 13 November 2000, para 287.

[225] *Wena* (n 16) para 99.

[226] *Mitchell*, Award (n 216) para 72.

taken should be avoided.[227] For example, if a state sequestrates a private investment with the view to deny potential benefits to the enemy party, such a measure can last for the whole duration of the conflict, which can be as quick as a few days or as long as several months or even years. It would be contrary to the practice of war tribunals to consider such measures as indirect expropriation merely because of their duration.[228]

In this regard, the *Mitchell* award,[229] in particular, is problematic because the tribunal based its decision solely on the impact the measures had on investment while ignoring the intent of the government and the public purpose driving the measures (according to the authorities, the investor had ties with the rebellion against the government and thus posed a threat to national security), and broader contextual circumstances (Congo was in a state of war).[230] The tribunal concluded that it did not have enough information to assess whether the government had a power to exercise its belligerent rights in that situation.[231] The more appropriate approach, endorsed in recent arbitral practice, would be to acknowledge Congo's 'police powers' and assess whether they were exercised proportionately (taking account not only of the duration and economic effect of the measure, but also the legitimacy of the objective, the ongoing armed conflict, and the emergency in the context of which the measure was adopted).[232] Following this approach, the tribunal would have had to determine whether the measure was suitable (capable of achieving the objective) and necessary (whether alternative measures interfering less with the investor's right would be possible) before engaging in the balancing exercise (proportionality *stricto sensu*) to establish whether the impact of the measure was proportionate to the aim that the state sought to achieve.

A helpful analogy for further guidance can be drawn from the human rights case law regarding the non-conviction-based confiscation or civil forfeiture which reflects a state's police powers. Human rights courts have held that a state authority can seize an individual's assets as a precautionary and preventive security measure as long as it can prove that those assets were likely to be used for facilitating unlawful conduct. In order to prevent abusive and arbitrary actions, the human rights courts have factored certain procedural requirements into the proportionality

[227] *Achmea BV v Slovakia* UNCITRAL, PCA Case no 2008-13, Final Award, 7 December 2012, para 289.

[228] See Chapter 2 C.1.a, in particular jurisprudence of the Eritrea–Ethiopia Claims Commission, e.g. *Eritrea's Civilian Claims* (n 166) para 128.

[229] The award was later annulled on the grounds that the law firm did not constitute an 'investment'. *Mitchell*, Annulment (n 214) paras 25–33.

[230] *Mitchell*, Award (n 216) para 74; *Mitchell*, Annulment (n 214) paras 51, 53, 56.

[231] *Mitchell*, Award (n 216) para 74.

[232] For an analysis of how investment tribunals have utilized variants of the proportionality analysis, see C Henckels, *Proportionality and Deference* (n 89) 83–171. See also A Stone Sweet and J Mathews, 'Proportionality Balancing and Global Constitutionalism' (2008) 47 Colum J Transnatl L 73; E Leonhardsen, 'Looking for Legitimacy: Exploring Proportionality Analysis in Investment Treaty Arbitration' (2012) 3(1) JIDS 95, 112.

equation.[233] In particular, they stressed that such measures had to be adopted by competent authorities and be supervised by judicial officials in line with due process (in *Mitchell*, the government measures were eventually overruled and the return of the assets was ordered by the military court);[234] that governmental authorities had to provide reasons justifying the measure (the Congolese authorities provided what they thought were sufficient security reasons justifying the intervention);[235] and that there should be no delays in returning the seized assets (this was a point of disagreement between the parties which the *Mitchell* tribunal rejected as irrelevant).[236]

Furthermore, in appraising Congo's measures, the tribunal would have to afford some deference to the government's analysis of the situation in which the police powers were exercised.[237] Instead of deferring to the factual and legal assessment of Congolese military authorities in the course of the armed conflict, the arbitrators held that they lacked sufficient information to themselves make a retrospective assessment about the legitimacy of the public purpose.[238] While such determinations about the decisions taken in times of security crises are undoubtedly extremely difficult,[239] the tribunal should have reviewed the measure on the basis of information available to the Congolese authorities on 5 March 1999, the day when the measures had been taken.[240] Given the importance of the protected public interest (national security), the context in which the measures was taken (war), and arbitrators' lack of expertise (none of them was an expert on public international law let alone security studies), a more deferential approach in ascertaining whether the measures fell within legitimate police powers would have been more apposite.[241] This is not to suggest that the tribunal should have given the Congolese authorities a blank check for their action. The fact that the measures included the imprisonment of

[233] See *Chaparro Álvarez and Lapo Iñiguez v Ecuador* Judgment of the IACtHR of 21 November 2017, paras 188, 197, 204, 209; *Memoli v Argentina* Judgment of the IACtHR of 22 August 2013, para 180; *Gogitidze and Others v Georgia* App no 36862/05, Judgment (ECtHR, 12 May 2015) paras 108–13; *Paulet v The United Kingdom* App no 6219/08, Judgment (ECtHR, 13 May 2014) para 65.

[234] *Mitchell*, Award (n 216) para 62.

[235] ibid para 74.

[236] ibid para 63.

[237] C Henckels, 'Indirect Expropriation and the Right to Regulate: Revisiting Proportionality Analysis and the Standard of Review in Investor-State Arbitration' (2012) 15(1) JIEL 223, 240.

[238] *Mitchell*, Award (n 216) para 74.

[239] *Metalpar SA and Buen Aire SA v Argentine Republic* ICISD Case no ARB/03/5, Award, 6 June 2008, para 198.

[240] The standard that the assessment of a state's action must be based on the circumstances and knowledge of the state or a commander at the time when the action was taken, was confirmed in Nuremberg trials. See *Hostage case* (*US v List et al*) (American Military Tribunal, Nuremberg, 1948) 11 NMT 1253, 1295–96. See also W Boothby, *Law of Targeting* (OUP 2012) 172; Y Dinstein, *The Conduct of Hostilities under the Law of International Armed Conflict* (3rd edn, CUP 2016) 166; G Corn, 'Humanitarian Regulation of Hostilities: The Decisive Element of Context' (2018) 51(3) VJTL 763, 766; M Newton, 'Reframing the Proportionality Principle' (2018) 51(3) VJTL 867, 882; See Chapter 2, n 155.

[241] Henckels, 'Revisiting Proportionality' (n 237) 245 (observing that more sensitive exercise of deference in situations concerning national security has been endorsed by ECtHR and European Court of Justice).

two employees could have importantly informed the proportionality analysis as to whether police powers were exercised appropriately.[242]

The last criterion commonly relied on by tribunals when identifying indirect expropriation is the effect that the measure had on the investor's reasonable expectations.[243] In other words, investors need to prove that their decision to invest in the host state was based on a state of affairs which did not anticipate the challenged governmental measures. Establishing the breach of legitimate and reasonable expectations is particularly difficult when the governmental measure is taken in the context of a volatile situation. On several occasions, tribunals stressed that investment treaties do not provide blank insurance for economic and political risks.[244] In the Iran–US Claims Tribunal case of *Starrett Housing Corp v Iran*, the US housing corporation challenged a series of government actions related to the Iranian Revolution, including a reduction in the project's work force owing to conditions in Iran, strikes and shortages of materials, the collapse of the banking system, the freezing of bank accounts, harassment of Starrett personnel by armed Revolutionary Guards, etc. The tribunal rejected the claim that several revolution-related governmental measures, either individually or taken together, constituted expropriation, and noted that:

> . . . investors in Iran, like investors in all other countries, have to assume a risk that the country might experience strikes, lock-outs, disturbances, changes of economic and political system and even revolution. That any of these risks materialised does not necessarily mean that property rights affected by such events can be deemed to have been taken. A revolution as such does not entitle investors to compensation under international law.[245]

In sum, some degree of political risk is inherent to the commercial nature of the investment, thus the assessment of investment-backed expectations for the purposes of determining the breach of the expropriation standard will be reasonably attuned

[242] As explained in Chapter 2 D, in the human rights field, in particular, the relevance of protected interests has been often factored in the assessment of proportionality of the measure. The detention of investor's employees (i.e. violation of the right to movement) would thus invite a stricter proportionality test than solely confiscation of the property. See e.g. *De Tommaso v Italy* App no 43395/09, Judgment (ECtHR, 23 February 2017) Joint Concurring Opinion of Judges Raimondi, Villiger, Šikuta, Keller, and Kjølbro, para 18. Generally, see J Boucht, *The Limits of Asset Confiscation: On the Legitimacy of Extended Appropriation of Criminal Proceeds* (Hart Publishing, Oxford, 2017) 174.

[243] See e.g. *Marvin Feldman* (n 76); Newcombe and Paradell, *Law and Practice* (n 33) 324. The condition has been included in some investment treaties, e.g. Canada–Peru BIT (2006) Annex B.13(1).

[244] See e.g. *MTD Equity Sdn Bhd and MTD Chile SA v Republic of Chile* ICSID Case no ARB/01/7, Award, 25 May 2004, para 178; *Maffezini v The Kingdom of Spain* ICSID Case no ARB/97/7, Award, 13 November 2000, para 64; *Waste Management Inc v United Mexican States* ICSID Case no ARB(AF)/00/3, Award, 30 April 2004, para 160.

[245] *Starrett Housing Corp v Iran (Case No 24)* (1983) 4 Iran–USCTR 122, 156.

with the broader political circumstances of the host state. A similar view has also been taken with respect to the content of the FET provision.

2. Fair and Equitable Treatment

The FET standard has been touted as one of the most important provisions in investment treaties, enabling investors to challenge a wide array of governmental actions that affect their investment.[246] The provision has been invoked by investors most frequently and with the best record of success.[247] Typically, tribunals have held that FET provides obligations to make all laws, regulations, and policies clear to foreign investors in advance; to maintain a stable and predictable legal framework; to behave in good faith and respect investors' legitimate expectations; to refrain from discrimination; and to provide due process.[248] In the context of a conflict, a host state's actions may be challenged with regard to the freezing of assets of investors coming from an enemy country, the harassment of investors coming from an enemy country or supporting an enemy regime, and the passing of laws and policies with a view to adjusting to extraordinary circumstances, among others.

During a conflict, or in the period immediately thereafter, host states often make the legal and policy changes that are necessary to adjust to their new realities. Should these legislative measures adversely affect investments, investors may be poised to invoke the FET provision, arguing that their expectations as to the stability of the host state's legal regime have been frustrated. Determining the scope of the investor's legitimate expectations will play a critical role. Whether the legitimate expectations of the investor will be assessed against the circumstances prevailing in the host state is not completely clear, as demonstrated by the conflicting conclusions in investment jurisprudence.[249] Some tribunals have held that the FET standard provides a guarantee of a stable legal environment and thus host states

[246] For an overview, see R Dolzer, 'Fair and Equitable Treatment' (2005) 39 Intl Lawy 87, 90; A Diehl, *The Core Standard in International Investment Protection: Fair and Equitable Treatment* (Kluwer 2012); McLachlan et al, *Substantive Principles* (n 32) 296–329; Salacuse, *Law of Investment Treaties* (n 32) 241–67.

[247] According to UNCTAD, the breach of the FET standard has been alleged in 433 cases, and found in 113 cases. See UNCTAD, Investment Dispute Settlement Navigator, <https://investmentpolicyhub.unctad.org/ISDS/FilterByBreaches> accessed 18 December 2018.

[248] Dolzer and Schreuer, *Principles* (n 56) 130–60.

[249] Tribunals held that a state's circumstances do not affect the fair and equitable treatment standard in e.g. *Sempra* (n 125) paras 303, 396; *Pantechniki* (n 21) para 76; *Tecmed* (n 18) para 154. On the other hand, tribunals examined the circumstances of the host state in e.g. *Bayindir Insaat Turizm Ticaret Ve Sanayi AS v Islamic Republic of Pakistan* ICSID Case no ARB/03/29, Award, 27 August 2009, paras 192–95; *Duke Energy Electroquil Partners v Republic of Ecuador* ICISD Case no ARB/04/19, Award, 18 August 2008, para 340; *National Grid* (n 125) para 179; *Parkerings* (n 52) paras 333–35; *Biwater* (n 27) para 217. See also the discussion on this subject in N Gallus, 'The Fair and Equitable Treatment Standard and the Circumstances of the State' in C Brown and K Miles (eds), *Evolution in Investment Treaty Law and Arbitration* (CUP 2011) 223; U Kriebaum, 'The Relevance of Economic and Political Conditions for Protection under Investment Treaties' (2011) 10 L & Prac of Intl Ct & Trib 383.

are not allowed to make material changes to law or policy governing foreign investment.[250] Other tribunals have upheld the opposite view. For example, the tribunal in *Duke Energy Electroquil Partners v Republic of Ecuador* contended that the investor's legitimate expectations must be assessed by taking 'into account all circumstances, including not only the facts surrounding the investment, but also the political, socioeconomic, cultural and historical conditions prevailing in the host State'.[251]

In reality, much will depend on the type of conduct of the state that is being challenged. For example, if the ground for invoking the FET standard is the denial of justice, the fact that the breach occurred in the context of a conflict or a post-conflict transition is unlikely to inform the determination of the state's liability. As explained by Arbitrator Paulsson in *Pantechniki v Albania*, regardless of the circumstances, foreign investors are always 'entitled to decision-making which is neither xenophobic nor arbitrary'.[252] Specifically, the ability to abide by this obligation does not hinge on the state's physical infrastructure, which may indeed be threatened under extraordinary circumstances, but rather on the 'human factor of obedience to the rule of law' which remains intact even in times of conflict.[253]

On the other hand, when in times of conflict or transition a host state is prompted to pass certain measures (e.g. freeze the assets of enemy investors) and make changes to its laws (e.g. introduce new tariffs or increase taxes), the better approach is to consider the influence of the broader political and factual circumstances of the FET. In this vein, the tribunal in *Toto v Lebanon* held that the investor's legitimate expectations as regards the stability of the investment's environment could not remain unaffected by the circumstances in a country in transition (in that period, there were bomb and terrorist attacks, a war with Israel, and two episodes of intense internal fighting in Lebanon).[254] The tribunal thus concluded that 'the post-civil war situation in Lebanon, with substantial economic challenges and colossal reconstruction efforts, did not justify legal expectations that custom duties would remain unchanged'.[255] Similarly, the tribunal in *Bayindir v Pakistan* rejected the investor's claim that his reasonable and legitimate expectations had been breached,

[250] See e.g. *Petroleum v Czech Republic* UNCITRAL, Final Award, 12 November 2010, para 285; *Tecmed* (n 18) para 154.

[251] *Duke Energy* (n 249) para 340.

[252] *Pantechniki* (n 21) para 76.

[253] ibid. It is worth reiterating the legal distinction between different types of enforcement activities. While the state compliance with some enforcement obligations (e.g. investigation and apprehension of perpetrators as part of the duty to protect) is measured against the flexible standard of due diligence, the fulfilment of other enforcement obligations (e.g. trial and execution of penalty) is not affected by external factors. See Pissilo-Mazzeschi, 'Due Diligence Rule' (n 52) 30.

[254] *Toto Costruzioni Generali SpA v Lebanon* ICSID Case no ARB/07/12, Award, 7 June 2012, paras 242, 245.

[255] ibid para 245.

by measuring the latter against the 'volatility of the political conditions prevailing in Pakistan'.[256]

In sum, tribunals appear to increasingly support the view that the legal expectations of investors with regard to the scope of protection they are afforded under the treaty will be assessed in the light of the circumstances during or after the conflict. In other words, investors have to adjust their legal expectations to align with the conditions of the host state. This could enable states to retain some degree of legal flexibility in dealing with the consequences of an extraordinary burden imposed by armed conflict.

E. Preliminary Conclusions

This chapter has shown that the substantive standards purporting to protect investors' physical security largely mirror the customary rules on the treatment of aliens. In the same vein, the tensions between investment expectations, on the one hand, and the state security interests and their individual circumstances, on the other hand, echo the nineteenth-century theories on state responsibility for conflict-related injuries to aliens. It has been argued that the treaty protections are not absolute. While host states are obliged to refrain from forceful interferences, this obligation is limited by their right to pursue measures necessary for protecting their security (as ensured by the police powers doctrine, exceptions in advanced armed conflict clauses etc). Similarly, while they are obliged to protect investors from the violence of non-state actors, fulfilment of this obligation is measured against the relative standard of due diligence. This notwithstanding, inconsistent and flawed interpretations in many arbitral awards may prompt reliance on other legal mechanisms with a view to protect states' freedom to act and regulate in times of conflict. The next chapter turns the focus to them.

[256] *Bayindir* (n 249) para 193. In a similar vein, the tribunal in *Parkerings* stated that in evaluating an investor's legitimate expectations regarding stability, the political environment at the time of investment had to be considered. For states in transition, legislative changes are more likely to occur. See *Parkerings* (n 52) paras 333–35.

5

Host State's Defences against Conflict-Related Investment Claims

A. Introduction

The previous chapter has shown that the scope of investment protections in times of conflict is limited, and that investment tribunals can take the circumstances in which losses arise into account. This notwithstanding, host states have often been held liable for breaching investment treaty protections. Inconsistent interpretations of treaty standards tend to create uncertainty, and therefore states may prefer to avoid justifying their measures within the scope of a treaty protection. Instead, they can try to prevent the measure from being subjected to the review of an investment tribunal in the first place. They can achieve this by invoking certain defence mechanisms that can either preclude the tribunal from hearing the claim and assessing the challenged state's measure, or, alternatively, preclude the state's responsibility for the found violation. These defences, which can be found in investment treaties and the general law of state responsibility, can prove to be vital for preserving the discretion of states in addressing threats to their national security.

This chapter seeks to examine the defence mechanisms that states are most likely to invoke against a conflict-related investment claim. Most reliable are those negotiated in applicable investment treaties. Security exceptions, in particular, are primarily designed with the purpose of addressing military threats. While in practice they have mostly been invoked with respect to economic crises, and subject to much controversy, their application to armed conflicts is not necessarily less problematic. This chapter also analyses the defences available in the general law of state responsibility, namely necessity, *force majeure*, and countermeasures. While their treatment in practice has been inconsistent, it is argued that their relevance for conflict-related claims is limited.

B. Security Exceptions

It is often argued that one of the strongest defence mechanisms that a state can negotiate in the drafting of an investment treaty is the security exception,[1] typically

[1] Another potentially relevant provision is the denial of benefits clause which enables the host state to refuse benefits of the investment treaty to companies owned by investors coming from an 'enemy'

The Protection of Foreign Investment in Times of Armed Conflict. First Edition. Jure Zrilič.
Published 2019 by Oxford University Press.

included in the non-precluded measures (NPM) clauses.[2] Such exceptions commonly specify that nothing in the investment treaty precludes a party from adopting measures that are 'necessary for' or 'directed to' safeguarding certain objectives such as essential security interests, national security, public order, or international peace and security. The rationale underlying the clause is similar to that of derogation clauses in human rights treaties, namely to secure a state's freedom to take certain measures necessary for the protection of its vital interests in extraordinary crisis situations. If the exception applies, the government is permitted to address the security concerns and military exigencies without breaching the investment treaty. Consequently, a host state will not be liable for losses that investors have suffered as a consequence of measures that meet the requirements formulated in an exception. As noted by White-Burke and von Staden, 'security clauses perform a risk-allocation function, transferring the costs of harming an investment from host States to investors in exceptional circumstances'.[3]

So far, only a minority of investment treaties contain security exceptions.[4] Among those that prominently feature these are the US investment treaties, following the tradition of US post-war treaties of friendship, commerce, and navigation (FCN).[5] This is not surprising, as the introduction of security exceptions in economic agreements was in fact a result of American Cold War anxieties and related concerns that the objectives of free trade and investment promotion would override military and security considerations, enmeshed with ideological underpinnings.[6]

While the US post-war programme of investment and trade agreements was formally motivated by the desire to sustain world peace through economic prosperity and co-dependence,[7] there was also a growing concern that another global war was

country that is not party to the investment treaty in question. Due to its limited scope and restrictive conditions, the provision is not discussed on this occasion.

[2] For a general overview, see W Burke-White and A von Staden, 'Investment Protection in Extraordinary Times: The Interpretation and Application of Non-Precluded Measures Provisions in Bilateral Investment Treaties' (2008) 48(2) Va J Intl L 308; A Newcombe and L Paradell, *Law and Practice of Investment Treaties* (Kluwer 2009) 482–500; UNCTAD, 'The Protection of National Security in IIAs' (UN 2009) Doc UNCTAD/DIAE/IA/2008/5 (UNCTAD National Security Report).

[3] Burke-White and von Staden, 'Non-Precluded Measures' (n 2) 314.

[4] According to UNCTAD, 15 per cent of investment treaties contain them. UNCTAD, International Investment Agreements Navigator <https://investmentpolicyhub.unctad.org/IIA/mappedContent> accessed 18 December 2018. For similar figures, see Burke-White and von Staden (n 2) 313; Newcombe and Paradell, *Law and Practice* (n 2) 488; UNCTAD National Security Report.

[5] See e.g. US–Italy FCN Treaty (1948) Art XXIV; US–Greece FCN Treaty (1948) Art XXIII. See also K Vandevelde, *United States Investment Treaties: Policy and Practice* (Kluwer Law and Taxation 1992) 222–27.

[6] K Vandevelde, *The First Bilateral Investment Treaties: U.S. Postwar Friendship, Commerce, and Navigation Treaties* (OUP 2017) 145; K Vandevelde, *Bilateral Investment Treaties: History, Policy, and Interpretation* (OUP 2010) 180; T Zeiler, *Free Trade, Free World, The Advent of GATT* (The University of North Carolina Press 1999) 64–65.

[7] See Chapter 7 B.1.

imminent, this time with the Soviet Union. Consequently, it was the priority of US foreign policy to secure wide enough room to wage war with the looming strategic and ideological adversary. This pro-military position was reflected in the negotiation of the Geneva Conventions, where the US, along with the UK, advocated that international humanitarian law (IHL) be drafted permissively, thus trying to ensure that their rights on the battleground would not be curtailed.[8] During the same period, the US was also pushing for the establishment of the International Trade Organization (ITO), which would promote freedom of trade and protection of foreign investment. The drafting history of the US proposal for the ITO Charter (also known as the Havana Charter) reveals a clash between the trade and the war departments as to the scope of a security exception, whereby the latter argued for an expressly self-judging exception that could be invoked at the discretion of the US even when the security interests warranting protection were less than 'essential'.[9] While the ITO project ultimately failed,[10] the investment provisions of the Havana Charter were transposed to the US FCN treaties, with some glaring departures: the language which confers on either party the power to determine whether its actions fall within the exception was absent; and the exception was not limited only to measures 'taken in time of war or other emergency in international relations'.

The abandonment of the reference to international armed conflict from the US FCN security exceptions was indicative of another, probably more controversial, rationale: the protection of Western values against communist ideology that could be spread around the world through revolutionary movements. While the US anxiety about the threat of the communist ideology was well documented during the negotiation of the Geneva Conventions as well as the Havana Charter,[11] the perceived role of security exceptions in fighting the threatening ideology was confirmed in their early invocations.[12] In two cases at the International Court of Justice (ICJ), *Nicaragua* and *Oil Platforms*, the US unsuccessfully relied on the exceptions to justify its unilateral military actions in Nicaragua and Iran, respectively (including mining Nicaraguan ports and attacking its facilities and vessels, and

[8] See O Barsalou, 'Making Humanitarian Law in the Cold: The Cold War, the United State and the Genesis of the Geneva Conventions of 1949' (2008) 11 IILJ Emerging Scholars Paper 11.

[9] Vandevelde, *First Bilateral Investment Treaties* (n 6) ch 3.

[10] The security exception was included in Art 99(1) of the Havana Charter, which stipulated that 'Nothing in this Charter shall be construed . . . to prevent a Member from taking . . . any action which it considers necessary for the protection of its essential security interests, where such action . . . is taken in time of war or other emergency in international relations ...'. Havana Charter for an International Trade Organization (adopted on 24 March 1948, not in force) UN Doc E/Conf.2/78.

[11] See Barsalou, 'Making Humanitarian Law' (n 8) 48; Vandevelde, *First Bilateral Investment Treaties* (n 6).

[12] S Gabriel and V Satish 'US Intervention in Nicaragua: A Success or Failure?' (1990) 51(4) Ind J Pol Sci 565, 568 (describing how the US's support for insurgency in Nicaragua was motivated by the desire to suppress communist ideology in a strategically important region); A Rubinstein, 'The Soviet Union and Iran under Khomeini' (1981) 57(4) Intl Aff 599, 600–01, 614 (describing how the politics of post-revolution Iran was a boost to the Communist Party in Iran and Soviet diplomacy, and how the US feared that the Soviet Union would exploit the Iran–US tensions to expand its influence in the region).

attacking Iranian oil platforms).[13] While the ICJ rejected the US's arguments that the exception is self-judging and held that its invocation was not justified, the arguments of the US government nonetheless revealed the type of situations in which they hoped the security exceptions would be applicable. More recently, in a case concerning the re-imposition of economic sanctions against Iran by the US, the ICJ reiterated that the security exception did not restrict its jurisdiction and indicated that sanctions concerning certain goods could not be justified thereunder.[14] The US expressed dissatisfaction with the ruling by announcing the termination of the treaty of amity with Iran.[15] One can but notice that the US-favoured, broad interpretation of exceptions that permits justification of unilateral forcible (including economic)[16] action outside of US territory is evocative of the interventionist practices of Western powers at the turn of the twentieth century.[17] Viewed in this light, the US FCN security exceptions could be said to present a refined manifestation of the Roosevelt Corollary.[18]

This ideologically dubious background notwithstanding, variations of exceptions (expressly referencing war and hostilities) were included in different multilateral attempts to codify the treatment of foreign investment.[19] While the inclusion of security exceptions in modern investment treaties was initially not popular, suggesting their limited relevance for states in times of armed conflict, recent studies have confirmed that they are common in multilateral agreements and appear in most of the free trade agreements with investment chapters,[20] as well as in bilateral investment treaties (BITs) concluded by a number of major participants

[13] *Military and Paramilitary Activities in and against Nicaragua (Nicaragua v US)* (Merits) [1986] ICJ Rep 14 (*Military and Paramilitary Activities*); *Oil Platforms (Iran v US)* (Judgment) [2003] ICJ Rep 161 (*Oil Platforms*). The invoked provisions were similar in wording to security exceptions in modern BITs (i.e. covering measures necessary to protect essential security interest). See US–Nicaragua Treaty of Friendship, Commerce and Navigation (1956) Art XXI(1)(d); US–Iran Treaty of Amity, Economic Relations and Consular Rights (1955) Art XX(1)(d).

[14] *Alleged Violations of the 1955 Treaty of Amity, Economic Relations, and Consular Rights (Iran v US)* (ICJ, Provisional Measures Order) (3 October 2018) paras 52, 70 (*Sanctions against Iran*).

[15] Secretary of State (Remarks to Media, 3 October 2018) <https://www.state.gov/secretary/remarks/2018/10/286417.htm> accessed 11 December 2018.

[16] In the aftermath of the *Nicaragua* case, during the discussion in the US Senate the concern was invoked that investment treaties could constrain the US freedom to impose economic sanctions on their partners for national security reasons. See J Alvarez, 'Political Protectionism and United States International Investment Obligations in Conflict: The Hazards of Exon-Florio' (1989) 30 Va J Intl L 1, 37–38.

[17] See Chapter 2 B.

[18] ibid. While the US pledged to abandon its interventionist tendencies with the Good Neighbour Policy in 1933, the arguments for Roosevelt Corollary resurfaced again with the start of the Cold War out of fear from the influence of the Soviet communism. See also T Peterson et al, *American Foreign Relations: A History Since 1895, Volume 2* (7th edn, Wadsworth 2010) 162–68.

[19] Abs-Shawcross Draft Convention on Investments Abroad (1960) 9 J Public L 116, Art V; Draft Convention on the International Responsibility of States for Injuries to Aliens, reprinted (1961) in 55 AJIL 545, Art 9 and commentary; OECD Draft Convention on the Protection of Foreign Property (1963) 2 ILM 241, Art 6; OECD Draft Convention on the Protection of Foreign Property (1968) 7 ILM 117, Art 6 (1967 OECD Convention).

[20] UNCTAD National Security Report, 3.

in international investment flows, including Germany, the Belgian–Luxembourg Economic Union, and India.[21] More importantly, there seems to be a notable tendency to include security exceptions in recent investment treaty negotiations.[22]

How effective exceptions are in protecting the state's right to adopt security measures during different types of conflict or the threat thereof depends on how they are drafted or interpreted.[23] In this regard, three aspects are particularly important: first, the scope of the treaty exceptions; second, the degree of autonomy that the provision accords to the state in ascertaining the threat and responding to it; and third, the relations between the exception and other treaty obligations. The following sections discuss them in turn.

1. Scope of Security Exceptions

In investment jurisprudence, the invocation of security exceptions attracted most attention with respect to economic measures. The Argentinian government relied on the defence to justify its policy measures in reaction to the severe economic crisis in 2001–02.[24] In those cases, the tribunals came to different conclusions as to whether the type of economic crisis suffered by Argentina could constitute such a threat to national security as to justify the derogation from the investment treaty protections.[25] More importantly for the purposes of this chapter, however, the tribunals seemed to agree that there was little doubt that the situations that security exceptions primarily covered were those that raised defensive, strategic, and geopolitical concerns, including situations of conflict.[26] What exactly is the type of situation that could give rise to the application of the security exception? This will likely depend on the objective of state measures that fall within the purview of the exception, or in other words, the type of interests protected thereunder. They can be divided into three, to an extent overlapping, groups.

[21] Burke-White and von Staden, 'Non-Precluded Measures' (n 2) 318.

[22] UNCTAD, Recent Trends in IIAs and ISDS (2015) 3; UNCTAD, World Investment Report 2017: Investment and the Digital Economy (2017) 122.

[23] Similarly, UNCTAD National Security Report, 72.

[24] See e.g. *CMS Gas Transmission Company v The Argentine Republic* ICSID Case no ARB/01/08, Award, 12 May 2005, paras 332–78; *CMS v The Argentine Republic* ICSID Case no ARB/01/08, Decision on Annulment, 25 September 2007, paras 101–50; *LG&E Energy Corp v The Argentine Republic* ICSID Case no ARB/02/1, Decision on Liability, 3 October 2006, paras 201–66; *Enron Corp v The Argentine Republic* ICSID Case no ARB/01/03, Award, 22 May 2007, paras 322–42; *Sempra Energy International v The Argentine Republic* ICSID Case no ARB/02/16, Award, 28 September 2007, paras 364–90; *Continental Casualty Company v The Argentine Republic* ICSID Case no ARB/03/9A, Award, 5 September 2008, paras 160–236.

[25] The tribunals in *CMS, Enron*, and *Sempra* held that the exception did not apply, whereas the tribunals in *LG&E* and *Continental Casualty* concluded that the economic crisis was such as to trigger the security exception.

[26] *CMS*, Award (n 24) para 362; *Sempra* (n 24) para 367; *Continental Casualty* (n 24) paras 177, 181.

(a) Protection of a host state's essential security interests

Compared to the FPS provisions and armed conflict clauses discussed above, security exceptions cover the narrowest category of violent situations—in other words, the applicability threshold is the most difficult to reach. Most commonly, the situations in which investment treaty exceptions can be invoked are subsumed under the broad wording 'essential security interests',[27] or 'national security'.[28] For example, the Economic Cooperation Agreement between India and Singapore (2005) provides in Article 6.12:

> 1. Nothing in this Chapter shall be construed: . . .
> b) to prevent a Party from taking any action which it considers necessary for the protection of its essential security interests . . . .[29]

Historically, the concepts of 'essential security interests' and 'national security' have been devised to address precisely the situations of military threats, in particular external ones.[30] While investment tribunals so far grappled only with the question of whether essential security interests cover severe economic crises, it has been uncontested that the situation of armed conflict is one of the examples that may constitute a threat to a state's 'essential security interest' or 'national security'. Whether or not this encompasses conflicts of both international and non-international character may not always be clear, however.

Some investment treaties include security exceptions that are more specific and expressly provide that measures taken for the protection of a state's essential security interest cover only measures 'taken in time of war or other emergency in international relations'.[31] Unless the term 'other emergency in international relations' is broadly interpreted, this provision would not include a non-international armed conflict with a purely local impact.[32] On the other hand, in some treaties the specific phrasing is used to ensure that non-international conflict situations are also covered by the exception. For example, the Israel–Japan BIT expressly

[27] UNCTAD National Security Report, 723. See e.g. 2012 US Model BIT Art 18(2).

[28] See e.g. 2008 UK Model BIT Art 7(1). According to *Oxford English Dictionary*, national security is defined as 'safety of a nation and its people, institutions, etc., especially from military threat or from espionage, terrorism'. UNCTAD National Security Report, 7.

[29] Economic Cooperation Agreement between India and Singapore (2005) Art 6.12. See also Hungary–Russia BIT (2005) Art 2; US–Croatia BIT (1996) Art XV; US–Senegal BIT (1983) Art X(1).

[30] UNCTAD National Security Report, 26. See also *Sempra* (n 24) para 374; *LG&E* (n 24) para 238; *CMS*, Award (n 24) para 360.

[31] See e.g. Austria–Yemen BIT (2003) Art 11(3); Energy Charter Treaty (1994) Art 24(3); Japan–Korea BIT (2002) Art 16(1); OCED, Multilateral Investment Agreement Draft (1998) DAFFE/MAI(98)7/REV1, 76, Part VI, General Exceptions (OECD MAI).

[32] C Schreuer, 'The Protection of Investments in Armed Conflicts' in F Baetens (ed), *Investment Law within International Law: Integrationist Perspectives* (CUP 2013) 3, 18. However, for a relatively broad conception of 'emergency in international relations' in a similarly worded security exception in GATT Art XXI(b)(iii), see the recent WTO decision *Russia – Measures concerning Traffic in Transit*, Panel Report (5 April 2019) WT/DS512/R, para 7.76 (noting that '[a]n emergency in international relations would . . . appear to refer generally to a situation of armed conflict, or of latent armed conflict, or of heightened tension or crisis, or of general instability engulfing or surrounding a state').

confirms that both international and internal armed conflict fall within the scope of the exception.[33] The Association Agreement between the EU and Egypt (2001) goes a step further and refers to the events of 'serious internal disturbances affecting the maintenance of law and order', which arguably covers even events of lesser intensity than non-international armed conflict, such as riots.[34]

In the absence of a reference to a particular type of conflict, an exclusive application of the security exception to international wars should not be presumed. Indeed, it is a truism that non-international armed conflicts are capable of amounting to the same level of intensity and produce equally devastating consequences for the state's existence and independence, and safety of its people like international ones.[35] Either way, the importance of these considerations and outlined semantic differences is reduced when the scope of the security exception is further broadened so as to cover measures required for the maintenance of public order.

(b) Maintenance of a host state's public order

Some investment treaties extend the scope of security exceptions to measures needed for the maintenance of a host state's public order.[36] Burke-White and von Staden noticed that the meaning of 'public order' was deeply influenced by the meaning it had in domestic legal and political practice, which could impact the interpretation of the concept by arbitral tribunals.[37] Typically, the notion can be found in criminal and police laws addressing powers for ensuring safety of the people in the community (e.g. for suppression of riots) and the general maintenance of the rule of law.[38] Viewed in this light, the exception of 'public order' in investment treaties would likely cover situations of lesser intensity and scope than 'essential security interest' exceptions, and primarily focus on internal disturbances, for example revolutions and riots.[39]

The OECD Draft Multilateral Agreement on Investment included a public order exception, clarifying in a footnote that '[t]he public order exception may be invoked only where a genuine and sufficiently serious threat is posed to one of the fundamental interests of society'.[40] A similar requirement attached to the public order exception can be found in some BITs,[41] and in the trade law

[33] Israel–Japan BIT (2017) Art 15(2).

[34] The Association Agreement between the EU and Egypt (2001) Art 83. See also the Association Agreement between the EU and Tunisia (1995) Art 87; and the Free Trade Agreement between the EFTA States and Egypt (2007) Art 22.

[35] See *Enron* (n 24) para 306; *Sempra* (n 24) para 348.

[36] See e.g. UK Model BIT (2008) Art 7(1); 2009 Germany Model BIT (2008) Art 3(2).

[37] Burke-White and von Staden, 'Non-Precluded Measures' (n 2) 360.

[38] ibid 357–60; J Kurtz, 'Adjudging the Exceptional at International Investment Law: Security, Public Order and Financial Crisis' (2010) 59(2) ICLQ 325, 361; OECD, Security-Related Terms in International Investment Law and National Security Strategies (May 2009) 8–10.

[39] Burke-White and von Staden (n 2) 359.

[40] OECD MAI, 76, n 2.

[41] See e.g. Colombia–Switzerland BIT (2006) Ad Art 2(2); Japan–Korea BIT (2002) Art 16(1)(d); Japan–Vietnam BIT (2003) Art 15(1)(d); Colombia–Japan BIT (2011) Art 15(1)(b).

context.[42] The clarification implies that internal disturbances would need to reach a certain threshold of intensity and scope in order for the state's actions to be justified under the exception. Conversely, in situations of isolated and less intense internal violence, a state would likely be still bound by BIT provisions.

These treaties, however, also demonstrate that 'essential security interests' and 'public order' exceptions essentially cover different types of situations, whereby the threshold for invoking 'essential security interest' appears to be higher.[43] The difference between the two concepts was discussed in the *Continental Casualty* case in which the claimant argued that 'public order' referred to a fundamental societal value, such as morality, whereas 'security interest' concerned the security of the state in relation to external threats.[44] The tribunal crisply rejected this narrow interpretation and held that 'public order' denoted 'public peace' that can be 'threatened by actual or potential insurrections, riots and violent disturbances of the peace'.[45] Arguably, this would include violent collective protests and widespread lootings caused by severe economic crises, as was experienced in the case in question. In contrast, the 'essential security interest' is a narrower concept, and whether or not it comprises internal threats to the national security and legal order as well will likely depend on the wording of a particular exception and the degree of severity of the threat.

(c) Maintenance or restoration of international peace and security

Security exceptions can also cover situations not directly related to a host state. For example, the US–Ukraine BIT provides in Article IX:

> This Treaty shall not preclude the application by either Party of measures necessary for the maintenance of public order, the fulfilment of its *obligations with respect to the maintenance or restoration of international peace or security*, or the protection of its own essential security interests.[46]

The exception concerning 'international peace or security' would typically provide a justification for military measures and, in particular, economic sanctions (e.g. the freezing of assets and travel bans targeting investors suspected of involvement in hostile activities) in reaction to conflicts or humanitarian crises (e.g. gross human rights violations) not taking place in the host state's territory, and which would be

[42] See WTO General Agreement on Trade in Services (15 April 1994), Marrakesh Agreement Establishing the World Trade Organization, Annex 1B, ILM 81 (1994) Art XIV(a), n 5. See also *WTO United States: Measures Affecting the Cross-Border Supply of Gambling and Betting Services*, Panel Report (10 November 2004) WT/DS285/R, para 6.467.

[43] e.g. Art 16 of the Japan–Korea BIT uses both 'essential security interests' and 'public order' as two separate grounds for invoking a security exception.

[44] *Continental Casualty* (n 24) para 174.

[45] ibid.

[46] US–Ukraine BIT (1994) Art IX (emphasis added). See also 2012 US Model BIT (2012) Art 18.

normally taken in compliance with the obligation that states have under the United Nations Charter (UN Charter).[47]

Some BITs expressly provide for an exception to measures taken 'in pursuance of [State party's] obligations under the United Nations Charter for the maintenance of international peace or security'.[48] At first glance, this articulation may appear legally gratuitous for the defence of the state measure complying with the UN Charter since the measure is likely to be justified even in the absence of such specification of its source due to superiority of the UN Charter obligations over investment treaty obligations, as confirmed by Article 103 of the UN Charter.[49] Centralized targeted sanctions under Chapter VII of the UN Charter are an important tool of effectuating international law and fostering peaceful relations between states. Article 39, for example, allows the UN Security Council (UNSC) to decide what measures shall be taken to 'maintain or restore international peace and security'. Following this authority, the UNSC has imposed financial sanctions against states and non-state actors in many countries for a number of humanitarian objectives.[50] Thus, in view of the UN Charter's primacy, it is unlikely that the host state's measure pursuant to the UNSC directive (e.g. freezing of assets of a foreign company specifically listed by the UNSC) would amount to an investment treaty violation.[51]

The rationale for including an express limitation to the 'obligations of the UN Charter' may lie in the intention of the treaty drafters to exclude from the ambit of the treaty security exception obligations under other collective security agreements, or measures that states adopted on their own.[52] Another question that arises is what exactly is meant by the 'pursuance of [State party's] obligations under

[47] *Continental Casualty* (n 24) para 181.

[48] See e.g. Canada Model BIT (2004) Art 10(4)(c). See also Japan–Vietnam BIT (2003) Art 15(1)(b); Japan–Republic of Korea BIT (2002) Art 16(1)(b).

[49] UN Charter, Art 103: 'In the event of a conflict between the obligations of the Members of the United Nations under the present Charter and their obligations under any other international agreement, their obligations under the present Charter shall prevail.' The principle has been widely accepted by the UN member states, international tribunals, and doctrine. See e.g. *Military and Paramilitary Activities* (n 13) para 107; Case T-315/01 *Kadi v Council and Commission* [2005] ECR II-3649, paras 183–204; Case T-306/01 *Yusuf and Al Barakaat v Council and Commission* [2005] ECR II-3533, paras 233–54. See also R Bernhard, 'Article 103' in B Simma et al (eds), *The Charter of the United Nations: A Commentary* (2nd edn, OUP 2002) 1292–302; B Conforti, 'Consistency among Treaty Obligations' in E Cannizzaro (ed), *The Law of Treaties Beyond the Vienna Convention* (OUP 2011) 189.

[50] See e.g. UNSC Res 1970 (26 February 2011) S/RES/1970 and UNSC Res 1973 (17 March 2011) S/RES/1973 (condemning 'the gross and systemic violation of human rights' in Libya and imposing mandatory sanctions which included targeted asset freezes against Qaddafi family members and some state officials); UNSC Res 1803, Annex I, II, II UN Doc S/RES/1803 (3 March 2008) (concerning Iran's nuclear programme). See generally, E Criddle, 'Humanitarian Financial Intervention' (2013) 24(2) EJIL 584, 594.

[51] A tribunal would not have the power to review the legality of the UNSC Resolution but could potentially review whether the state's measure corresponded to it. See e.g. *Kadi* (n 49) paras 198–99; *Bosphorus Hava Tollari v Ireland* App no 45036/98, Judgment (ECtHR, 30 June 2005) para 156.

[52] e.g. this reason was raised during the negotiation of the MAI. See OECD, 'The Multilateral Agreement on Investment: Commentary to the Consolidated Text' (1998) DAFFE/MAI(98)8/REV1, 41.

the UN Charter'? Does this include only mandatory UNSC sanctions, or also recommendations or even General Assembly sanctions? Given the UNSC's central role in coordinating action to 'address any threat to peace, breach of peace, or act of aggression',[53] the preferred interpretation would appear to restrict such state actions to their obligation under UNSC mandatory resolutions.[54]

Sometimes countries decide to implement sanctions against another state's nationals without the prior approval of the UNSC, often when it is impossible to obtain due to political disagreements.[55] Narrowly worded security exceptions limiting the scope of their application to the compliance with UN Charter obligations will provide little room for defence of such decentralized targeted sanctions (unless a state decides to justify it as a response to a threat to its own 'essential security interests').[56] One could argue, however, that if the exception includes the wording 'in pursuance with', the flexible interpretation could accommodate those state sanctions that were adopted prior to the UN action, but were later retroactively approved by the UNSC resolution.[57]

On the other hand, broadly worded security exceptions not limited to the UN Charter obligations, like those in the US BITs, that encompass measures 'necessary for fulfilment of [State's] obligations with respect to the maintenance or restoration of international peace or security',[58] would arguably also cover sanctions by the host states that were taken in compliance with regional collective security agreements.[59] While some scholars have suggested that such clauses even cover measures by states acting on their own and not following any treaty-based obligations,[60] this proposition is problematic. It is grounded in the idea that there is a general legal obligation for states to intervene in cases of conflict or humanitarian crises in other countries, which remains controversial in international law and could reflect the above-discussed interventionist tendencies.[61] Thoughtful criticism against the potential application of a similarly worded security exception for justifying unilaterally imposed economic sanctions was recently articulated by Judge Trindade

[53] UN Charter Arts 39, 41.

[54] See, however, Art 6 of the 1967 OECD Convention, which extended application of the security exception to recommendations of the UNSC and General Assembly, but only because the exception expressly provided so. 1967 OECD Convention, Notes and Comments to Article 6 (n 19) 31.

[55] e.g. the US and EU sanctions against Russian and Ukrainian nationals in 2014.

[56] See e.g. *Sanctions against Iran* (n 14).

[57] e.g. the US and EU freezing of Libyan assets before the SC Res 1970 was adopted.

[58] e.g. US–Ukraine BIT (1994) Art IX(1).

[59] For some support for this view, see e.g. Commentary to OECD MAI (n 52) 41. See also letters of submittal of the US–Lithuania BIT, US–Albania BIT, the US–Jamaica BIT, which state that the obligations arising out of the Chapter VII of the UN Charter are only an example of obligations with respect to the maintenance or restoration of international peace or security.

[60] A van Aaken, 'International Investment Law and Decentralized Targeted Sanctions: An Uneasy Relationship' Columbia FDI Perspectives, No 164 (4 January 2015).

[61] See n 159. Generally, see A Orford, 'Moral Internationalism and the Responsibility to Protect' (2013) 24(1) EJIL 83;
ME O'Connell 'Responsibility to Peace: A Critique of R2P' (2010) 4(1) J Interv Statebuilding 39.

in an ICJ case brought by Iran against the US.[62] In his Separate Opinion, he noted that such unilateral actions themselves could undermine international peace and security, and that more attention should be paid 'to international security than to State susceptibilities as to their own "national security" interests or strategies'.[63] Importantly, he stressed that extra-territorial sanctions should comply with the UN Charter and be authorized by the UNSC.[64]

2. Degree of State Autonomy in Reacting to a Threat

While the afore outlined state interests protected under the security exceptions determine the type of situations and measures that fall within their scope, successful invocation of exceptions will further depend on whether the state has discretion to decide whether there is a threat to its interests and how it wishes to respond. These aspects are largely determined by the self-judging nature of the exceptions, briefly reviewed in the next two sections.

(a) Self-judging exceptions

If the security clause is self-judging, that is it explicitly permits the state to take such measures that the state itself considers necessary for the protection of its security interests,[65] the said measure will be largely exempt from the review by the arbitral tribunal.[66] This gives the state a high degree of autonomy in classifying a particular situation as a legitimate threat to its security interest, and consequently in deciding the type of measure most appropriate for addressing such a threat. International courts and tribunals have agreed that a security clause has a self-judging character only if its language expressly provides for it.[67]

Even in such cases, however, the tribunal could still perform a limited review of whether the state's invocation of the security exception has been made in good faith in accordance with Article 26 of the Vienna Convention on the Law of Treaties (VCLT).[68] What the scope of this scrutiny is in practice is unclear due to the lack

[62] *Sanctions against Iran*, Separate Opinion of Judge Cançado Trindade (n 14).

[63] ibid para 91.

[64] ibid para 85 (referring to the UN Special Rapporteur (I Jazairy) of the UN Office of the High Commissioner on Human Rights on the Negative Impact of the Unilateral Coercive Measures on the Enjoyment of Human Rights).

[65] See e.g. US–Uruguay BIT (2005) Art 18; US–Rwanda BIT (2008) Art 18; US–Mozambique BIT (1998) Art 25. Some investment agreements go a step further and exclude judicial reviewability in express terms. See e.g. US–Peru FTA (2006) Art 22.2, n 2; India Model BIT (2016) Art 33, Annex 1.

[66] UNCTAD National Security Report, 39.

[67] See e.g. *Military and Paramilitary Activities* (n 13) 116, para 222; *Oil Platforms* (n 13) 183, para 43; *Enron* (n 24) para 336; *Sempra* (n 24) para 383; *LG&E* (n 24) para 213; *Devas et al v India* PCA Case no 2013-09, Award on Jurisdiction and Merits, 25 July 2016, para 219. Only a small minority of investment treaties (around 5 per cent) provide for self-judging exceptions. UNCTAD Navigator (n 4).

[68] Art 26 of the VCLT stipulates that '[e]very treaty in force is binding upon the parties to it and must be performed by them in good faith.' See also *Certain Questions of Mutual Assistance in Criminal Matters (Djibouti v France)* (Judgment) [2008] ICJ Rep 177, 229, para 145; UNCTAD National Security

of case law regarding the interpretation of the good faith principle.[69] Burke-White and von Staden proposed that a good faith review is twofold: the first part looks into whether the state was honest and fair when asserting the exception, while the second part requires the establishment of a rational basis for the invocation.[70] The first element, which requires honesty and lack of deception in the state's dealings, has gained some support in practice,[71] and its assessment would likely focus on whether the state has provided reasons justifying its measure, whether the measure was taken by those who have the requisite authority,[72] and whether there is any evidence of bad faith, that is evidence of potential abuse of the exception with a view towards pursuing ulterior economic or political motives.

On the other hand, the second requirement for a 'rational basis' is somewhat problematic, because it brings the good faith review closer to the scrutiny typically carried out under non-self-judging clauses or substantive treaty standards and may result in a tribunal second-guessing a host state's decisions on security matters.[73] The better view is that the good faith review should not be concerned with reasonableness of the decision,[74] but rather with *prima facie* finding of manifest lack of connection between a state's measure and the objective pursued thereunder, that suggests an intentional misapplication of the exception.

(b) Non-self-judging exceptions

In the absence of the self-judging language, arbitral tribunals will carry out a review of whether the situation in question amounted to a threat to a national security (or other interest protected under exception), and whether the state's reaction to it was warranted.[75] What matters is not whether the host state considered the measure to be necessary, but rather whether the measure was justified from an objective, neutral point of view. This does not imply a complete disregard of a

Report, 40; Burke-White and von Staden, 'Non-Precluded Measures' (n 2) 376; K Vandevelde, 'Of Politics and Markets: The Shifting Ideology of the BITs' (1993) 11 Intl Tax Bus Law 159, 176–77. See also *Russia – Traffic in Transit* (n 32) paras 7.132–7.133, 7.63–7.65 (noting that the phrase 'which it considers' was not intended to make a self-judging security exception in GATT Art XXI subject to a Member's unilateral determination).

---

69 UNCTAD National Security Report, 40; Burke-White and von Staden, 'Non-Precluded Measures' (n 2) 379.

70 Burke-White and von Staden, ibid 379–80.

71 See e.g. 1935 Harvard Research on the Law of Treaties, *Codification of International Law*, 29 AJIL (supplement) 1, 981, cited in Burke-White and von Staden, ibid 379.

72 *Mutual Assistance in Criminal Matters* (n 68) para 145.

73 *LG&E* (n 24) para 214 (implying that there is little difference between the good faith review and substantive examination). For a position acknowledging the difference between two types of review, see *Enron* (n 24) para 339.

74 See e.g. *Mutual Assistance in Criminal Matters* (n 68) para 135 (Djibouti relied on reasonableness and good faith as separate concepts); *Russia – Traffic in Transit* (n 32) paras 7.138–7.139 (linking the obligation of good faith to the reqirement of plausible connection between the measure and the protected essential security interests, rather than reasonableness).

75 UNCTAD National Security Report, 41; *Devas* (n 67) para 229.

state's determination. In particular when a measure is taken in reaction to a military threat against the existence of a state and safety of its people, the state's assessment of the security situation should inform the tribunal's evaluation.[76] The extent to which this will be done is not always clear.[77]

The degree of deference paid to a state's determination will depend on a treaty's language, whereby broad wording describing permissible objectives and defining a nexus requirement will increase the deference to a state's own assessment.[78] Conversely, more specific treaty language reduces the degree of deference, since it already provides the tribunal with objective standards needed for the evaluation of a state's measure.[79] The most difficult aspect of a tribunal's assessment will be determination of the nexus requirement, that is a link between a state measure and the objective protected in the exception, commonly formulated as 'necessary for'. Investment treaties typically do not to provide interpretive guidance as to the meaning of the nexus requirement,[80] which further minimizes predictability as to who will bear the risk of a state's action in security crises.[81]

This conclusion echoes the deeply flawed reasoning in *Mitchell v Congo*,[82] the only case in which the security exception was addressed in the context of armed conflict. In that case, which concerned the seizure of an investor's premises due to a perceived threat to the security of a country in war, the government invoked the non-self-judging security exception only in the annulment stage which probably contributed to its limited analysis.[83] While the Annulment Committee did not make a final decision on the raised objection, its reasoning suggested that since the tribunal did not have 'enough information to evaluate, under all pertinent angles, the situation as it existed' at the time when the challenged

[76] See e.g. *Continental Casualty* (n 24) para 181 (highlighting that the 'objective assessment must contain a significant margin of appreciation' for a state taking the security measure); *Devas* (n 67) paras 245, 354 (largely heeding the state's assessment of its essential security interests). See also Burke-White and von Staden, 'Non-Precluded Measures' (n 2) 371; H Lauterpacht, *The Function of Law in the International Community* (Archon Books 1933) 188 (expressing doubts that any tribunal could override a state's assessment of its security interests).

[77] See UNCTAD National Security Report, 41–42; Burke-White and von Staden (n 2) 370–76 (proposing the application of the margin of appreciation doctrine, commonly used by the European Court of Human Rights).

[78] This includes exceptions with reference to broadly defined objectives without any specific guidance, and loosely defined nexus that does not require the measure to be 'necessary'. See e.g. Hungary–India BIT (2003) Art 12; Peru–Singapore BIT (2003) Art 11. See also *Devas* (n 67) paras 233–41 (recognizing that the nexus formulated as 'directed to', as opposed to 'necessary for', widens a state's discretion); UNCTAD National Security Report, 42, 95; Burke-White and von Staden (n 2) 371.

[79] Burke-White and von Staden, ibid.

[80] ibid 348.

[81] For an overview of different interpretative approaches regarding the nexus requirement, see Burke-White and von Staden, ibid; Kurtz, 'Adjudging the Exceptional' (n 38) 365; A Reinisch, 'Necessity in International Investment Arbitration—An Unnecessary Split of Opinions in Recent ICSID Cases? (2007) 8 JWIT 191, 201.

[82] *Patrick Mitchell v Democratic Republic of Congo* ICSID Case no ARB/99/7, Annulment Decision, 1 November 2006, para 51.

[83] Art X(1) of the US–Congo BIT (1990) provides that 'the treaty shall not preclude . . . measures necessary for . . . the protection of its own essential security interests.'

action had been taken, it also did not have enough information to determine whether there was a threat to the security of the state and whether the measures that the state adopted were necessary.[84] This is troubling, since it will rarely be possible for a tribunal to dispose of all relevant information concerning the security measure and the context in which it was taken, and more importantly, this is not necessarily needed for making a reasoned conclusion on whether the state's reaction to a threat was warranted. As explained above,[85] it is precisely in this type of situations when reliance on a state's assessment of a security situation could be justified. Instead of paying deference to the government's evaluation, the Committee held that the gaps in the available information would likely preclude the successful invocation of the security exception. The decision thus illustrates how the inclusion of a security exception in an investment treaty does not automatically preserve a state's freedom to react to a perceived security threat in a desired manner.

3. The Relationship between Security Exceptions and other Investment Treaty Provisions

The effectiveness of security exceptions in safeguarding a state's policy space further depends on their relationship with other investment treaty provisions. This relationship is shaped by two factors: first, the express limitations of the scope of their application; and second, their legal effect. With respect to the former, three drafting approaches can be distinguished: some investment treaties provide for no limitations and exceptions can apply to all investment treaty obligations;[86] some stipulate that security exceptions will only apply with respect to certain investment treaty provisions;[87] while yet others specify provisions that do not fall within the ambit of the exception.[88] The last two approaches suggest state parties' preference for defending their actions within specified substantive obligations rather than by invoking a security exception. Thus, for example, should the Energy Charter Treaty apply, a claim regarding the destruction of investment property by a host state's forces could only be defeated by relying on the 'necessity of the situation'

[84] *Mitchell*, Annulment (n 82) para 58.

[85] See Chapter 4 D.1. See also *Continental Casualty* (n 24) para 181 (noting that 'a time of grave crisis is not the time for nice judgments, particularly when examined by others with the disadvantage of hindsight').

[86] See e.g. US and Canadian BITs.

[87] e.g. the application of security and public order exceptions is limited only to the national and most-favoured-nation standard in Benin–Germany BIT (1978) Protocol 2(a); China–Germany BIT (2003) Protocol, 4(a); and to the full protection and security standard in Morocco–Turkey BIT (1997) Art 2.2; BLEU–Sudan BIT (2005) Art 2.2; BLEU–Ethiopia (2006) Art 3; BLEU–Botswana (2006) Art 3.

[88] e.g. according to Art 24(1) of the Energy Charter Treaty, the security exception does not apply to the armed conflict clause and the expropriation provision.

embedded in the advanced armed conflict clause,[89] since the application of the security exception is explicitly excluded for such situations.

More controversial is the second question, namely what are the legal consequences that exceptions carry?[90] Should they be interpreted as limitations of the scope of substantive obligations and thus as effectively suspending their application for state measures falling within the exception's purview?[91] Or alternatively, are they merely justifications for a state conduct that is otherwise inconsistent with investment treaty provisions?[92] While no consensus emerged from case law on this interpretive question, the former position, which is more in line with principles of interpretation (especially when exceptions are formulated as part of NPM clauses),[93] has gained more support in legal doctrine.[94]

Defining the legal effect of security exceptions bears importance for the relationship with other substantive treaty provisions, in particular for the defence mechanisms incorporated therein such the 'necessity of the situation' in armed conflict clauses or the police powers doctrine. Construing exceptions as justification presupposes that a state's action would breach a treaty obligation were it not for the exceptional circumstances defined in the security exception. This could deprive a state of the chance to try to justify its conduct within the relevant substantive obligation. Namely the two types of defence tools (security exceptions and justifications within a primary rule, e.g. the police powers doctrine, exceptions in advanced armed conflict clauses) would not be able to operate in parallel—a choice between them would have to be made and arbitral tribunals would likely prefer to assess a state's conduct within a security exception as otherwise its inclusion in an investment treaty would be meaningless, and thus contra *effet utile* interpretation.[95] Since the requirements for determining the application of exceptions are often understood to be stricter than for assessing a state's compliance with the primary norm,[96] their presence in investment treaties could thus actually create a risk of limitation of a state's space to react to a security threat.[97]

[89] Energy Charter Treaty Art 12(2).

[90] Generally on this question, see C Henckels, 'Scope Limitation or Affirmative Defence? The Purpose and Role of Investment Treaty Exception Clauses' in F Paddeu and L Bartels (eds), *Exceptions and Defences in International Law* (OUP 2019); J Viñuales, 'Sovereignty in Foreign Investment Law' in Z Douglas et al (eds), *Foundations of International Investment Law* (OUP 2014) 329.

[91] This view gained support in *CMS*, Annulment (n 24) para 129; *Continental Casualty* (n 24) para 164; *Devas* (n 67) para 293.

[92] This view gained support in *Mitchell*, Annulment (n 82) para 55; *CMS*, Award (n 24) para 356; *Sempra* (n 24) paras 372–73; *Enron* (n 24) para 339; *LG&E* (n 24) para 261; *Bear Creek Mining Corp v Peru*, ICSID Case no ARB/14/21, Award, 30 November 2017, para 473.

[93] Burke-White and von Staden, 'Non-Precluded Measures' (n 2) 388.

[94] ibid 388; Vandevelde, *History* (n 6) 181; Newcombe and Paradell, *Law and Practice* (n 2) 483; Henckels, 'The Purpose and Role' (n 90); Viñuales, 'Sovereignty' (n 90) 349.

[95] On the principle of effectiveness, see Chapter 3, n 129.

[96] See n 81.

[97] For similar views see A Newcombe, 'The Use of General Exceptions in IIAs: Increasing Legitimacy or Uncertainty' in A De Mestral and C Levesque (eds), *Improving International Investment Agreements* (Routledge 2012) 278; Henckels, 'The Purpose and Role' (n 90).

Concerns about the relevance of defence mechanisms at the level of treaty standards when pitted against exceptions are illustrated in the reasoning of the award in *Bear Creek v Peru*. In that case, the tribunal held that there was no need to consider the state's arguments relying on the police powers doctrine since the fact that the investment treaty included the exception led 'to the conclusion that no other exceptions from general international law or otherwise can be considered in this case'.[98]

By contrast, if one interprets the legal effect of security exceptions as a limitation of the investment treaty's scope, both types of defence will operate autonomously.[99] Should it be determined that the state's measure falls within the scope of the security exception, the substantive treaty obligations will not apply. If, however, the measure would fall outside of the exception's ambit, the defence tools on the level of treaty standards could still be considered. While according to this approach, the state preserves its regulatory freedom better, the risk of its limitation still exists, especially if the assessment of the state's measure under the unsuccessfully invoked security exception with a rigorous nexus requirement would influence the tribunal's subsequent assessment of the same measure under the relevant treaty standard.

The lack of clarity as to how treaty provisions relate to security exceptions and tribunals' general tendency to place the burden of proving requirements in exceptions, regardless of how their legal effect is understood, on a host state invoking them,[100] casts doubt about their usefulness in defending a state's freedom to act and regulate. It may even lead to states making a strategic choice to defend their actions primarily on the level of compliance with treaty obligations despite the availability of security exceptions. This is what likely happened in *Mitchell* case, in which the government defended itself by relying on police powers to protect its security interests, and only invoked the security exception in the annulment stage.[101] The case is a good example of how the objectives expressly stated in the exceptions are capable of being preserved already at the level of a particular treaty provision but also illustrates the risk of a tribunal's interpretation that is oblivious to this.

These uncertainties raise a question as to why at all are security exceptions included, and increasingly so, in investment treaties. As long as the institutional and normative investment environment is characterized by divergent interpretations of vaguely worded treaty standards,[102] security exceptions can play an important role in preventing the outcome of overly broad and legally erroneous interpretations

[98] *Bear Creek* (n 92) para 473.
[99] Viñuales, 'Sovereignty' (n 90) 357.
[100] ibid 348–49. Generally on a burden of proof, see C Brown, *A Common Law of International Adjudication* (OUP, 2007) 92–97.
[101] *Mitchell*, Annulment (n 82).
[102] It has been demonstrated in Chapter 4 how jurisprudential and doctrinal disagreements exist about many standards that could be relevant in conflict-related cases, including full protection and security, armed conflict clauses, and the application of the police powers doctrine.

that may unexpectedly hamper a state's regulatory flexibility.[103] However, to carry out this role effectively and prevent simply replacing interpretive divisions at the level of treaty standards with those at the level of exceptions, they need to be drafted in a specific and clear enough manner to avoid any confusion as to their actual purpose.

C. General Defences in the Law of State Responsibility

Failing to successfully rely on defence mechanisms in the investment treaty, a state could potentially escape responsibility for the alleged breach by invoking defences available under customary international law. The general rules on state responsibility predict circumstances that can preclude the wrongfulness of a state's measures and are codified in Chapter V of the Articles on the Responsibility of States for Internationally Wrongful Acts (ARS).[104] In the light of the strong historical link between the investment treaty regime and the general international law of state responsibility, outlined in Chapter 2, it is not surprising that investment tribunals have routinely referred to the general principles on state responsibility as codified in ARS and articulated in the jurisprudence of the ICJ and arbitral tribunals.[105]

In principle, the usefulness of these defences is limited for several reasons. The first is rooted in the conceptual distinction between primary rules and secondary rules,[106] and explains why the defences embedded in investment treaties either as part of substantive standards or security exceptions (primary rules) will always take priority in application over circumstances precluding wrongfulness. Namely, as a secondary rule the defence in the law of state responsibility can only apply when the breach of an international obligation has already been established.[107] In other words, a tribunal will first have to consider defences under the treaty law (e.g. the police powers doctrine, the 'necessity of the situation' in an advanced armed conflict clause, the security exception) to determine if the breach has indeed taken place, and only if it has, will the circumstance precluding wrongfulness come into play.

[103] Newcombe, 'The Use of General Exceptions' (n 97) 268, 277.

[104] International Law Commission, 'Draft Articles on the Responsibility of States for Internationally Wrongful Acts with Commentaries' UN GAOR, 56th Sess, Supp 10, Ch 4, (2001) UN Doc A/56/10 (ARS).

[105] J Zrilič, 'Jurisprudential Interaction between ICSID Tribunals and the International Court of Justice' in A Bjorklund (ed), *Yearbook on International Investment Law & Policy 2013–2014* (OUP 2015) 305.

[106] ILC Commentary to ARS, 31. The foundation for the distinction were laid down already by Special Rapporteur Roberto Ago. See R Ago, 'Second Report on State Responsibility'in ILC, *Yearbook of the International Law Commission, 1970, Vol II*, UN Doc A/CN.4/233, 178. See also E David, 'Primary and Secondary Rules' in J Crawford et al (eds), *The Law of International Responsibility* (OUP 2010) 27.

[107] ILC Commentary to ARS, Chapter V, paras 2–4, 7; *CMS*, Annulment (n 24) paras 129, 132–34; Kurtz, 'Adjudging the Exceptional' (n 38) 344.

Second, the application of these defences is limited by narrowly defined conditions for their invocation, often more stringent than the requirements entailed in investment treaty defences. For example, a state will not be able to rely on such a defence if it caused or contributed to the situation that gives rise to it (e.g. a conflict), a condition that is not stipulated for invoking a treaty security exception.[108]

Third, the question of whether successful application of defences in the law of state responsibility precludes the obligation to pay compensation, has not been settled in international law.[109] Since investment claims are normally filed for compensation, the lack of certainty as to consequences of a successfully invoked plea further reduces its practical significance.

The following sections consider the potential of the defences that are most likely to be raised by a state against the conflict-related investment claim: necessity, *force majeure*, and countermeasures.[110]

1. Necessity

In the absence of a security exception in the investment treaty, the state could justify the same type of measure by invoking the plea of necessity under customary international law, as codified in Article 25 ARS.[111] Although the purpose of this

[108] ARS Art 23(2)(a) and ILC Commentary to ARS Art 23, para 9 (*force majeure*); ARS Art 25(2)(b) and ILC Commentary to ARS Art 25, para 20 (necessity).

[109] ARS Art 27. See also *Gabčíkovo-Nagymaros Project* (*Hungary v Slovakia*) [1997] ICJ Rep 7, 39, para 48. For conflicting decisions on the obligation to pay compensation following the successful invocation of necessity, see *LG&E* (n 24) para 264 (deciding that damages should be borne by the investor); *CMS*, Award (n 24) paras 383–94 and *EDF International S.A. v Argentina* ICSID Case no ARB/03/23, Award, 11 June 2012, para 1177 (noting that the successfully invoked plea of necessity does not exclude the duty to compensate). See also Newcombe and Paradell, *Law and Practice* (n 2) 523–24; M Paparinskis, 'Circumstances Precluding Wrongfulness in International Investment Law' (2016) 31(2) ICSID Rev 484, 500.

[110] This chapter will not discuss the circumstances of distress (ARS Art 24) and self-defence (ARS Art 21) as they have not been applied in the context of international investment law and are less likely to play a role in the future. The defence of distress mirrors the conditions of necessity, but is limited to the threat to human life (i.e. the life of a state agent or individuals entrusted to its care). Self-defence, on the other hand, mostly encompasses state's actions that inflict losses on another state's territory, thus barring the investment treaty claim on jurisdictional grounds. Moreover, self-defence presupposes the anterior breach of international obligation (use of force) owed to a particular state and not an individual, thus its invocation as a defence against an investor's claim raises similar challenges to the invocation of countermeasures (see Section 5 C.3).

[111] The article provides that:

1. Necessity may not be invoked by a State as a ground for precluding the wrongfulness of an act not in conformity with an international obligation of that State unless the act:
   (a) is the only way for the State to safeguard an essential interest against a grave and imminent peril; and
   (b) does not seriously impair an essential interest of the State or States towards which the obligation exists, or of the international community as a whole.
2. In any case, necessity may not be invoked by a State as a ground for precluding wrongfulness if:
   a) the international obligation in question excludes the possibility of invoking necessity; or
   b) the State has contributed to the situation of necessity.

defence mechanism—the protection of a state's essential interests—suggests a high potential for justifying measures in situations of conflict, the record of the successful invocation of necessity is poor.[112] For a long time, the plea of necessity was not widely accepted as a defence to state responsibility.[113] It was a notion charged with controversy related to the right of self-preservation, and was subjected to additional scepticism after being used as justification for a number of historical occupations and annexations, such as the German invasion of Belgium in 1914.[114] The defence gained greater acceptance when domestic legal systems started to include it in their legislation,[115] and more importantly for international law, when the International Law Commission (ILC) embarked on the project of codifying the plea in ARS.

This notwithstanding, the plea of necessity has hardly ever been successfully invoked in international fora.[116] One of the reasons for this is that the conditions for its application are very narrowly defined and difficult to satisfy. As pointed out by the ILC, the measure taken must be 'the only way for the State to safeguard an essential interest against a grave and imminent peril'.[117] That a threat to national security could qualify as an essential interest was never questioned, as the plea of necessity in its original conception purported to cover exactly the kind of situations which may compromise the very existence and independence of a state.[118] Such situations, however, would have to meet a high threshold of gravity in order to constitute 'grave and imminent peril', a condition lacking in many investment cases which led the tribunals to reject the plea.[119] This could prevent the application of

Generally on necessity, see D Desierto, *Necessity and National Emergency Clauses: Sovereignty in Modern Treaty Interpretation* (Martinus Nijhoff 2012); R Sloane, 'On the Use and Abuse of Necessity in the Law of State Responsibility' (2012) 106 AJIL 447; S Heathcote, 'Circumstances Precluding Wrongfulness in the ILC Articles on State Responsibility: Necessity' in J Crawford et al (eds), *Law of International Responsibility* (n 106) 491.

---

[112] For its unsuccessful invocation in international fora, see e.g. *Gabčíkovo* (n 109) para 51; *Enron* (n 24) para 303; *CMS*, Award (n 24) para 331.

[113] Heathcote, 'Necessity' (n 111) 492; F Paddeu, 'A Genealogy of Force Majeure in International Law' (2012) 82(1) BYIL 381, 444.

[114] Paddeu, ibid.

[115] ibid 445.

[116] The first time a state successfully invoked the plea of necessity was in the investment treaty case *LG&E v Argentina*. While the tribunal based its decision on Art XI of the Argentina–US BIT (1991), it supported the analysis of the provision by referencing ARS Art 25. *LG&E* (n 24) para 258.

[117] ILC Commentary to ARS Art 25, at 80.

[118] Special Rapporteur Ago gave some examples of what would constitute 'essential interests': the existence of the state, its political and economic survival, the continued functioning of its essential services, the maintenance of its internal peace, the survival of part of its population etc. See R Ago, 'Addendum to the Eighth Report on State Responsibility' in ILC, *Yearbook of the International Law Commission, 1980, Vol II*, UN Doc A/CN.4/318/Add.5-7 (Part 1) 14. See also *Enron* (n 24) para 306; *CMS*, Award (n 24) para 319; *LG&E* (n 24) paras 251, 257; *Sempra* (n 24) para 334.

[119] See e.g. *CMS*, Award (n 24) para 355; *Enron* (n 24) para 307; *Sempra* (n 24) para 349; *AWG Group Ltd v Argentine Republic* UNCITRAL, Decision on Liability, 30 July 2010, para 265; *EDF* (n 109) para 1171. However, for a different conclusion see *LG&E* (n 24) para 257; *Continental Casualty* (n 24) paras 168, 233.

necessity in small-scale internal disturbances, such as riots. Conversely, the fact that a state proclaims a state of emergency due to widespread internal strife does not mean that the threshold for the necessity defence has been met, since such a declaration in itself can amount to or include the contested state's wrongful measures.[120] Furthermore, a number of adjudicative bodies confirmed the rule that the state's conduct can only be justified if it was 'the only way' of achieving a legitimate policy objective.[121] If the protection of the state's essential interests is achievable by the use of other means, even if more expensive or less convenient, the plea of necessity would not be applicable.[122]

In investment arbitration, necessity has come under the spotlight mostly due to the conflation by tribunals of this plea with the security exception. Namely, in some arbitral cases emerging in the aftermath of the Argentine financial crisis, the rigorous requirements of the customary necessity defence were read into conditions of the investment treaty security exceptions, thus making it more cumbersome for the state to safeguard its regulatory space.[123] While these cases were rightfully criticized in the literature,[124] scholars have overlooked that the same approach effectively merging different types of defences was espoused even before the Argentine 'economic measures' cases, namely in the context of armed conflict.

Thus, the Annulment Committee in *Mitchell v Congo* held that the security exception is merely a codification of the customary necessity defence, and as such a circumstance precluding wrongfulness rather than a provision delimiting the scope of the application of the investment treaty.[125] This position misunderstands the role and the nature of the two defences and is oblivious to their conceptualization as primary and secondary rules. As aptly noted by another Annulment Committee in *CMS v Argentina*, despite some similarities in the language of security exception and the defence of necessity, the two concepts have a 'different operation and content'.[126] The customary necessity will become relevant as a defence only once the wrongfulness of the state conduct has been established, that is after the investment treaty defence mechanisms, including security exceptions, have failed to provide cover for state action. If the 'grave and imminent' peril is a security threat, the presence of a security exception in an investment treaty will render the

[120] *Enron* (n 24) para 71.

[121] *Gabčíkovo* (n 109) paras 51, 52, 55; *Oscar Chinn* (*UK v Belgium*) [1934] PCIJ Rep Series A/B No 63, Separate Opinion of Judge Anzilotti, 114; *CMS*, Award (n 24) para 323; *Enron* (n 24) para 308; *Sempra* (n 24) para 350.

[122] ILC Commentary to ARS Art 25, at 83, para 15.

[123] *CMS*, Award (n 24) paras 316–31; 353–78; *Enron* (n 24) paras 314–42; *Sempra* (n 24) paras 159–223; *El Paso Energy v Argentina* ICSID Case no ARB/03/15, Award, 31 October 2011, para 665.

[124] See e.g. Kurtz, 'Adjudging the Exceptional' (n 38) 341–51; Viñuales, 'Sovereignty' (n 90) 353; Newcombe and Paradell, *Law and Practice* (n 2) 497.

[125] *Mitchell*, Annulment (n 82) paras 55, 57.

[126] *CMS*, Annulment (n 24) paras 129, 131. Similarly, *Continental Casualty* (n 24) para 167; *Devas* (n 67) para 254.

possibility of the defence of necessity merely theoretical.[127] On the other hand, the defence will retain relevance for measures aiming at protecting those essential interests that fall outside of the scope of security exceptions (e.g. environmental). That said, even in the absence of a security exception, the fact that the customary necessity covers only the most severe, catastrophic threats,[128] presents a more difficult path for the state to establish its case,[129] and the consequences of a potentially successful plea are unclear,[130] reduces the appeal of this avenue of defence.

2. *Force majeure*

The wrongfulness of a state conduct can be further precluded if the state's act was due to *force majeure*.[131] It has been long undisputed that the event giving rise to *force majeure* could be not only a natural disaster (e.g. an earthquake) but also a man-made situation, such as war, revolution, or mob violence. In fact, it was due to the latter type of events that *force majeure* entered prominently onto the international legal plane. Historically, the defence was frequently raised against claims of foreign investors for losses they suffered in conflict situations. Related to the arguments on state non-responsibility for injuries to aliens in times of conflict, discussed in Chapter 2, countries in the nineteenth and early twentieth centuries often declared international and civil wars, as well as other types of internal strife, as *force majeure* in an attempt to preclude all claims for reparations by aliens and their home states.[132] While it was widely accepted that *force majeure* was a universal rule of international law (e.g. it was referred to as a general principle of law in the Hague

[127] In similar vein, the IHL treaties exclude, by its object and purpose, the application of necessity to obligations regulated therein (already covered by military necessity). See ARS, Commentary to Art 25, para 21; *CMS*, Award (n 24) para 353.

[128] UNCTAD National Security Report, 36.

[129] Apart from the more demanding nexus requirement, the customary law defence can never be self-judging, unlike investment treaty exceptions. Furthermore, the latter are not limited by the requirement to prove that there was no alternative to the state's measure.

[130] See n 109.

[131] For a more detailed analysis, see J Zrilič, 'Armed Conflict as Force Majeure in International Investment Law' (2019) 16(1) Manchester Journal of International Economic Law 28. Parts of this section summarize the argument made in the paper. See also, Paddeu, 'Genealogy' (n 113); A Bjorklund, 'Emergency Exceptions: State of Necessity and Force Majeure' in P Muchlinski et al (eds), *The Oxford Handbook of International Investment Law* (OUP 2008) 499.

[132] e.g. the Venezuelan government rejected the responsibility for acts of insurgents during guerrilla action in 1858 by arguing that injuries sustained by foreigners in such internal disturbances 'are disasters for which Governments cannot humanely be held responsible, just as they are not answerable for fires, plagues, earthquakes or other disorders arising from physical causes.' See Study by the Secretariat, '"Force majeure" and "Fortuitous event" as Circumstances Precluding Wrongfulness: Survey of State Practice, International Judicial Decisions and Doctrine' in *Yearbook of the International Law Commission, 1978, Vol II*, UN Doc A/CN.4/315 (Part 1) (Secretariat Study) 110, 131; J Goebel, 'The International Responsibility of States for Injuries Sustained by Aliens on Account of Mob Violence, Insurrections and Civil Wars' (1914) 8 AJIL 802, 847–48; C Calvo, *Le droit international théorique et pratique, vol 3* (3rd edn, Pedone-Lauriel 1880) 429; Paddeu, 'Genealogy' (n 113) 412.

Conference for the Codification of International Law in 1930),[133] disagreement existed as to what it actually meant.[134] The violent events of that era thus presented an opportunity for statesmen, adjudicators, and scholars to assert and establish their views about the content and role of *force majeure* in international law. Those developments importantly influenced the codification of *force majeure* in ARS.

According to Article 23 of ARS,[135] three main conditions must be met for the successful invocation of this defence.[136] First, the event of *force majeure* must be due to either an irresistible force or an unforeseen event.[137] Second, the *force majeure* act must be beyond the control of the state.[138] Third, the unforeseeable, irresistible, and uncontrollable event must make it materially impossible for the state to perform the obligation. The condition of 'material impossibility' signifies that merely the increased difficulty of performance is insufficient for a successful invocation of the plea. The Commentary to ARS emphasizes that '[*f*]*orce majeure* does not include circumstances in which performance of an obligation has become more difficult, for example due to some political or economic crisis'.[139] What exactly this means has been subject to disagreement. The arbitral tribunal in the *Rainbow Warrior Affair* famously equated material impossibility with 'absolute impossibility'.[140] This view was later criticized by James Crawford[141] and implicitly rejected by the ICJ in the *Gabčíkovo-Nagymaros Case*,[142] both maintaining the distinction between 'material impossibility' under *force majeure* and the stricter

[133] Secretariat Study, 68, 83.

[134] Secretariat Study, 88 (citing the statement of Mexico on the United Nations Conference on the Law of the Treaties in 1968: 'Force Majeure was a well-defined notion in law; the principle that "no person is required to do the impossible" was both a universal rule of international law and a question of common sense.'). On the other hand, representatives of other countries voiced concerns that 'force majeure lacked precision' (the US), and 'had not been clearly defined and had no precise meaning in international law' (the Soviet Union).

[135] The article states:

1. The wrongfulness of an act of a State not in conformity with an international obligation of that State is precluded if the act is due to force majeure, that is the occurrence of an irresistible force or an unforeseen event, beyond the control of the State, making it materially impossible in the circumstances to perform the obligation.
2. Paragraph 1 does not apply if:
   a. the situation of force majeure is due, either alone or in combination with other factors, to the conduct of the State invoking it;
   b. the State has assumed the risk of that situation occurring.

[136] *Sempra* (n 24) para 246.

[137] It suffices that either the event is unforeseeable or foreseeable but irresistible. Secretariat Study, 61, 70.

[138] This does not mean that it must be absolutely external to the state invoking the defence. *Force majeure* can be applied even in cases when the activities or omissions giving rise to it stem from the state itself, as long as they are not attributed to it as a result of its wilful behaviour. Secretariat Study, 69.

[139] ILC Commentary to ARS Art 23, at 76, para 3.

[140] *Rainbow Warrior Affair* (*New Zealand v France*) (1990) 20 RIAA 217, 253. The tribunal found that 'the test of applicability of [draft article 31] is of absolute and material impossibility' and consequently rejected France's defence by emphasizing that 'a circumstance rendering performance more difficult or burdensome does not constitute a case of force majeure'.

[141] J Crawford, 'Second Report on State Responsibility' 1999, UN Doc A/CN.4/498, paras 257–59.

[142] *Gabčíkovo* (n 109) para 102.

standard of 'absolute impossibility' under the rule of supervening impossibility to perform, as codified in Article 61 of the VCLT.[143] The support for this position can be found also in the comments of the Special Rapporteur Ago who described material impossibility as 'relative impossibility', the threshold of which was met when the performance would result in a 'sacrifice that could not be reasonably required.'[144] This understanding of 'material impossibility' will become relevant in particular when the defence is invoked due to financial impossibility to pay (e.g. a state's failure to make certain payments to investors) during and in the aftermath of conflicts when a state's budget is impoverished and its resources are needed for defence or the post-conflict rebuilding of the economy.[145]

As noted above, historically, *force majeure* defence was commonly invoked when states were accused of violating the obligation to protect foreign investors against violence of non-state actors.[146] While revolutions, insurrections, and civil wars were often described as situations of *force majeure* in arbitral decisions,[147] legally, those cases were not decided by analysing specific *force majeure* conditions, but rather by assessing whether governments exercised due diligence in protecting aliens. This gives rise to an important question as to what is the relationship between the due diligence obligation and *force majeure* as a legal defence in international law. Can a *force majeure* defence be effectively invoked in cases of non-performance of obligations that involve the duty of due diligence?

In theory, *force majeure* can be invoked with respect to any international obligation. However, this does not mean that the content of primary obligations cannot affect the applicability of the *force majeure* defence. The application of *force majeure* can be excluded by the content of the specific international obligation.[148] Some special regimes of international law provide for their own *force majeure* exception or similar limitations as part of the primary rules,[149] which effectively prevents the operation of *force majeure* as a circumstance precluding wrongfulness. It is submitted that the same applies for the obligations containing a standard of due

[143] See Chapter 3 C.1.

[144] R Ago, 'Eighth Report on State Responsibility' in ILC, *Yearbook of the International Law Commission, 1979, Vol II*, UN Doc A/CN.4/SER.A/1979.1 (Part 1) 48–49, paras 103, 106.

[145] That economic impossibility can be covered by the *force majeure* defence was confirmed in the case of *French Company of Venezuelan Railroads*, in which the umpire held that the situation of internal conflict necessitated the consumption of all the government's resources in the same fashion as it deprived the company of the proceeds of its ordinary business. See *1888 French Company of Venezuelan Railroads* (*France v Venezuela*) (1904) 10 RIAA 285, 314. See also Ago, 'Eighth Report' (n 144) 59; *Sylvania Technical Systems v Iran* (1985) 8 Iran–USCTR 309–10. For a different view, see S Szurek, 'Circumstances Precluding Wrongfulness in the ILC Articles on State Responsibility: Force Majeure' in J Crawford et al (eds) *Law of International Responsibility* (n 106) 475, 479; Paddeu, 'Geneology' (n 113) 443 (arguing that necessity is more appropriate defence for this kind of situations).

[146] For the general overview of case law, see Secretariat Study.

[147] See e.g. *Mena Case* (*Spain v Venezuela*) (1903) 10 RIAA 748, 749; *Spanish Zone of Morocco* (*Great Britain v Spain*) (1924) 2 RIAA 615, 639, 642.

[148] Secretariat Study, 220.

[149] See e.g. Art 18 of the United Nations Convention on the Law of the Sea, which provides for an exception concerning the right to stop and anchor during passage in foreign waters due to *force majeure*.

diligence. It is difficult to imagine a situation where the wrongfulness of a state's failure to sufficiently protect an investor during conflict would be precluded by the *force majeure* defence pursuant to Article 23 ARS. Namely, whether the state has violated this obligation will be measured against the duty of due diligence, taking into account different circumstances which may largely coincide with the conditions of a *force majeure* defence. As explained in Chapters 2 and 4, arbitral tribunals often held that the state was unable to protect aliens because the situation in question was sudden (and thus unforeseeable),[150] intensely violent (and thus irresistible),[151] or it occurred in the part of the territory which is outside of the state's control (and thus uncontrollable).[152] If no breach of the obligation to protect is found, there is also no need for invoking *force majeure*—the elements of latter are already implicitly incorporated in the due diligence rule.

While a *force majeure* defence is possible in principle, its invocation in such situations would be incompatible with the purpose of investment law obligations of prevention. Both *force majeure* and the due diligence rule are tools that international law uses for allocating risks concerning states' failure to comply with primary international obligations. These risks are defined by certain characteristics such as unforeseeability, impossibility, and uncontrollability. Since the application of the due diligence standard in the context of armed conflict already reduces the risk for a state's responsibility, the application of *force majeure* as a secondary tool for allocating the same risk in the same circumstances and against the same parameters, is gratuitous.[153] The reverse position (i.e. the application of *force majeure* before the breach of the obligation to protect has been ascertained through the due diligence analysis) would not only be legally inaccurate but could potentially result in a decision that a state has to pay compensation for the losses that investors sustained during conflict.

In sum, it appears safe to conclude that the potential of *force majeure* as a defence against conflict-related investment claims is significantly reduced. The flexibility of the due diligence standard excludes the application of *force majeure* for certain primary obligations, in particular the obligation to protect.[154] It should be noted,

[150] See e.g. *US Diplomatic and Consular Staff in Teheran Case (US v Iran)* (Judgment) [1980] ICJ Rep 3, 33; *Ampal-America Israel Corp v Arab Republic of Egypt* ICSID Case no ARB/12/11, Decision on Liability, 21 February 2017, paras 285, 289.

[151] See e.g. *Spanish Zone of Morocco* (n 147) 644–45; *GL Solis* (*US v Mexico*) (1928) 4 RIAA 358, 362; *Pantechniki SA Contractors & Engineers v The Republic of Albania* ICSID Case no ARB/07/21, Award, 30 July 2009, para 82.

[152] See e.g. *Wipperman Case*, reported in J Moore, *History and Digest of International Arbitrations to which United States has been a Party* (GPO 1898) 3041; *Spanish Zone of Morocco* (n 147); *Ampal* (n 150) paras 285, 289.

[153] For a similar view, see C Eagleton, *The Responsibility of States in International Law* (New York University Press 1928) 156. See also Secretariat Study, 215, 217.

[154] The overlap between the due diligence rule and the defence of *force majeure* was indirectly acknowledged in *Ampal* (n 150) paras 274, 239. See also Zrilič, 'Armed Conflict as Force Majeure' (n 131) 45.

however, that contract-based claims can be rebutted by invoking contractual *force majeure*, often contained in investment contracts governed by domestic and international commercial law.[155] While a comparison of the two defences is beyond the scope of this chapter,[156] parties should be mindful of the importance of carefully drafting contractual clauses in order to maximize *force majeure* protection.

3. Countermeasures

The measure of a host state that adversely affects foreign investors can be taken with a specific aim to address an internationally wrongful act perpetrated by the investor's home state. While there may be no armed conflict in the host state, the measure may purport to achieve the end of a conflict or conflict-related atrocities in the targeted state, or some other state. Such a measure that breaches an international obligation owed to another state, in response to that state's prior breach of international law, is called a countermeasure.[157] In situations when a host state's measure, designed to induce certain behaviours from another state, amounts to a violation of an investment treaty between these two states, the question is whether the host state's conduct can be justified under the defences of the law of state responsibility.

Typically, such measures take the form of economic sanctions and may pursue various objectives.[158] Most often, the host state will direct banks to freeze the accounts of the target state or its nationals in order to compel the targeted state to change its practices pertaining to forceful attacks, war crimes, or violations of fundamental human rights. Although their use is not without controversy,[159] and

[155] Contractual *force majeure* has been invoked more commonly against conflict-related claims. See e.g. *Autopista Concesionada v Republic of Venezuela* ICSID Case no ARB/00/5, Award, 23 September 2003; *RSM Production Corp v Central African Republic* ICSID Case no ARB/07/02, Decision on Jurisdiction and Liability, 7 December 2010; *Gujarat State Petroleum Corporation Ltd v the Republic of Yemen and the Yemen Ministry of Oil and Minerals* ICC Arbitration no 19299/MCP, Award, 10 July 2015; *National Oil Corporation v Sun Oil* ICC Case no 4462/1985 and 1987, XVI Yearbook Commercial Arbitration 54–78 (1991); *Ampal-America Israel Corp v Arab Republic of Egypt* ICC Case no 18215/GZ/MHM, Final Award, 4 December 2015.

[156] Such *force majeure* clauses are often tailored to the needs of parties entering into long-term commercial transactions and are consequently drafted in broad terms, thereby widening the scope of situations in which they can be applied, and lowering the impossibility threshold to the level of commercial impracticability. For a more detailed analysis see Zrilič, 'Armed Conflict as Force Majeure' (n 131) 46–55.

[157] Generally, see ILC Commentary to ARS, 128–39; Ago, 'Eighth Report' (n 144) 39–47 (referring to countermeasures as 'legitimate application of a sanction'); N White and A Abass, 'Countermeasures and Sanctions' in M Evans (ed), *International Law* (2nd edn, OUP 2006) 509–21; O Elagab, *The Legality of Non-Forcible Counter-Measures in International Law* (Clarendon Press 1988).

[158] Criddle, 'Humanitarian Financial Intervention' (n 50) 584.

[159] For the argument that economic measures are prohibited under Art 2(4) of the UN Charter, see O Elagab, 'Economic Measures against Developing Countries' (1992) 41 ICLQ 682, 688. See also the critique of economic sanctions as a tool of powerful countries for exerting control over weaker countries and meddling with their domestic affairs: S D Murphy, *Humanitarian Intervention: The United Nations in an Evolving World Order* (U Pen Press 1996) 10; Criddle (n 50) 591.

disagreement exists as to their effectiveness,[160] economic sanctions have become a popular alternative to the use of physical force in responding to external security threats, conflicts, and humanitarian crises abroad. In the context of investment law, the measures become problematic when they target investors due to their links with the targeted state, possibly giving rise to claims of expropriation, violation of the fair and equitable treatment standard, and other investment treaty provisions.

In the absence of authorization by the UNSC and broadly worded security exceptions in investment treaties, discussed above,[161] the state measures could be potentially defended by relying on the customary international law of countermeasures, as codified in ARS.[162] The ILC has confirmed that economic sanctions, like the freezing of foreign assets, are permitted under customary international law when necessary to address another state's breach of international law.[163] However, the potential of countermeasures as a defence tool against investment claims is undermined due to uncertainty inherent to their application in certain contexts.

First, with respect to measures taken in time of war, the ARS provide in Article 50(1)(c) that 'countermeasures shall not affect . . . obligations of a humanitarian character prohibiting reprisals'. As noted in Chapter 2, the IHL treaties governing international armed conflicts prohibit reprisals against civilians and civilian property.[164] A state embroiled in armed conflict would not be able to preclude the wrongfulness of non-compliance with these obligations by invoking countermeasures. The rationale of this prohibition is to reduce mutually injurious conduct, prevent the escalation of violations, and in this way facilitate the principle of humanity in wartime. In an attempt to clarify the rule, the International Criminal Tribunal for the Former Yugoslavia articulated that the prohibition has become customary and that it applies to non-international armed conflicts too.[165] This view has been subjected to doubt and criticism by some commentators and countries, notably the US and the UK, who held that in extreme circumstances, the injured state could lawfully resort to reprisals to coerce the enemy into respecting the law.[166]

[160] See e.g. O Hatchway and S Shapiro, 'Outcasting: Enforcement in Domestic and International Law' (2011–2012) 121 Yale L J 252, 302 (arguing that sanctions are an effective tool for enforcing the change of behaviour of a targeted state); J MacMillian, *On Liberal Peace: Democracy, War and the International Order* (I.B. Tauris, 1998) 114–24 (arguing that economic sanctions can exacerbate the conflict).

[161] Section 5 B.1.c.

[162] ARS Arts 22, 49–54.

[163] ARS Commentary Arts 49–54.

[164] See e.g. Fourth Geneva Convention Art 33; Additional Protocol I (AP I), Arts 51(6), 52(1). The International Committee of the Red Cross (ICRC) stressed that the ban on all forms of reprisals is absolute and mandatory. ICRC Commentary to the Fourth Geneva Convention Art 33, 225; ICRC Commentary to AP I, Art 51(6), para 1984.

[165] See *Prosecutor v Kupreškić* (Trial Judgment) IT-95-16 (14 January 2000) paras 527–33; *Prosecutor v Martić* (Review of the Indictment Pursuant to Rule 61) IT-95-11 (8 March 1996) paras 10–19.

[166] See e.g. F Kalshoven, 'Reprisals and the Protection of Civilians: Two Recent Decisions of the Yugoslavia Tribunal' in LC Vohran et al (eds), *Man's Inhumanity to Man: Essays on International Law in Honour of Antonio Cassese* (Kluwer 2003). While the US is not a party to AP I, the UK expressed reservations concerning reprisals when ratifying it. See Department of the Navy, the Commander's Handbook on the Law of Naval Operations (2007) para 6.2.4; UK Ministry of Defence, The Manual of the Law

Second, while peacetime bilateral countermeasures are universally recognized as a self-help tool for injured states,[167] the existence of a non-injured state's right to take so-called solidarity or third-party countermeasures has been traditionally contested.[168] Scholars observed that the view that states can take countermeasures against a state, whose breach of an international norm does not directly affect them, has gained more acceptance over time, in particular since the ICJ's recognition of the concept of obligations *erga omnes*, that is obligations owed to all members of the international community.[169] While the ARS endorse *erga omnes* obligations in Article 48, the Commentary specifies that 'the current state of international law on countermeasures taken in the general or collective interest is uncertain' and thus the ILC 'leaves the resolution of the matter to the further development of international law'.[170]

Third, the successful invocation of the defence in the context of investment claims depends on the nature of the investor's rights. Paparinskis highlighted the relevance of different approaches to conceptualizing investors' rights under investment treaties for the application of countermeasures.[171] Thus, sanctions against investors could be justified under countermeasures if investors' rights are seen as belonging to home states only, or as derived from the state's rights to the investor as a third-party beneficiary.[172] On the other hand, investors' assets cannot be targeted with countermeasures if investment treaties bestow on investors direct rights, thus making them a third party to a countermeasure.[173] The investment jurisprudence tends to be more inclined to support the direct rights approach that would

of Armed Conflict (2004) 423, n 62. The ICRC was careful not to declare the prohibition the custom; however, it noted a strong trend towards outlawing the practice of reprisals. See J-M Henckaerts and L Doswald-Beck, *International Committee of the Red Cross, Customary International Humanitarian Law, vol I, Rules* (2005 CUP) 523, Rules 145 and 147. For views supportive of limited use of armed reprisals, see M Newton, 'Reconsidering Reprisals' (2010) 20(361) Duke J Comp Intl L 361; C Greenwood, 'The Twilight of Belligerent Reprisals' in *Essays on War in International Law* (Cameron May 2006) 295, 299.

---

[167] ARS Arts 42, 49.

[168] See S Talmon, 'The Constitutive versus the Declaratory Theory of Recognition: Tertium non Datur?' (2004) 75 BYIL 101, 162–81.

[169] Criddle, 'Humanitarian Financial Intervention' (n 50) 596. See also C Tams, *Enforcing Obligations Erga Omnes in International* Law (CUP 2010); M Dawidowicz, *Third-Party Countermeasures in International Law* (CUP 2017) (arguing that third-party countermeasures are permitted under customary international law).

[170] ILC Commentary to ARS, 139.

[171] M Paparinskis, 'Investment Arbitration and the Law of Countermeasures' (2008) 79 BYIL 264, 354. See also Z Douglas, 'The Hybrid Foundations of Investment Treaty Arbitration' (2003) 74 BYIL 151; Z Douglas, *The International Law of Investment Claims* (CUP 2009) ch 1; R Volterra, 'International Law Commission Articles on State Responsibility and Investor-State Arbitration: Do Investors Have Rights?' (2010) 25(1) ICSID Rev-FILJ 218.

[172] Paparinskis (n 171) 334. See e.g. *Archer Daniels Midland Company v Mexico* ICSID AF Case no ARB/(AF)/04/5, Award, 21 November 2007, paras 161–80. See also A Roberts, 'Triangular Treaties: the Nature and Limits of Investment Treaty Rights' (2015) 56(2) HILJ 353.

[173] See e.g. *Corn Products Int'l Inc v Mexico* ICID AF Case no ARB/(AF)/04/1, Decision on Responsibility, 15 January 2008, paras 161–79; *Cargill v Mexico* ICSID Case no ARB(AF)/05/2, Award, 18 September 2009, paras 420–28.

preclude the host state's countermeasure defence because the sanction infringes on the investor's own rights rather than the rights of his home state.

These observations suggest the limited utility of the defence of countermeasures to a host state that implemented sanctions against foreign investors. This does not mean, however, that the passing of such measures necessarily results in the host state's liability. Some tribunals have taken into account investors' illegal conduct when deciding jurisdictional or admissibility issues,[174] or assessing the compliance of a host state with the substantive standards.[175] This practice could provide support for an equitably adjusted direct rights approach, according to which the state could take a countermeasure against the foreign investor only if the latter was closely associated with the targeted regime and directly contributed to the home state's internationally illegal actions. Because of the close connections to the governing regime and contribution to the wrongful act, the property of those investors would be perceived as being coalesced with the home state's public assets and could thus be legitimately targeted by interstate countermeasures.[176] While policy objectives for such piercing of an investor's personality are understandable, the legal justification remains questionable and untested.

Alternatively, if a tribunal finds the state liable for passing the contested measure, the final amount of compensation could still be reduced by taking into account the contribution of a the injured investor to the damage it has suffered.[177] The principle of contributory fault has been applied by tribunals in assessment of conflict-related damages when the investors' contribution was in the form of their lack of caution that should be reasonably exercised in conditions of hostilities,[178] or their

[174] Jurisdictional defence has been only available if the illegality occurred at the stage of investment acquisition. See e.g. *Inceysa Vallisoletana v Republic of El Salvador* ICSID Case no ARB/03/26, Award, 2 August 2006, paras 225–44; *World Duty Free Company Ltd v Republic of Kenya* ICSID Case no ARB/00/7, Award, 4 October 2006, paras 148, 157; *Plama Consortium Ltd v Republic of Bulgaria* ICSID Case no ARB/03/24, Award, 27 August 2008, para 135; *Phoenix Action, Ltd v Czech Republic* ICSID Case no ARB/06/5, Award, 15 April 2009, para 101; *Gustav F W Hamester GmbH & Co KG v Ghana* ICSID Case no ARB/07/24, Award, 18 June 2010, paras 123–24; *SAUR International SA v Argentine Republic* ICSID Case no ARB/04/4, Decision on Jurisdiction and Liability, 6 June 2012, para 308; *Niko Resources Ltd v Republic of Bangladesh and Others* ICSID Case no ARB/10/18, Decision on Jurisdiction, 19 August 2013, paras 431–33; *Liman Caspian Oil BV and NCL Dutch Investment BV v Republic of Kazakhstan* ICSID Case no ARB/07/14, Award, 22 June 2010, para 194; *David Minnotte and Robert Lewis v Republic of Poland* ICSID Case no ARB(AF)/10/1, Award, 16 May 2014, para 131.

[175] *Yukos Universal Ltd v The Russian Federation* UNCITRAL, Final Award, 18 July 2014, para 1355; *Fraport AG Frankfurt Airport Services Worldwide v Republic of Philippines* ICSID Case No ARB/03/25, Award, 16 August 2007, para 354.

[176] e.g. in the *Yukos* case, Russia argued that the claimant's corporate personality should be disregarded due to its criminal activity. *Yukos* (n 175) para 1276.

[177] Principle of contributory fault is codified in Art 39 of ARS. See also *LaGrand (Germany v US)* (Judgment) [2001] ICJ Rep 466, 487 (para 57), 508 (para 116).

[178] In *Lillie Kling* case, the presiding Commissioner held that the shooting by Mexican soldiers of an American employee at the oil company was partially caused by the 'shots fired in the air' by some of the victim's companions 'in a very imprudent manner in view of the hour and the conditions of constant alarm and insecurity which then prevailed . . .' See *Lillie Kling v Mexico* (1930) 4 RIAA 575, 585.

indirect,[179] or direct contribution to a conflict situation.[180] It goes without saying that the investor's contribution would need to be clearly established for the application of the principle in the context of countermeasures.

D. Preliminary Conclusions

It has been shown that a host state's best chance of defeating a claim against its security-related measure lies in investment treaty-based defences. While security exceptions provide for the most reliable defence, their efficiency in safeguarding a state's discretion in reacting to security threats will depend on their language and the meaning given to them by arbitral tribunals. This chapter has warned against imprecise and overly broad drafting, which has resulted in interpretations that have undermined a state's freedom to act, rather than strengthened it. Furthermore, it has argued that defences in the law of state responsibility have limited value, among others, because the treaty-based defences (i.e. police powers, exceptions, due diligence) will often render the reliance on the secondary rules superfluous.

[179] In *Bear Creek* case, the respondent argued that the investor contributed to the social unrest by failing to conduct responsible community outreach. While the tribunal found no such contribution, the dissenting arbitrator, Philippe Sands, came to a different conclusion, recommending a reduction in compensation of 50 per cent. *Bear Creek* (n 92) paras 560, 569; Dissenting Opinion of Philippe Sands, para 39.

[180] In *Copper Mesa* case, the mining company planned and induced violent acts (e.g. by recruiting and using armed men) against the local residents who opposed the investment, which exacerbated the conflict situation. *Copper Mesa Mining v Republic of Ecuador* PCA no 2012-2, Award, 15 March 2016, paras 6.99–6.102.

6
The Interplay of Investment Law and International Humanitarian Law

A. Introduction

In addition to the possible defences presented in the preceding chapter, states can try to defend their measures by relying on the obligations that exist in another legal regime. Chapter 2 showed that different substantive areas of international law co-exist with investment treaty law in times of armed conflict. Which body of law is used by the tribunal to assess the conduct of the host state with respect to foreign investment can become important when the norms from different legal frameworks regulate a specific situation differently, attaching different consequences to a state's actions. For example, a problem may arise if certain conduct is mandated or permitted under the international humanitarian law (IHL), while also constituting a breach of the investment treaty provision. In such a case, the interaction between the two regimes can give rise to a normative conflict.

Concerns about the interaction between different areas of international law have long preoccupied legal scholars. Such interactions are the consequence of the fragmented nature of the international legal order and have been perceived as problematic since they can create normative conflicts between different legal regimes. In 1953, Wilfred Jenks famously stated that such conflicts present 'an inevitable incident of growth' of international law, and called for the formulation of principles that could resolve such conflicts when they emerge.[1] Since then, the pursuit of finding an antidote to the 'problem' of fragmentation has been undertaken with great enthusiasm by academics,[2] international courts and tribunals,[3] as well as

[1] W Jenks, 'Conflict of Law-Making Treaties' (1953) 30 BYIL 401, 405.

[2] See Bruno Simma, 'Self-Contained Regimes' (1985) XVI Nl Ybk 111; M Koskenniemi and P Leino, 'Fragmentation of International Law? Postmodern Anxieties' (2002) 15 Leiden J Intl L 553; J Pauwelyn, *Conflict of Norms in Public International Law: How WTO Law Relates to Other Rules of International Law* (CUP 2003); B Simma and D Pulkowski, 'Of Planets and the Universe: Self-contained Regimes in International Law' (2003) 17(3) EJIL 484; E Vranes, 'The Definition of "Norm Conflict" in International Law and Legal Theory' (2006) 17(2) EJIL 396; M Milanović, 'Norm Conflicts, International Humanitarian Law and Human Rights Law' in O Ben-Naftali (ed), *International Human Rights and International Humanitarian Law* (OUP 2011) 95.

[3] See e.g. ICJ jurisprudence: *Legality of the Threat or Use of Nuclear Weapons* (Advisory Opinion) [1996] ICJ Rep 240, para 25 (*Nuclear Weapons*); *The Legal Consequences of the Construction of a Wall in the Occupied Palestinian Territory* (Advisory Opinion) [2004] ICJ Rep 178, para 106 (*Israeli Wall*); *Armed Activities on the Territory of the Congo (Democratic Republic of the Congo v Uganda)* (Judgment) [2005] ICJ Rep 168, paras 216–20 (*Armed Activities*).

the International Law Commission (ILC).[4] The topic has not escaped the attention of international investment law scholars. As arbitral awards have been relentlessly criticized for demonstrating pro-investor bias at the expense of other objectives, many have observed that this was due to the investment regime's insufficient or inadequate engagement with other co-existing legal regimes, such as human rights law and environmental law.[5] However, only a few scholars have addressed the interaction of investment treaties with IHL.[6] They have argued that IHL is a more suitable framework for regulating the situations of armed conflict and should thus either displace investment law protections or inform their interpretation.[7] This chapter will challenge these views and advocate investment rules as capable of regulating the protection of an investor's property during times of armed conflict. There is no general international rule determining whether investment law or IHL is the more special law (*lex specialis*). It will be argued that this is not problematic because investment treaty provisions often complement and extend IHL's focus on protecting civilians and civilian property.

The chapter will proceed by first considering the arguments that the interaction between IHL and investment law norms gives rise to the normative conflicts. It will then analyse the award in *AAPL v Sri Lanka* as a case study to demonstrate the complementary nature of the two legal regimes.[8] Finally, it will propose a methodology that can help tribunals address potential normative tensions in the future.

B. Normative Conflicts

In most cases, the relationship between different legal regimes whose subject matter partially overlaps will not be cause for concern. There is no normative conflict if the

[4] ILC Study Group, 'Fragmentation of International Law: Difficulties Arising from the Diversification and Expansion of International Law' (2006) UN Doc A/CN.4/L.682 (ILC Fragmentation Report).

[5] See e.g. F Baetens (ed), *Investment Law within International Law: Integrationist Perspectives* (CUP 2013); PM Dupuy, EU Petersmann, and F Francioni (eds), *Human Rights in International Investment Law and Arbitration* (OUP 2009); MC Cordonier Segger, M Gehring, and A Newcombe (eds), *Sustainable Development in World Investment Law* (Kluwer 2010).

[6] See G Hernández, 'The Interaction between Investment Law and the Law of Armed Conflict in the Interpretation of Full Protection and Security Clauses' in F Baetens (ed), *Investment Law Within International Law: Integrationist Perspectives* (CUP 2013) 21; O Mayorga, 'Arbitrating War: Military Necessity as a Defence to the Breach of Investment Treaty Obligations' (Policy Brief, August 2013) Program on Humanitarian Policy and Conflict Research Harvard University; H Bray, 'SOI—Save Our Investments! International Investment Law and International Humanitarian Law' (2013) 14(3) JWIT 578; W Burke-White, 'Inter-Relationships between the Investment Law and Other International Legal Regimes' (Think Piece, October 2015) E15 Task Force on Investment Policy.

[7] See Hernández, 'The Interaction between Investment Law and the Law of Armed Conflict in the Interpretation of Full Protection and Security Clauses' (n 6); Mayorga, 'Arbitrating War: Military Necessity as a Defence to the Breach of Investment Treaty Obligations' (n 6); Bray, 'SOI—Save Our Investments! International Investment Law and International Humanitarian Law' (n 6); Burke-White, 'Inter-Relationships between the Investment Law and Other International Legal Regimes' (n 6).

[8] *AAPL v Republic of Sri Lanka* ICSID Case no ARB/87/3, Award, 27 June 1990.

substantive norms of the two regimes either address different issues (e.g. IHL provisions on the protection of wounded soldiers are irrelevant to the investment law context) or they are complementary (e.g. IHL provisions prohibiting pillaging are in line with the full protection and security (FPS) and advanced armed conflict provisions in investment treaties). In the latter case, the norms are in a harmonious relationship, supporting each other without creating any divergence.[9]

The co-existence of different legal regimes becomes problematic, however, if 'a party to two treaties cannot simultaneously comply with its obligations under both treaties'.[10] According to this traditional definition devised by Jenks,[11] and followed by some international tribunals,[12] the normative conflict only exists in situations of mutually exclusive obligations. Should one adhere to this definition to inspect the relationship between IHL and investment law, the investigation would likely be short-lived, as there appear to be no such conflicting obligations in the respective regimes. This should not be surprising as both, at its core, were created to protect the interests of individuals against certain forceful interferences, or the effects thereof.

Jenks' definition has been criticized for being too narrow and for not accommodating the possibility of equally problematic divergences between permissive norms, on the one hand, and prescriptive or prohibitive norms, on the other, or discrepancies between obligations which, although not mutually exclusive, have incompatible content.[13] These incompatibilities are covered by a broader definition put forward by Pauwelyn, according to whom there is a normative conflict if a substantive norm pertaining to one regime 'constitutes, had led to, or has a potential to lead to, a breach of the norm from another regime'.[14] The broad notion of conflict, which is adopted also in the influential ILC Fragmentation Report,[15] has served as a basis for claims that during war a state could take actions in compliance with IHL that would conflict with the investment treaty obligations. While this chapter does not purport to rule out on the intricacies of a definition of a normative conflict, it does aim to show that whichever definition one subscribes to, the conclusion will likely be the same: the two normative regimes are not incompatible.

[9] ILC Fragmentation Report, 16, para 19. See also *Suez v Argentine Republic* ICSID Case no ARB/03/19, Decision on Liability, 30 July 2010, para 262; *Armed Activities* (n 3) para 220.

[10] Jenks, 'Conflict of Law-Making Treaties' (n 1) 426.

[11] For a similar view see also W Karl, 'Conflicts between Treaties' in R Bernhardt (ed), *Encyclopedia of Public International Law* (North-Holland 1984) 467, 468; G Marceau, 'Conflict Norms and Conflicts of Jurisdictions: The Relationships between the WTO Agreement and MEAs and other Treaties' (2001) 35 JWT 1081.

[12] See in particular decisions of the WTO panels: *Indonesia-Certain Measures Affecting the Automobile Industry* Panel Report (23 July 1998) WT/DS54/R, WT/DS59/R, WT/DS64/R, para 649; *Turkey-Restrictions on Imports of Textile and Clothing Products* Panel Report (31 May 1999) WT/DS34/R, para 9.88.

[13] Vranes, 'Definition of Norm Conflict' (n 2) 404; Pauwelyn, *Conflict of Norms* (n 2) 171.

[14] Pauwelyn, ibid 176.

[15] ILC Fragmentation Report, 19, para 25.

The broad understanding of normative conflict enables a helpful distinction between apparent and genuine conflicts.[16] In the latter case, the norms are incompatible and their application leads to opposite outcomes.[17] The resolution of such a conflict will require a determination as to which norm will prevail over the other.[18] By contrast, in apparent conflicts, the content of two norms only seem contradictory, and the emergence of the conflict can still be avoided by the use of certain interpretative tools. By applying these tools, the interpreters of a particular norm are paying heed to the norm of a distinct legal system, signalling their awareness thereof, harmonizing them, and dispelling the fear of the conflict between them.[19]

Scholars have invoked in particular three examples of a genuine conflict between the norms of IHL and investment law. First, some have argued that a conflict could arise between the investment treaty's FPS standard and the IHL principle of military necessity, which permits a belligerent state to attack lawful targets.[20] For example, the destruction of property 'due to necessity of war' would be justified under Article 23(g) of the Hague Regulations, but violate the state's investment treaty obligation to abstain from forceful interference under FPS. While an investment treaty imposes an obligation on a state not to destroy investment property, the IHL treaty provides a similar obligation but adds an express permission for such destruction in certain circumstances. Consequently, the relationship between these norms would fall within the broad definition of a normative conflict because the compliance with the IHL norm and activation of the 'military necessity' permission entailed therein would violate the FPS standard. This legal construction would be valid if the state's obligation to abstain under FPS was absolute. However, as shown in Chapter 4, this is not the case and states are arguably allowed to rely on their 'police powers' to protect their security interests or 'reasonably' exercise belligerent rights without violating FPS. Advanced armed conflict clauses, included in some investment treaties, simply reinforce this state's prerogative by providing for the permission in express terms, echoing IHL more closely. It follows thus that compliance with the IHL norms providing for 'military necessity' does not violate the FPS provision.

Another example of incompatibility has been said to exist in regulation of sequestration of enemy investment property.[21] According to this view, such seizures of investor property amount to indirect expropriation and must be compensated

[16] Pauwelyn, *Conflict of Norms* (n 2) 272; Vranes, 'Definition of Norm Conflict' (n 2) 414; Milanović, 'Norm Conflicts' (n 2) 103; C Borgen, 'Resolving Treaty Conflicts' (2005) 37 Geo Wash Intl L Rev 573, 605–06.

[17] *The Loewen Group, Inc and Raymond Loewen v United States of America* ICSID Case no ARB(AF)/98/3, Award, 26 June 2003, para 160 (noting that the normative conflict emerges in situations where explicit stipulations 'are at variance with the continued operation of the relevant rules of international law'.)

[18] ILC Fragmentation Report, 25, para 36.

[19] ibid.

[20] Mayorga, 'Arbitrating War' (n 6) 7.

[21] T Cole, *The Structure of Investment Arbitration* (Routledge 2013) 79.

for under investment treaty rules, although this is not required by the standards of IHL rules. However, here too, the normative conflict is only apparent since the state's 'police powers', commonly used as a defence against claims of indirect expropriation in investment law,[22] accommodate the state's right to temporarily seize assets for security reasons. Conversely, IHL norms and practice provide that such property must be eventually returned or compensation paid.[23]

Lastly, it has been argued that a normative conflict also emerges in relation to the obligation of due diligence in taking precautions in military operations.[24] Unlike in the previous examples where the normative conflict has been alleged to exist between an investment prescriptive norm and an IHL permissive norm, in this case the conflict would emerge between two norms that are not mutually exclusive but are nonetheless incompatible. Thus, the argument is that the state is held to a stricter due diligence standard under the FPS than under the IHL provisions regulating precautions.[25] Since this issue was at the core of disagreement between arbitrators in the *AAPL v Sri Lanka* case and it sets out a clear example of the interplay between investment law and IHL, the argument is discussed in greater detail and ultimately disproved in the next section.

C. *AAPL v Sri Lanka*: A Case against Fragmentation

The question of the relationship between investment law and IHL can become relevant when a particular investment claim seeks to redress losses sustained in an armed conflict that meets the IHL applicability threshold. This occurred in the case of *AAPL v Sri Lanka* as it emerged out of the civil war.[26] The case gave rise to several complex questions and provides a convenient investment treaty case study for an examination of the relationship between international investment law and IHL.

It has been shown in Chapters 2 and 4 that in the different legal frameworks applicable to investors, the host state's responsibility to protect is assessed against the standard of due diligence. Despite many commonalities, the manner in which the standard is applied may differ depending on the legal framework that the adjudicator applies in a particular case. These differing approaches are reflected in the *AAPL* case, where the majority ultimately found that Sri Lanka was liable for its failure to exercise due diligence in protecting the foreign investor. The tribunal's analysis was strongly disputed by the dissenting arbitrator, Professor Samuel

[22] See Chapter 4. D.1.
[23] See e.g. The Hague Regulations Arts 52, 53. See Chapter 2 C.1.a.
[24] I Ryk-Lakhman, 'Foreign Investments as Non-Human Targets' in B Baade et al (eds), *International Humanitarian Law in Areas of Limited Statehood—Adaptable and Legitimate or Rigid and Unreasonable?* (Nomos 2018) 171, 191–92.
[25] Additional Protocol I to the Geneva Conventions (AP I), Arts 57 and 58.
[26] For a general overview, see M Rasaratnam, *Tamils and the Nation: India and Sri Lanka Compared* (OUP 2016) 166–213.

Asante, and subjected to criticism by some scholars.[27] The core of the critique appeared to be the majority's inadequate appraisal of the due diligence rule, in particular its application in times of civil war where the standards governing the law of armed conflict would have been more appropriate. The due diligence rule thus presents itself as another area in which the co-influence of principles existing in parallel legal frameworks can come into play.[28] The following sub-sections examine this interplay through an analysis of the *AAPL* decision.

1. The Tribunal's Analysis

Having found that there was insufficient evidence that Sri Lankan armed forces had destroyed the investor's property, and having established that the said destruction took place in a combat action, the *AAPL* tribunal found that the state was not liable under the advanced armed conflict clause of Article 4(2) of the UK–Sri Lanka BIT.[29] It then moved to investigate if its responsibility could be sustained under customary international law and the FPS provision in Article 2(2). Although the tribunal arrived at customary international law through the misinterpretation of Article 4(1),[30] it explicitly referred to the due diligence obligation of the host state as encompassed in both the minimum standard of customary international law and Article 2(2).[31]

Referring extensively to the arbitrations and mixed commissions of the early twentieth century[32] and authorities like Brownlie and Freeman,[33] the tribunal restated that state responsibility could emerge from the failure to exercise due diligence in protecting foreign investors, and that this principle did not cease to apply in the period of insurgency. In determining the content of due diligence, the tribunal relied specifically on Brownlie's formulation that 'substantial negligence to take reasonable precautionary and preventive action' was deemed a sufficient ground to create 'responsibility for damage to foreign public or private property in the area'.[34] In the absence of conclusive evidence of what caused the destruction of the Serendib farm, this element proved to be crucial for establishing the responsibility of the Sri Lankan government.

[27] Mayorga, 'Arbitrating War' (n 6); J Gathii, 'War's Legacy in International Investment Law' (2009) 11 ICLR 353, 370; M Sornarajah, *The International Law on Foreign Investment* (4th edn, CUP 2017) 252; S Vasciannie, 'Bilateral Investment Treaties and Civil Strife: The AAPL/Sri Lanka Arbitration' (1992) 39(3) Nl ILR 332.

[28] For other areas of interplay, see the discussion on 'combat action' and 'necessity of the situation' in Chapter 4 C.3.

[29] See Chapter 4 C.3.a.

[30] See Chapter 4 C.2.

[31] *AAPL* (n 8) paras 67, 68, 70, 78.

[32] ibid paras 72–75.

[33] ibid paras 76–77.

[34] ibid para 76, citing I Brownlie, *Principles of Public International Law* (3rd edn, Oxford 1979) 452.

Both parties gave a different account of what happened on 28 January 1987. The investor claimed that the Serendib farm was not a terrorist base, that the attack by the Sri Lankan Special Forces was not met with violent resistance from the farm, and that the damage and killing was caused by Sri Lankan security forces not required by the exigencies of the situation.[35] The Sri Lankan government rejected these points and argued that the farm was used by Tamil Tiger insurgents as a base of their operations, that the farm's management cooperated with the terrorists, that the Tigers violently resisted the military operation of the Sri Lankan forces, and that any destruction of the farm facilities was caused directly by the Tigers.[36]

Being unable to ascertain what actually happened, the tribunal decided to focus on the facts upon which both parties agreed. First, it was uncontested that the area where the Serendib farm was located was infiltrated by rebels and was consequently out of the government's control for several months before the military operation.[37] It was also established that at the time when the relevant events took place, the farm came under exclusive control of the security forces.[38] Second, it was uncontested that Serendib farm's management established a cordial relationship with the government's security forces and offered their cooperation with respect to identifying and removing any undesirable persons from the farm. More specifically, just ten days before the attack, the security forces assured the management that they had no suspicions about any of the staff on the farm. This led the tribunal to conclude that the security forces failed to undertake precautionary measures to remove suspected persons peacefully from the farm before launching the attack. This could have been achieved through the voluntary cooperation offered by the Serendib management or by ordering the company to expel any suspected persons.[39] According to the tribunal, 'this would have been essential to minimise the risks of killings and destruction when planning to undertake a vast military counterinsurgency operation in that area for regaining lost control'.[40] Sri Lanka's inaction and omission was a violation of 'its due diligence obligation which requires undertaking [of] all possible measures that could reasonably [be] expected to prevent the eventual occurrence of killing and property destruction'.[41]

Professor Asante contested the majority's view on several points. Most importantly, he disagreed with the majority's analysis of the due diligence obligation under customary international law, and, arguably, under investment treaty provisions. While citing similar early twentieth-century jurisprudence and authorities, much like the majority,[42] he placed an emphasis on the exceptional character of the

[35] ibid paras 79, 80.
[36] ibid para 82.
[37] ibid para 84.
[38] ibid para 84(d).
[39] ibid para 85(d).
[40] ibid para 85(b).
[41] ibid.
[42] *AAPL*, Dissenting Opinion, ibid 590.

state responsibility in times of armed conflict. According to Asante, the rule was that the host state was not liable for losses sustained by foreigners during insurrections and civil commotion, and while there might be some limited exceptions, the due diligence principle did not apply with regard to areas in which the government of the host state had temporarily lost control.[43]

Asante's narrow interpretation of the due diligence rule was necessary to rebut the majority's ruling that the government ought to have taken certain precautionary measures in the conduct of its operation. According to him, there was no such obligation of diligence incumbent on the host state. He thus contested the majority's decisions on the ground that the due diligence rule in the context of armed conflict did not entail an obligation to take precautions.

2. Precautions in Attack

Asante held that it was not 'feasible or reasonable' to expect the Sri Lankan government to undertake any precautions in advance of operation 'Day-Break' against the Tiger rebels:

> The precautionary measure envisaged by the majority opinion would have been a reasonable police measure if the situation to be addressed was no more than an ordinary case of civil disorder. However, in the face of a major insurrection launched by well-armed insurgents engaged in a sophisticated guerrilla warfare against Government forces, it seems unrealistic to expect a major counter-insurgency operation to be preceded by routine police warnings.[44]

According to Asante, precautionary measures were not appropriate with regard to the actions targeting military objectives, which Serendib farm constituted according to the Sri Lankan government. Asante contrasted this to lesser types of internal disorder, where the requirement to undertake precautions would have been acceptable. This view, which prioritizes the state's unfettered discretion in targeting operations, has gained support from some commentators. Some, for example, argued that requiring the host state to carry out precautions in such situations could frustrate the objectives of military operations.[45] Moreover, they suggested that the requirement to exercise due diligence by undertaking such precautions clashes with the laws of war and thus creates a normative conflict between investment treaties and the law of targeting.[46] Along the same line, other commentators argued

43 ibid.
44 ibid 594.
45 Mayorga, 'Arbitrating War' (n 6) 4.
46 ibid 4, 6.

that the FPS obligation under investment treaties requires a higher threshold of diligence in taking precautions than the relevant IHL provisions, thus creating a normative conflict.[47]

These observations appear to be inaccurate. First, as shown in Chapter 2,[48] IHL imposes the due diligence obligation on belligerent parties, including the duty to take certain precautions during an attack. Article 57(1) of Additional Protocol I to the Geneva Conventions (AP I) thus clarifies that '[i]n the conduct of military operations, constant care shall be taken to spare the civilian population, civilians and civilian objects'. That the duty to exercise care by issuing precautions in attacks is part of the customary international law has been acknowledged by the International Committee of the Red Cross (ICRC), human rights bodies, and adjudicative tribunals.[49] The precautions should not only be taken with respect to the planned military operations of the belligerent party (active precautions), but also against the effects of attacks by the other side (passive precautions).[50] Article 57(1) AP I lists the types of precautionary measures that belligerent parties have to follow before they launch an attack, including doing everything feasible to verify that the targeted objectives are neither civilians nor civilian objects.[51] The obligation to verify the military nature of the objective to be attacked presupposes a focus on collection, assessment, and quick dissemination of information on potential targets.[52] While this provision imposes an obligation of conduct, largely dependent on the availability and quality of state's means of intelligence or reconnaissance,[53] the duty of due diligence extends also to the development of such means as needed to comply with the obligations under the Additional Protocols.[54]

The Commentary to AP I further emphasizes the importance of the duty of care in identifying the military objective, by stating that in case of doubt, additional information must be gathered before an attack can be carried out.[55] In other words,

[47] Ryk-Lakhman, 'Non-Human Targets' (n 24) 191–92.

[48] See Chapter 2 C.1.a.

[49] *Western Front, Eritrea's Claims, Claim 26* (Partial Award of 19 December 2005) 26 RIAA 291, 327, para 95. This duty applies to both international and non-international armed conflicts. See J-M Henckaerts and L Doswald-Beck, *Customary International Humanitarian Law* (CUP 2005) (ICRC Study) Rules 15–21; UN Human Rights Council, 'Report of the United Nations Fact Finding Mission on the Gaza Conflict' (2009) UN Doc A/HRC/12/48, 130; 2006 Manual on the Law of Non-International Armed Conflict, International Institute of Humanitarian Law (San Remo 2006) (NIAC Manual) 25, para 2.1.2.

[50] See AP I, Art 58, which requires the belligerent parties, among others, to protect civilians and civilian objects against the dangers resulting from military operations, 'to the maximum extent feasible'. Generally on precautions in IHL, see Chapter 2 C.1.a.

[51] AP I, Art 57(2)(a)(i).

[52] J-F Queguiner, 'Precautions under the Law Governing the Conduct of Hostilities' (2006) 88(864) IRRC 793, 797.

[53] ibid 797–78; K Trapp, 'Great Resources Mean Great Responsibility: a Framework of Analysis For Assessing Compliance with API Obligations in the Information Age' in D Saxon (ed), *International Humanitarian Law and the Changing Technology of War* (Martinus Nijhoff 2013) 153, 156; E Jaworski, '"Military Necessity" and "Civilian Immunity": Where is the Balance?' (2003) 1 Chinese Intl L 201.

[54] ICRC Commentary to Art 48 of AP I, para 1871; Trapp (n 53) 158–57. See Chapter 2 C.1.a.

[55] ICRC Commentary to AP I, 680, para 2195. On the other hand, see W Boothby, *The Law of Targeting* (OUP 2012) 122 (expressing scepticism about this approach).

an attack that is launched merely on the basis of suspicion as to the military nature of the target (e.g. that a civilian object is used by enemy forces) would breach the principle of distinction.[56] In the *AAPL* case, the tribunal held that the military reports submitted by the government as evidence that the prawn farm became a 'terrorist facility' were contradictory, inconsistent, lacking credibility, and thus unpersuasive.[57] This would suggest a likely breach of a due diligence duty in verifying the military nature of the AAPL farm, had the IHL been applied.

Furthermore, under IHL a belligerent party is obliged to take all feasible precautions in the choice of means and methods of attack in order to avoid, or at least minimize, collateral damage to civilians and civilian objects.[58] It is accepted in doctrine and jurisprudence that feasible precautions are 'those precautions which are practicable or practically possible, taking into account all circumstances ruling at the time, including humanitarian and military considerations'.[59] While the 'feasibility' of precautions will often be context dependent, parties should always be guided by the overarching duty of due diligence and act in good faith.[60] This would, for example, require the belligerent party to pay attention to the timing of the attack with a view to avoiding or minimizing collateral damage. Hence, in practical terms, attacks on civilian objects used for military purposes (e.g. factories) should be carried out at night or over the weekend, in order to minimize the harm to the staff working there.[61] Applying this principle to the context of the *AAPL* case, the fact that the 'Day-Break' operation was launched on a Wednesday during working hours, and thus resulted in the death of managers and more than twenty members of staff on Serendib farm indicates a likely breach of this principle.

Moreover, Article 57(2)(c) AP I requires the state to issue an effective warning prior to attacks affecting civilian populations, 'unless circumstances do not permit'. This is a well-established rule that enables civilians to vacate the targeted object before it is attacked.[62] In the past, such warnings took the form of evacuations of

[56] AP I, Art 52(3). See Queguiner, 'Precautions' (n 52) 798; Y Dinstein, *The Conduct of Hostilities under the Law of Armed Conflict* (3rd edn, CUP 2016) 112. The US has argued that this rule does not reflect customary international law. See US Department of Defense Report to Congress on the Conduct of the Persian Gulf War—Appendix on the Role of the Law of War (1992) 31 ILM 612, 627.

[57] *AAPL* (n 8) para 85(c). Human Rights Watch reported that ten years later, army personnel in Batticaloa admitted to their involvement in the atrocities committed in the Kokkaddicholai area (including the 'prawn farm massacre'). Human Rights Watch, *World Report: Events of 2001* (2002) 255.

[58] AP I, Art 57(2)(a)(ii).

[59] ICRC Study, 54, 70. Eritrea–Ethiopia Claims Commission explained that feasible precautions are not precautions that are practically impossible. See *Ethiopia's Central Front Claims: Ethiopia's Claim 2* (Partial Award of 28 April 2004) 26 RIAA 155, 190, para 110.

[60] Dinstein, *Conduct of Hostilities* (n 56) 165; M Bothe, 'Legal Restraints on Targeting: Protection of Civilian Population and the Changing Faces of Modern Conflicts' (2001) 31 Is YHR 35, 45.

[61] ICRC Commentary to AP I, Art 52(2), 682, para 2200; Dinstein (n 56) 171; Queguiner, 'Precautions' (n 52) 800; UK Ministry of Defence, *The Manual of the Law of Armed Conflict* (OUP 2005) (UK Manual) para 5.32.6; US Department of Defense, *Law of War Manual* (Office of General Counsel 2015) (US Manual) s 5.11.3.

[62] A Cassese, 'The Geneva Protocols of 1977 on the Humanitarian Law of Armed Conflict and Customary International Law' (1984) 2 UCLA Pacific Basin LJ 55, 84; Queguiner (n 52) 806.

targeted areas, issuing notices over the radio or by means of pamphlets, making a general announcement that a particular type of object would be attacked, etc.[63] The vaguely worded derogation to this rule allows belligerents to launch an attack without warning civilians in situations where the element of surprise is a condition of the success of the military operation. What exactly constitutes an effective warning, and when can it be left out, is not easy to ascertain.[64] In recent years, human rights bodies have interpreted the duty to issue effective warnings narrowly, limiting the scope of the exception.[65] In the context of the *AAPL* case, the absence of a prior warning could hardly be justified on the ground that the element of surprise was crucial for the success of the military operation. The goal of the Sri Lankan government was to dismantle the rebel base as part of its plan to regain control over the general area. This could have likely been achieved even with prior warning, thereby enabling the non-rebel workers to escape the farm before the attack was launched.

Even the loss of a state's control over part of its territory does not constitute an automatic exemption from its responsibility should it fail to exercise due diligence in the planning of its military operations. While reduced control over the territory is indeed an important variable that affects the assessment of due diligence in preventing injuries at the hands of non-state actors, the state's duty to exercise due diligence in the planning of forceful operations persists regardless of the type of conflict and loss of control. In this context, the forgiving character of due diligence, as discussed in Chapter 4, is diminished. In other words, the dual nature of due diligence is revealed: on the one hand, the strict standard applies to prevent damage resulting from the activities of state organs, while on the other hand, diligence in preventing harm at the hands of non-state actors is measured against a more flexible standard. This is in line with IHL, whereby the obligation to take passive precautions (i.e. precautions against the attack of enemy forces) exists only in so far as the civilian persons and objects to be protected are under the defending state's control.[66] Conversely, the duty to exercise diligence in taking active precautions knows

[63] ICRC Commentary to AP I, Art 57(2)(c), 687, paras 2224–25. Deceiving or misleading warnings that would be contrary to the proper function of the warning have been deemed unacceptable. See UK Manual, para 5.32.8; US Manual, s 5.11.5.2; 2010 Harvard University Humanitarian Policy and Conflict Research Program, Manual on International Law Applicable to Air and Missile Warfare, March 2010, 132, rule 37; Boothby, *Law of Targeting* (n 55) 128.

[64] Dinstein, *Conduct of Hostilities* (n 56) 172; Queguiner, 'Precautions' (n 52) 808; Boothby (n 55) 128.

[65] See e.g. *Isayeva v Russia* App no 57950/00, Judgment (ECtHR, 24 February 2005) para 191 (*Isayeva II*) para 187. See also UN Human Rights Council, 'Report on the Gaza Conflict' (n 49) 130.

[66] AP I, Art 58. See M Bothe, K Partsch, and W Solf, *New Rules for Victims of Armed Conflicts: Commentary on the Two 1977 Protocols Additional to the Geneva Conventions of 1949* (2nd edn, Martinus Nijhoff 2013) 41; M Sassoli, 'Targeting: The Scope and Utility of the Concept of Military Objectives for the Protection of Civilians in Contemporary Armed Conflict' in D Whippman and M Evangelista (eds), *New Wars, New Laws? Applying the Laws of War in 21st-Centry Conflicts* (Transnational Publishers 2005) 209; WH Parks, 'Air War and the Law of War' (1990) 32(1) Air Force L Rev 153–54. See also US Manual, s 5.2.1 (stating that 'party controlling the civilian population generally has the greater opportunity to minimize risk to civilians').

no such requirement as it prescribes the conduct to be followed in attacks, typically occurring on the territory under the control of the enemy forces. The control may still be a factor informing the due diligence assessment,[67] but not to the same extent as it is with respect to passive precautions and definitely does not preclude the obligation to take precautions in planning of the attack (i.e. deciding which objects will be targeted, what methods and means of attack will be deployed etc.). In other words, the necessary pre-condition for applying a due diligence rule in regard of activities of a state's own organs is not control over the territory, but rather control over the situation from which the harmful effects are likely to emerge (e.g. military attack). The higher the degree of control over such a situation, the higher is the standard of diligence a state is expected to exercise.[68]

The above analysis of the relevant IHL provisions, clearly confirms that the duty to exercise care in launching military attack coincides substantively with the due diligence obligation imposed on host states under investment law. The argument that obliging states to take precautions in launching military attacks would be inappropriate[69] can be linked to an early ambiguity as to the meaning of 'feasible' precautions used in Article 57 AP I. Namely, at the time of signing of the Protocol, the British delegation advocated a broad interpretation of the phrase that would cover 'everything that was practicable or practically possible, taking into account all the circumstances at the time of the attack, including *those relevant to the success of military operations*'.[70] The last criterion of the success of the military operation was considered controversial, as it ostensibly prioritized military interests over humanitarian obligations.[71] While the UK delegation eventually amended its declaration,[72] a relaxed interpretation of 'feasible precautions' has been adopted in the US Law of War Manual.[73] This understanding of 'feasibility' completely ignores the considerations of humanity, does not reflect the state of law, and has been rejected by the ICRC.[74]

67 ICRC has noted that the use of certain precautions and warnings may depend on who has control of the airspace. ICRC Commentary to AP I, Art 57, at 682, 686, paras 2200, 2224.

68 For a similar view in the context of extraterritorial application of human rights, see V Tzevelekos, 'Reconstructing the Effective Control Criterion in Extraterritorial Humans Rights Breaches: Direct Attribution of Wrongfulness, Due Diligence, and Concurrent Responsibility' (2014) 36(1) Mich J Intl L 129, 175.

69 *AAPL*, Dissenting Opinion (n 8) 594; Mayorga, 'Arbitrating War' (n 6) 4.

70 See ICRC Commentary to AP I, Art 57(2)(a), 628, para 2198 (emphasis added); Official Records of the Diplomatic Conference on the Reaffirmation and Development of International Humanitarian Law Applicable in Armed Conflicts, Geneva (1974–1977) Vol 6 (Swiss Federal Political Department, Bern, 1978) 214; Queguiner, 'Precautions' (n 52) 810; E Jensen, 'Precautions against the Effects of Attacks in Urban Areas' (2016) 98(1) IRRC 147, 165.

71 Queguiner (n 52).

72 ibid.

73 The US Law of War Manual states that 'if a commander determines that taking a precaution would result in operational risk (i.e., a risk of failing to accomplish the mission) or an increased risk of harm to their own forces, the precaution would not be feasible and would not be required'. US Manual, s 5.2.3.2.

74 The Commentary expressly rejects the 'success of operation' as the circumstance that factors in the assessment of 'feasibility' of precautions. ICRC Commentary to Art 57 of AP I, para 2198. On the other

Similarly, the argument that the IHL regime is more permissive in measuring state diligence in taking precautions than is investment law[75] is open to serious doubt. As shown in Chapters 2 and 4, in both regimes the standard of diligence is relative and takes into account the state's existing capabilities, including its financial and technical resources. Moreover, it has been argued that the obligation to take precautions under IHL is not measured only against a state's effort in using its existing resources, but also against its effort to develop resources that are needed for complying with IHL obligations, which arguably reflects the objective aspect of due diligence.[76] It would thus appear that there is no evidence that the investment law creates a stricter due diligence obligation than IHL in taking precautions. The subsequent analysis of the principle of proportionality further buttresses this point.

3. Proportionality

Article 57(1)(a)(iii) AP I stipulates that the precautions should include refraining from launching an attack which may be expected to violate the principle of proportionality. It is widely accepted that the principle achieved the status of customary international law and is equally applicable to non-international armed conflicts.[77] In the law of targeting, it purports to prohibit an attack expected to cause 'incidental loss' that would be excessive in relation to the 'concrete and direct' military advantage anticipated.[78] The principle has been criticized as being imprecise and open to interpretation by military commanders.[79] The ICRC Commentary admits the flaws that stem from the vague language of the provision, but defends the provision as a step forward from the arbitrary conduct of the belligerents and as a 'reasonable compromise' between the conflicting interests.[80] As mentioned above,[81] it is often asserted that the proportionality test in IHL is based on the elusive standard of a reasonable military commander who must carefully weigh the humanitarian

hand, Boothby, critical of this approach, places emphasis on the 'reality of the military context' in determination of 'feasibility'. Boothby, *Law of Targeting* (n 55) 123.

---

75 Ryk-Lakhman, 'Non-Human Targets' (n 24).

76 Chapter 2 C.1.a.

77 ICRC Study, 46, Rule 14; NIAC Manual, 22, para 2.1.1.4. See also HCJ 769/02: *The Public Committee against Torture in Israel et al v The Government of Israel et al* Supreme Court of Israel (Judgment, 11 December 2006) (*Targeted Killing*) para 43; J Gardam, *Necessity, Proportionality and the Use of Force by States* (CUP 2004) 121, 125.

78 ICRC stresses that such military advantage must be 'substantial and close'. ICRC Commentary to AP I, Art 57, para 2209. According to Bothe 'concrete' denotes specific and perceptible to the senses, while 'direct' means without necessitating any intervening agency. Bothe, *Commentary* (n 66) 365. Dinstein is also critical of the ICRC and argues against the 'substantial' condition. Dinstein, *Conduct of Hostilities* (n 56) 161.

79 ICRC Commentary to AP I, Art 57(1)(a)(iii), para 2210.

80 ibid para 2219.

81 See Chapter 2 C.1.a.

(collateral damage to civilian persons and objects) and military interests (concrete military advantage expected from an attack) at stake.[82] To abate the uncertainty, the ICRC Commentary stressed that in complex and difficult situations, the care for civilians and civilian objects should always be prioritized.[83]

Interestingly, one of the grounds on which the AAPL based its claim against Sri Lanka was the breach of proportionality in the military attack on Serendib farm:

> [t]he complete destruction and cold-blooded killings by the Government's security forces were completely out of proportion to what was necessary to meet the specific exigencies of the situation which actually existed at the SSL facility.[84]

Moreover, the claimant (represented by the public international lawyer and expert on human rights law, Heribert Golsong) seems to have invoked the strict standard of proportionality according to which the attack would only be permissible if there was no less restrictive alternative. Thus, the AAPL argued that the destruction and the killings were not needed since 'less destructive action—short of wholesale destruction and murder—could surely have been taken by the Sri Lankan special security forces'.[85] While the language of the tribunal resembled the law of targeting terminology of minimizing the risks of death and destruction,[86] the standard according to which the state's conduct was measured was arguably proportionality commonly utilized by human rights bodies. The tribunal tacitly used proportionality as part of the assessment of the government's due diligence in planning of the military operation and ultimately found the government responsible for the breach of the customary international minimum standard (and arguably FPS), without reference to relevant IHL provisions.[87] The majority conceded to the claimant's view that the attack was not proportionate since there were other peaceful alternatives available (e.g. judicial investigations against the suspected persons, and measures to peacefully remove the suspected persons from the farm) that could have been attempted first.

While the tribunal missed the opportunity to consider proportionality in more express and detailed terms, the close reading of the award reveals that most stages of a proportionality analysis, as typically applied by human rights courts, were actually addressed.[88] Thus the tribunal, exercising appropriate deference, acknowledged the legitimacy of the aim of operation and the suitability of the measure to

[82] M Wells-Greco, 'Operation "Cast Lead: Jus in Bello Proportionality"' (2010) 57 NILR 397, 407; APV Rogers, 'The Principle of Proportionality' in HM Hensel (ed), *The Legitimate Use of Military Force: The Just War Tradition and the Customary Law of Armed Conflict* (Ashgate 2008).

[83] ICRC Commentary to AP I, Art 57, para 2215.

[84] *AAPL* (n 8) para 28.

[85] ibid para 79.

[86] ibid para 85(b).

[87] ibid paras 67, 70, 86.

[88] The proportionality analysis is comprised of the assessment of the legitimacy of the measure's objective, the assessment of the measure's suitability and necessity, and lastly cost-benefit balancing or so-called proportionality *stricto sensu*. For a general overview, see C Henckels, *Proportionality and*

achieve this aim. The government's case, however, failed at the necessity analysis, which required the security organs to consider the alternative measures that would have impacted the investor's rights to a lesser extent. Having established that less restrictive viable options were clearly available to the authorities, the tribunal did not have to proceed to the most controversial stage,[89] proportionality *stricto sensu*, which would require explicit weighing of the national security interests against the rights of the investor, although the reasoning indicates that the fact that the state measure's impact included the loss of human lives (as opposed to property destruction only), would have importantly informed such a balancing exercise.

The government defended the failure to take precautions by arguing that the entire management of the farm was suspected of supporting the terrorists.[90] Leaving aside the fact that those suspicions were not buttressed by any convincing evidence,[91] it was uncontested between the parties that the management of the farm established a relationship of cooperation with the security forces and was willing to comply with their reservations or follow their instructions as to the hiring or removal of suspicious staff.[92] No such reservations or requests were ever made by the security forces. Furthermore, even if one accepts that the farm was indeed a terrorist base, the fact remains that there were still civilians working there and no precautions were taken to remove them from the farm or warn them about the incoming attack. According to IHL, the presence of civilians used as a shield on the military objective does not automatically protect that site from an attack,[93] however, the attacking party must still comply with the obligation to take all necessary precautionary measures to limit loss or damage to the civilian population and objects.[94] Moreover, the presence of civilians arguably raises the degree of diligence that armed forces are expected to exercise in taking precautions.[95]

Deference in Investor-State Arbitration: Balancing Investment Protection and Regulatory Autonomy (CUP 2015); G Bücheler, *Proportionality in Investor-State Arbitration* (OUP 2015).

---

[89] The criticism is directed against the subjective nature of the balancing exercise and the related risk of overly intrusive assessment of measures. See e.g. C Henckels, 'Indirect Expropriation and the Right to Regulate: Revisiting Proportionality Analysis and the Standard of Review in Investor-State Arbitration' (2012) 15(1) JIEL 223, 237.

[90] *AAPL* (n 8) para 85(d).

[91] ibid para 85(c).

[92] ibid para 85(b)(d).

[93] The intentional intermingling of civilians and combatants in order to render certain areas immune from military operation is a breach of IHL. See AP I, Art 51(7); ICRC Study, 337. Human Rights Watch observed that during civil war in Sri Lanka, both sides frequently used civilians as an involuntary 'human shield'. See Human Rights Watch, 'War on the Displaced: Sri Lankan Army and LTTE Abuses against Civilians in the Vanni, Report' (February 2009) <https://www.hrw.org/report/2009/02/19/war-displaced/sri-lankan-army-and-ltte-abuses-against-civilians-vanni#> accessed 18 December 2018.

[94] AP I, Art 51(8); Queguiner, 'Precautions' (n 52) 812–13; Boothby, *Law of Targeting* (n 55) 137; Dinstein, *Conduct of Hostilities* (n 56) 185 (noting, however, that in such situations 'the number of civilian casualties can be foreseen to be higher than usual').

[95] ICRC Commentary to AP I, Art 51, para 1923 (stressing that the protection of innocent civilians against danger arising from hostilities is one of the most important objectives of the Protocol). See also Queguiner (n 52) 814.

These circumstances must be taken into account when the attacking commander is applying the principle of proportionality in the planning and launching of the attack.[96] While the *AAPL* tribunal did not refer to IHL, its spirit permeates the tribunal's analysis and the application of the principle of proportionality, which appears to have been informed by the presence of innocent civilians on the farm and the subsequent human losses.[97] The tribunal's decision that a higher degree of precaution was needed due to staff working on the farm demonstrates how proportionality can be used as a yardstick for adjusting the level of expected diligence based on the objective of protection.

The tribunal's approach is evocative of the approach followed subsequently in the human rights framework. As shown in Chapter 2,[98] the European Court of Human Rights (ECtHR) has held that states have the obligation to exercise requisite care in times of armed conflict, including the obligation to issue precautions to minimize the perilous effects of hostilities on human life or property. Like the *AAPL* tribunal, the ECtHR restricted the state's discretion in launching attacks in conflict situations by applying the proportionality test.[99] However, proportionality did not require merely avoiding excessive incidental damage, as commonly postulated in the context of IHL,[100] but rather doing whatever was necessary to minimize the number of potential casualties. For example, in *McCann v United Kingdom*, the Court, ultimately finding that England violated the right to life by killing three Irish Republican Army terrorists, stressed that 'the use of lethal force would be rendered disproportionate if the authorities failed, whether deliberately or through lack of proper care, to take steps which would have avoided the deprivation of life of the suspects without putting the lives of others at risk'.[101] In *Ergi v Turkey*, the Court considered it necessary to establish whether an anti-terrorist operation conducted by Turkish security forces 'had been planned and conducted

[96] *Santo Domingo Massacre v Colombia* Judgment of the IACtHR of 30 November 2012, paras 228, 235. UK Manual notes that in the assessment of alternative means and methods of attack, factors that should be taken into account include 'the factors affecting incidental losses or damage, such as the proximity of civilians, civilian objects in the vicinity of the target or other protected objects . . .' It, however, also states that the proportionality assessment is informed not only by the presence of civilians on the military objective but also by the fraudulent conduct of the party under attack who uses civilians as a shield. See UK Manual, paras 5.32.5 and 5.22.1.

[97] *APPL* (n 8) para 85(d).

[98] See Chapter 2 D.1.

[99] See e.g. *Isayeva II* (n 65) paras 180–81, 187; *Isayeva, Yusupova and Bazayeva v Russia* App nos 57947/00, 57948/00, and 57949/00, Judgment (ECtHR, 24 February 2005) (*Isayeva I*) paras 178–81; *McCann and Others v The United Kingdom* App no 18984/91, Judgment (ECtHR, 27 September 1995) paras 202–14.

[100] Dinstein, *Conduct of Hostilities* (n 56) 155 (noting that the destruction of a whole village along with civilians living there would not be 'excessive', if an enemy artillery would operate from within that village).

[101] *McCann* (n 99) para 235.

in such a way as to avoid or minimise, *to the greatest extent possible*, any risk to the lives of the villagers'.[102]

Some domestic constitutional courts have also used proportionality restrictively in assessing the legality of a state's military operations. Famously, in the *Targeted Killings* judgment, the Supreme Court of Israel, drawing heavily on the ECtHR case law, held that a terrorist may not be targeted if less harmful means can be employed, that is if he can be captured and put on trial.[103] The Israeli Court acknowledged that arrest, investigation, and trial were not always possible, however, they were preferable to use of force and the possibility of their employment had to always be considered.[104] While some scholars stressed that there is no such rule that prescribes 'less harmful means' in IHL as combatant or civilian participating directly in hostilities can be lawfully killed,[105] the ECtHR and Israeli Court framed it within the principle of proportionality.[106] The link with the IHL understanding of proportionality in targeted attacks becomes more apparent when the state's failure to use 'less harmful means' results in incidental losses of civilian lives, as was the case in *AAPL v Sri Lanka*. In other words, the rule is that the state must refrain from attacking combatants and terrorists 'if the damage expected to be caused to nearby innocent civilians is not proportionate to the military advantage in harming the combatants and terrorists'.[107] It should be reiterated that such proportionality test is informed by the importance of the protected interests: the standard is stricter if the likely incidental losses include human lives rather than the property alone. The *AAPL* tribunal adhered to this approach.

4. Towards Convergence

The principle of proportionality—what it means and how it is applied in practice—has been one of the most controversial topics in IHL. As described in Chapter 2,[108] the permissive principle that places the emphasis on the assessment of a military advantage by a 'reasonable military commander' has been favoured by large military powers, such as the UK and the US,[109] as well as the military legal

[102] *Ergi v Turkey* App no 23818/94, Judgment (ECtHR, 28 July 1998) para 79 (emphasis added). Similarly, the Court held that Russia should have issued warnings against the effects of the rebels' actions in *Albekov and Others v Russia* App no 68216/01, Judgment (ECtHR, 9 October 2008) paras 84–85.

[103] *Targeted Killing* (n 77).

[104] ibid para 40.

[105] See e.g. Dinstein, *Conduct of Hostilities* (n 56) 42; M Milanović, 'Lessons for Human Rights and Humanitarian Law in the War on Terror: Comparing Hamdan and the Israeli Targeted Killings Case' (2007) 89(886) IRRC 373, 390.

[106] *Targeted Killing* (n 77) paras 40, 46.

[107] ibid para 46.

[108] See Chapter 2 C.1.a.

[109] *Official Records of the Diplomatic Conference on the Reaffirmation and Development of International Humanitarian Law Applicable in Armed Conflicts, Geneva* (1974–77), vol 14 (1981) 64, 67.

doctrine.[110] On the other hand, already during the negotiation of the Geneva Conventions and AP I, many developing countries expressed the fear of abuse of the principle in favour of imperialist forces.[111] Moreover, international lawyers have long been critical of the military perspective and sought to promote an interpretation that was more susceptible to human rights values and lent itself to a truly humanitarian body of law, rather than one that was humanitarian in name only.[112] Such proposals have been often described by military lawyers as detached from military and political reality, idealistic, and operationally impractical.[113] This opposition notwithstanding, the shift towards more humanitarian interpretation of IHL, including the principle of proportionality, has been advanced towards the end of the twentieth and at the beginning of the twenty-first centuries, in particular through the work of non-governmental organizations, international criminal tribunals, human rights bodies, and academic writings.[114]

The decisions of the human rights bodies, rejecting the overly permissive interpretation of proportionality, do not contradict the rules governing armed conflict. As demonstrated, the provisions of IHL treaties require due diligence in the planning of military attacks, including undertaking precautions, and likewise they apply proportionality to gauge the appropriateness of the military measures. The fact that the traditional military doctrine and scarce military practice, mostly by the US and its military partners, suggests an interpretation that is deferential to the state's autonomy in taking such measures does not necessarily create a normative conflict with the interpretation prevailing in the human rights setting. Ultimately, both frameworks have a common object and purpose when it comes to their application in the context of armed conflict, that is to limit the adverse effects of war on

[110] See e.g. Dinstein, *Conduct of Hostilities* (n 56) 159; W Parks, 'Air War and the Law of War' (1992) 32 Air Force L Rev 1,173–75; G Roberts, 'The New Rules of Waging War: The Case against Ratification of Additional Protocol I' (1985–1986) 26 Va J Intl L 109, 146; J Parkerson, 'United States Compliance with Humanitarian Law Respecting Civilians during Operation Just Cause' (1991) 133 Mil L Rev 31, 535; P Kahn, 'Lessons for International Law from the Gulf War' (1992–1993) 45 Stan L Rev 425, 435; M Newton, 'Reframing the Proportionality Principle' (2018) 51(3) VJTL 867, 885; Lieutenant Colonel R Katzir, 'Four Comments on the Application of Proportionality under the Law of Armed Conflict' (2018) 51(3) VJTL 857; G Corn, 'Humanitarian Regulation of Hostilities: The Decisive Element of Context' (2018) 51(3) VJTL 763.

[111] *Official Records of the Diplomatic Conference* (n 109) 61.

[112] T Meron, 'The Humanization of Humanitarian Law' (2000) 94 AJIL 239, 244; D Kennedy, *The Dark Sides of Virtue: Reassessing International Humanitarianism* (2004) 267; I Gunning, 'Modernizing Customary International Law: The Challenge of Human Rights' (1990–1991) 31 Va J Intl L 211, 220; L Doswald-Beck and S Vité, 'International Humanitarian Law and Human Rights Law' (1993) 293 IRRC 94, 109; A Cassimatis, 'International Humanitarian Law, International Human Rights Law, and Fragmentation of International Law' (2007) 56 ICLQ (2007) 623; C Byron, 'A Blurring of the Boundaries: The Application of International Humanitarian Law by Human Rights Bodies' (2006–2007) 47 Va J Intl L 839.

[113] See e.g. Roberts, 'New Rules' (n 110) 146; Newton, 'Reframing the Proportionality' (n 110) 885; Y Dinstein, 'Keynote Address: The Recent Evolution of the International Law of Armed Conflict: Confusions, Constraints, and Challenges' (2018) 51(3) VJTL 701, 705, 709; Corn, 'Humanitarian Regulation' (n 110) 771, 778, 783.

[114] For the historical account of this shift, see A Alexander, 'A Short History of International Humanitarian Law' (2015) 26(1) EJIL 109.

innocent people. Consequently, the desirable interpretation is one that affords the greatest protection for victims of armed conflicts. Many scholars have thus argued that rather than contradicting IHL, the human rights framework may be seen as complementing it, thus contributing to its further development.[115] In this sense, human rights bodies are filling in the gaps in the law of armed conflict, gradually humanizing it. Recent developments with respect to precautions and proportionality by some military powers are illustrative of this trend.[116]

The same reasoning, *mutatis mutandis*, applies to the relationship between humanitarian and investment law. It has been shown that the *AAPL* tribunal would have likely come to the same conclusion, had it applied IHL. The award is imbued with the humanitarian sensibilities and restrains the right to decide to launch an attack when no requisite precautions were taken and the alternatives less harmful to civilians were not considered first. It is in particular noteworthy that the *AAPL* tribunal reached this decision long before similar conclusions were adopted by human rights courts. In a way, the award was an overlooked harbinger of the shift towards more humanitarian rules governing the conduct in the course of hostilities, foreshadowing the progress accelerated later by more traditional IHL participants.

In view of the above, the doctrinal arguments that there is a strong potential for a normative conflict between investment law and IHL (which should be resolved with the displacement of the former to the benefit of the latter),[117] should be treated cautiously. This school of thought is based on the premise that investment law is an inappropriate regulatory framework in situations of armed conflict, and that IHL norms should apply instead. It emerged in response to the approach taken by the *AAPL* tribunal, which placed an emphasis on the strongest protection for victims of armed conflict. The *AAPL* decision, however, clearly shows how the investment treaty standards can be applied without giving rise to a normative conflict with the IHL provisions. The majority based its decision on the requirement to diligently undertake precautions in the planning of attacks and, arguably,

[115] Meron, 'Humanization' (n 112); D McGoldrick, 'Human Rights and Humanitarian Law in the UK Courts' (2007) 40 Is L R (2007) 527, 531; Milanović, 'Norm Conflicts' (n 2) 101; Milanović, 'Lessons for Human Rights and Humanitarian Law' (n 105) 390; A Gioia, 'The Role of the European Court of Human Rights in Monitoring Compliance with Humanitarian Law in Armed Conflict' in O Ben-Naftali (ed), *International Human Rights and International Humanitarian Law* (OUP 2011) 226, 233; W Abresch, 'A Human Rights Law of International Armed Conflict: The European Court of Human Rights in Chechnya' (2005) 16(4) EJIL 741; L Hill-Cawthorne, 'Humanitarian Law, Human Rights Law and the Bifurcation of Armed Conflict' (2015) 64 ICLQ 293; Alexander, 'Brief History' (n 114).

[116] See e.g. the Obama presidential policy guidance requiring that 'direct action will be taken only if there is near certainty that the action can be taken without injuring or killing non-combatants'. 'Procedures for Approving Direct Action against Terrorist Targets Located outside the United States and Areas of Active Hostilities' (22 May, 2013) <perma.cc/N53N-NWJH> accessed 18 December 2018. See also G Corn, 'War, Law, and Oft Overlooked Value of Process as a Precautionary Measure' (2015) 42 Pepp L Rev 419, 455; G McNeal, 'Targeted Killing and Accountability' (2014) 102 Georget L J 681, 745.

[117] Hernández, 'The Interaction' (n 6) 47; Mayorga, 'Arbitrating War' (n 6); Ryk-Lakhman, 'Non-Human Targets' (n 24).

to do so by applying proportionality, both of which are well-established standards of IHL. The assertion that there is no such obligation for states in civil wars or that the required standard of diligence is lower in IHL than in investment law does not reflect the current state of law. Rather, it is aspirational in nature and presents a step back from the effort of restraining the arbitrary conduct of belligerent states during hostilities.[118]

Regretfully, the tribunal did not make use of the opportunity to explicitly clarify the exact standard of proportionality reflected in the award. Moreover, the way it merged the IHL approach (the precautionary obligation measured against due diligence) and the human rights approach (proportionality in the obligation to refrain) leaves much to be desired in terms of legal reasoning. This notwithstanding, the *AAPL* decision, like the above-mentioned jurisprudence of human rights bodies, is an example of how investment law and IHL can be applied in a co-influential fashion, reconciling the normative tensions rather than giving rise to a genuine normative conflict.

D. Methodology for Addressing Normative Tensions

The *AAPL* case has demonstrated that there are several areas in which the investment regime may interact with the IHL framework. While it was argued that the tribunal applied the investment treaty provisions consistently with IHL, the backlash that the decision has sparked calls for a more systemic parsing of the tools for addressing the normative overlap between the two regimes. Admittedly, concerns about the incompatibility of investment law and the IHL are rooted in overly broad and vague language of some investment treaty and IHL norms and they are further bred by inconsistent interpretations that these norms are given by the relevant actors in the respective regimes. While this can create an impression of an antagonism between the two regimes, the accurate interpretation and application of norms yields no actual conflict. The uncertainty as to the exact content of legal norms creates a field of normative tension that can be alleviated only when the norms are interpreted and applied. This section examines the methods, some of which relied on by the *AAPL* tribunal, for reducing this tension.

Some scholars have suggested that states should start raising IHL defences in their pleadings as this would force tribunals to better and more expressly address such normative interactions.[119] There are certain political and jurisdictional obstacles to this preposition, which can result in norm conflict avoidance.

[118] The ICTY noted that IHL norms (in that case Arts 57 and 58 of AP I) 'must be interpreted so as to construe as narrowly as possible the discretionary power to attack belligerents, and by the same token, so as to expand the protection accorded to civilians'. *Prosecutor v Kupreškić* (Trial Judgment) IT-95-16 (14 January 2000) para 525.

[119] Mayorga, 'Arbitrating War' (n 6) 9; Burke-White, 'Inter-Relationships' (n 6) 6.

1. Political Hurdle

States are unlikely to raise IHL-based arguments as they often try to avoid the application of IHL to internal violent situations for political reasons. Namely, acknowledging that the violent situation constitutes an armed conflict and that the *jus in bello* framework applies would have certain political consequences that states normally wish to avoid, particularly if the violent situation is ongoing. For example, to resort to IHL would mean that the state tacitly admits that it is losing control over its internal matters and is unable to stop large-scale violence, that rebels have the requisite international personality to carry on diplomacy and participate in peace conferences, and that the rebels are accorded prisoner-of-war status and immunity from criminal prosecution.[120] It would also invite the international community's intervention and the state would acknowledge that *jus in bello* obligations apply. Finding that the political costs of implied admission would likely exceed the benefits of the IHL application, states often decide to downplay the intensity of the situation by claiming to carry out an operation to maintain public order.[121] As shown in Chapter 2, in conflict-related cases brought before human rights bodies, states were reluctant to resort to humanitarian law and preferred to defend their actions under provisions in the applicable human rights instruments. Not surprisingly, host states in investment cases opted for a similar strategy and did not raise defences under IHL.[122] Consequently, the states' reluctance to bring normative conflict as an argument in their defence is a way of preventing the emergence of such a conflict.[123]

2. Jurisdictional Hurdle

Another potential challenge to the direct application of IHL principles lies in the jurisdictional bar and limitations as to the applicable law.[124] Generally speaking, jurisdictional clauses in investment treaties can be divided into two categories: while some restrict the tribunal's jurisdiction to disputes concerning

[120] Abresch, 'Human Rights Law' (n 115) 756–57.

[121] ibid; A Cullen, *The Concept of Non-International Armed Conflict in International Humanitarian Law* (CUP 2010); S Vité, 'Typology of Armed Conflicts in International Humanitarian Law: Legal Concepts and Actual Situations' (2009) IRRC 94.

[122] e.g. the Sri Lankan government, which did not rely on IHL in the *AAPL* case, disallowed the Red Cross from entering the country until 1989 as this could have implied the existence of a civil war. ME O'Connell, 'Humanitarian Assistance in Non-International Armed Conflict, The Fourth Wave of Rights, Duties and Remedies' (2001) 31 Is Ybk HR 183, 195. Similarly, the government of Congo did not invoke IHL in the *Mitchell* case, although it relied on the fact that there was a state of war to justify its actions. *Patrick Mitchell v Congo* ICSID Case no ARB/99/7, Award, 9 February 2004.

[123] ILC Fragmentation Report, 28, para 43.

[124] Generally, see C Schreuer, 'Jurisdiction and Applicable Law Clause in Investment Treaties' (2014) 1(1) McGill J Disp Resol 1.

the investment treaty standards (e.g. 'interpretation and application' of the BIT),[125] others open up the jurisdictional scope as to cover 'any dispute related to the investment'.[126] An arbitral tribunal whose jurisdiction is limited to disputes arising under the investment treaty will be not be able to adjudicate claims or counter-claims based on the sources other than investment treaties (including for the alleged breaches of IHL norms), and will be typically reluctant to apply rules from other subfields of international law.[127] Conversely, broadly defined jurisdictional clauses (as was the one applied by the *AAPL* tribunal) that refer to any disputes concerning the investment arguably provide for wider discretion in hearing not only claims arising under the investment treaty standards but also claims for the violations of other international norms (e.g. customary international law).[128]

Even the narrowly drafted jurisdictional clauses do not create an absolute bar to the application of the norms from a distinct legal framework. As noted in the ILC Fragmentation Report, a distinction should be maintained between jurisdiction and applicable law, whereby the scope of the latter is not necessarily limited by the former.[129] Thus, if an investment treaty extends the applicable law to the 'rules of international law' either by means of a specific clause,[130] or an overarching procedural instrument under which the arbitration is conducted,[131] tribunals constituted under such treaties would be able to engage with IHL rules in their analysis. While such applicable law clauses cannot be used to widen the tribunal's jurisdiction,[132] a tribunal would be able to engage with IHL norms (as part of the applicable 'rules of international law') in considering parties' arguments,[133] for example, a host state's

[125] See e.g. Paraguay–Venezuela BIT (1996) Art 9(1); Switzerland–Turkey BIT (1988) Art 8(1); Germany–Zimbabwe BIT (1995) Art 8(1).

[126] See e.g. Switzerland–Paraguay BIT (1992) Art 9(1); UK–Sri Lanka BIT (1980) Art 8.

[127] See e.g. *The Rompetrol Group BV v Romania* ICSID Case no ARB/06/3, Award, 6 May 2013, paras 169–72; *Iberdrola Energia v Guatemala* ICSID Case no ARB/09/5, Award, 17 August 2012, para 306. See also Sornarajah, *International Law* (n 27) 252 (arguing that investment tribunals were not designed to deal with such political issues as the characterization of armed conflict, the legality of force used to suppress an insurrection, etc).

[128] See e.g. *SGS v Paraguay* ICSID Case no ARB/07/29, Decision on Jurisdiction, 12 February 2010, para 183; *Metal-Tech v Uzbekistan* ICSID Case no ARB/10/3, Award, 4 October 2014, para 378.

[129] ILC Fragmentation Report, 29, para 45. See also *Mox Plant Case (Ireland v UK)* PCA Case no 2002-01, Procedural Order No 3, 24 June 2003, 126 ILR 310, para 19; L Bartels, 'Applicable Law in WTO Dispute Settlement Proceedings' (2001) 35 JWT 499, 501–02.

[130] See e.g. Paraguay–Switzerland BIT (1992) Art 9(6); Paraguay–Venezuela BIT (1997) Art 9(5); Germany–Zimbabwe BIT (1995) Art 10(5).

[131] See e.g. ICSID Convention Art 42(1). See also *MTD Equity v Republic of Chile* ICSID Case no ARB/01/7, Decision on Annulment, 21 March 2007, para 61.

[132] See e.g. *Bernhard von Pezold v Zimbabwe* ICSID Case no ARB/10/15, Procedural Order no 2, 26 June 2012, paras 57–61; *Case Concerning Application of the Convention on the Prevention and Punishment of the Crime of Genocide* (*Bosnia-Herzegovina v Serbia and Montenegro*) (Judgment) [2007] ICJ Rep 43, 104, para 147. On the other hand, see *Arbitration Regarding the Delimitation of the Maritime Boundary between Guyana and Suriname* (17 September 2007) 30 RIAA 113, para 406.

[133] For similar conclusion, see *Urbaser v Argentina* ICSID Case no ARB/07/26, Award, 8 December 2016, paras 1201–02; *Bear Creek v Peru* ICSID Case no ARB/14/21, Award, 30 November 2017 (Partial Dissenting Opinion of Professor Philippe Sands) paras 10–11.

defence that its conduct, contested by an investor, was authorized by IHL norms. In other words, such applicable law clauses do not open the door to IHL-based claims but rather grant permission to entertain IHL-based arguments to the extent this is necessary for determining whether there was a breach of the relevant investment treaty standard. In addition, as will be discussed below, consideration of the insights from other disciplines of international law is made possible by means of rules on treaty interpretation (Article 31(3)(c) of the Vienna Convention on the Law of Treaties (VCLT)).[134]

Apart from these political and jurisdictional considerations that can hamper the engagement of investment tribunals with IHL, there are other mechanisms for dealing with normative interactions between the legal systems. Depending on whether they predict the interaction in advance, or in the adjudicatory phase after the apparent normative conflict has already emerged, one can distinguish between *ex ante* and *ex post* methods for addressing the normative interactions.

3. *Ex Ante* Methods

The most direct way of minimizing potential normative tensions is by incorporating the requisite solution into investment treaties. As explained in previous chapters, this can be done either by means of security exceptions or, more specifically, through advanced armed conflict clauses and express and precise demarcation of substantive standards (e.g. police powers). By negotiating such exceptions and justifications in investment treaties, states do not only shift the risk of bearing some conflict-related losses to foreign investors, but arguably also reduce the scope for apparent conflict between the investment treaty obligations and IHL.

The disadvantage of this method is that the mere inclusion of exceptions in investment treaties does not necessarily resolve normative tensions. Much will depend on the degree of specificity of their wording and, subsequently, the room left for differing interpretations by the investment tribunals. Moreover, vaguely worded exceptions could give rise to new normative tensions. For example, while the advanced armed conflict clauses build a bridge to IHL, they also complicate the relationship between the two frameworks by covering a wider array of conflict situations, thus raising questions as to the meaning of necessity and combat action. The shortcomings of the drafting solutions can still be remedied *ex post*, however.

[134] *AAPL* (n 8) paras 12, 37; *Urbaser* (n 133) paras 1200, 1204; *Tulip Real Estate and Development Netherlands BV v Republic of Turkey* ICSID case no ARB/11/28, Decision on Annulment, 30 December 2015, paras 86–92. See also ILC Fragmentation Report, 212, para 423.

4. *Ex Post* Methods

Investment treaties that tribunals commonly have to apply do not contain adequate mechanisms for addressing the interaction of competing legal obligations. In those situations, it is up to the arbitrators how they will address the normative tensions, if at all. Three often overlapping methods particularly stand out when it comes to the interplay of investment and humanitarian law: (1) the role of *jus in bello* normative elements as a factual circumstance in the investment treaty framework; (2) the role of rules and principles of general international law in bridging the differences between the two special regimes; and (3) the interpretative dialogue enabled by the principle of systemic integration. Before they are discussed, however, the use of another popular method for resolving normative conflicts will be briefly assessed, namely the *lex specialis* rule.

(a) *Lex specialis*

The content and the role of the maxim *lex specialis derogat legi generali* in dealing with normative conflicts is controversial.[135] In its simplest form, the principle means that a more special law overrides the general law. It applies when two norms regulate the same subject matter, but cannot be construed consistently. In order for the normative conflict to be resolved, a decision must be made as to which law regulates the subject matter more specifically and, arguably, was intended to govern the subject matter by the states. This law will replace the more general one in regulating that matter. Consequently, this is a method of resolving genuine normative conflicts.[136]

Some scholars subscribe to a wider understanding of *lex specialis*.[137] According to this view, *lex specialis* is a tool for avoiding the normative conflict (i.e. a tool for addressing an apparent rather than a genuine conflict) since its role is reduced to assisting in the interpretation of general norms by reference to more specific norms from the other branch.[138] This view is formulated in the *Nuclear Weapons* Advisory Opinion where the ICJ described IHL as a *lex specialis* in relation to international human rights law.[139] According to the Court, the effect of the principle was that the norm in a human rights treaty must be interpreted in the light of the more specific IHL norm.[140] In other words, the special law did not override the general law, but

[135] For an overview, see ILC Fragmentation Report, 30–114.

[136] ibid 35, para 57.

[137] ibid paras 56, 66. See e.g. J Mus, 'Conflicts between Treaties in International Law' (1998) 45 NILR 207, 218.

[138] Milanović, 'Norm Conflicts' (n 2) 113; J Pejić, 'Conflict Classification and the Law Applicable to Detention and the Use of Force' in E Wilmshurst (ed), *International Law and the Classification of Conflicts* (OUP 2012) 113.

[139] *Nuclear Weapons* (n 3) 240, para 25.

[140] The Court held that the meaning of the 'arbitrary deprivation of life' under Art 6(1) of International Covenant on Civil and Political Rights should be determined by IHL as *lex specialis*. *Nuclear Weapons*, ibid.

rather informed its interpretation. The technique that the Court has deployed indeed falls within the interpretative approach of avoiding the normative conflict, namely one that is coalesced with the principle of systemic integration.[141] As such, *lex specialis* is used to identify which norm is more appropriate for providing an interpretive direction to the other. It is not concerned with distinguishing between the special law and the general law, but rather with integrating the content of the external norm into the meaning of the standard applicable and immediately available norm. The result is that both norms are construed consistently by pursuing the same purpose. The normative conflict is only apparent, so there is no need to apply the *lex specialis*.[142] If, however, the normative conflict was indeed genuine, then the 'modified application' of the general law denotes its *de facto* displacement by the more specific rule, whereby the language of 'concurrent application' or 'modification' is only used to rationalize and legitimize the judicial interpretive exercise. While there is lack of consensus and consistent practice on the meaning of the *lex specialis* maxim,[143] it is submitted that the view closer to its animating spirit is that this is primarily a technique that aims to resolve a normative conflict by replacing a general norm with a special norm.

Having established this, the question is if the rule can be applied to the relationship between investment and humanitarian law? If so, which law is *lex specialis*? Hernández, drawing on the Advisory Opinion of the ICJ in *Israeli Wall*, suggested that IHL is the special regime that displaces the investment treaty regime.[144] In *Israeli Wall*, the ICJ reinforced its view in *Nuclear Weapons* that IHL in general (not just a specific norm) is *lex specialis* in relation to the human rights regime.[145] According to Hernández, the precedence of IHL over investment law is supported by the 'intransgressible' nature of IHL which is 'designed to provide a floor for human rights protection in times of armed conflict'.[146] He buttressed his argument by stating that it would be untenable to interpret investment treaty provisions into the IHL norms, which, in his view, would have happened if investment law had been designated as *lex specialis*.[147] This view, based on the broader understanding of *lex specialis*, is oblivious to the fact that the content of investment treaty standards has been influenced by the law of state responsibility for injury to foreigners under customary international law, often clarified in the nineteenth and early twentieth-century conflict-related jurisprudence that also informed the content

141 VCLT Art 31(3)(c).

142 A similar view was held by the ECtHR in *Neumeister v Austria* App no 1936/63, Judgment (ECtHR, 7 May 1974) paras 28–31, and by the Dispute Settlement Body of the WTO in *Turkey-Restriction on Imports* (n 12) paras 9.92–9.96. See Pauwelyn, *Conflict of Norms* (n 2) 240–44, 386; ILC Fragmentation Report, 49, para 88.

143 The ILC Study Group supported the application of *lex specialis* even in the absence of a genuine normative conflict. ILC Fragmentation Report, paras 88–97.

144 Hernández, 'The Interaction' (n 6) 28–29, 47.

145 *Israeli Wall* (n 3) 199, para 157.

146 Hernández, 'The Interaction' (n 6) 29, 47.

147 ibid 29.

of the IHL rules on the protection of civilian property. Thus, given the historical linkage and resemblance of the investment and IHL rules governing the treatment of private property, the recourse to international investment law (especially its case law) to determine the content of an IHL norm does not seem untenable—quite the opposite. As seen in Chapter 2, the war manuals of some countries still refer to the nineteenth-century arbitration decisions concerning the protection of foreign investors during civil wars to substantiate the meaning of military rules.[148]

It seems that Hernández's conclusion was necessitated by the urge to make a decision as to which law is *lex specialis*. This technique does not provide the answer, nor is there any other rule in international law that could provide guidance to the arbitral tribunal. It is submitted that the question is best left unanswered. First, as argued above, the relationship between investment law and IHL likely gives no rise to a genuine normative conflict and hence no recourse to a norm conflict resolution is needed. Second, the *lex specialis* doctrine can be effectively applied only in certain contexts.[149] For example, in the relationship between provisions within the same legal framework (e.g. investment treaty provisions),[150] or norms of general international law and its specialized fields, or, in particular, when the more general treaty expressly 'contracted out' to the more special treaty, as is the case with the Articles on the Responsibility of States.[151] Deciding which of the *leges speciales* with no clear norm relation should be displaced is inherently controversial as it creates a quasi-hierarchical relationship between the norms of two regimes, or between the regimes themselves.[152] If no clear evidence is given that this reflects the intention of the state parties (e.g. an investment treaty provision that expressly derogates to IHL), the use of this tool to address normative tensions is best avoided.[153]

148 e.g. American war manuals are supporting the rules regulating targeting of war-sustaining facilities by referring to the nineteenth-century case law involving the protection of aliens. See US Manual, s 5.17.2.3; US Department of the Air Force, *Commander's Handbook on the Law of Armed Conflict* (1980) (AFP 110–34); US Department of the Navy, *Commander's Handbook on the Law of Naval Operation* (1987) 2–3(a).

149 A Lindroos, 'Addressing Norm Conflicts in a Fragmented Legal System: The Doctrine of Lex Specialis' (2005) 74 Nordic J Intl L 27, 39 (arguing that the maxim can be successfully applied only where norm-relations are pre-determined by the hierarchical and institutional structures of the legal order).

150 ILC Fragmentation Report, 41, para 70–73.

151 Art 55 of Articles on Responsibility of States for Internationally Wrongful Acts.

152 Some other scholars have expressed scepticism of *lex specialis* in the context of the relationship between IHL and human rights law. See L Hill-Cawthorne, 'Just Another Case of Treaty Interpretation? Reconciling Humanitarian Law and Human Rights Law in the ICJ' in M Andenas and E Bjorge (eds), *A Farewell to Fragmentation: Reassertion and Convergence in International Law* (CUP 2015); A Orakhelashvili, 'The Interaction between Human Rights and Humanitarian Law: Fragmentation, Conflict, Parallelism, or Convergence' (2008) 19 EJIL 161.

153 This is the approach that the ICJ took in the *Armed Activities* case in which it did not refer to the *lex specialis* maxim to determine the relationship between IHL and human rights law, but instead applied both bodies of law in parallel and found that they outlaw the same conduct. *Armed Activities* (n 3) paras 217–20.

(b) *Jus in bello* normative elements as a factual circumstance

While a certain circumstance may be an important normative element in IHL, but not in the investment framework, the tribunals can still take it into account as a factual circumstance modifying the investment treaty obligation. For example, the existence of an armed conflict is a prerequisite for the application of IHL, but not for the application of most investment treaty provisions. Nevertheless, the fact of an armed conflict could be relevant as a circumstance informing the content of the investment treaty obligation, for example, the obligation of due diligence. Many investment tribunals applied the due diligence principle with great sensitivity, taking into account the conflict situation in which the investor sustained the loss. It should be noted, however, that what is relevant for the purposes of assessing compliance with the due diligence standard is not the legal status of armed conflict per se, but rather the factual conditions constituting it (the intensity of the conflict, the scope, how it affected the state's ability to protect investors, etc). The same level of standard could thus apply to the situations of turmoil, which are not recognized as armed conflicts under IHL, should the factual circumstances in which the losses occurred effectively be the same in both types of situation. Conversely, and as shown in *AAPL v Sri Lanka*, the mere outbreak of a civil war is not a sufficient ground for exempting the host state from the due diligence obligation. In the same vein, the existence of an armed conflict could be used to support the application of the security exception. Notably, however, armed conflict as such is neither a necessary nor a sufficient condition for the applicability of such exceptions to state responsibility.

Another example concerns the legal status of combatants. IHL distinguishes between civilians and combatants, whereby the latter do not benefit from the protections guaranteed to the former.[154] Thus, combatants may be attacked on the basis of their status, even when they pose no immediate danger to the adversary. Investment law recognizes no such distinction, which begs the question of whether a state should be liable for the measures targeting an investor (or his employees, or management) who was involved in the combat.[155] While human rights law does not differentiate between civilians and combatants either, the human rights bodies seem to have taken a more nuanced approach to this question, and have, to some extent, taken into account the fact that a targeted person, whose right to life has been violated, participated in hostilities.

Thus, the ECtHR considered the fact that the targeted person was effectively a fighter in a conflict in its analysis of Article 2(2) of the European Convention on Human Rights (ECHR), in particular when assessing the legitimacy of the

[154] AP I, Arts 51 and 52.

[155] Art 51(3) of AP I states that civilians shall enjoy the protections 'unless and for such time as they take a direct part in hostilities'.

attack.[156] The Court, however, adopted a restrictive approach in factoring in this consideration, first, by imposing a requirement that the targeted person had to be directly involved in the combat,[157] and second, by imposing a requirement that the state had to acquire adequate information to establish that the targeted person was directly involved in the hostilities before the attack materialized.[158] In case of doubt, the target would need to be carefully verified.[159]

In a similar vein, investment tribunals could take the 'combatant' status into account as a factual consideration in the application of investment treaty standards, for example as part of the exercise of its police powers, one of the elements in considering due diligence, or when assessing the 'combat action' or 'necessity' within the armed conflict clause. In *AAPL*, the tribunal did not base its analysis on the rebel status of the staff on Serendib farm; however, it held that the state failed to provide convincing evidence that there were terrorists on the farm and that a different, less destructive, course of action should have been taken against the suspected persons.[160]

(c) Rules and principles of general international law

The two specialized fields of international law could be further brought together by the application of the rules and principles of general public international law.[161] A tribunal faced with a legal question that could yield different outcomes in two different legal settings could thus seek out the common denominator in the body of general international law applicable in both frameworks. In this way, it would avoid having to choose one norm over the other, a dilemma that could spark legitimacy concerns about the inadequate balancing of competing values and establishing artificial normative hierarchies. The rules that could help the legal regimes communicate better could either take the form of customary international law or general principles of international law *stricto sensu*.[162] The application of such rules does not need to be justified by a recourse to Article 31(3)(c) VCLT—as stressed by the ILC Study Group, they form an interpretive background for special treaty provisions and are 'applicable as a function of their mere "generality"'.[163] It has been shown that investment tribunals, while

[156] See e.g. *Ahmet Özkan and Others v Turkey* App no 21689/93, Judgment (ECtHR, 6 April 2004) paras 305–06; *Isayeva II* (n 65) paras 180–81.
[157] See e.g. *Gül v Turkey* App no 22676/93, Judgment (ECtHR, 14 December 2000) para 82; *Oğur v Turkey* App no 21594/93, Judgment (ECtHR, 20 May 1999) para 81.
[158] See e.g. *Mansuroğlu v Turkey* App no 43443/98, Judgment (ECtHR, 26 February 2008); *Khatsiyeva and Others v Russia* App no 5108/02, Judgment (ECtHR, 17 January 2008) paras 134–37.
[159] This reasoning was followed also in *Targeted Killing* (n 77) para 40, referring to the ICRC Study, 24.
[160] *AAPL* (n 8) para 85(c)(d).
[161] ILC Fragmentation Report, 211, para 421.
[162] Statute of the International Court of Justice, Art 38(b) and (c).
[163] ILC Fragmentation Report, paras 421, 468. See also, *North Sea Continental Shelf Cases (Federal Republic of Germany/Denmark; Federal Republic of Germany/Netherlands)* (Judgment) [1969] ICJ Rep, 38–39, para 63.

reluctant to borrow from specialized legal regimes, do not shy away from applying the rules and principles of general international law in relation to a broad range of issues.[164]

Both international investment law and IHL are normatively related as subfields of the same body of general international law, thus they share some common principles. The link is even stronger in the light of their historical connections going back to the nineteenth-century conflict-related arbitrations addressing the losses of aliens. As seen in Chapter 2, that jurisprudence has strongly influenced the evolution of both humanitarian and investment treaty law, and clarified the international minimum standard, part of which is the principle of due diligence. Thus, one way for an investment tribunal to bridge the gap with humanitarian law in the area of overlap is to inform the content of the treaty standard with the customary international law, or to apply the latter directly. In this way, the common foundation of some of the investment and IHL norms may help avoid a normative conflict between the two regimes.[165] For example, the *AAPL* tribunal based its decision on the customary international minimum standard while linking its analysis of the due diligence principle to the jurisprudence emerging from late nineteenth- and early twentieth-century civil wars. This method avoids the controversial, and, for arbitrators, less appealing, reference to the IHL treaty law, while arguably arriving at the same outcome. In the words of Campbell McLachlan, the reference to custom is appealing because it may inhibit 'the unfettered discretion of the adventurist arbitrator'.[166]

Another normative link is provided by the general principles of international law that are binding upon states because of their ubiquity in various municipal systems across the world. An example of such a general principle is good faith,[167] or similar principles rooted in equity, which could be used to account for the 'combatant' status of the investor. As noted above, the involvement of the investor in the hostile activities would likely need to pass a high threshold in order to be taken into account as a relevant circumstance in the assessment of state responsibility under the investment treaty standards. However, equity-based principles provide

[164] J Commission, 'Precedent in Investment Treaty Arbitration: A Citation Analysis of a Developing Jurisprudence' (2007) 24(2) JIA 129, 152; O Fauchald, 'The Legal Reasoning of ICSID Tribunals—An Empirical Analysis' (2008) 19(2) EJIL 301, 342; J Zrilič, 'Jurisprudential Interaction between ICSID Tribunals and the International Court of Justice' in A Bjorklund (ed), *Yearbook on International Investment Law & Policy 2013–2014* (OUP 2015) 305.

[165] The ILC Study Group highlighted the relevance of customary international law as a means for achieving systemic integrity. ILC Fragmentation Report, 237–38. See also Cassimatis 'International Humanitarian Law' (n 112) 633–37.

[166] C McLachlan, 'Is there an Evolving Customary International Law on Investment?' (2016) 41(2) ICSID Rev 257, 258.

[167] See e.g. *Nuclear Tests* (*Australia v France*) Judgment [1974] ICJ Rep 253, 268, para 46. For an overview, see B Cheng, *General Principles of Law as Applied by International Courts and Tribunals* (CUP 2006) 105–160.

a tribunal with another ground to take into account the 'bad faith' of the foreign investor.[168]

Another tool used to allay the normative strain between investment and humanitarian values is the principle of proportionality. Whether or not proportionality has attained the status of a general principle,[169] or it merely operates as an interpretive technique, it is frequently used by international courts, in particular the ECtHR, as a device that enables them to balance the competing values. The case *Tecmed v Mexico* is often celebrated as the first in which proportionality was applied in investment arbitration.[170] It has been shown, however, that more than ten years before the *Tecmed* decision, the *AAPL* tribunal arguably applied proportionality in its assessment of the state's conduct. While not being extensive, the reasoning of the majority clearly implies that the state's measures, that is the lack of adequate precautions, were considered disproportionate, which led to the finding of Sri Lanka's responsibility. The application of proportionality was likely influenced by its invocation by the claimant, as well as its generally accepted role in the law of targeting. Along the same lines, the awards in the *Pantechniki* and *Lesi* cases advocated the use of proportionality in evaluating states' due diligence in taking measures of protection against physical violence that does not involve targeting operations.[171]

Apart from being used to assess a state's active (*AAPL*) and passive (*Pantechniki, Lesi*) precautions within the due diligence rule, proportionality can be also applied in considering the legality of measures that a state has taken to protect its security interests and that have directly or indirectly harmed investors' interests. Such use of proportionality has been introduced in reasoning of several arbitral awards with an aim to establish the presence of compensable expropriation, often alongside the police powers doctrine.[172] The two concepts are not incompatible; rather, they are in a mutually supportive relationship whereby proportionality helps to prevent the abuse of state's police powers. As argued in Chapter 4, the use of police powers (and proportionality) should be encouraged beyond indirect expropriation to cover

[168] At the very least, an investor's improprieties could inform the arbitral decision-making process and be taken into account in the assessment of the host state's liability and the amount of awarded compensation. See Chapter 5, nn 174–80.

[169] See Bücheler, *Proportionality* (n 88) Chapter 3, and n 11 (listing authorities who agree and disagree that proportionality is a general principle of law). For a view that proportionality is not a general principle of law and should not be applied in an investment law context, see in particular M Sornarajah, *Resistance and Change in the International Law of Foreign Investment* (CUP 2015) 365–82.

[170] *Tecmed v United Mexico* ICSID Case no ARB(AF)/00/2, Award, 29 May 2003, paras 116, 122, 123. In that case, the tribunal transposed the concept of proportionality directly from the ECtHR jurisprudence.

[171] *Pantechniki SA Contractors & Engineers v The Republic of Albania* ICSID Case no ARB/07/21, Award, 30 July 2009, para 77; *LESI v Algeria* ICSID Case no ARB/03/08, Award, 10 January 2005, para 181. The view that the due diligence assessment should include a proportionality analysis was advocated already by nineteenth-century jurists. See W Hall, *A Treatise on International Law* (2nd edn Clarendon Press 1884) 196.

[172] See Chapter 4, n 89.

alleged breaches of FPS provisions as well. This aligns the investment framework with the IHL which in a similar vein uses proportionality to determine the legality of military measures that result in the harm of civilians.

(d) Principle of systemic integration

Finally, the commonly advocated tool for ensuring unity between investment and humanitarian law is the principle of systemic integration set out in Article 31(3)(c) of the VCLT, which requires that other applicable rules of international law be taken into account when interpreting a treaty.[173] The principle provides tribunals with a legal justification for considering other rules of international law in their interpretation and application of a treaty provision and thus enables them to avoid the normative conflict.[174] It can either function on its own or support other methods of avoiding normative conflict. Importantly, it goes beyond a mere restatement of the applicability of general international law, for which, as mentioned above, no formal reference to Article 31(3)(c) would be necessary.[175] Rather, the scope of integration is extended to bring in the rules from other specialized fields of international law.[176] This can be done either by using a norm from an extraneous legal regime to inform the interpretation of the content of the investment treaty provision, or by cross-fertilizing the ideas articulated in the decisions of a distinct adjudicative system. The principle of systemic integration and the corresponding jurisprudential interaction have been largely touted as a panacea to the problem of 'fragmentation'.[177] For example, in his study of the case law of different international courts and tribunals, Charney observed that international courts have largely applied international law consistently, partly because of the cross-fertilization of ideas among them.[178]

Interestingly, the *AAPL* tribunal explicitly embraced systemic integration by stressing that a BIT is not a 'self-contained closed legal system' and that 'recourse to the rules and principles of international law has to be considered a necessary

[173] For an overview of the principle, see in particular ILC Fragmentation Report, paras 410–93; C Mclachlan, 'The Principle of Systemic Integration and Article 31(3)(c) of the Vienna Convention' (2005) 54(2) ICLQ 279, 280; P Sands, 'Treaty, Custom and the Cross-fertilization of International Law' (1998) 1(1) Yale HRDLJ 85.

[174] For an overview of the principle, see in particular ILC Fragmentation Report, paras 410–93; Mclachlan, 'The Principle of Systemic Integration' (n 173); Sands, 'Treaty, Custom and the Cross-fertilization of International Law' (n 173).

[175] ILC Fragmentation Report, paras 415, 421–22.

[176] ibid paras 422, 470.

[177] ibid para 420.

[178] J Charney, 'The Impact on the International Legal System of the Growth of International Courts and Tribunals' (1999) 31 NYU JILP 697, 707. For a similar view in support of cross-fertilization between different normative regimes see B Simma, 'Universality of International Law from the Perspective of a Practitioner' (2009) 20 EJIL 265, 282–84; *Case Concerning Ahmadou Sadio Diallo (Republic of Guinea v Democratic Republic of the Congo)* (Judgment on Compensation) [2012] ICJ Rep 324, Declaration of Judge Greenwood 391, 394.

factor providing guidance within the process of treaty interpretation'.[179] It then used the armed conflict clause as an example of an investment treaty provision that is susceptible to such borrowing from distinct legal systems. As discussed above, the tribunal informed the content of the armed conflict clause and the standard of due diligence by engaging with the war-related cases of international and domestic adjudicatory bodies and the customary law clarified therein.[180] Such references may be preferred to direct references to IHL treaties, whose application, even if only in the background as an interpretative tool, may be complicated. The complications are not only as a result of politics (i.e. reflecting an implicit acknowledgement of the existence of civil war), but also due to their limited scope in the context of non-international conflict and the requirement that the host state must be the party to the relevant IHL convention or protocol.[181]

While there are many benefits to this method of avoiding normative conflict, there are also certain risks. It may lead to the misinterpretation of the foreign norms and concepts,[182] conflicting jurisprudence,[183] and the development of investment law in the wrong direction.[184] It is also problematic because it endows tribunals with tremendous discretion in formulating the applicable norm. It most certainly is not a panacea that could establish a perfect cross-balancing of competing regimes. For example, the scholars who have argued for better accounting of states' security interests in investment law have proposed systemic integration as an interpretative device to achieve this goal;[185] however, the *AAPL* tribunal appears to have used the exact same method to arrive at an outcome that was detrimental to the state's position. Systemic integration is only a means, a legal justification, to the tribunal opening the door to the norms and standards of other branches of international law. How these norms are interpreted and applied—either to support the investor's interests or the non-investment values—will depend on each tribunal.[186] The fragmented nature of the investment treaty adjudicative system further exacerbates the problem by creating inconsistencies in the application of systemic

[179] *AAPL* (n 8) paras 21 and 37 Rule (D). The tribunal buttressed this statement by reference to the VCLT Art 31(3)(c).

[180] The tribunal could have invoked the rules of general international law even without the express reference to VCLT Art 31(3)(c). See ILC Fragmentation Report, para 459, 468.

[181] The latter limitation may be mitigated insofar as the relevant rule in the treaty has a status of customary international law. ILC Fragmentation Report, 237–38, paras 471–72.

[182] See e.g. J Kurtz, 'The Use and Abuse of the WTO Law in Investor-State Arbitration: Competition and its Discontents' (2009) 20 EJIL 794.

[183] ibid.

[184] Zrilič, 'Jurisprudential Interaction' (n 164) 326; C Brown, *A Common Law of International Adjudication* (OUP 2007) 149.

[185] Hernández, 'The Interaction' (n 6) 48; Mayorga, 'Arbitrating War' (n 6); Burke-White, 'Inter-Relationship' (n 6).

[186] See M Waibel 'Uniformity versus Specialisation (2): A Uniform Regime of Treaty Interpretation?' in C Tams et al (eds), *Research Handbook on the Law of Treaties* (Edgar Elgar 2014); and 'Interpretive Communities in International Law' in A Bianchi et al (eds) *Interpretation in International Law* (OUP 2015).

integration and cross-fertilization, and thus sparks legitimacy concerns. This casts a shadow of doubt over the proposition that systemic integration should be used as the primary interpretative tool for avoiding normative conflicts. Nonetheless, if tribunals decide to engage in an interpretive dialogue and draw analogies with an external system, they should do so with great sensitivity and awareness of the shared values and conceptual differences between the legal regimes.[187]

E. Preliminary Conclusions

This chapter has set out to examine the interplay between the norms of investment treaties and IHL. It has done so by analysing the award in *AAPL v Sri Lanka*. The political context in which the case arose has invited criticism from scholars who saw the majority's decision as unfairly suppressing the state's sovereign right to defend itself, and as paying insufficient heed to the norms and principles of IHL. These claims have been rejected, and it has been argued that the tribunal's final decision, albeit flawed in its reasoning, was accurate and fair in its outcome, and did not contradict the norms of IHL. Moreover, it has been argued that the potential for a genuine normative conflict to materialize between the two regimes is unlikely for practical, political, and legal reasons. For example, it has been shown that in certain contexts, such as targeting operations, the due diligence standard in IHL and investment law converges, and should be applied in a way that best protects the innocent party. Investment law equips tribunals with sufficient tools to mitigate normative tensions between regimes, and some of those tools were effectively employed by the *AAPL* tribunal.

[187] Zrilič, 'Jurisprudential Interaction' (n 164).

7

Investment Treaty Claims and Post-Conflict Justice

A. Introduction

It has been shown that host states will typically try to defend their detrimental actions or omissions during times of conflict by citing the impossibility of meeting their obligations as a result of the circumstances, or by referring to the need to prioritize national security interests over investors' rights. In the post-conflict period another competing interest emerges, namely the interest of the host state, and broadly, that of the international community, to ensure that the conflict does not resurface and that the host state recovers from the crisis. In particular, the host state's obligation to clean up after its past misdeeds by paying hefty compensation to foreign investors can, presumably, hamper the state's efforts to facilitate post-conflict economic recovery and ensure just and sustainable peace.

Traditionally, conflict-related claims by foreign investors have been dealt with in peace treaties or their functional equivalents, that is through resolution on a government-to-government basis. This classical approach reflects the practical necessities of peacemaking, as the presence of claims controlled by individuals potentially complicates the perpetually difficult process of establishing peace. Governments will usually base their decision to raise a conflict-related claim on a number of political and strategic considerations, such as the financial ability of the other side to pay damages and the conditions for durable peace, among others. In contrast, investors pursuing claims directly against host states would not typically be concerned with the broader implications that financial awards may have on the process of peacemaking. Claims for compensation may amount to hundreds of millions of dollars, payment of which may impose a heavy financial burden on an impoverished state that seeks to return to lasting peace. Against this background, this chapter aims to examine whether investment treaties are likely to assist or complicate the transition from conflict to peace.[1]

Following this route, the chapter first sketches out the role of investment treaties in the post-conflict framework. It then compares the traditional methods of settling

[1] A shorter version of this chapter has been published in a special volume looking at the interaction of investment law and post-conflict justice. See J Zrilič, 'International Investment Law in the Context of Jus Post Bellum: Are Investment Treaties Likely to Facilitate or Hinder the Transition to Peace?' (2015) 16 JWIT 604.

post-conflict international claims with investment treaty arbitration and examines how investment treaty claims may interfere with peacemaking. Following that, it discusses various methods for incorporating *jus post bellum* considerations in determining compensation modalities.[2] In the end, it reflects on different ways that states can regain more control in the process of post-conflict settlements.

B. Investment Treaties in the Post-Conflict Framework

The role of investment treaties in the post-conflict framework is twofold. First, and according to the conventional view, as a modern fabric of international economic governance they promote economic development and thus contribute to maintaining peace. Second, they provide foreign investors with an avenue to pursue financial reparations for conflict-related losses. On both macro- and microeconomic levels, however, investment treaties are a double-edged sword. While they may indeed contribute to peace by facilitating stability and development in the host state, they may also be the source of (renewed) conflict. Similarly, as indemnifying investors for conflict-related losses is a just and necessary step in the process of peaceful transition, it may also interfere with the peacemaking process in the host state.[3]

1. Macroeconomic Effect: Investment as a Condition for Peace

Many scholars have touted economic rebuilding as a relevant element of post-conflict justice.[4] As noted by Boon, 'the establishment of a durable peace is widely perceived to include . . . economic reconstruction'.[5] It is believed that an important part of economic development depends on the inflow of foreign direct investment (FDI). The nexus between the FDI and peace has been to a certain extent

[2] The term *post bellum*/post-conflict justice is associated with objectives of establishing durable peace, the fairness and inclusiveness of peace settlements, the humanization of reparations and sanctions etc. For an overview, see C Stahn, 'Mapping the Discipline(s)' in C Stahn and J Kleffner (eds), *Jus Post Bellum: Towards a Law of Transition From Conflict to Peace* (TMC Asser Press 2008) 105; C Stahn, J Easterday, and J Iverson (eds), *Jus Post Bellum: Mapping the Normative Foundations* (OUP 2014).

[3] See e.g. C Tomuschat, 'Individual Reparation Claims in Instances of Grave Human Rights Violations, The Position under General International Law' in A Randelzhofer and C Tomuschat (eds), *State Responsibility and the Individual, Reparation in Instances of Grave Violations of Human Rights* (Kluwer Law International 1999) 1, 23.

[4] See I Österdahl and E van Zadel, 'What Will Jus Post Bellum Mean? Of New Wines and Old Bottles' (2009) 14 JCSL 175, 182–83; A Bellamy, 'The Responsibilities of Victory: Jus Post Bellum and the Just War' (2008) 34 Rev Intl Studies 601, 615; L Jubilut, 'Toward a New Jus Post Bellum: The United Nations Peacebuilding Commission and the Improvement of Post-Conflict Efforts and Accountability' (2011) 20 Minnesota J Intl L 26, 57; K Boon, 'Obligations of the New Occupier: The Contours of Jus Post Bellum' (2009) 31 Loyola LA Intl and Comp L Rev 57, 58.

[5] Boon, ibid.

proven by empirical studies, according to which FDI links between countries, particularly when symmetrical, significantly diminish the chances of conflict occurring between them.[6] Such links are more likely to reduce hostilities than, for example, trade links.[7] It is thus not surprising that governments often encourage FDI in conflict-prone areas, or in countries recovering from armed conflict, in the hopes of stabilizing their economic and political situations.[8] For example, after the Second World War, US foreign economic policy (which included treaties on protection of foreign investment) was based on the idea that a new world war could only be avoided if the global economy was stable and prosperous.[9] Thus, the goal was to increase economic interdependence which in turn would increase the costs of conflict between states.

Furthermore, commentators from the field of political economy have observed that post-conflict policy choices are crucial for determining whether the state will be able to emerge from the cycle of violence and poverty to achieve enduring economic recovery and political stability (poverty–conflict trap).[10] Following this reasoning, countries would be incentivized to create mechanisms that would attract FDI—in other words, to create the conditions for good governance. Empirical evidence also shows that weak economic governance, particularly as it concerns the protection of property rights, negatively affects the inflow of FDI.[11] The insecurity that investors face when investing abroad, especially in countries where the political risks are high and the domestic institutions are weak, creates the need for *ex ante* precautionary measures that mitigate some of these risks.[12] The conventional view is that investors will be reluctant to invest unless a state credibly commits to guarantee certain protections and constrain its future conduct.[13] This belief is also one of the reasons why countries decide to enter into investment treaties.

[6] R Rosenrance and P Thompson, 'Trade, Foreign Investment and Security' (2003) Annu Rev Polit Sci 377.

[7] ibid.

[8] Rosenrance and Thompson have noted that the present-day investment from Taiwan to China aims 'to improve the political relationship and to create a situation in which neither political unit can think realistically of getting along without the other'. ibid 391.

[9] Hence, the post-Second World War US FDI in Berlin, France, and Italy. See K Vandevelde, *The First Bilateral Investment Treaties: U.S. Postwar Friendship, Commerce, and Navigation Treaties* (OUP 2017) ch 1; P Hearden, *Architects of Globalism: Building a New World Order During World War II* (The University of Arkansas Press 2002) xi.

[10] Some studies suggest that leaders of post-conflict countries are more likely to limit their sovereignty by entering into bilateral investment treaties (BITs) in order to attract much needed foreign capital, escape the poverty-conflict trap, and thus retain political power. See e.g. S Blomberg and G Hess, 'The Temporal Links between Conflict and Economic Activity' (2002) 46(1) J Conflict Resol 74; P Collier et al, *Breaking the Conflict Trap: Civil War and Development Policy* (World Bank Publications 2003).

[11] A Dixit, 'International Trade, Foreign Direct Investment and Security' (2011) 3 Ann Rev Econ 191; S Globerman and D Shapiro, 'Governance Infrastructure and US Foreign Direct Investment' (2003) 34 J Int Bus Stud 19.

[12] Dixit, ibid; C Daude and E Stein, 'The Quality of Institutions and Foreign Direct Investment' (2007) 19(3) Econ Pol 317.

[13] A Guzman, 'Explaining the Popularity of Bilateral Investment Treaties' in K Sauvant and L Sachs (eds), *The Effect of Treaties on Foreign Direct Investment* (OUP 2009) 81; E Neumayer and L Spess, 'Do Bilateral Investment Treaties Increase Foreign Direct Investment to Developing Countries' in Sauvant

While the above narrative seems logical and sound, it is by no means undisputed. First, the link between investment and peace has predominantly been considered with respect to international conflicts, while the link to internal conflicts lacks a convincing empirical foundation.[14] History also shows that the drivers of conflict, when they exist, can be extremely intense, ranging from ethnic divisions to differences in religious beliefs, ideological disagreements, and the struggle for resources.[15] Often these forces will offset the gains for economic cooperation. Second, it has been contended in some empirical surveys that the correlation between investment treaties and the inflow of FDI is rather tenuous.[16] This is in particular the case in politically unstable, conflict-prone countries where investment treaties alone may not be enough to counterbalance the lack of security.[17]

Moreover, the investment treaty regime has often been criticized as being modelled on a neoliberal project and thus favouring the rights of foreign investors at the expense of capital-importing, traditionally developing countries and their public policy objectives.[18] The prospect of investors' compensation claims may deter governments from passing certain regulatory measures that would benefit society.[19] Alternatively, passing such regulatory measures may result in investment disputes and hefty compensation, which may impose a heavy burden on the host state's population and its well-being. This can contribute to conditions resulting in public

and Sachs, 230; A Dreher and S Voigt, 'Does Membership in International Organizations Increase Governments Credibility? Testing the Effects of Delegating Powers' (2011) 39(3) J Comp Econ 326.

---

[14] One recent study, however, suggests that BITs and FDI are an appealing and effective policy choice for economic recovery after civil war. See T Billing and AD Lugg, 'Conflicted Capital: Bilateral Investment Treaties and Post-Conflict Economic Recovery' (2019) 63(2) J Conflict Resol (2019) 373.

[15] See e.g. I De Soysa, 'Paradise Is a Bazaar? Greed, Creed, and Governance in Civil War, 1989–1999' (2002) 39(4) J Peace Res 395, 413; L Diamond and M Plattner (eds), *Nationalism, Ethnic Conflict, and Democracy* (Johns Hopkins University Press 1994); J Fearon and D Laitin, 'Violence and the Social Construction of Ethnic Identity' (2000) 54(4) Intl Org 845.

[16] J Yackee, 'Bilateral Investment Treaties, Credible Commitment, and the Rule of (International) Law: Do BITs Promote Foreign Direct Investment?' (2008) 42 L & Soc Rev 805; UNCTAD, 'The Role of International Investment Agreements in Attracting Foreign Direct Investment to Developing Countries' (UN 2009) UNCTAD/DIAE/IA/2009/5; K Vandevelde, 'The Economics of Bilateral Investment Treaties' (2000) 41 HILJ 469; M Hallward-Driemeier, 'Do Bilateral Investment Treaties Attract Foreign Direct Investment? Only a Bit . . . And They Could Bite' (2003) World Bank Policy Research Working Papers No WPS 3121.

[17] Vandevelde, *First Bilateral Investment Treaties* (n 9) 249 (noting that this is how the US State Department explained the lack of FDI in politically unstable countries despite the conclusion of the post-war FCN treaties with those countries).

[18] See M Sornarajah, *The International Law on Foreign Investment* (4th edn, CUP 2017) 171; A Shalakany, 'Arbitration and the Third World: A Plea for Reassessing Bias under the Specter of Neo-Liberalism' (2000) 41 HJIL 419; J Gathii, 'War's Legacy in International Investment Law' (2009) 11 ICLR 353, 385.

[19] On so-called 'regulatory chill', see S Schill, 'Do Investment Treaties Chill Unilateral State Regulation or Mitigate Climate Change?' (2009) 24(5) J Intl Arb 496; K Tienhaara, 'Regulatory Chill and the Threat of Arbitration: A View from Political Science' in C Brown and K Miles (eds), *Evolution in Investment Treaty Law and Arbitration* (CUP 2011) 606; D Schneiderman, 'Investing in Democracy? Political Process and International Investment Law' (2010) 60(4) U Toronto L J 909, 910.

discontent, the rise of nationalism, riots, and other types of violence.[20] More directly, foreign investors can threaten the peace or worsen the security situation in a host state by meddling with the domestic democratic processes,[21] through deployment of private security firms in order to suppress local opposition to investment,[22] by helping terrorist organizations or insurrectional movements that aim to topple a government,[23] or by assisting the governments responsible for humanitarian atrocities.[24]

Additionally, when the transition from conflict to peace overlaps with the transition from an authoritarian regime to a new political order, the new government will often be pressured to redistribute the economic rents monopolized by the elites favoured by the previous regime to the supporters of the new regime.[25] The government may be inclined to pursue such actions in order to enhance its legitimacy, consolidate its control, and thereby secure the regime's viability.[26] Investment treaties may constrain this process by placing a high price on such redistribution. In response to governmental actions, in particular, investors protected under investment treaties can initiate expensive lawsuits before arbitration tribunals.[27] In

[20] See e.g. Cochabamba's 'Water War', featuring widespread violence and protests against the foreign investor, Aguas del Tunari, in response to the raising of the water rates in Bolivia. *Aguas del Tunari SA v Republic of Bolivia* ICSID Case no ARB/02/3. See also the riots in response to the increase in the road tolls in *Autopista Concesionada de Venezuela v Venezuela* ICSID Case no ARB/00/5, Award, 23 September 2003.

[21] e.g. foreign business groups were believed to assist in the overthrow of the government of Allende in Chile and his replacement with Pinochet in 1973. Sornarajah, *International Law* (n 18) 177. Recently, the role of foreign media investors in undermining democracies has come under greater attention. e.g. Russian and Hungarian investors in a media sector have been accused of fuelling the right-wing populist wave in some European countries. See e.g. P Kingsley, 'Safe in Hungary, Viktor Orban Pushes His Message Across Europe' *New York Times* (18 June 2018) <https://www.nytimes.com/2018/06/04/world/europe/viktor-orban-media-slovenia.html accessed> accessed 15 October 2018.

[22] See e.g. *Copper Mesa Mining Corp v Ecuador* PCA no 2012-2, Award, 15 March 2016. See also P Smith, 'Shell Accused of Fuelling Violence in Nigeria by Paying Rival Militant Gangs' *the Guardian* (3 October 2011) <https://www.theguardian.com/world/2011/oct/03/shell-accused-of-fuelling-nigeria-conflict> accessed 7 November 2018.

[23] In several arbitration cases, governments tried to justify their measures by invoking alleged association between investors and rebellions or terrorist groups. See *Patrick Mitchell v Congo* ICSID Case no ARB/99/7, Award, 9 February 2004; *AAPL v Sri Lanka* ICSID Case no ARB/87/3, Final Award, 27 June 1990; *Al Jazeera Media Network v Arab Republic of Egypt* ICSID Case no ARB/16/1 (pending).

[24] See e.g. *Doe I v. Unocal Corp*, 395 F.3d 932 (9th Cir. 2002), in which the American court had to assess whether the US corporation allowed and supported the human rights violations by the Myanmar government, committed in the course of the investor's project. See also E Black, *IBM and the Holocaust: The Strategic Alliance between Nazi Germany and America's Most Powerful Corporation* (Dialog Press 2012); J Harri, 'How the World's Biggest Corporations are Fuelling Genocide in Sudan' *Independent* (19 November 2004) <https://www.independent.co.uk/voices/commentators/johann-hari/how-the-worlds-biggest-corporations-are-fuelling-genocide-in-sudan-533753.html> accessed 7 November 2018.

[25] J Bonnitcha, 'Investment Treaties and Transition from Authoritarian Rule' (2014) 15 JWIT 965, 979; S Mazumder, 'Can I Stay a Bit Longer? The Effect of Bilateral Investment Treaties on Political Survival' (2016) 11(4) Rev Intl Org 477.

[26] See Saul, 'Creating Popular Governments in Post-Conflict Situations' in Stahn et al (n 2) 451.

[27] The interim Egyptian government has been facing this problem in the aftermath of the revolution in 2011. While it has been reluctant to re-nationalize investments that were sold for less than market value by the Mubarak administration, fearing that this would lead to costly arbitrations and scare off future foreign investment, the national courts and the Egyptian people have been vocal in their discontent

this context, the investment treaties, and FDI, more broadly, do not facilitate a peaceful transition, but rather contribute to destabilizing and exacerbating political and social tensions in the post-conflict phase.

2. Microeconomic Effect: Reparations

Paying reparations is a fundamental element of *jus post bellum* and is also usually the most controversial part of the post-conflict period. On the one hand, the claims of victims as a result of the losses they suffered are just, and their adjudication is necessary as it re-establishes the rule of law in post-conflict societies and signals to investors that the legal environment is stabilizing. On the other hand, meeting these claims may impose a heavy burden on a country and its people who have been shattered by the conflict, and thereby slow down the process of recovery and fuel further frustration. One only needs to recall the excessive imposition of reparations on Germany after the First World War, which is believed to have significantly contributed to the collapse of the German economy in the 1920s and consequently led to another war.[28] Drawing on this unsatisfactory experience, a more nuanced and constructive approach was taken as to the treatment of war-related claims after the Second World War. For instance, the US insisted that the post-Second World War reparations policy be moderate and compatible with the broader goal of creating a free global economy and establishing the conditions for peace.[29] Along the same lines, the Allied powers concluded at the Potsdam Conference that reparations had to reflect Germany's capacity to pay, and should not result in the punishment of the German people.[30]

On which end of the spectrum (either the victim-oriented, or the more holistic, peace-aiming sides of the spectrum) the settlement of post-conflict reparations will lean ultimately depends on the choice of a post-conflict remedial mechanism. While in the past the reparation structures catered to the broader concept of post-conflict justice, some of the more recent models tend to place a greater emphasis

regarding the government's unwillingness to clean up the corruption of the previous regime. See M Fick, 'Egypt Drags Its Feet in Privatisation Tussle' *Reuters* (29 May 2013) <https://uk.reuters.com/article/us-egypt-renationalisation/egypt-drags-its-feet-in-privatization-tussle-idUKBRE94S0Q420130529> accessed 5 May 2014.

[28] See e.g. J Keynes, *The Economic Consequences of the Peace* (Harcourt, Brace and Howe 1919); I Seidl-Hohenveldern, 'Reparations' in 4 *Encyclopaedia of Public International Law* 178 (Rudolf Bernardt 2000); R Buxbaum, 'A Legal History of International Reparations' (2005) 23(2) Berkeley J Intl L 314, 323–26.

[29] See US State Department, II Foreign Relations of the United States: Diplomatic Papers 620–21 (1945), cited in Buxbaum, ibid 326–27; R Dolzer, 'The Settlement of War-Related Claims: Does International Law Recognize a Victim's Private Right of Action—Lessons after 1945' (2002) 20(1) Berkeley J Intl L 296, 338. See also M Waibel, *Sovereign Defaults before International Courts and Tribunals* (CUP 2011) 147–48.

[30] Protocol of the Proceedings of the Potsdam Conference (1 August 1945) para 19.

on justice for the injured individual. What is common to most, however, is that they have prioritized compensation over restitution as a means of redressing damages.[31] The following discussion is thus limited to post-conflict compensation programmes.

(a) Interstate arbitrations and diplomatic protection

As illustrated in Chapter 2, foreigners have often raised compensation claims for property losses that took place during conflicts abroad. Historically, conflict-related injuries to foreigners have been remedied through interstate arbitration and diplomatic protection.[32] From the second half of the nineteenth century until the outbreak of the Second World War, such arbitrations often took place before mixed claims commissions, which usually heard a series of claims.[33] In that period, international arbitration was celebrated as a means of achieving two intertwined objectives: first, promotion of free trade and investment; and second, fostering of peaceful relations.[34] The US and the UK were at the forefront of the movement pushing for arbitration, often in the aftermath of conflicts in Latin America,[35] as an effective way to world peace.[36]

Under some of these arbitral tribunals and commissions, individuals had private standing which required the prior consent of the state of their nationality. Such consent was limited only to the past event giving rise to the reparations (e.g. war or revolution), and in addition, the private claimant was subjected to control by the agent of their state. In the majority of cases, however, such claims could only be raised by the alien's home state. The injured individual had to ask the state of its nationality to espouse the claim, and if the state agreed—which it was not obliged to do—the state was fully in control of the claim. This meant that state could

[31] While in investment law a distinction is maintained between compensation and damages (the former presenting a payment for lawful expropriation, while the latter for the breach of other investment treaty provisions), here, the terms are used interchangeably, describing a monetary form of reparation (see Art 36 of the Articles on Responsibility of States for Internationally Wrongful Acts).

[32] For a general account of the claims commissions and other remedial structures, see arbitration reports cited in Chapter 2, n 11. See also H Van Houtte et al, *Post-War Restoration of Property Rights under International Law* (CUP 2008); K Parlett, *The Individual in the International Legal System* (CUP 2011); M Matheson, *International Civil Tribunals and Armed Conflict* (Brill/Nijhoff 2012).

[33] The peak was reached in the interwar period with the post-First World War mixed tribunals, and the claims commission following the Mexican Revolution between 1910 and 1920. See A Feller, *The Mexican Claims Commission 1923–1934: A Study in the Law and Procedure of International Tribunals* (Macmillan Company 1935).

[34] M Koskenniemi, 'The Ideology of International Adjudication and the 1907 Hague Conference' in Y Dauded (ed), *Topicality of the 1907 Hague Conference, the Second Peace Conference* (Martinus Nijhoff 2008) 127, 130–32; C Tams, 'World Peace through International Adjudication?' in HG Justenhoven et al (eds), *Peace Through Law: Reflections on Pacem in Terris from Philosophy, Law, Theology, and Political Science* (Nomos 2016) 215.

[35] See Chapter 2 B.

[36] Koskenniemi, 'Ideology of International Adjudication' (n 34); M Mazower, *Governing the World. The History of an Idea* (Penguin 2013) 85–93.

determine the damages sought or even decide to settle a dispute. In the absence of such an espousal, the individual had no direct action to international legal order.

Under diplomatic protection rules, a government would necessarily render its decision about raising a claim against another government in the broader context of their political relations and strategic concerns. As aptly noted by Rudolf Dolzer, this meant that the conflict-related claim would be evaluated in the light of 'issues of reconciliation, punishment, assessment of the individual claim within the full range of potential claims, the ability of the other side to pay damages, and generally of the conditions for desirable peace . . .'[37] The advantage of the government-to-government approach in deciding reparations for peacemaking was evident. The government stayed in control of the claims and could use its knowledge of non-legal information to strike a nuanced balance between the competing interests of providing redress to its injured nationals, on the one hand, and ensuring strategic prospects for future relations with the counterpart country and sustainable peace, on the other hand. Such a policy-oriented approach thus sought to strike a balance between international claims expectations and the requirements of post-conflict community aspirations.

Interstate arbitration proved to be rather effective for addressing claims arising from internal conflicts in that it provided the two involved states with enough flexibility in designing the process and tailoring it to their unique needs, while also ensuring a degree of predictability in the outcome since all claims between two states were arbitrated against the same factual background, often by the same arbitrators.

However, the catastrophic events that started unfolding in 1914 presented a sobering moment to the advocates of arbitration's peacekeeping ability. Even less satisfactory was the adjudication of claims for losses related to the First World War. The Treaty of Versailles established mixed commissions and arbitral tribunals, and more controversially, reparations commissions, between Germany and the Allied powers,[38] but their outcomes were perceived as unjust by Germany and further deteriorated its relationships with the winning states. Notably, injured individuals were granted stronger procedural rights under the peace treaties, and in some cases, they had full control over their claims.[39] Arguably, the consequences of that post-conflict arrangement were detrimental to the maintenance of hard-won peace.[40] Whether the escalation of the new World War was facilitated by the work of mixed commissions that were deciding property and contract claims, or the reparations commissions established to determine reparations for personal

[37] Dolzer, 'War-Related Claims' (n 29) 304.

[38] Treaty of Peace between Allied and Associated Powers and Germany (28 June 1919), Arts 304–05.

[39] See e.g. the mixed arbitral tribunals with the Allied powers (excluding the US) and the Upper Silesian Mixed Commission and Arbitral Tribunal. See Treaty of Versailles, Arts 297–98; Treaty of Neuilly (27 November 1919) s IV; Treaty of St Germain-en-Laye (10 September 1919) s IV; Treaty of Trianon (4 June 1920) s IV. Parlett, *The Individual* (n 32) 72–77.

[40] Keynes, *Economic Consequences* (n 28).

injuries and death, forced labour and damage to governmental property, the winning powers decided to seek alternative arrangements for remedying losses related to the Second World War.

(b) Lump sum settlements

After the Second World War, state espousal and international arbitration were increasingly replaced by lump sum settlements.[41] According to a lump sum agreement, the respondent state agrees to pay a lump sum compensation to the claimant state who then distributes the settlement to its nationals who made the claim, usually by establishing national claims commissions.[42] They were perceived as a quicker and more politically feasible alternative to interstate arbitrations for addressing war-related claims on a massive scale. Since the Second World War, states have entered into more than 200 lump sum agreements, making it the most popular method for settling international claims concerning the treatment of foreign nationals and their property.[43] While the majority of the lump sum settlements concerned the payment of compensation for nationalization, the second most common subject has been war claims.[44] Those agreements were often merely a fulfilment of obligations originally undertaken by the respondent states in the peace treaties.[45] Consequently, such agreements were negotiated by taking into account different extra-legal—economic, social, and political—considerations.[46]

This was particularly reflected in two aspects of the settlements. First, the agreements typically avoided the question of state liability under international law.[47] In this sense, they could be seen as successors of the nineteenth-century practices of paying conflict-related gratuities without expressing an admission of liability.[48]

41 See R Lillich and B Weston, *International Claims: Their Settlements by Lump Sum Agreements, Part I: The Commentary* (University Press of Virginia 1975); G Yates, 'State Responsibility for Nonwealth Injuries to Aliens in the Postwar Era' in R Lillich (ed), *International Law of State Responsibility for Injuries to Aliens* (University Press of Virginia 1983) 213. While there were still some interstate commissions dealing with war-related property claims (e.g. Japanese commissions), the control of individuals was limited compared to the post-First World War arrangements. See also S Murphy, T Snider, and W Kidane, *Litigating War: Mass Civil Injury and the Eritrea-Ethiopia Claims Commission* (OUP 2013) 33; Parlett, *The Individual* (n 32).

42 For more on compensation commissions, see Waibel, *Sovereign Defaults* (n 29) 189–201.

43 D Bederman, 'Lump Sum Agreements and Diplomatic Protection' (2002) Report for the International Law Association Committee on Diplomatic Protection of Persons and Property, 70th Conference New Delhi.

44 C Gray, *Judicial Remedies in International Law* (OUP 1987) 179. While the majority of them were concluded with respect to injuries inflicted during the Second World War, some of them concerned compensation for losses caused to foreigners in riots and demonstrations. See e.g. an agreement between Panama and the US, cited in Lillich and Weston, *International Claims* (n 41) Treaty No 11. See also the settlement between China and the US for the damage done to the respective state diplomatic and consular properties during the NATO air bombing of Belgrade, and violent protests in China, reported in Murphy et al, *Litigating War* (n 41) 34.

45 Lillich and Weston, *International Claims* (n 41) 204 (citing lump sum agreements between former Axis powers of Bulgaria, Hungary, Italy, Japan, and Rumania).

46 ibid.

47 Gray, *Judicial Remedies* (n 44) 179.

48 See Chapter 2 B.1.

The second aspect concerned the amount of the agreed compensation, which usually did not represent the true level of the loss, and the deferred payment of compensation. That feature has been controversial in debates over the contribution of lump sum settlements to the development of customary international law. While some scholars have argued that the large body of the settlements impacted the standard of compensation in international law,[49] the adjudicative bodies treated them as *sui generis* political agreements and as such were not capable of shaping international custom.[50]

While the appeal of lump sum agreements is that they provide states with more flexibility to accommodate post-conflict political necessities, the downside is that the injured victims are further removed from the process that directly concerns them. The amount of compensation is not decided by ascertaining the state's liability and a careful assessment of the evidence, but is typically agreed upon at a very early stage in the process, before the scope and nature of the claims are entirely known.[51] The complete lack of transparency and the prospect of receiving only partial recovery problematizes lump sum settlements as a remedial structure for achieving optimal post-conflict justice.

(c) Special tribunals

In the second half of the twentieth century, new models for remedying conflict-related losses evolved, giving more control to injured individuals. The most notable example is the Iran–US Claims Tribunal, which was the first tribunal after the Second World War to address a large number of investment claims arising from a conflict situation. The tribunal was created as part of the 1981 Algiers Accords to address claims by the US and Iran, as well as their respective nationals, arising out of the 1979 Iranian Revolution.[52] The tribunal, which still operates from The Hague, has thus far issued more than 600 awards, while the majority of the claims were settled.

The novelty of this tribunal is that not only governments, but also their nationals, can bring forward economic claims arising out of contracts, expropriations, and other measures adopted during the Iranian Revolution that affected investors' property rights. Another novel feature is the distinction it makes between large claims (filed for amounts of $250,000 or more) that can be brought by the nationals themselves, and low-value claims (filed for amounts of less than $250,000) that are filed by the nationals' governments. The advantage of this arrangement is

[49] See Lillich and Weston, *International Claims* (n 41).

[50] See e.g. *Barcelona Traction (Belgium v Spain)* (Merits) [1970] ICJ Rep 3, 40.

[51] Murphy et al, *Litigating War* (n 41) 35.

[52] See e.g. W Mapp, *The Iran-United States Claims Tribunal, The First Ten Years, 1981–1991* (MUP 1996); C Brower and J Brueschke, *The Iran-United States Claims Tribunal* (Nijhoff 1998); J Sharpe, 'Iran-United States Claims Tribunal' in C Giorgetti (ed), *The Rules, Practice, and Jurisprudence of International Courts and Tribunals* (Nijhoff 2012).

that investors suffering large losses (presumably big businesses) gain full control over the process, how their claims are presented and potentially settled. Around 1,000 such claims have been submitted by private entities.[53] With respect to small claims, the control over the process becomes less relevant, particularly in view of the impracticality of administering the large number of private claims as well as the benefits of allocating the litigation costs from injured individuals to their governments.[54]

Another ad hoc remedial structure that addressed a large number of conflict-related claims was the UN Compensation Commission (UNCC).[55] The UNCC was created as a subsidiary organ of the UN Security Council (UNSC) to administer claims and pay compensation for losses resulting from Iraq's invasion and the occupation of Kuwait between 1990 and 1991.[56] Since Iraq's liability for the harm and losses suffered by numerous states and their nationals was already determined by the UNSC,[57] the UNCC was only mandated to process the claims, verify their validity, evaluate losses, and pay the compensation to successful claimants from a special UN account funded mostly from the proceeds of Iraq's oil exports. In this sense, it was not an adjudicative, but rather an administrative, body performing a fact-finding function. The Commission accepted several categories of claims, including claims of foreign investors ('category E'), which also covered losses related to the destruction or seizure of business assets.[58] In contrast to the Iran–US Claims Tribunal, those claims could not be brought by investors themselves, but were submitted by the seventy governments representing the nationalities of those affected. Preventing individuals from submitting their own claims was reasonable in view of the sheer number of claims that that the Commission received (approximately 2.69 million, compared to around 3,900 claims finalized by the Iran–US Claims Tribunal), and the large number of nationalities involved. In addition, direct control over submitting a claim was of lesser importance since the question of liability had already been decided.

While the UNCC has been praised as a cost-effective and time-efficient (it concluded the processing of claims in 2005) post-conflict remedial structure, and nominated as a potential universal model for the future resolution of post-conflict

[53] Murphy et al, *Litigating War* (n 41) 44.
[54] ibid 45.
[55] See T Feighery, 'The United Nations Compensation Commission' in C Giorgetti (ed), *The Rules, Practice, and Jurisprudence of International Courts and Tribunals* (Nijhoff 2012) 515; H van Houtte, H Das, and B Delmartino, 'The United Nations Compensation Commission' in P De Greiff (ed), *The Handbook of Reparations* (OUP 2008) 321, 326.
[56] UNSC Res 687 (3 April 1991) S/RES/687, paras 16–19.
[57] The SC Resolutions found that Iraq 'is liable, under international law, for any direct loss, damage, including environmental damage and the depletion of natural resources, or injury to foreign governments, nationals and corporations, as a result of Iraq's unlawful invasion and occupation of Kuwait'. ibid para 16.
[58] The Commission received more than 6000 E category claims. See <http://www.uncc.ch/claims> accessed 15 June 2015.

claims,[59] this is unlikely to happen. The success of the UNCC should be considered in the context of a variety of different factors surrounding its establishment, including the involvement of the UNSC, the fact that the question of liability did not need to be adjudicated and that Iraq was capable of funding the administration of the UNCC and pay the compensation demanded.[60] Should the wrongdoing state lack such resources, or be impoverished by its own direct losses in the conflict, such a remedial structure would unlikely be effective and would also complicate the transition to peace.

(d) Direct access to justice

The above remedial structures were created especially to consider the claims pertaining to a particular conflict situation. However, states are not always willing to set up such post-conflict remedial programmes. They may consider it politically unacceptable, they may be unable or unwilling to provide funds for setting up a special tribunal, or simply, they may consider the conflict in question to be an internal matter and potential claims capable of being resolved by municipal courts. In those situations, the claims of injured investors against the host state for conflict-related injuries could still be brought before international remedial structures with more general jurisdiction, that is to bodies that were not designed specifically for the purpose of hearing conflict-related claims. Two international regimes in particular are important as they have empowered individuals with direct access to international justice. First, the regional human rights courts, like the European Court of Human Rights (ECtHR), are enabled to hear not only interstate claims, but also petitions by individuals against states for breaches of human rights instruments. As seen in Chapter 2, such claims by individuals not uncommonly referred to conflict-related injuries that constituted human rights violations, including the right to property.[61] If the court finds the violation, it can decide that the applicant must be compensated for the damage sustained. There are, however, limitations to human rights remedies. In particular, human rights courts can only hear claims against states that are parties to the relevant human rights instruments and have accepted the jurisdiction of the court. Moreover, injured individuals can only bring the claim to the court after they have exhausted all domestic remedies. In this way, the state is first given the opportunity to provide redress for the alleged injury at the national level.

The latter obstacle is removed in investor–state arbitration. The investment treaty regime introduced a significant change in this regard by allowing foreign investors to directly bring a claim against the wrongdoing state before the investor–state arbitration tribunals without the prior espousal or consent of their

59 Murphy et al, *Litigating War* (n 41) 48.
60 ibid 49; Van Houtte et al, 'The United Nations Compensation Commission' (n 55) 326.
61 Chapter 2 D.1.

home state, and without the admissibility requirement to first exhaust all local remedies. Since then, hundreds of investor–state arbitrations have been launched.[62] In contrast to the practice of mixed claims commissions and diplomatic protection, the investor is in control of every aspect of the claim. Investor–state arbitration has thus been praised as strengthening the protection of investors abroad and depoliticizing investor-state disputes.[63] Needless to say, investors' claims do not pose the kind of economic, financial, and political questions as relations among states in transition between conflict and peace. Normally, they will merely focus on redressing the consequences of the conflict that affected them individually. Similarly, investment tribunals, often composed of lawyers with a background in commercial law,[64] will not look at the case from the same multifaceted perspective as the government, but will be understandably confined to the contours and legal setting of a particular case.[65] Can the post-conflict considerations of ensuring a peaceful transition be taken into account at all in the compensation stage of the investment proceedings? The next section sets out to discuss this.

C. Determining Post-Conflict Compensation

When it comes to determining post-conflict compensation, tribunals are faced with the dilemma of weighing competing interests: investors need to be indemnified for their losses, but at the same time, the financial load imposed on the wrongdoing state and its population should not make the process of recovering from the hardship of conflict overly difficult.[66] This delicate balance is important for achieving just and sustainable peace.[67]

Contemporary developments in international law show that there is a trend towards moderate reparations and the prohibition of excessive claims.[68] This is reflected in various international norms. For example, the former Article 42(3) of

[62] UNCTAD, 'World Investment Report 2013, Global Value Chains: Investment and Trade for Development' (UN 2013) 102, 111.

[63] See I Shihata, 'Towards a Greater Depoliticization of Investment Disputes: The Role of ICSID and MIGA' (1986) 1 ICSID Rev-Foreign Inv L J 1, 11–12; K Vandevelde, 'The Bilateral Investment Treaty Program of The United States' (1988) 21 Cornell Intl L J 201, 256–58. See also A Roberts, 'State-to-State Investment Treaty Arbitration: A Hybrid Theory of Interdependent Rights and Shared Interpretive Authority' (2014) 55 HILJ 11.

[64] A Roberts, 'Clash of Paradigms: Actors and Analogies Shaping the Investment Treaty System' (2013) 107 AJIL 45.

[65] Waibel, *Sovereign Defaults* (n 29) 322 (noting that arbitrators lack sufficient information to decide policy trade-offs, especially in turbulent periods).

[66] In the context of sovereign defaults, Waibel similarly argued that striking the right balance between the protection of creditors and a fresh start for a state is vital for the legitimacy of investment arbitration. ibid 326.

[67] L May, 'Jus Post Bellum, Grotius and Meionexia' in Stahn et al (n 2) 18.

[68] C Stahn, 'Jus ad Bellum, Jus in Bello . . . Jus Post Bellum?—Rethinking the Conception of the Law of Armed Force' (2006) 17 EJIL 921, 939.

the 1996 Draft Articles on State Responsibility stated that reparation shall 'in no case . . . result in depriving the population of a State of its own means of subsistence'. Similarly, Article 1(2) of the International Covenant on Civil and Political Rights provides that '[i]n no case may a people be deprived of its own means of subsistence'.[69] The ECtHR has repeatedly applied the doctrine of 'fair balance' between the demands of the general community and the requirement to protect the individual's fundamental rights when determining the compensation for expropriation.[70] More pointedly, the practice of peace agreements and lump sum settlements demonstrates the importance of assessing the compensation claims in the light of the economic potential of the wrongdoing state and their implications for the welfare of its citizens.

The central aspect of peacemaking concerns the nexus between the amount of the reparations and the timing of the payment by the wrongdoing state. In lump sum settlements, these modalities have been frequently addressed. Since the investment treaties remove the control of the governments over the post-conflict compensation claims and their potential effect on the transition to peace, the question arises as to whether the investment treaty practices accommodate the discussed *post bellum* principle. As a rule, if a state has breached an investment treaty, the investor is entitled to recover the full market value of the loss. As shown above, the quantum amount can be reduced in accordance with the investor's contribution to the conflict-related loss.[71] Beyond that, however, the question remains if there is room to balance between the competing interests at the compensation stage?

According to the investment tribunal in *Al-Kharafi v Libya*, there is not. The case confirms that concerns about the negative effects of exorbitant compensation resonate well into the present.[72] In that case, which concerned the cancellation of an investment project, the arbitration was initiated against the Libyan government during the civil war in 2011. In the final award issued in 2013, the tribunal ordered Libya, a country facing formidable financial and political challenges, to pay almost $1 billion, one of the largest ever compensation awards in the history of investment treaty arbitration. The award represented 1.3 per cent of Libyan GDP in 2013 and, needless to say, imposed a huge burden on the country that is experiencing an ongoing conflict between different rival groups for control over Libyan territory. Such a disproportionate award may deprive the state of the funds that are needed for it to rebuild its war-torn infrastructure and combat the rival groups that are trying to overpower the democratically elected government.

[69] The Eritrea–Ethiopia Claims Commission invoked this provision to explain why the hefty compensation could not be awarded. *Eritrea's Damages Claims* (Final Award of 17 August 2009) 26 RIAA 505, 522, paras 19–20.

[70] See e.g. *Papachelas v Greece* App no 31423/96, Judgment (ECtHR, 25 March 1999) para 48; *Former King of Greece and Others v Greece* App no 25701/94, Judgment (ECtHR, 23 November 2000) para 89. See also S Ripinsky with K Williams, *Damages in International Investment Law* (BIICL 2008) 81.

[71] Chapter 5, nn 177–80.

[72] *Mohamed Al-Kharafi & Sons Co v Libya* Ad hoc Arbitration, Award, 22 March 2013, paras 380–82.

The *Al-Kharafi* award is illustrative of the approach that is ill suited to the post-conflict compensation settlement context. It is submitted that there are four sometimes overlapping ways for *post bellum* considerations to feed into the determination of compensation modalities: a reasonable standard of compensation for conflict-inflicted losses, the valuation of damages, equity, and a deferred payment of compensation.

1. Reasonable Standard of Compensation

The standard of compensation, in particular in cases of expropriation, used to be one of the most controversial issues in international investment law. While the view of developed countries was that compensation should be prompt, adequate, and effective, the developing countries advocated more flexible standards, often reflecting principles existing in their national jurisdictions.[73] Eventually, the former view prevailed and became increasingly accepted in investment treaties. In other words, it has become settled that compensation must reflect the full market value of the investment. A different standard is often applied for determining the amount of damages for breaches of other investment provisions that are not accompanied by an explicit rule. In such cases, investment tribunals have often referred to the rule of customary international law, articulated famously by the Permanent Court of International Justice (PCIJ) in *Chorzów Factory* case: '[R]eparation must, as far as possible, wipe out all the consequences of the illegal act and re-establish the situation which would, in all probability, have existed if that act had not been committed'.[74] In practice, this will often lead to a similar outcome as achieved by the application of the compensation standard for expropriation.[75]

Some investment treaty provisions, however, do specify a different compensation standard. Most notably, some armed conflict clauses provide that compensation for losses inflicted by the host state during armed conflict should be 'reasonable' or 'just' rather than 'adequate'.[76] The origin of this expression can be traced to the nineteenth century, when home states of aliens who sustained losses at the hands of a host state's armed forces during hostilities, sometimes urged for the payment of 'reasonable compensations' that took into account 'the peculiar hardships' of situations.[77] What the 'reasonable compensation' means is unclear, but it could be argued that in view of the departure from the wording commonly used

[73] For an overview, see Chapter 4, n 212.

[74] *Case Concerning the Factory at Chorzów (Germany v Poland)* (Merits) [1928] PCIJ Rep Series A No 17, 47 (*Chorzów Factory*).

[75] See e.g. *Siag and Vecchi v Egypt* ICSID Case no ARB/05/15, Award, 11 May 2009, para 542. See also B Sabahi, *Compensation and Restitution in Investor–State Arbitration: Principles and Practice* (OUP 2011) 102.

[76] See e.g. UK–Hong Kong BIT (1998) Art 4(2); Croatia–Ukraine BIT (1998) Art 6(2).

[77] J Moore, *A Digest of International Law* (Vol 6, GPO 1906) 892.

for expropriation standards, it implies that an amount of compensation should be adjusted to the circumstances, and is ultimately less than the full market value of the investment. Some BITs even go a step further and delegate the determination of the amount of compensation to the domestic laws of the host state.[78] This clearly reflects the views of the developing countries regarding the appropriate standard of compensation commonly voiced in the last century. So far, the tribunals have not been faced with a case where compensation would have to be decided for a breach of the armed conflict clause. It is submitted that especially in cases where the provision uses explicitly different wording, like 'reasonable' or 'just' compensation, the amount awarded should not reflect the usual compensation paid for the breach of the investment treaty standard. The methods explained next, equity, in particular, can be used to aid this interpretation.

2. Valuation of Damages

The extraordinary circumstances in which the host state found itself may be taken into account in the valuation of the property that has been damaged through the breach of an investment treaty obligation. Many cases demonstrate that tribunals have the ability to take into account the circumstances of the state when awarding damages. For example, the higher risk of investing in a politically unstable country can be factored in determination of a rate of return.[79] Furthermore, the tribunal may lower the amount of damages for the loss of future profits, or completely discard the claim for it, if it considers that future gains would have been unlikely given the political, economic, or security crisis.[80]

In *AAPL v Sri Lanka*, the tribunal, taking into account all the circumstances, including civil war, concluded that the 'future profitability' of the injured investor could not be established and thus the prospective earnings did not constitute part of the total value of the property for the purposes of determining compensation.[81] The tribunal in *AMT v Zaire* similarly rejected the claim for future profits by noting that:

> [I]t is apparent that the situation remains precarious and that the *lucrum cessans* or the loss of profit is not at all measurable without a solid base on which to found

[78] See e.g. Mauritius–Singapore BIT (2000) Art 7(2); Singapore–Ukraine BIT (2006) Art 6(2). See UNCTAD Report, 'Bilateral Investment Treaties 1995–2006: Trends in Investment Rule Making' (UN 2007) 55.

[79] See e.g. *Active Partners Group Ltd v The Republic of South Sudan* PCA Case no 2013/4, Award, 27 January 2016, paras 366–68. The tribunal lowered the claimant's 35 per cent profit margin to a 25 per cent 'reasonable rate of return'.

[80] *CMS Gas Transmission Company v Argentine Republic* ICSID Case no ARB/01/8, Award, 12 May 2005, paras 356, 406.

[81] *AAPL* (n 23) paras 104–6.

> any profit to take or predicting the growth or expansion of the investment made. It would be neither practical nor reasonable to apply the method of assessment of compensation in a way so removed from the striking realities of the current situation.[82]

Somewhat less satisfactory was the adjustment of the amount of compensation in *Mitchell v Congo*. While the tribunal stated it had taken into account 'the economic and political environment of the Congo' when assessing the fair market value of investment,[83] the government of Congo argued that this was merely lip service and that future profits were awarded 'without taking account of political circumstances and of the state of war in Congo, which had profoundly disrupted the Congolese economy.'[84] The tribunal's approach was indeed cautious and overly legalistic: while it took into account factors that existed at the time of the violation of the investment treaty and it could feed into the assessment of the value of the investment, it disregarded the circumstances at the time of calculating the compensation (i.e. the financial ability of the state to pay, the potential effect of the compensation on a state's welfare, and the potential effect on the re-escalation of conflict). It is submitted that the latter considerations can be accommodated by relying on the principle of equity,[85] discussed next.

3. Principle of Equity

Equity is a general principle of law that may be applied by international adjudicators without specific authorization of the parties with an aim to correct unjust outcomes that could result from the strict application of the rules of law.[86] It has been often referred to in maritime and territorial delimitation cases.[87] In some cases, it has been relied on to determine the amount of compensation,[88] along with factors such as the economic situation caused by war.[89]

[82] *AMT v Zaire* ICSID Case no ARB/93/1, Award, 21 February 1997, para 7.14.

[83] *Mitchell*, Award (n 23) para 93.

[84] *Patrick Mitchell v Democratic Republic of Congo* ICSID Case no ARB/99/7, Annulment Decision, 1 November 2006, para 64.

[85] Although in practice, these two approaches may be conflated, as tribunals will be reluctant to acknowledge they adjusted the compensation beyond the valuation of the investor's property. For a detailed discussion about the role of equity in post-conflict investment disputes, see Zrilič 'International Investment Law in the Context of Jus Post Bellum' (n 1).

[86] For more on equity, see Judge Weeramantry's analysis of equity in *Jan Mayen (Denmark v Norway)* (Separate Opinion) [1993] ICJ Rep 38, 250; C Rossi, *Equity and International Law, A Legal Realist Approach to International Decisionmaking* (Transnational Publishers 1993); G Schwarzenberger, 'Equity in International Law' (1972) 26 YB of World Aff 346.

[87] See *North Sea Continental Shelf (Germany v Netherlands)* (Judgment) [1969] ICJ Rep 3, 53; *Frontier Dispute Case (Burkina Faso v Mali)* (Judgment) [1986] ICJ Rep 554, 633.

[88] See *Corfu Channel (UK v Albania)* (Assessment of the Amount of Compensation) [1949] ICJ Rep 4, 244, 248; *Libyan American Oil Company (LIAMCO) v Libyan Arab Republic* (1981) 62 ILR 140, 150–52, 160.

[89] See *Serbian Loans (France v Serb-Croat-Slovene)* [1929] PCIJ Ser A No 20; *Brazilian Loans (France v Brazil)* [1929] PCIJ Ser A No 21.

The post-conflict remedial structures discussed above often adjusted the amount of compensation based on equity. For example, in the *Sea-Land* case, the Iran–US Claims Tribunal stated that equity requires that factual circumstances be taken into account when calculating compensation before rejecting the claim for the loss of future profit.[90] An approach based on equity was also followed by the UNCC and Eritrea–Ethiopia Claims Commission (EECC), where, due to a large number of claims, the payment of full compensation would have clearly imposed a disproportionate financial burden on the compensating country.[91] The most clearly expressed justification for equity was provided by the EECC which, when assessing the claims for damages, took into account the economic positions of the parties (both countries were among the poorest in the world), the fact that the amounts sought were huge (both in absolute terms and in relation to the parties' financial capacity), and the fact that the award of full compensation would have likely imposed a crippling burden on the countries transitioning from war, as well as their people.[92] The ECtHR has also been guided by equity when awarding financial compensation, by taking into account the position of the applicant, public interest concerns, the local economic circumstances, and the overall context in which the breach of the treaty provision occurred.[93] Consequently, the compensation awarded has often been smaller than the actual value of the damage suffered.[94]

Some investment treaty tribunals have found that regardless of the actual damage to the claimant, they can adjust the compensation to ensure that it is equitable.[95] Commentators seem to support this application of equity in investment disputes and they perceive it as a 'pragmatic solution to deal with real life problems'.[96] Wälde and Sabahi noted that 'tribunals ultimately when choosing between competing and equally plausible and legitimate valuation methods . . . cannot avoid exercising discretion. This is where they will be influenced by the equitable considerations.'[97] In this vein, the tribunal in *AMT v Zaire* decided to opt for 'a method that is most plausible and realistic in the circumstances of the case, while rejecting all other methods of assessment which would serve unjustly to enrich an investor, who rightly or wrongly, has chosen to invest in Zaire'.[98] It pointed out that

[90] *Sea-Land Service Inc v Iran* (1984) 6 Iran–USCTR 149, 169.

[91] C Gray, 'Remedies in International Dispute Settlement' in C Romano, K Alter, and Y Shany (eds), *The Oxford Handbook of International Adjudication* (OUP 2013) 871, 896.

[92] *Ethiopia's Damages Claims* (Final Award of 17 August 2009) 26 RIAA 631, paras 18–23.

[93] See Gray, 'Remedies' (n 91) 891.

[94] ibid.

[95] See e.g. *AMT* (n 82) para 7.17. See also N Gallus, 'The Fair and Equitable Treatment Standard and the Circumstances of the State' in C Brown and K Miles (eds), *Evolution in Investment Treaty Law and Arbitration* (CUP 2011) 243.

[96] Sabahi, *Compensation and Restitution* (n 75) 187; T Wälde and B Sabahi, 'Compensation, Damages, and Valuation in International Investment Law' in P Muchlinski, F Ortino, and C Schreuer (eds), *The Oxford Handbook of International Investment Law* (OUP 2008).

[97] Wälde and Sabahi, ibid 1049, 1105.

[98] *AMT* (n 82) paras 7.15, 7.16.

by applying the equitable principle it fully took into account the situation in Zaire when determining the amount of compensation.[99]

Even more significant was the contrast between the amount sought and compensation awarded in *AAPL v Sri Lanka*. While in this situation the tribunal did not expressly pay heed to equitable considerations, its application of such can be inferred from the tribunal's choice of method to calculate the compensation. Without providing much explanation, the tribunal decided to award US $460,000, a rather small amount compared to the more than $8 million sought. In 1987, when the claim was filed, $8 million presented 1.3 per cent of the Sri Lankan government's total annual expenditure.[100] Taking into account that during that period, the monetary cost of the civil war in Sri Lanka was around US $500 million annually, and that by 1986, 17 per cent of the Sri Lankan national budget was spent on defence matters,[101] awarding the amount claimed would have possibly negatively affected Sri Lankan security policy. While these considerations are not discussed in the final award, one can assume that they played some role in arriving at the final outcome.[102]

While some scholars have been critical of such application of equitable considerations to damages in investment law as being in conflict with the principle of full reparation,[103] this view seems too narrow and oblivious to the post-conflict practice of awarding equitably adjusted compensation. As clarified by the EECC:

> Huge awards of compensation by their nature would require large diversions of national resources from the paying country—and its citizens needing health care, education and other public services—to the recipient country. In this regard, the prevailing practice of States in the years since the Treaty of Versailles has been to give very significant weight to the needs of the affected population in determining amounts sought as post-war reparations.[104]

In fact, the EECC did not find such adjustments of the amount of compensation contradictory to the *Chorzów Factory* principle. According to the Commission's interpretation of the principle, the role of compensation is to restore the injured party to the extent that it is possible. It performs a remedial, not punitive, function.[105]

[99] ibid paras 7.18, 7.21.

[100] The general government expenditure in 1987 was $663,654,800. See World Bank's Report <http://data.worldbank.org.liverpool.idm.oclc.org/country/sri–lanka> accessed 20 May 2016.

[101] G Samaranayaka, *Political Violence in Sri Lanka, 1971–1987* (Gyan Publishing House 2008) 348.

[102] The reticence to explain the role of equity in the quantum of compensation is not only characteristic of investment tribunals. Adjudicative bodies in general are often vague when it comes to explaining how they calculate the sums they award and how they factor in equitable considerations. See Gray, 'Remedies' (n 91) 895.

[103] Bonnitcha, 'Transition from Authoritarian Rule' (n 25) 1006–07.

[104] *Ethiopia's Damages Claims* (n 92) para 21.

[105] ibid para 27.

The use of equity to adjust the amount of compensation to reflect post-conflict realities does not imply creating new laws or changing and correcting the existing law. Rather, it enables arbitrators to arrive at a just outcome through their use of judicial discretion (e.g. by choosing between different methods of calculating the compensation), or through applying an equitable interpretation of treaty provisions, thereby tempering the rigidity of the law (e.g. by leniently interpreting 'just', 'reasonable', or 'prompt' compensation). Such treatment of equity is *infra legem* and, as demonstrated above, has a long tradition in judicial and arbitral practice.[106]

4. Deferred Payment

The fourth method refers to the transfer of the compensation due and is reflected in some of the investment treaties' advanced armed conflict clauses. Such clauses allow the state that is experiencing balance of payments difficulties—arguably as a result of its involvement in the conflict—to place limits on the amount transferred, which would help the state to handle the financial burden over an extended period of time. Thus, for instance, the UK–Papua New Guinea BIT provides that:

> However, in the event of extreme balance of payments difficulties, transfer of such payments [of compensation] may be restricted to the extent necessary to meet the difficulties, provided the amount permitted to be transferred shall not be less than 10 per cent per annum and the total shall be transferred within five years of the due date.[107]

This condition mirrors the practice of lump sum settlement agreements where the payment of the compensation was often by instalments over a number of years, and whereby the period of five years was considered to be reasonably adequate in most cases.[108] A similar clause permitting the payment of compensation by instalment was included in the Harvard Convention on the International Responsibility of States for Injuries to Aliens, for losses related to nationalization undertaken in 'furtherance of a general program of economic and social reform . . .'[109] The provision in the Harvard Convention was severely criticized, especially by the US representatives who held that it constituted a departure from the traditional international law principle requiring prompt payment of adequate and effective compensation.[110]

[106] See also *CME v Czech Republic*, UNCITRAL, Separate Opinion of Professor Brownlie (14 March 2003) paras 79, 80 (arguing for a quantum adjustment by drawing on the *post bellum* practice of peace treaties).

[107] See e.g. UK–Papua New Guinea BIT (1981) Art 4(2); UK–Jamaica BIT (1987) Art 4(2).

[108] See Lillich and Weston, *International Claims* (n 41) 210.

[109] Harvard Convention on the International Responsibility of States for Injuries to Aliens (1961) Art 10(14) in *Yearbook of the International Law Commission, 1969, Vol II*, UN Doc A/CN.4/217 144.

[110] See Harvard Convention, Draft No 11 with Explanatory Notes, 111–12.

The 'payment by instalment' clause, as included in investment treaties, is restricted only to situations of state liability for losses arising out of armed conflict—which is a less common case than the taking of property for the 'furtherance of economic or social reform'. In addition, the applicability of the clause is conditioned upon the host state's extreme balance of payment difficulties. Although the exception is more restricted than the one in the Harvard Convention, it is only featured in a few investment treaties.

The question is thus whether the investment tribunal would be able to order a deferred payment of compensation even in the absence of such an explicit clause. Unlike expropriation clauses in BITs that, as a rule, require 'prompt, adequate and effective compensation', some armed conflict clauses provide that compensation needs only to be adequate and freely transferable, leaving out the 'promptness' requirement.[111] Applying *a contrario* interpretation, such a provision would give more room to arbitrators with regard to the method of payment of compensation. When the payment without delay is required explicitly,[112] however, such ordering would be questionable. One could consider whether the payment by instalment could be subsumed under the principle of equity. While equity has been applied with respect to the amount of compensation when it is sometimes impossible to quantify losses with certainty, it is less clear if arbitrators could exercise the same discretion with respect to the payment period when prompt compensation is required. If the equitable principle allows arbitrators to make adjustments with respect to the amount of compensation, there appear to be fewer convincing reasons to disallow a similar compromise in the timing and method of payment. In this context, equity would be used to advance a lenient interpretation of the treaty rule, that is the meaning of 'prompt' compensation, thus tempering its rigidity. Arguably, such an application would make the award more just for the state facing financial difficulties in the aftermath of a conflict, which would be in line with the objective of equity. In support of this view is the practice of the post-conflict lump sum agreements, according to which the payment by instalment may be regarded as compatible with the promptness requirement.[113]

D. Reflections on Post-Conflict Dispute Resolution

While the application of equity and other methods of determining the *post bellum* compensation discussed above can alleviate concerns about the interference of investment treaty claims with post-conflict transitions, it certainly does not eliminate them. First, the consistent application of these methods

[111] See e.g. UK–Argentine Republic BIT (1990) Art 4(2); Israel–Ukraine BIT (1994) Art 4(2).
[112] See e.g. Finland–Ukraine BIT (2004) Art 6(1); Austria–Libya BIT (2002) Art 5(2).
[113] See Lillich and Weston, *International Claims* (n 41) 216.

cannot not be guaranteed in a heavily fragmented investment-arbitration system. Whether, and how, investment tribunals will decide to deploy them is left to their discretion, which gives rise to a great deal of uncertainty and unpredictability.

Second, the negative effect of post-conflict damages is but one aspect that renders investor–state arbitration a questionable choice for remedying conflict-related losses. Another concerns the suitability of arbitral tribunals to decide on measures that the host state has passed with a view to safeguard certain security interests, or failed to pass because of supervening circumstances created by a conflict. As seen in previous chapters, such measures can be taken to prevent the conflict, to suppress it, or to maintain the newly established peace. The arbitral tribunal's assessment of those measures could be seen as curtailing the host state's most sovereign of all sovereign rights, namely the prerogative to fight for its existence.[114] There is a wealth of scholarship criticizing investment arbitration as a venue for solving such highly charged disputes that involve a strong 'public' dimension.[115] Some scholars have also questioned the suitability of investor–state arbitration to decide on politically sensitive cases concerning a host state's security interests.[116]

Investment claims arising from the conflict or post-conflict setting are inherently politically charged and their litigation before investment tribunals should be approached with a degree of caution and scrutiny. The political dimension stems from the broader ramifications of the state's measure that is challenged before the tribunal (e.g. the state's measure was passed to prevent certain political change, like the overthrowing of a government or occupation by an enemy power), or the post-conflict ramifications of the tribunal's decision (e.g. the impact of the quantum award on the host state's finances and the maintenance of peace). This dimension gives rise to several complex questions and it would be careless, to say the least, for the adjudicator not to consider the underlying public interests in resolving such disputes. Yet, investment tribunals have been continuously denounced for failing to do so.[117] This prompts the question of whether investor–state arbitration is an appropriate venue at all for settling conflict-related disputes.

[114] *AAPL*, Dissenting Opinion of Samuel Asante (n 23) 651.

[115] See e.g. G Van Harten, *Investment Treaty Arbitration and Public Law* (OUP 2007); D Schneiderman, *Constitutionalizing Economic Globalization: Investment Rules and Democracy's Promise* (CUP 2008); S Frank, 'The Legitimacy Crisis in Investment Treaty Arbitration: Privatizing Public International Law through Inconsistent Decisions' (2005) 73 Fordham L Rev 1521; J Maupin, 'Differentiating among International Investment Disputes' in Z Douglas, Joost Pauwelyn, and J Viñuales (eds), *The Foundations of International Investment Law: Bringing Theory Into Practice* (OUP 2014) 469.

[116] See e.g. Gathii, 'War's Legacy' (n 18) 382; Sornarajah, *International Law* (n 18) 252.

[117] See Waibel et al (eds), *Backlash against Investment Arbitration* (Kluwer 2010).

1. Oscillating between State and Investor Control

It has been demonstrated above[118] how investors gradually achieved direct access to, and more control over, the settlement of post-conflict claims. To conclude that there was a straightforward and smooth process from state-centric to more inclusive remedial regimes would be somewhat simplistic. Rather, the trajectory has been characterized by the dynamic of reactionary oscillation, whereby the type of remedial regime was determined in response to the challenges specific to a particular conflict situation.[119] In the context of post-conflict claims settlements, the choices were often influenced by extra-legal considerations, like the political implications that such remedial programmes might bear on the maintenance of peace.

To briefly recall: from the mid-nineteenth century until the interwar period in the twentieth century, the prevailing mode for settling conflict-related claims was characterized by the strong role of the states in deciding when and how the conflict-related claims of their nationals against other states would be litigated. The claims could be espoused by means of diplomatic protection and pursued by the home state on its own behalf through interstate arbitrations and mixed claims commissions. The home state had full control over the commencement, prosecution, and settlement of the claim, and the disposal of the final compensation. This changed after the First World War when the peace treaties gave more control to injured individuals, thus enabling them to pursue their own claims before mixed arbitral tribunals and commissions. That, coupled with the multiplication of such commissions and the disregard for the economic and political realities in the aftermath of the First World War, created discontent with this remedial structure. After the Second World War, the pendulum thus swung back towards the control of the state, but eliminated the politically contentious nature of post-conflict international adjudication. Reparations for conflict-related losses were negotiated in lump sum agreements between the home state of the victims and the compensating state. These compensations were settled behind closed doors, where the redress for the injured nationals was but one of many extra-legal considerations in the negotiations. That proved unsatisfactory for victims as the sums awarded were often just a small amount of the actual damages sustained.

The next step was to bestow more control on the investors who were directly affected. While some of the conflicts towards the end of the twentieth century yielded nuanced arrangements falling somewhere between state control and direct individual claims, investors gained unfettered access to international justice with the investor–state arbitration clauses in modern investment treaties. By permitting investors to sue the host state directly, the disputes were devoid of the home

[118] Section 7 B.2.

[119] More generally, a similar observation was made by Parlett with respect to the individual's power in international procedure. Parlett, *The Individual* (n 32) 369.

state's political whims and considerations of extra-legal factors. The depoliticizing of investor-state disputes has been celebrated as a contribution to peaceful international relations.[120] However, this development, which primarily aimed at promoting foreign investment, had a darker side that was revealed in disputes with particularly accentuated public dimensions. Investor-state arbitral tribunals came under fire for allegedly displaying pro-investor bias and ignoring the host state's public interests when interpreting often broadly and vaguely worded investment treaty provisions.[121] Investor control manifests itself in the pleadings in which investors' commonly advocate broad interpretations favouring their own commercial interests; and in the appointment of arbitrators, often resulting in tribunals composed of lawyers with commercial backgrounds who lack an understanding of the complexities brought about by the public component of investor-state disputes.[122] Although the tribunals, as shown in the preceding chapter, have become increasingly willing to consider the host state's public policy objectives and take account of other fields of public international law, the challenge persists and is exacerbated by the system's inherent lack of consistency. This is in contrast to post-conflict commissions and interstate arbitrations where claims were shaped by home states and commonly adjudicated by arbitrators with a good knowledge of public international law.

Following these concerns, could one conclude that investor–state arbitration is not a suitable venue for conflict-related disputes? Ultimately, the answer will depend on different factors,[123] in particular, the type of armed conflict and the number and nature of potential claims. If armed conflict spawned a large number of claims (e.g. protracted intense conflicts or conflicts that resulted in a change of territory), and the transition to peace is likely to be a fragile and complicated process, a single post-conflict tribunal would seem to be a better option. Such a tribunal could take the form of a mixed claims commission, or a hybrid tribunal where claims could be brought by either investors alone or by both investors and their governments. Since arbitrators would be appointed by the state parties and not by the investors, this would enable the adjudication of claims by lawyers with

[120] C Schreuer and U Kriebaum, 'From Individual to Community Interest in International Investment Law' in U Fastenrath et al (eds), *From Bilateralism to Community Interest, Essays in Honour of Bruno Simma* (OUP 2011) 1079, 1080; F Orrego Vicuña, 'Maintenance and Restoration of International Peace and Security Through Arbitration and Judicial Settlement' in A von Arnauld et al (eds), *100 Years of Peace Through Law: Past and Future* (Duncker & Humblot Berlin 2015) 53–65.

[121] See e.g. Letter from Alliance for Justice, to Members of Congress (11 March 2015) <https://www.afj.org/press-room/press-releases/more-than-100-legal-scholars-call-on-congress-administration-to-protect-democracy-and-sovereignty-in-u-s-trade-deals> accessed 18 December 2018 (more than 100 US law professors signed the letter asking Congress to reject investment arbitration in US trade agreements); L Williams, 'TTIP: Three Million People Sign Petition to Scrap Controversial Trade Deal' *The Independent* (5 October 2015) <www.independent.co.uk/news/business/ttip-threemillion-people-sign-petition-to-scrap-controversial-trade-deal-a6680411.html> accessed 18 December 2018.

[122] Roberts, 'Clash of Paradigms' (n 64).

[123] For an overview of practical considerations, see Murphy, *Litigating War* (n 41) 49; H Holtzmann and E Kristjansdottir, *International Mass Claims Processes* (OUP 2007).

the knowledge of public international law, as well as minimize the appearance of the pro-investor bias. It could also provide greater flexibility in determining the applicable law and shaping the proceedings, reduce the risk of inconsistent decisions, and improve the predictability of the final outcome. In view of being faced with a large number of claims, such a tribunal would likely be more perceptive of the host state defences,[124] and would be more likely to take into account the underlying political context and the negative effect that multiple compensation awards could have on a transitioning state. Following the example of historical post-conflict commissions, the procedure would be transparent and decisions would be published, thus contributing to the development of the rules on protection of foreign investment in times of armed conflict.[125] Furthermore, if the situation in question would meet the threshold for application of international humanitarian law (IHL), such a tribunal would present a truly independent and neutral adjudication of inter-regime conflicts (i.e. external to both IHL and investment law).[126] Lastly, by bringing two governments together and engaging them in a post-conflict dialogue, establishing such a forum could be seen as a step forward towards promoting stable and peaceful relations.

A relatively recent example of a remedial structure that exhibited such characteristics was the Eritrea–Ethiopia Claims Commission, established in 2000 under the Algiers Agreement to adjudicate claims arising from the 1998–2000 conflict.[127] While not designed specifically to address the claims for the losses of investors, these were among the claims filed. While both the governments and the injured individuals (including investors from each state) could bring a claim, in practice even claims of individuals were presented by the government (but on behalf of the individuals and not as the state's own claims). The challenge with such a structure is that it presupposes the political willingness of the concerned states to enter into an agreement that creates the jurisdiction of the tribunal. This is further complicated if injured investors have different nationalities, which would require the involvement of their home states or result in the lack of standing for the investors whose nationalities are not covered by the founding agreement. For example, the EECC

[124] Roberts, 'State-to-State Investment Treaty Arbitration' (n 63) 68 (arguing that a tribunal hearing a multitude of claims may reach a different conclusion on necessity than multiple tribunals hearing individual claims). See also R Howse, 'The Concept of Odious Debt in Public International Law' (2007) UNCTAD Discussion Paper no 185 UNCTAD/OSG/DP/2007/4, 22 (arguing that a single transitional tribunal would be an attractive solution to apply equitable defences).

[125] Despite the ongoing promotion of transparency in investment arbitration, many disputes continue to be governed by confidentiality, with jurisdictional and final awards not available to public, including claims against Russia related to the Crimea conflict. See Chapter 1, n 8.

[126] ILC Study Group, 'Fragmentation of International Law: Difficulties Arising from the Diversification and Expansion of International Law' (2006) UN Doc A/CN.4/L.682, 142, 166; A Cassimatis, 'International Humanitarian Law, International Human Rights Law, and Fragmentation of International Law' (2007) 56 ICLQ 623, 627, 631.

[127] Agreement, Eritrea–Ethiopia (12 December 2000) 2138 UNTS 94.

held that it did not have jurisdiction for losses and injury to property owned by non-nationals of Ethiopia or Eritrea.[128]

The success of such a mechanism could be further hampered if investors decided to pursue their claims in other fora. Their home state could try to preserve the exclusive jurisdiction of the instituted settlement programme by waiving the reparation claims of recalcitrant investors. While it is generally accepted that states can waive the civil claims of their nationals against other states, and in fact, they have often done so in peace treaties,[129] it is less clear what would be the effect of such a waiver on investment treaty claims. While further analysis is beyond the scope of this work, the answer will likely depend on whether the rights under investment treaties are conceptualized as pertaining to states or investors. Should one subscribe to the increasingly popular view that investment treaties grant direct rights to investors, then, arguably, home states would not be able to waive investors' procedural rights.[130]

2. Reclaiming State Control in Investment Treaties

In the absence of an agreement that would create a post-conflict *sui generis* remedial structure, or without the right to seize such a structure, the most appealing alternative to seek redress for the injured investor would be investor–state arbitration, provided that the relevant investment treaty is in place. The concerns of procedural inefficiency and inconsistent decisions in arbitrating a large number of claims resulting from the same armed conflict could be addressed by either consolidating the claims or by submitting individual mass claims. Both devices raise complex procedural questions and neither tackles the problematic lack of state control in politically sensitive disputes. Thus, a more important question is whether the existing investment treaty regime provides for any mechanism that would enable states to reassert their role in a post-conflict dispute settlement.[131]

An important mechanism serving this end, which can be found in most investment treaties, is a dispute resolution clause allowing state-to-state arbitration in cases concerning treaty interpretation and/or application.[132] While underutilized in practice, the state-to-state arbitration clause has been celebrated by Anthea

[128] *Port Claims: Ethiopia's Claim 6* (Final Award, 19 December 2005) 26 RIAA 489, 495, paras 5–6.

[129] See e.g. San Francisco Treaty between the Allied powers and Japan (8 September 1951) 136 UNTS 45, Art 14(b). On this basis, municipal courts have rejected claims of individuals. See also A McNair, 'The Effects of Peace Treaties upon Private Rights' (1939–1941) 7 Cambridge Law Journal 379, 386; Dolzer, 'Settlement of War-Related Claims' (n 29) 312; Van Houtte et al, *Post-War Restoration* (n 32) 304.

[130] M Paparinskis, 'Investment Treaty Arbitration and the (New) Law of State Responsibility (2013) 24(2) EJIL 617, 645.

[131] Generally on this question, see A Kulick (ed), *Reassertion of Control over the Investment Treaty Regime* (CUP 2017).

[132] e.g. 2012 US Model BIT Art 37(1).

Roberts as a 'progressive mechanism by which treaty parties can re-engage with the system in order to correct existing imbalances and help shape its development from within'.[133] She has divided the interstate claims that can be brought under the clause into three categories: (1) diplomatic protection claims (when home state files a diplomatic protection claim for the losses suffered by its investors);[134] (2) pure interpretive disputes (a home or host state seeks interpretation of a treaty provision);[135] and (3) claims for declaratory relief (a home or host state brings a request for a declaratory relief on a matter that may arise in investor–state arbitration).[136]

While depending on the circumstances, all of these categories could be relevant in the context of conflict-related losses, the claims for declaratory relief would likely present the best alternative to a post-conflict tribunal. Thus, where a number of investors sustained losses as a consequence of the host state's conduct in times of conflict, their home state could seek a declaration that the host state violated the investment treaty. This would provide for a consistent and efficient means of determining major factual and legal questions, such as liability. Following the interstate arbitral award, investors could then file claims for damages before investor–state arbitration.[137]

On the other hand, a host state facing several conflict-related claims could potentially also bring a claim for declaratory relief before the state-to-state arbitration, benefiting from all claims being considered by a single tribunal whose composition would not be influenced by investors, rather than by multiple tribunals with investor-appointed arbitrators.[138] The effectiveness of such a procedure would depend on whether the state-to-state arbitral award would be considered binding, or at least highly persuasive, on the subsequent investor–state arbitration. The possibility of interstate arbitration under investment treaties raises several complex questions that are beyond the scope of this chapter. It suffices to note that state-to-state arbitration clauses provide states with a viable, albeit untested in practice, venue for influencing the resolution of conflict-related claims, and thereby minimizes their interference with the post-conflict transition to peace.

A more certain and straightforward way of shifting control back to the state would be through re-drafting of investment treaties. For example, state parties could exclude investor–state arbitration either completely or partially for conflict-related cases, that is for claims concerning measures that the host state

[133] Roberts, 'State-to-State Investment Treaty Arbitration' (n 63) 5. For a more cautious approach, see C Schreuer, 'Investment Protection and International Relations' in A Reinisch and U Kriebaum (eds), *The Law of International Relations, Liber Amicorum Hanspeter Neuhold* (Eleven 2007) 345, 348.

[134] *Republic of Italy v Republic of Cuba* Ad hoc Arbitration, Interim Award, 15 March 2005; *Republic of Italy v Republic of Cuba* Ad hoc Arbitration, Final Award, 15 January 2008.

[135] *Ecuador v United States* UNCITRAL, Request for Arbitration, 28 June 2011.

[136] *Cross-Border Trucking Services (Mexico v US)* Case No USA-MEX-98-2008-01 (NAFTA Ch 20 Arb Trib Panel Decision, 6 February 2001).

[137] Roberts, 'State-to-State Investment Treaty Arbitration' (n 63) 67.

[138] ibid 68.

has adopted for the protection of its security interest or for the maintenance of peace. While such carve-outs are rare, an example is provided in Article 12 of the BIT between Mexico and the Netherlands, which states that '[t]he dispute settlement provisions of this Schedule shall not apply to the resolutions adopted by a Contracting Party for national security reasons'.[139] By applying the insights of other conflict-related remedial structures, the following conditions to investor–state arbitration could also be considered in the negotiation of future investment treaties: requirement that the arbitrators have strong background in public international law,[140] requirement of the approval of all state parties to the treaty before the conflict-related claim could be brought before arbitration, requirement for mandatory mediation as a condition of initiating arbitration, or introducing monetary thresholds whereby claims above a certain amount would require the consent of the investor's home state, or could only be adjudicated via state-to-state arbitration.

In sum, the aim of this section was not to argue that investor–state arbitration should be dismissed entirely. It has been shown throughout this book that investment law is mostly capable of addressing claims for conflict-related losses, and in some cases tribunals have done this with aplomb. The fact that investor–state arbitration is often the only international forum that is in a position to address the state arbitrary and violent actions during armed conflicts (IHL does not provide an equivalent remedial mechanism), should also not be neglected. There lies an important symbolic value in having an international adjudicative body finding the state liable for abusing its power, especially when the latter resulted in civilian losses and without the passing of too much time after the wrongful act had been committed. *AAPL v Sri Lanka* is a case in point. While it took many years for the international community to start paying attention to atrocities perpetrated during the Sri Lankan civil war,[141] the *AAPL* tribunal was the first and the only international body that adjudicated a claim emerging therefrom.[142] The award in which the government was found liable of breaching international law was paid without delay, possibly brought some comfort to the relatives of the farmers murdered in

[139] Mexico–the Netherlands BIT (1998) Schedule Art 12. More common are exceptions that limit the dispute settlement procedures to the security-related measures passed at the stage of the acquisition of domestic enterprise. See e.g. Iceland–Mexico BIT (2005) Art 23; Germany–Mexico (1998) Art 20.

[140] See 2018 Draft Netherlands Model BIT Art 20(5). It is the lawyers with formidable knowledge in public international law and appreciation of its different subfields, who often enriched the case law with nuanced reasoning. See e.g. Heribert Golsong's arguments as a representative of the claimant in the *AAPL* case; or his Separate Opinion in the *AMT* case.

[141] The recommendation for the establishment of a human rights monitoring mission was made at the UN Human Rights Council only in 2006, although various non-governmental organizations and human rights bodies voiced concerns about Sri Lanka's violations of human rights and war atrocities long before. 'Special Rapporteur on Extrajudicial Executions Urges Establishment of Human Rights Monitoring Mission in Sri Lanka' UN General Assembly (20 October 2006) GA/SHC/3859. See also D McConnel, 'The Tamil People's Rights to Self-Determination' (2008) 21(1) Camb Rev Intl Aff 59, 70.

[142] Asia does not have a regional human rights court equivalent to ECtHR.

the prawn farm massacre (the investor shared the awarded money with the murdered men's families),[143] and more broadly, presented a step towards reconciliation.

On the other hand, it has been also shown that for every good and legally accurate award, there is at least one where tribunals have failed to interpret the rules properly or, as argued here, arrived at inaccurate and unjust conclusions, thus failing to provide a consistent, predictable, and fair post-conflict dispute resolution framework. This merely reflects the systemic flaws inherent to the investor–state arbitration system, discussed in various other substantive contexts outside the present topic.[144] The often-voiced plea applies to the conclusion of this analysis: unless appropriate reforms are introduced to the system,[145] its potential in fulfilling the role of effective and appropriate means for resolving conflict-related disputes will be unlikely to be realized.

E. Preliminary Conclusions

This chapter set out to explore whether investment treaties are likely to facilitate or hinder the transition to peace. It observed that interaction between investment law and peace occur on two levels: the macroeconomic level, where it is widely believed that investment treaties facilitate stability and consequently contribute to lasting peace; and the microeconomic level, where individual investors are empowered to directly seek redress for conflict-related losses sustained by the host states. As for the former level, it was argued that the role of investment treaties as a facilitator of peace has been doubtful, at the least. The chapter's focus was, however, on the second level of interaction, that is the post-conflict investment treaty claims and the negative effects of compensation awards on peacemaking. The chapter has identified the various methods used to take into account humanitarian considerations when awarding damages in conflict-related cases. The chapter has also compared investor–state arbitration to other post-conflict reparations mechanisms,

[143] M Trawick, 'Lessons from Kokkadichcholai' paper presented at International Conference on Tamil Nationhood and Search for Peace in Sri Lanka (21–22 May 1999) <http://tamilnation.co/conferences/cnfCA99/trawick.html> accessed 18 December 2018.

[144] The literature on different systemic problems pervading investor–state arbitration (including the lack of transparency, insufficient expertise of arbitrators, inconsistent interpretations, conflict of interests, etc) is vast. See e.g. Frank, 'Legitimacy Crisis' (n 115); M Langford, D Behn, and R Lie, 'The Revolving Door in International Investment Arbitration' (2017) 20 JIEL 301; C Giorgetti 'Who Decides Who Decides In International Investment Arbitration?' (2013) 35 U Pa J Intl L 431.

[145] Currently, reforms of the investment system are on the agenda of several institutions. See e.g. UNCITRAL, 'UNCITRAL Working Group III: Investor-State Dispute Settlement Reform' (2017) <http://www.uncitral.org/uncitral/en/commission/working_groups/3Investor_State.html> accessed 18 December 2018; European Commission, 'Multilateral Investment Court' (2017) <http://trade.ec.europa.eu/doclib/docs/2017/september/tradoc_156042.pdf> accessed 18 December 2018; ICSID Secretariat Bank, 'Proposal for Amendment of the ICSID Rules—Working Paper' (2 August 2018) <https://www.google.co.uk/search?hl=en&q=icsid+rules+reform&meta=&gws_rd=ssl> accessed 18 December 2018.

tracing the historical oscillation between state and investor control over remediation processes. It concluded that the appropriateness of the structure depends on various factors, in particular the type of conflict situation, whereby the most intense conflicts resulting in large-scale responsibility matters could warrant the re-emergence of state control over international claims.

8
Conclusion

A. Conflicting Interests

The all-encompassing and perpetual tension between private and public has long been recognized as inherent to investment treaties. This divide is reflected in the normative (how treaty provisions are articulated and interpreted) as well as the institutional (how the investment treaty disputes are adjudicated) dimensions of the regime. Investment treaties impose certain obligations on contracting parties concerning the treatment of foreign investment, and consequently restrain the states' sovereign right to regulate their affairs in their territory, including measures in the area of national security. This creates the potential for a clash to occur between the objective of protection of foreign investment, on the one hand, and protection of the host state's security concerns, on the other. The outward perception of the unfair prioritization of investors' interests over states' security concerns undermines confidence and trust in the system, and gives rise to a legitimacy backlash. Thus, it is imperative for states and other stakeholders benefitting from the system to find an appropriate balance—one that allows a state to sufficiently safeguard its security interests while at the same time debars opportunistic behaviour resulting in abuse of force and consequently violation of investors' rights. This contribution has shown that the tension between investors' and host states' objectives manifests itself on four different levels.

First, on the level of the application of investment treaties, the answer to the question of whether the treaties or relevant treaty provisions continue to operate in times of armed conflict is split between two demands: on the one hand, there is the requirement for the stability and predictability of relations between different states, and on the other hand, the practical and security necessities allowing states to adjust their treaty relationship to an extraordinary change in circumstances. If the latter prevails, the treaty, or treaty provisions, will be suspended at the very least. Given the strong preference of the international community for a stable and predictable legal framework, a high threshold is set for any aberration in the continued application of international treaties.

Second, on the level of the responsibility of a host state, the central conflict exists between the expectations of investors that their rights are protected against the adverse interference of the host state and non-state actors, and the host state's right to protect certain security interests that can justify such adverse interference. Which interest takes precedence will be decided by evaluating a host state's conduct

The Protection of Foreign Investment in Times of Armed Conflict. First Edition. Jure Zrilič.
Published 2019 by Oxford University Press.

against a particular investment treaty standard, as well as assessing the defences that exist in investment treaties and customary international law.

Third, on the level of compensation/damages, the tension between private and public seeps into the post-conflict stage. On the one hand, injured investors have an interest in fully recovering the losses they have sustained from the breach of the investment treaty. On the other hand, the wrongdoing state, as well as the international community, has an interest in creating and maintaining the conditions for an uninterrupted transition to peace, and minimizing the suffering of the population of a state emerging from a conflict. Achieving the latter objective can be threatened by the payment of full compensations to injured investors.

Lastly, on the level of dispute resolution, there is a conflict between the right of foreign investors to have unfettered access to international justice, and the right of states to retain some degree of control in how politically sensitive disputes are processed and adjudicated. While investment treaties largely provide for the former, it has been shown that there can be valid reasons, but limited options, for reintroducing the stronger role of states in the process of resolving conflict-related disputes.

Following the preliminary conclusions of the different chapters, it is submitted that how the tensions between these conflicting interests are resolved can be explained by two different theories: the theory of the dominant paradigm and the theory of the type of conflict (see Figure 8.1, below). While the former is based on the normative narrative pervading the applicable investment treaty and interpretative process, the latter is concerned with the factual circumstances in which the investment claim originates. The effectiveness and appropriateness of investment treaty protections depends on the combination of both theories.

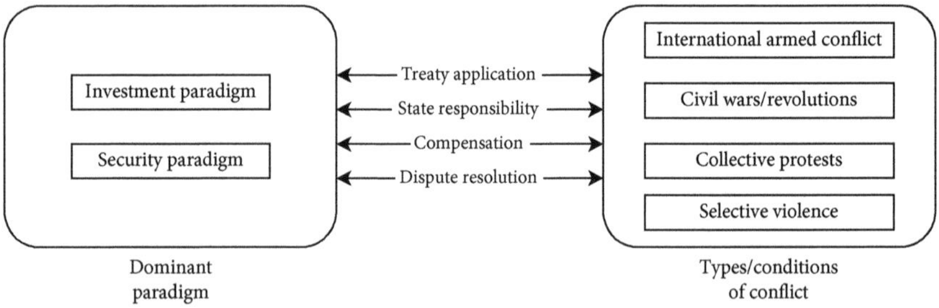

Figure 8.1 Framework for evaluating investment treaties in times of armed conflict

B. Types/Conditions of Conflict

The development of the rules on protection of foreign investment in times of armed conflict has been importantly influenced by different historical conflict situations. This is similar to international humanitarian law (IHL), with American Civil War,

Battle of Solferino in 1859, and the Second World War, among others, often being regarded as defining moments in its evolution.[1] Armed conflict has played a two-fold role in the development of relevant investment law rules. First, it gave rise to jurisprudence of post-conflict arbitrations and commissions which clarified the principles and rules governing state conduct, as well as provoked doctrinal discussions (e.g. nineteenth- and early twentieth-century revolutions and civil wars in Latin America; the Mexican Revolution of 1919–20; the 1979 Iranian Revolution; and recent conflicts in North Africa, the Middle East, and the Ukraine). Second, it also exposed the flaws in the conventional law and inspired drafting innovations like armed conflict clauses and security exceptions (in particular, the Second World War and Cold War). Those events thus mark the milestones in the evolution of legal protections of foreign investment in armed conflict.

In addition, as demonstrated throughout this book, the situation of conflict (including the conditions constituting it, such as its international dimension, the intensity of the lethal violence, scope and scale of the conflict, motivation etc) has been an essential element in determining the effectiveness and appropriateness of the investment treaty protections. Chapter 2 showed that at the turn of the last century, some scholars differentiated between different types of conflict by attaching different consequences to the state's responsibility for the harm caused to aliens. Those proposals became part of some of the private codifications of state responsibility but were ultimately rejected by the International Law Commission (ILC). Rightly so, as experience has shown that state responsibility can emerge in all types of conflict and it would be wrong to exempt it by squaring a particular case in an arbitrarily created category of conflict rather than by assessing it on its own merits. This notwithstanding, the experience has also shown that states are less likely to be found liable for losses inflicted in some type of situations than they are in others.

The same observations can be made with respect to the modern investment treaty framework. As noted in Chapter 1, unlike the IHL framework, investment treaties place different types of conflict on the same footing; however, the application of treaty protections may likely yield different outcomes depending on the conditions of the conflict. It has been shown that how investment treaty standards or state defences will be applied will often depend on the type of volatile situation in which the losses were incurred.[2] While distinguishing between different types of

[1] American Civil War gave rise to the first example of the codification of the laws on war conduct, i.e. the Lieber Code; the Battle of Solferino in 1859 inspired Henry Dunant to found the Red Cross movement; while the Second World War prompted the overhaul of the IHL. See A Alexander, 'A Short History of International Humanitarian Law' (2015) 26(1) EJIL 109, 112; D Schindler, 'International Humanitarian Law: Its Remarkable Development and Its Persistent Violation' (2003) 5 J Hist Intl L 165, 167.

[2] A similar trend towards recognizing the distinction between different categories of conflict has been recently identified in the international human rights framework, which traditionally advocated the elimination of any differentiation of conflict situations similar to that in IHL. L Hill-Cawthorne, 'Humanitarian Law, Human Rights Law and the Bifurcation of Armed Conflict' (2015) 64 ICLQ 293;

conflict as absolute legal categories in investment law should be generally rejected, acknowledging the differences may nonetheless provide a useful insight into the functioning of the investment treaty framework in volatile times. Therefore, a list of the categories of conflict that indicates when the investment treaty protections could be effective and appropriate could be a helpful tool for understanding the complexities of conflict-related investment disputes. The following observations can be made based on the typology proposed in the introductory chapter:

- *International armed conflicts*, especially if intense and protracted, are more likely to result in the suspension of treaty protections, either by rendering relevant treaty provisions inoperative, or by applying treaty security exceptions or general defences in the law of state responsibility. Given the potentially high number of conflict-related claims, different sources of state responsibility (most injuries are likely to be caused by the enemy state, while some, especially against enemy aliens, are caused by the host state) and highly sensitive political contexts, investor–state arbitration is unlikely to be a suitable venue for adjudicating the claims. Instead, resolution by a single post-conflict tribunal established to hear all the conflict-related claims, or concluding a lump sum settlement agreement would appear more appropriate.
- While in *internal armed conflicts (including civil wars and revolutions)* investment treaties likely continue to apply even when the threshold for the application of IHL is met, defences like treaty security exceptions or justifications on the level of treaty standards (police powers, due diligence, exceptions in advanced armed conflict clauses) could provide the host state with sufficient room to refute potential claims. If the resolution of conflict-related claims takes place against the backdrop of political instability, limited state resources, a large number of claims, or the transition to a new regime, some degree of state control in the dispute resolution process (e.g. a single post-conflict tribunal or state-to-state arbitration with respect to the liability) could provide for a more suitable remedial option than investor–state arbitration.
- The effectiveness of investment protections for remedying injuries sustained in violent *collective protests* will depend on various circumstances. While security exceptions and defences under the law of state responsibility will be difficult to establish, determining the failure of the host state to protect investors will depend on circumstances like suddenness and magnitude of such events, state resources and the availability of relevant information needed to prevent or suppress the violence on time, and reasonableness and proportionality in a state's response to violence (e.g. xenophobic mob lootings warrant different reaction than protests of a concerned local community).

D Kretzmer, 'Rethinking the Application of IHL in Non-International Armed Conflict' (2009) 42 Isr L Rev 8.

- In the event of *selective violence* in particular, investment treaty protections have a potential to be effective and offer an appropriate venue for adjudicating investors' claims. This is true even when targeted attacks are carried out against the background of one of the above categories, as long as such events do not result in a multitude of claims (the *AAPL* award is a good example).

This list illustrates a sliding scale whereby moving up in the categories of conflict renders the effectiveness and appropriateness of investment treaties increasingly questionable. As mentioned above, these categories should be understood in instructive, rather than absolute and exhaustive, terms. The conditions of conflict (e.g. its intensity, magnitude, motivation behind it, the degree of control that a host state exercises over its territory, the organization of armed groups) may be fluid across different categories or may have a bearing on how the treaty standards are applied within the same type of conflict. Nevertheless, the typology rather accurately reflects the context in which investment treaty disputes have arisen most frequently in the past, namely in the last category.

In the end, how the competing interests will be balanced will depend on both the conditions of the conflict and the prevailing normative paradigm. Thus, the security paradigm will make moving up the scale of conflict significantly more difficult, likely rendering claims for losses from internal armed conflicts ineffective. On the other hand, should the investment paradigm dominate a particular dispute, investors will have an easier job litigating the claims emerging from a conflict higher up on the scale.

C. Dominant Paradigms

How effective investment treaty protections are for foreign investors in times of armed conflict will largely depend on how the treaties are drafted and how their provisions are interpreted. Whether the pendulum will swing towards stronger investment protections or to a wider space for the host state to address its national security matters is driven by the normative and interpretative paradigm that dominates a particular conflict-related case.[3] Both the investment and the security paradigms have an important role to play in how the competing interests described above are balanced at different stages of an investment dispute: the operation of the investment treaty, the ascertainment of the host state's responsibility, the determination of the amount of compensation, and the manner in which disputes are resolved in the first place.

[3] For a general account of competing paradigms in investment law, see A Roberts, 'Clash of Paradigms: Actors and Analogies Shaping the Investment Treaty System' (2013) 107 AJIL 45.

1. The Investment Paradigm

The investment paradigm is derived from the common understanding of the objective and purpose of investment treaties as the promotion of foreign investment achieved by guaranteeing a certain level of investment protection and ensuring a certain degree of legal stability. While this view has been a source of debate,[4] it has been continuously upheld by arbitral tribunals and investment law scholars,[5] implying that it is the paradigm that has traditionally dictated the narrative of how conflict-related disputes were resolved.

According to the investment paradigm, the outbreak of armed conflict, including that of the highest intensity, like international wars, does not disrupt the operation of investment treaties. The application of treaty provisions is not affected by the Effects of Armed Conflicts on Treaties (EACT) or Vienna Convention on the Law of Treaties (VCLT) doctrines. The paradigm further manifests in the absence of security exceptions and advanced armed conflict clauses in investment treaties. The wording of treaty provisions implies heightened protections compared to those in customary international law, and the substantive standards are broadly interpreted (e.g. the objective standard of due diligence in full protection and security (FPS) provisions, the sole effect doctrine or limited application of the police powers doctrine). Once the responsibility of the host state for a treaty violation is established, full compensation must be paid, including that for the loss of future profit, regardless of the post-conflict circumstances. There are no limits placed on the investor's access to arbitration, and little room for a home state's interference in the dispute resolution process.

The investment paradigm emerged in diplomatic protection cases of the nineteenth and early twentieth centuries when developed states were starting wars to protect the interests of their businesses abroad. While the theories of absolute responsibility were rejected by mixed claims commissions, the rule that was confirmed was that in some cases, host states could still be responsible for losses that foreigners sustained in times of conflict (Chapter 2). The same rule has been transplanted into modern investment treaties where the ascertainment of the host state's liability will often depend on the assessment of the host state's due diligence

[4] See M Waibel et al (eds), *The Backlash against Investment Arbitration: Perceptions and Reality* (Kluwer Law International 2010).

[5] See e.g. *BG Group v Republic of Argentina* UNCITRAL, Final Award, 27 December 2007, paras 133, 307; *Occidental Exploration and Production Company v Ecuador (I)* LCIA Case no UN3 4 67, Final Award, 1 July 2004, paras 66, 183; *CMS Gas v Republic of Argentina* ICSID Case no ARB 01/08, Final Award, 12 May 2005, paras 337, 353; *Sempra Energy International v Republic of Argentina* ICSID Case no ARB/02/16, Award, 28 September 2007, para 300. See also O Fauchald, 'The Legal Reasoning of ICSID Tribunals—an Empirical Analysis' (2008) 19(2) EJIL 301, 322 (observing that most arbitrators held that 'the object and purpose' of investment treaties was evident and no special substantiation was needed); R Dolzer, 'The Impact of International Investment Treaties on Domestic Administrative Law' (2006) 37 Intl L and Pol 952; A Rigo Sureda, *Investment Treaty Arbitration: Judging Under Uncertainty* (CUP 2012) 130.

obligation. As seen above, on several occasions, investment tribunals have found that states did not do everything they should have, and could have, to protect investors from physical violence. Furthermore, some tribunals have failed to efficiently conceptualize the space within which states can react to security threats, holding them liable for actions taken in the course of armed conflict (Chapters 4 and 5). The message ostensibly conveyed is that the interference constituting a breach of the investment treaty in a tumultuous period is no different from interference during peacetime, and the harm arising from it should be remedied accordingly.

On the policy level, the paradigm translates into an incentive for unstable countries to do their best to maintain the rule of law and legal stability in times of conflict and during the post-conflict transition. This, in turn, may facilitate more foreign investment and foster economic recovery—one of the conditions for stability itself. Furthermore, the investment paradigm partially resembles the international human rights framework in that it places an emphasis on the protection of individuals, seeks to restrain the state's arbitrary conduct in times of hostilities, and empowers individual victims to seek remedies (Chapters 6 and 7).

A vital aspect of the investment paradigm is that it emancipates investors from the control of their home state in their pursuit of post-conflict justice. In addition, the possibility of investor–state arbitration alleviates the burden of the home states since they are no longer faced with the pressure of initiating litigation against another state, and in so doing exacerbate delicate interstate relationships in a precarious post-conflict period (Chapter 7). In other words, investor–state arbitration is set to depoliticize conflict-related disputes and create a venue where claims ought to be decided on a purely legal basis.

2. The Security Paradigm

The security paradigm is premised on the state's sovereign right to protect its security interests and safeguard peace, on the recognition of extraordinary and uncontrollable circumstances that armed conflict can create, and on the need for sensitivity when dealing with post-conflict compensation claims. The state's inability to meet its commercial obligations to foreign investors can be justified by its role as a sovereign protector of its people. Since the manner in which investment treaty claims for losses sustained by investors in conflicts are resolved has traditionally been influenced by the investment paradigm, it would appear, at first sight, that the security paradigm (while introduced to the investment treaties of some major powers) has mainly been used by scholars or dissenting arbitrators as a lens for examining and highlighting the systemic flaws.

According to the security paradigm, investment treaty provisions could be terminated or suspended as a result of the outbreak of armed conflict by the application of VCLT doctrines or the EACT, for which notification procedures are not mandatory. Substantive standards in investment treaties do not provide stronger protections than those accorded in customary international law, and their interpretation takes into account the circumstances and interests of the host state (e.g. the subjective standard of due diligence, broad application of the police powers doctrine). Investment treaties contain specific exceptions provided for in advanced armed conflict clauses or broadly worded self-judging security exceptions, covering a wide array of state actions. At the level of compensation, it manifests in expressly provided lower standards of compensation and the deferred payment thereof for the breach of an armed conflict clause, and more generally, in the equitable adjustments of compensation in post-conflict settings. Lastly, the paradigm is also reflected in the treaty provisions excluding or limiting investor–state arbitration from adjudicating security-related claims.

The doctrinal origins of the security paradigm are found in the views of the Latin American scholars and diplomats of the nineteenth century who strongly rejected the responsibility of host states for conflict-related losses, and the international adjudication of investors' claims (Chapter 2). While these views were dismissed by the international community and did not translate into customary international law, they resurfaced in the second half of the twentieth century as part of the Third World critique against the modern international economic order.[6] In the context of investment law, the fact that the majority of the countries being sued for breaching investment treaties have been capital-importing countries, and that the claimants have been predominantly investors from powerful capital-exporting countries, gave rise to the neo-colonialism claim. According to that, investment treaties still reflect the exploitative nature of colonial rule and they have only repackaged the inequalities between developed and developing countries.[7] With respect to the conflict-related claims, scholars have argued that the investment treaty regime severely hindered the host state's sovereign right to protect its security interests, and that investment tribunals, promoting the investment paradigm, should not be enabled to hear such cases (Chapters 6 and 7). Their views are critical of normative and institutional proposals put forward to address the systemic flaws of the regime. Rather, they see the whole system as inherently unfair and unbalanced, and as such inappropriate for addressing claims concerning conflict-related losses.

A more lenient expression of the security paradigm is the view that IHL should take precedence over international investment law when there is an inevitable conflict between the norms of the respective regimes. Some scholars thus argued that IHL norms should be applied directly or through an informed interpretation

[6] See e.g. M Bedjaoui, *Towards a New International Economic Order* (Holmes & Meier 1979); JT Gathii, 'War's Legacy in International Investment Law' (2009) 11 ICLR 353, 363–70.

[7] JT Gathii, *War, Commerce and International Law* (OUP 2010); M Sornarajah, *The International Law on Foreign Investment* (4th edn, CUP 2017); M Sornarajah, *Resistance and Change in the International Law of Foreign Investment* (CUP 2015).

of investment treaty provisions to the investment cases (Chapter 6). This view is grounded on legal (IHL as *lex specialis*) and policy arguments (the need to preserve a host state's rights on the battleground). Unlike the critics of neo-colonialism, these scholars are not dismissive of investment law in its entirety, but rather call for a better engagement with a regime primarily designed to regulate a state's conduct in times of armed conflict.

Lastly, post-Arab Spring events in Egypt and Libya have seen the emergence of a new argument highlighting the problematic nature of the investment treaty framework in the period of transition from conflict to peace (Chapter 7). The prospect of paying hefty compensation awards could complicate post-conflict reforms, destabilize weak transitional governments, and pose a threat to a newly established peace. This is in stark contrast to the investment paradigm, which sees investment awards as an opportunity for a state to signal its stability and return to the strong rule of law to prospective investors abroad.

Table 8.1 illustrates how the dominant paradigms are manifested in investment treaties:

Table 8.1 Dominant paradigms in investment treaties

	Investment paradigm	Security paradigm
The application of investment treaties or investment treaty provisions	- Continue to apply in time of conflict - Mandatory notification procedure	- Suspension or termination under the EACT or VCLT doctrines - No mandatory notification procedure
The responsibility of a host state	- Absence of security exceptions and advanced armed conflict clauses - Broad interpretation of FPS (objective standard of due diligence, the police powers doctrine does not apply) and other treaty protections	- Self-judging, broadly interpreted security exceptions - Advanced armed conflict clauses - Narrow interpretation of FPS (subjective standard of due diligence, the police powers doctrine applies) and other treaty protections
Compensation/ Damages	- Full and prompt compensation	- Reasonable or just standard of compensation for the breach of advanced armed conflict clauses - Deferred payment clause - Equitable adjustments
Dispute resolution	- Unlimited access to investor–state arbitration	- Limitations to investor–state arbitration - State-to-state arbitration clause

3. Shifting the Paradigms

The examination of the investment protections in times of armed conflict can be undertaken in two ways. First, through the lens of historical oppression of Western, capital-exporting countries over developing, capital-importing countries.[8] Second, through the lens of restraint of the arbitrary and violent conduct in the course of conflict. In this book, the emphasis was on the latter. However, since the two narratives are interwoven, it was also necessary to apply the former lens to shed light on the historical context and ideological environment from which modern investment law emerged. The origins of the rules on protection of foreign investment showed that investment and security approaches have been often used as part of the same rhetoric, re-enforcing and justifying each other. Thus, Western diplomats and international lawyers often referred to order- and security-based justifications when discussing the legal framework for protection of Western capital abroad (Chapters 2 and 7). Such use of the argument of 'peace' and 'security' to rationalize the frameworks and actions for protecting investment has often been opportunistic, favouring the pro-investor foreign policy. The views of the powers, however, have shifted through time, depending on the type of state conduct being regulated, strategic interests, and geopolitical context.

With regard to the state's failure to protect foreign investors from the violent acts of non-state actors, the limits of space within which a host state would be responsible for related losses was framed by the clash of views of Western powers, on the one hand, and capital-importing and politically unstable Latin American states, on the other. The arguments from both sides were pragmatic, reflecting the powers' interests and circumstances, with a strict standard of responsibility favoured by the former, and tools for escaping responsibility, like *force majeure*, advocated by the latter. While these disagreements attracted much controversy and fuelled the narrative of investment law as tool of Western imperialism for decades to come, jurisprudence of post-conflict commissions as well as modern investment tribunals eventually struck a balance in between these extremes, giving way to a relative standard of due diligence as a mechanism for evaluating such situations.

On the other hand, a state's proactive conduct undertaken in pursuit of its own security, strategic, or military goals, has attracted less attention in the investment community but has been no less problematic. In the past, Western powers routinely justified their military interventions for protecting their investors abroad under the guise of fostering security and order. As such conduct became outlawed under international law and as the conflicts moved from the periphery and semi-periphery to the centre, the concern that the protection of economic interests in international agreements would outweigh the state security considerations

[8] Gathii, *War, Commerce* (n 7).

became more urgent for Western states. Thus, it is countries like the US and the UK that have become most ardent advocates of provisions protective of their security interests in investment treaties. This reflected the traditional position of the two military powers: protective of their freedoms on the battleground, and both critical of the general trend to humanize IHL. Modern treaty making has thus marked the start of a shift from investment to security paradigm, with both developed and developing countries welcoming such limitations to investment treaty obligations. Given the ongoing geopolitical tensions (shift of economic and political power from West to East, the 'war on terror', and the increasing number of internal conflicts and the rise of populist revolt), it is unlikely that this trend will discontinue.

While this book has been generally supportive of drawing the investment system closer to the pole of the security paradigm, and aimed to identify and clarify under-utilized avenues for protecting a state's security interests (e.g. the EACT and the police powers doctrine), it still remained critical of the latter. Times of political crisis are often accompanied by a great variety of negative views that are often directed at foreigners. History shows that foreign businesses, in particular, may find themselves blamed for the malaise, which in turn may give rise to violence against them,[9] or cause them to be exploited for their strategic value in combat situations.[10] Chalking up every injury sustained in a period of conflict as a political risk that one takes when investing abroad would significantly undermine the rule of law and create an environment adverse to further investment and economic development.[11] In those circumstances, the prospect for establishing the conditions necessary for political stability would be hampered. Moreover, prioritizing security approaches could not only authorize a state's strategic opportunism but also threaten the overall peace and stability.

This book has been further cautious about the security paradigm's calls for prioritizing IHL over investment law. It has been shown that the genuine normative conflicts between the two regimes are unlikely to happen, and that the normative tensions can be minimized by certain *ex ante* and *ex post* methods. The investment treaty rules do not directly contradict the *jus in bello* framework, although in some cases investment tribunals have applied them in a way that appears to be more

[9] See e.g. the riots in South Africa targeting small business owners coming from other African countries. 'Xenophobic Violence in Democratic South Africa' (South African History Online, 17 April 2015) <https://www.sahistory.org.za/article/xenophobic-violence-democratic-south-africa> accessed 19 December 2018; *Al Jazeera Media Network v Arab Republic of Egypt* ICSID Case no ARB/16/1 (pending).

[10] See e.g. *Ampal-American Israel Corporation and Others v Arab Republic of Egypt* ICSID Case no ARB/12/11, Decision on Liability, 21 February 2017, para 65. The investor alleged that Egypt's passivity in providing adequate protection against selective terrorist attacks at its infrastructure was because the investor had been delivering gas to Israel.

[11] See e.g. Chinese investor's attempt to reduce its billions of dollars' worth of involvement in the Mes Aynak mines, situated in a conflict-ridden area of Afghanistan, due to lack of security. L O'Donnell, 'China's MCC Turns Back on US$3b Mes Aynak Afghanistan Mine Deal' *South China Morning Post* (20 March 2014).

protective of investors, or in other words, more restrictive of the state's discretion in conducting military operations (Chapter 6). Rather than condemning such practices, those cases could be seen as an opportunity to contribute to the development of the rules governing the state's conduct in armed conflict.

It has been argued that cases like *AAPL v Sri Lanka* could help clarify the obligations that states waging civil wars owe to civilians, including the duty to exercise due diligence in protecting them.[12] Views that states have no such duty in times of internal armed conflict are arguably driven by the lack of understanding of the relevant legal frameworks or ideological desires to replace *lex lata* with *lex ferenda*, and accordingly have been challenged. The *AAPL* arbitration, in particular, illustrates the clash of the 'imperialist oppression' narrative and the 'restraint of violence' narrative. While the case has been cited as an example of investment law's pro-West and pro-investor inclinations,[13] such views rest on partial or incomplete understanding of the way the due diligence rule operated in that particular context. As shown in Chapters 4 and 6, the case was not decided on the basis of a failure to protect the investor from the rebels, as sometimes thought,[14] but rather on the basis of the state's failure to take precautions in planning and execution of the armed attack, which would have minimized or avoided the loss of civilian lives and property. In other words, the award did not extend the developing state's responsibility for losses outside of its control (the view popular with Western powers in the past), but rather held the government to account for not taking certain mandatory steps in a military operation over which it had control (the view not popular with Western military powers). By applying investment rules in such a way, investment tribunals, in a similar manner to human rights bodies, could contribute to more humane state conduct in times of armed conflict, which, after all, is the objective of IHL. Despite the potential of investment tribunals to emerge as an unconventional actor in contributing to 'humanization' of rules governing conduct in hostilities, the argument has remained realistic: without essential reforms, this potential is unlikely to be fulfilled on a systemic level.

Rather than denouncing the investment treaty regime or subjugating it to IHL, the book has advocated a more balanced system where changes can be achieved from within. While neither investment nor security paradigms provide the optimal solution for addressing conflict-related investment claims, a nuanced equilibrium can be established by combining the elements of both into a mixed, investment-security paradigm at all levels of balancing the competing interests. To a certain

[12] *Asian Agricultural Products Ltd (AAPL) v Republic of Sri Lanka* ICSID Case no ARB/87/3, Award, 27 June 1990.

[13] Gathii, 'War's Legacy' (n 6) 382, 384; Sornarajah, *International Law* (n 7) 278.

[14] E De Brabandere, 'Host States' Due Diligence Obligations in International Investment Law' (2015) 42(2) Syracuse J Intl & Com 320, 335; S Alexandrov and J Robbins, 'Proximate Causation in International Investment Disputes' in K Sauvant (ed), *Yearbook on International Investment Law & Policy 2008-2009* (OUP 2009) 317.

extent, this is already reflected in some aspects of the investment treaty regime (e.g. relative due diligence standard as an integral part of the FPS provision). This book has pointed out several other areas in which a similar balance can be achieved. For example, it has challenged the prevailing view in investment law scholarship that the outbreak of armed conflict can never affect the operation of investment treaty provisions, or that the police powers doctrine cannot be applied to provisions other than indirect expropriation, as well as cautioned against the inappropriate interpretation of security exceptions. It has further highlighted the potential of some principles like proportionality in determining a host state's responsibility, or equity in adjusting the post-conflict compensation modalities. In other words, having recognized the inadequacies of the current system, the book has sought to find venues for modifying the investment paradigm with a view to curtailing the negative effects that investment treaty claims may have on host states in a conflict and post-conflict setting.

Such modifications of the investment regime can be achieved through the necessary systemic overhaul, encompassing the changes in the text of investment treaties and transformation of the current model of dispute resolution. Until legislative and institutional changes are introduced, how the interplay between the investment and security approaches will play out in a particular case will largely depend on the investment tribunal's interpretation of the existing rules. States can exert some influence by issuing interpretative guidelines with respect to specific provisions, by how they shape defences in their pleadings, and by appointing arbitrators with good knowledge of public international law. Moreover, they can try to agree on other means of settling post-conflict claims, such as setting up a single hybrid tribunal or agreeing for state-to-state arbitration as provided for in investment treaties. This would be a desirable solution, especially if the dispute includes politically sensitive questions and there is the possibility of there being a large number of conflict-related claims. These solutions do not imply setting the clock back to times of diplomatic protection. Rather, they reflect the typical trajectory of settling conflict-related investment disputes, according to which the increase of the investor's power over the process has not been linear, but reactionary.

D. Concluding Remarks

This book has traced the legal protections of foreign investment in times of armed conflict across different legal regimes and at different levels of a conflict-related investment claim. It has demonstrated that the legal protections have evolved over time, with the investment treaty regime providing the strongest legal framework for protecting investors yet. How effective investment law protections are in redressing the conflict-related losses will depend on how the investment treaties are drafted and construed. While investment interests have traditionally been prioritized, there has been an apparent shift towards a security paradigm in recent treaty making and this is being promoted in investment scholarship. This book has been critical of both paradigms, perceiving them as two extremes on the spectrum of possibilities for the regulation of a state's conduct vis-à-vis foreign investment in times of hostilities. Instead, it has argued for a more nuanced approach that draws on both investment- and security-based approaches and is centred on the balancing of competing interests at different levels of investment claims set against the backdrop of various conflict situations.

The book has further established that the concept of armed conflict and its relevance in applying protections has also evolved and taken different forms across different legal regimes. While in some other legal frameworks conflict has been used to define the applicable rules, investment treaties generally apply at all times. However, it has been shown that the type and conditions of a conflict situation, while generally not determinative of the applicable rules, have played an important role in how the competing objectives are balanced on different investment treaty protection levels. Different types of conflicts lend themselves to different types of standards and yield different outcomes as a result of their application. This book has linked the paradigm theory and the conflict theory in an attempt to provide a richer understanding of how foreign investors are protected in times of armed conflict. In view of the current hostilities and political instabilities, it is hoped that the proposed framework can abate uncertainties regarding investment protections in volatile times and contribute to the ongoing debate over the future development of international investment law.

It seems apt to conclude the book where it started. The *AAPL* arbitration, which has been at the centre of the present analysis, is in many ways emblematic of concerns the book has aimed to address. The prawn farm massacre, which gave rise to the *AAPL* case, has achieved a somewhat mythical status in the Sri Lankan Tamil community. It is a reminder of their oppression and a testament to their perseverance. On the other hand, in the investment law community, the award has been celebrated as a landmark for different reasons. It was the first decision in which the tribunal established jurisdiction based on the dispute resolution clause in the investment treaty, thus opening the way for hundreds of arbitrations that have forever changed the face of international investment law. And yet, this book has pointed to another virtue extolled in the case and commonly forgotten in successive arbitrations, namely the essence of investment protection rules, once they are stripped of their problematic origin. The case stands as a reminder of not what investment law was necessarily meant to be, but what it could have become.

Bibliography

Abresch W, 'A Human Rights Law of International Armed Conflict: The European Court of Human Rights in Chechnya' (2005) 16(4) EJIL 741

Akande D, 'Classification of Armed Conflict: Relevant Legal Concepts' in Wilmshurst E (ed), *International Law and the Classification of Conflicts* (OUP 2012)

Alexander A, 'A Short History of International Humanitarian Law' (2015) 26(1) EJIL 109

Alexandrov S and Robbins J, 'Proximate Causation in International Investment Disputes' in K Sauvant (ed) *Yearbook on International Investment Law & Policy 2008-2009* (OUP 2009) 317

Alfredsson G, 'Article 17' in Eide A et al (eds), *The Universal Declaration of Rights: A Commentary* (OUP 1992) 255

Alvarez J, 'The Human Right of Property' (2018) 72 U Miami L Rev 580

Alvarez JE, 'Political Protectionism and United States International Investment Obligations in Conflict: The Hazards of Exon-Florio' (1989) 30 Va J Intl L 1

Ambrus M et al (eds), *Risk and the Regulation of Uncertainty in International Law* (OUP 2017)

Amerasinghe CF, *Diplomatic Protection* (OUP 2008)

Anghie A, *Imperialism, Sovereignty and the Making of International Law* (CUP 2004)

Arias H, 'The Non-liability of States for Damages Suffered by Foreigners in the Course of a Riot, an Insurrection or a Civil War' (1913) 7 AJIL 724

Aust A, *Modern Treaty Law and Practice* (2nd edn, CUP 2007)

Baetens F (ed), *Investment Law Within International Law: Integrationist Perspectives* (CUP 2013)

Bannelier-Christakis K, 'Cyber Diligence: A Low-Intensity Due Diligence Principle for Low-Intensity Cyber Operations? (2014) 14 Baltic YB Intl L 1

Barnidge RP, 'The Due Diligence Principle under International Law' (2006) 8 ICLR 81

Barsalou O, 'Making Humanitarian Law in the Cold: The Cold War, the United State and the Genesis of the Geneva Conventions of 1949' (2008) 11 IILJ Emerging Scholars Paper 1–52

Bassiouni M, 'The Normative Framework of International Humanitarian Law: Overlaps, Gaps and Ambiguities' (1998) 8 Trans L Contemp Probs 199

Bederman DJ, 'Lump Sum Agreements and Diplomatic Protection' (2002) Report for the International Law Association Committee on Diplomatic Protection of Persons and Property, 70th Conference New Delhi

Bedjaoui M, *Towards a New International Economic Order* (Holmes & Meier 1979)

Bell C, 'Of Jus Post Bellum and Lex Pacificatoria' in Stahn C, Easterday JS, and Iverson J (eds), *Jus Post Bellum: Mapping the Normative Foundations* (OUP 2014) 197

Bellamy AJ, 'The Responsibilities of Victory: Jus Post Bellum and the Just War' (2008) 34 Rev of Intl Studies 601

Bellinger J III and Haynes W II, 'A US Government Response to the International Committee of the Red Cross Study Customary International Humanitarian Law' (2007) 89 IRRC 44

Bentwich N, *The Law of Private Property in War with a Chapter on Conquest* (Sweet & Maxwell 1907)

Benvenuti P, 'The ICTY Prosecutor and the Review of the NATO Bombing Campaign against the Federal Republic of Yugoslavia' (2001) 12 EJIL 503

Bernhard R, 'Article 103' in Simma B et al (eds), *The Charter of the United Nations: A Commentary* (2nd edn, OUP 2002) 1292

Bernstorff von J, 'The Use of Force in International Law before World War I: On Imperial Ordering and the Ontology of the Nation-State' (2018) 29(1) EJIL 233

Billing T and Lugg A, 'Conflicted Capital: Bilateral Investment Treaties and Post-Conflict Economic Recovery' (2019) 63(2) J Conflict Resol 373

Bjorklund AK, 'Emergency Exceptions: State of Necessity and Force Majeure' in Muchlinski P, Ortino F, and Schreuer C (eds), *The Oxford Handbook of International Law* (OUP 2008) 499

Black E, *IBM and the Holocaust: The Strategic Alliance between Nazi Germany and America's Most Powerful Corporation* (Dialog Press 2012)

Blomberg SB and Hess GD, 'The Temporal Links between Conflict and Economic Activity' (2002) 46 (1) J Conflict Resol 74

Bonnitcha J, 'Investment Treaties and Transition from Authoritarian Rule' (2014) 15 JWIT 965

Bonnitcha J, Poulsen L, and Waibel M, *The Political Economy of the Investment Treaty Regime* (OUP 2017)

Boon KE, 'Obligations of the New Occupier: The Contours of Jus Post Bellum' (2009) 31 Loyola LA Intl and Comp L Rev 57

Boothby W, *The Law of Targeting* (OUP 2012)

Borchard E, '"Responsibility of States" at the Hague Codification Conference' (1930) 24 AJIL 517

Borchard EM, *Diplomatic Protection of Citizens Abroad* (The Banks Law Publishing 1915)

Bothe M, 'Legal Restraints on Targeting: Protection of Civilian Population and the Changing Faces of Modern Conflicts' (2001) 31 Is YHR 35

Bothe M, 'The Protection of the Civilian Population and NATO Bombing on Yugoslavia: Comments on a Report to the Prosecutor of the ICTY' (2001) 12 EJIL 531

Bothe M et al, *New Rules for Victims of Armed Conflicts: Commentary on the Two 1977 Protocols Additional to the Geneva Conventions of 1949* (2nd edn, Martinus Nijhoff 2013)

Boucht J, *The Limits of Asset Confiscation. On the Legitimacy of Extended Appropriation of Criminal Proceeds* (Hart Publishing 2017)

Bray HL, 'SOI—Save Our Investments! International Investment Law and International Humanitarian Law' (2013) 14(3) JWIT 578

Brower CN and Brueschke JD, *The Iran-United States Claims Tribunal* (Nijhoff 1998)

Brown C, *A Common Law of International Adjudication* (OUP 2007)

Brown C, *Commentaries on Selected Model Investment Treaties* (OUP 2013)

Brownlie I, *System of the Law of Nations: State Responsibility State Responsibility, Part I* (Clarendon Press 1983)

Brownlie I, Principles of Public International Law (OUP 2008)

Bücheler G, *Proportionality in Investor-State Arbitration* (OUP 2015)

Burke-White WW, 'Inter-Relationships between the Investment Law and Other International Legal Regimes' (Think Piece, October 2015) E15 Task Force on Investment Policy 1–19

Burke-White WW and von Staden A, 'Investment Protection in Extraordinary Times: The Interpretation and Application of Non-Precluded Measures Provisions in Bilateral Investment Treaties' (2008) 48(2) Va J Intl L 308Buxbaum RM, 'A Legal History of International Reparations' (2005) 23(2) Berkeley J Intl L 314

Byron C, 'A Blurring of the Boundaries: The Application of International Humanitarian Law by Human Rights Bodies' (2006–2007) 47 Va J Intl L 839
Calvo C, 'De la Non-Responsibilité des États a Raison des Dommages Soufferts par des Étrangers en Cas d'Émeute ou de Guerre Civile' (1869) 1 (1d series) Revue de Droit International et de Legislation Comparee 427
Calvo C, *Le droit international théorique et pratique, vol 3* (3rd edn, Pedone-Lauriel 1880)
Cassese A, 'The Geneva Protocols of 1977 on the Humanitarian Law of Armed Conflict and Customary International Law' (1984) 2 UCLA Pacific Basin LJ 55
Cassimatis A, 'International Humanitarian Law, International Human Rights Law, and Fragmentation of International Law' (2007) 56 ICLQ 623
Charney J, 'The Impact on the International Legal System of the Growth of International Courts and Tribunals' (1999) 31 NYU JILP 697
Cheng B, *General Principles of Law as Applied by International Courts and Tribunals* (CUP 2006)
Chinkin CM, 'Crisis and the Performance of International Agreements: The Outbreak of War in Perspective' (1981) 7 Yale J World Pub Ord 177–208
Colby E, 'How to Fight Savage Tribes' (1927) 21 AJIL 279
Cole T, *The Structure of Investment Arbitration* (Routledge 2013)
Collier P et al, *Breaking the Conflict Trap: Civil War and Development Policy* (World Bank Publications 2003)
Commission JP, 'Precedent in Investment Treaty Arbitration: a Citation Analysis of a Developing Jurisprudence' (2007) 24(2) JIA 129
Conforti, B, 'Consistency among Treaty Obligations' in Cannizzaro E (ed), *The Law of Treaties Beyond the Vienna Convention* (OUP 2011)
Conforti B and Labella A, 'Invalidity and Termination of Treaties: The Role of National Courts' (1990) 1 EJIL 44
Cordero Moss G, 'Full Protection and Security' in Reinisch A (ed), *Standards of Investment Protection* (OUP 2008)
Cordonier Segger MC et al, *Sustainable Development in World Investment Law* (Kluwer 2010)
Corn G, 'War, Law, and Oft Overlooked Value of Process as a Precautionary Measure' (2015) 42 Pepp L Rev 419
Corn G, 'Humanitarian Regulation of Hostilities: The Decisive Element of Context' (2018) 51(3) VJTL 763
Corten O and Klein P (eds), *The Vienna Conventions on the Law of Treaties, The Commentary* (OUP 2011)
Costelloe D, 'Treaty Succession in Annexed Territory' (2016) 65 ICLQ 343
Coupland R, 'Humanity: What Is It and How Does It Influence International Law' (2001) 83(844) IRRC 969–89
Cox J, *Expropriation in Investment Treaty Arbitration* (OUP 2019)
Coyle JF, 'The Treaty of Friendship, Commerce and Navigation in Modern Era' (2012) 51 Columb J Trans L 302
Crawford J, *State Responsibility, General Part* (CUP 2013)
Criddle EJ, 'Humanitarian Financial Intervention' (2013) 24(2) EJIL 584
Cullen A, *The Concept of Non-International Armed Conflict in International Humanitarian Law* (CUP 2010)
Daude C and Stein E, 'The Quality of Institutions and Foreign Direct Investment' (2007) 19(3) Econ Pol 317
Davenport F (ed) *Two European Treaties Bearing on the History of the United States and Its Dependencies, 1650-1697* (Washington Carnegie 1929)

David E, 'Primary and Secondary Rules' in Crawford J et al (eds), *The Law of International Responsibility* (OUP 2010) 27

Dawidowicz M, *Third-Party Countermeasures in International Law* (CUP 2017)

De Brabandere E, 'Host States' Due Diligence Obligations in International Investment Law' (2015) 42(2) Syracuse J Intl Com 320

De Mestral A and Gruchalla-Wesierski T, *Extraterritorial Application of Laws of Export Control Legislation* (Brill 1990)

Delaume G, 'Excuse for Non-Performances and Force Majeure in Economic Development Agreements' (1971) 10 Columb J Trans L 242

Delbrück J, 'War, Effect on Treaties' in Bernhardt R (ed), *Encyclopedia of Public International Law: Vol* IV (Amsterdam Elsevier 1982) 311

Desierto DA, *Necessity and National Emergency Clauses: Sovereignty in Modern Treaty Interpretation* (Martinus Nijhoff 2012)

Detter I, *The Law of War* (2nd edn, CUP 2000)

Diamond L and Plattner L eds, *Nationalism, Ethnic Conflict, and Democracy* (Johns Hopkins University Press 1994)

Diehl A, *The Core Standard in International Investment Protection: Fair and Equitable Treatment* (Kluwer 2012)

Dijn P and Van Hoof GJH, *Theory and Practice of the European Convention on Human Rights* (2nd edn, Kluwer 1990)

Dinstein Y, *The Conduct of Hostilities under the Law of Armed Conflict* (3rd ed, CUP 2016)

Dinstein Y, 'Keynote Address: The Recent Evolution of the International Law of Armed Conflict: Confusions, Constraints, and Challenges' (2018) 51(3) VJTL 701

Dixit A, 'International Trade, Foreign Direct Investment and Security' (2011) 3 Annual Rev Econ 191

Dolzer R, 'The Settlement of War-Related Claims: Does International Law Recognize a Victim's Private Right of Action-Lessons after 1945' (2002) 20(1) Berkeley J Intl L 296

Dolzer R, 'Fair and Equitable Treatment' (2005) 39 Intl Lawy 87

Dolzer R, 'The Impact of International Investment Treaties on Domestic Administrative Law' (2006) 37 Intl L and Pol 952

Dolzer R and Schreuer C, *Principles of International Investment Law* (2nd edn, OUP 2012)

Dörr O and Schmalenbach K, *Vienna Convention on the Law of Treaties* (Springer 2011)

Doswald-Beck L and Vité S, 'International Humanitarian Law and Human Rights Law' (1993) 293 IRRC 94

Douglas Z, 'The Hybrid Foundations of Investment Treaty Arbitration' (2003) 74 BYIL 151

Douglas Z, *The International Law of Investment Claims* (CUP 2009)

Dreher A and Voigt S, 'Does Membership in International Organizations Increase Governments Credibility? Testing the Effects of Delegating Powers' (2011) 39(3) J Comp Econ326

Dumberry P, 'Requiem for Crimea: Why Tribunals Should Have Declined Jurisdiction over the Claims of Ukrainian Investors against Russian under the Ukraine-Russia BIT' (2018) 9 JIDS 506

Dunn FS, *The Protection of Nationals: A Study in the Application of International Law* (The Johns Hopkins Press 1932)

Dupuy PM et al (eds), *Human Rights in International Investment Law and Arbitration* (OUP 2009)

Duxbury A, 'Drawing Lines in the Sand—Characterising Conflicts for the Purpose of Teaching International Humanitarian Law' (2007) 8 MJIL 259

Eagleton C, *The Responsibility of States in International Law* (The New York University Press 1928)
Economides C, 'Content of the Obligation: Obligations of Means and Obligations of Result' in Crawford J et al (eds), *The Law of International Responsibility* (OUP 2010) 371
Elagab O, *The Legality of Non-Forcible Counter-Measures in International Law* (Clarendon Press 1988)
Elagab O, 'Economic Measures against Developing Countries' (1992) 41 ICLQ 682
Elias O, 'General International Law in the European Court of Justice: From Hypothesis to Reality' (2000) 31 NYIL 3
Fauchald OK, 'The Legal Reasoning of ICSID Tribunals—an Empirical Analysis' (2008) 19(2) EJIL 301
Fearon J and Laitin D, 'Violence and the Social Construction of Ethnic Identity' (2000) 54(4) Intl Org 845
Feighery TJ, 'The United Nations Compensation Commission' in Giorgetti C (ed), *The Rules, Practice, and Jurisprudence of International Courts and Tribunals* (Nijhoff 2012) 515
Feller AH, *The Mexican Claims Commission 1923–1934: A Study in the Law and Procedure of International Tribunals* (Macmillan Company 1935)
Fitzmaurice GG, 'The Juridical Clauses of the Peace Treaties' (1948) 73 Recueil Des Cours 260
Fitzmaurice GG, 'The Law and Procedure of the International Court of Justice: Treaty Interpretation and Certain Other Treaty Points' (1951) 28 BYIL 1
Fitzmaurice M and Elias O, *Contemporary Issues in the Law of Treaties* (Eleven 2005)
Fleck D (ed), *The Handbook of Humanitarian Law in Armed Conflict* (OUP 1995)
Forrest CJS, 'The Doctrine of Military Necessity and the Protection of Cultural Property during Armed Conflict' (2007) 37(2) Calif West Intl L J 177
Foster G, 'Recovering "Protection and Security": The Treaty Standard's Obscure Origins, Forgotten Meaning, and Key Current Significance' (2012) 45 VJTL 1095
Franck S, 'The Legitimacy Crisis in Investment Treaty Arbitration: Privatizing Public International Law Through Inconsistent Decisions' (2005) 73 Fordham L Rev 1521
Freeman A, *Responsibility of States for Unlawful Acts of their Armed Forces* (AW Sijthoff 1957)
Gabriel S and Satish V, 'US Intervention in Nicaragua: A Success or Failure?' (1990) 51(4) Ind J Pol Sci 565
Gallus N, 'The Influence of the Host State's Level of Development on International Investment Treaty Standard of Protection' (2005) 6 JWIT 711
Gallus N, 'The Fair and Equitable Treatment Standard and the Circumstances of the State' in Brown C and Miles K (eds), *Evolution in Investment Treaty Law and Arbitration* (CUP 2011)
Garcia Mora MR, 'The Calvo Clause in Latin American Constitutions and International Law' (1950) 33 Marquette L Rev 205
García-Amador FV, Sohn L, and Baxter R, *Recent Codification of the Law of State Responsibility for Injuries to Aliens* (Brill 1974)
Gardam J, 'Proportionality and Force in International Law' (1993) 87 AJIL 391
Gardam J, *Necessity, Proportionality and the Use of Force by States* (CUP 2004)
Gardiner R, *Treaty Interpretation* (OUP 2008)
Garner B, *A Dictionary of Modern Legal Usage* (2nd edn, OUP 1995)
Garner JW, 'Responsibility of States for Injuries Suffered by Foreigners within their Territories on Account of Mob Violence, Riots and Insurrection' (1927) 21 ASIL Proceedings 49
Gathii JT, 'War's Legacy in International Investment Law' (2009) 11 ICLR 353

Gathii JT, *War, Commerce and International Law* (OUP 2010)
Gathings JA, *International Law and American Treatment of Alien Enemy Property* (American Council of Public Affairs 1940)
Ginty RM, 'Looting in the Context of Violent Conflict: a Conceptualisation and Typology' (2007) 25(5) TWQ 857
Gioia A, 'The Role of the European Court of Human Rights in Monitoring Compliance with Humanitarian Law in Armed Conflict' in Ben-Naftali O (ed), *International Human Rights and International Humanitarian Law* (OUP 2011) 226
Giorgetti C, 'Who Decides Who Decides In International Investment Arbitration?' (2013) 35 U Pa J Intl L 431
Globerman S and Shapiro D, 'Governance Infrastructure and US Foreign Direct Investment' (2003) 34 J Int Bus Stud 19
Goebel J, 'The International Responsibility of States for Injuries Sustained by Aliens on Account of Mob Violence, Insurrections and Civil Wars' (1914) 8 AJIL 802
Gong G, *The Standard of Civilization in International Society* (Clarendon Press 1984)
Goodman R, 'The Obama Administration and Targeting "War-Sustaining" Objects in Non-International Armed Conflict (2016) 110 AJIL 663
Gray C, *Judicial Remedies in International Law* (OUP 1987)
Gray C, 'Remedies in International Dispute Settlement' in Romano C, Alter KJ, and Shany Y (eds), *The Oxford Handbook of International Adjudication* (OUP 2013) 871
Greenwood C, 'The Twilight of Belligerent Reprisals' in *Essays on War in International Law* (Cameron May 2006)
Greenwood C, 'Historical Development and Legal Basis' in Fleck D and Bothe M (eds), *The Handbook of International Humanitarian Law* (OUP 2007) 1
Grotius H, *De jure belli ac pacis libri tres* (Clarendon Press 1925)
Gudgeon K, 'United States Bilateral Investment Treaties: Comments on Their Origin, Purposes, and General Treatment Standards' (1986) 4(1) Berkeley J Intl L 105
Gunning I, 'Modernizing Customary International Law: The Challenge of Human Rights' (1990–1991) 31 Va J Intl L 211
Gurr R, *Why Men Rebel* (Routledge 1970)
Guzman A, 'Explaining the Popularity of Bilateral Investment Treaties' in Sauvant K and Sachs L (eds), *The Effect of Treaties on Foreign Direct Investment* (OUP 2009)
Hall W, *A Treatise on International Law* (2nd edn, Clarendon Press 1884)
Hallward-Driemeier M, 'Do Bilateral Investment Treaties Attract Foreign Direct Investment? Only a Bit . . . And They Could Bite' (2013) World Bank Policy Research Working Papers No WPS 3121
Hamilton A, *The Defence No. Xxii (Oct. 14, 1795), reprinted in* 19 *The Papers of Alexander Hamilton* (Harold C. Syrett ed, 1973)
Happ R and S Wuschka S, 'Horror Vacui: Or Why Investment Treaties Should Apply to Illegally Annexed Territories' (2016) 33 J Intl Arb 245
Hatchway O and Shapiro S, 'Outcasting: Enforcement in Domestic and International Law' (2011–2012) 121 Yale L J 252
Hayashi, N, 'Military Necessity As A Normative Indifference' (2013) 44 Georget J Intl L 50
Hearden PJ, *Architects of Globalism: Building a New World Order During World War II* (The University of Arkansas Press 2002)
Heathcote S, 'Circumstances Precluding Wrongfulness in the ILC Articles on State Responsibility: Necessity' in Crawford J et al (eds), *Law of International Responsibility* (OUP 2010) 491

Heintze H, 'On the Relationship between Human Rights Law Protection and International Humanitarian Law' (2004) 86(856) IRRC 798

Henckaerts JM, 'Concurrent Application of International Humanitarian Law and Human Rights Law: Victim Perspective' in Arnold R and Quénivet NR (eds), *International Humanitarian Law and Human Rights Law: Towards a New Merger in International Law* (Brill 2008) 250

Henckaerts JM and Doswald-Beck L, *International Committee of the Red Cross, Customary International Humanitarian Law, vol I, Rules* (CUP 2005)

Henckels C, 'Indirect Expropriation and the Right to regulate: Revisiting Proportionality Analysis and the Standard of Review in Investor-State Arbitration' (2012) 15(1) JIEL 223

Henckels C, *Proportionality and Deference in Investor-State Arbitration: Balancing Investment Protection and Regulatory Autonomy* (CUP 2015)

Henckels C, 'Scope Limitation or Affirmative Defence? The Purpose and Role of Investment Treaty Exception Clauses' in Paddeu F and Bartels L (eds), *Exceptions and Defences in International Law* (OUP 2019)

Henderson I, *The Contemporary Law of Targeting* (Martinus Nijhoff 2009)

Hernández G, 'The Interaction Between Investment Law and the Law of Armed Conflict in the Interpretation of Full Protection and Security Clauses' in Baetens F (ed), *Investment Law Within International Law: Integrationist Perspectives* (CUP 2011) 21

Hibbs D, *Mass Political Violence: A Cross-National Causal Analysis* (Wiley-Interscience Publication 1973)

Hill-Cawthorne L, 'Humanitarian Law, Human Rights Law and the Bifurcation of Armed Conflict' (2015) 64 ICLQ 293

Hill-Cawthorne L, 'Just Another Case of Treaty Interpretation? Reconciling Humanitarian Law and Human Rights Law in the ICJ' in Andenas M and Bjorge E (eds), *A Farewell to Fragmentation: Reassertion and Convergence in International Law* (CUP 2015)

Holtzmann HM and Kristjánsdóttir E, *International Mass Claims Processes* (OUP 2007)

Howse R, 'The Concept of Odious Debt in Public International Law' (2007) UNCTAD Discussion Paper No 185 UNCTAD/OSG/DP/2007/4

Huffcut EW, 'International Liability for Mob Injuries' (1891) 2 Ann Am Acad Pol Soc Sci 69

Hull I, *A Scrap of Paper: Making and Breaking International Law during the Great War* (Cornell University Press 2014)

Hurst CJB, 'The Effect of War on Treaties' (1921) 2 BYIL 37

Hyde CC, *International Law Chiefly as Interpreted and Applied by the United States* (Little Brown 1922)

Ishay M, *The Human Rights Reader* (Routledge 1997)

Jaworski E, '"Military Necessity" and "Civilian Immunity": Where is the Balance?' (2003) 1 Chinese J Intl L 201

Jenks W, 'Conflict of Law-Making Treaties' (1953) 30 BYIL 401

Jensen E, 'Precautions against the Effects of Attacks in Urban Areas' (2016) 98(1) IRRC 147

Jochnick C and Normand R, 'The Legitimation of Violence: A Critical History of the Laws of War (1994) 35 HILJ 49

Jubilut LL, 'Toward a New Jus Post Bellum: The United Nations Peacebuilding Commission and the Improvement of Post-Conflict Efforts and Accountability' (2011) 20 Min J Intl L 26

Kahn P, 'Lessons for International Law from the Gulf War' (1992–1993) 45 Stans L Rev 425

Kalshoven F, 'Reprisals and the Protection of Civilians: Two Recent Decisions of the Yugoslavia Tribunal' in Vohran LC et al (eds), *Man's Inhumanity to Man: Essays on International Law in Honour of Antonio Cassese* (Kluwer 2003)

Karl W, 'Conflicts between Treaties' in Bernhardt R (ed), *Encyclopedia of Public International Law* (North-Holland 1984) 467
Katzir R 'Four Comments on the Application of Proportionality under the Law of Armed Conflict' (2018) 51(3) VJTL 857
Keen MH, *The Laws of War in the Late Middle Ages* (Keegan Paul 1965)
Keen MH, *Chivalry* (Yale University Press 1984)
Keene E, *Beyond the Anarchical Society: Grotius, Colonialism and Order in World Politics* (CUP 2002)
Kennedy D, *The Dark Sides of Virtue: Reassessing International Humanitarianism* (2004)
Keynes JM, *The Economic Consequences of the Peace* (Harcourt, Brace, and Howe 1919)
Klabbers J, 'Re-inventing the Law of Treaties: The Contribution of the EC Courts' (1999) 30 NYIL 45
Koivurova T, *Due Diligence*, in *Max Planck Encyclopaedia of International Law* (OUP 2010)
Koskenniemi M and Leino P, 'Fragmentation of International Law? Postmodern Anxieties' (2002) 15 Leiden J Intl L 553
Kretzmer D, 'Rethinking Application of IHL in Non-International Armed Conflict' (2009) 42 Isr L Rev 8
Kriebaum U, 'The Relevance of Economic and Political Conditions for Protection under Investment Treaties' (2011) 10 L and Prac of Intl Ct and Trib 383
Kriebaum U and Reinisch A, 'Property, Right to, International Protection' in Wolfrum R (ed), *Max Planck Encyclopedia of Public International Law* (OUP 2009)
Kulick A (ed), *Reassertion of Control over the Investment Treaty Regime* (CUP 2017)
Kunz J, 'The Laws of War' (1956) 50 AJIL 313
Kunz JL, 'The Chaotic Status of the Law of War and the Urgent Necessity of their Revision' (1951) 45(1) AJIL 37
Kurtz J, 'The Use and Abuse of the WTO Law in Investor-State arbitration: Competition and its Discontents' (2009) 20 EJIL 794
Kurtz J, 'Adjudging the Exceptional at International Investment Law: Security, Public Order and Financial Crisis' (2010) 59(2) ICLQ 325
Langford M, Behn D, and Lie R, 'The Revolving Door in International Investment Arbitration' (2017) 20 JIEL 301
Lauren PG, *The Evolution of International Human Rights* (University of Pennsylvania Press 1998)
Lauterpacht H, *The Function of Law in the International Community* (The Clarendon Press 1933)
Lauterpacht H, 'Restrictive Interpretation and the Principle of Effectiveness in the Interpretation of Treaties' (1949) 26 BYIL 48
Legarre S, 'The Historical Background of the Police Power' (2007) 9 U Pa J Const L 745
Leonhardsen E, 'Looking for Legitimacy: Exploring Proportionality Analysis in Investment Treaty Arbitration' (2012) 3(1) JIDS 95
Lillich R (ed), *International Law of State Responsibility for Injury to Aliens* (The University Press of Virginia 1983)
Lillich RB and Weston BH, *International Claims: Their Settlements by Lump Sum Agreements, Part I: The Commentary* (University Press of Virginia 1975)
Lindroos A, 'Addressing Norm Conflicts in a Fragmented Legal System: The Doctrine of Lex Specialis' (2005) 74 Nordic J Intl L 27
Lissitzyn OJ, 'Treaties and Changed Circumstances (Rebus sic Stantibus)' (1967) 61 AJIL 895
Littauer RM, 'Confiscation of the Property of Technical Enemies' (1942–43) 52 Yale L J 739
Lorca A, *Mestizo International Law: A Global Intellectual History 1842–1933* (CUP 2014)

MacMillian J, *On Liberal Peace: Democracy, War and the International Order* (I.B. Tauris 1998)
Maier CS, 'Targeting the Cities: Debates and Silences about the Aerial Bombing of World War II' (2005) 87(859) IRRC 429
Mapp W, *The Iran-United States Claims Tribunal, The First Ten Years, 1981–1991* (MUP 1996)
Marceau G, 'Conflict Norms and Conflicts of Jurisdictions: The Relationships between the WTO Agreement and MEAs and other Treaties' (2001) 35 JWT 1081
Marshall M, *Third World War* (Rowman & Littlefield 1999)
Matheson M, *International Civil Tribunals and Armed Conflict* (Brill/Nijhoff 2012)
Maupin JA, 'Differentiating among International Investment Disputes' in Douglas Z, Pauwelyn J, Viñuales JE (eds), *The Foundations of International Investment Law: Bringing Theory Into Practice* (OUP 2014) 469
Mayorga O, 'Arbitrating War: Military Necessity as a Defence to the Breach of Investment Treaty Obligations' (Policy Brief, August 2013) Program on Humanitarian Policy and Conflict Research Harvard University
Mayorga O, 'Occupants, Beware of BITs: Applicability of Investment Treaties to Occupied Territories' (2017) 19 Palestine YB Intl L 136
Mazumder S, 'Can I Stay a Bit Longer? The Effect of Bilateral Investment Treaties on Political Survival' (2016) 11(4) Rev Intl Org 477
McConnell D, 'The Tamil People's Right to Self-Determination' (2008) 21(1) Camb Rev Intl Aff 59
McCoubrey H, *International Humanitarian Law: Modern Developments in the Limitation of Warfare* (Ashgate 1998) 1
McDougal MS and Feliciano F, 'International Coercion and World Public Order: The General Principles of the Law of War' (1958) 67 Yale L J 771
McGoldrick D, 'Human Rights and Humanitarian Law in the UK Courts' (2007) 40 Is L R 527
Mcintyre S, *Legal Effects of World War II on Treaties of the United States* (Martinus Nijhoff 1958)
Mclachlan C, 'The Principle of Systemic Integration and Article 31(3)(c) of the Vienna Convention' (2005) 54(2) ICLQ 279
Mclachlan C, 'Is there an Evolving Customary International Law on Investment?' (2016) 41(2) ICSID Rev 257
Mclachlan C, Shore L, and Weiniger M, *International Arbitration: Substantive Principles* (2nd edn, OUP 2017)
McNair A, *International Law* Opinions (CUP 1956)
McNair AD, 'The Effects of Peace Treaties upon Private Rights' (1939–1941) 7 Cam L J 379
McNair AD, *The Law of Treaties* (OUP 1961)
McNeal G, 'Targeted Killing and Accountability' (2014) 102 Georget L J 681
Mégret F 'From Savages to Unlawful Combatants: A Postcolonial Look at International Law's "Other"' in Orford A (ed), *International Law and Its Others* (CUP 2006) 265
Meron T, *Human Rights and Humanitarian Norms as Customary Law* (Clarendon Press 1989)
Meron T, 'The Humanization of Humanitarian Law' (2000) 94 AJIL 239
Meron T, *The Humanization of International Law* (Martinus Nijhoff 2006)
Milanović M, 'Lessons for Human Rights and Humanitarian Law in the War on Terror: Comparing Hamdan and the Israeli Targeted Killings Case' (2007) 89(886) IRRC 373

Milanović M, 'Norm Conflicts, International Humanitarian Law and Human Rights Law' in Ben-Naftali O (ed), *International Human Rights and International Humanitarian Law* (OUP 2011) 95

Miles K, *The Origin of International Investment Law: Empire, Environment and the Safeguarding of Capital* (CUP 2014)

Miller H, *Treaties and Other International Acts of the United States of America*, vol 2 (Government Printing Office 1931)

Moore J, *History and Digest of International Arbitrations to which United States has been a Party* (GPO 1898)

Moore J, *A Digest of International Law: As Embodied in Diplomatic Discussions, Treaties and Other International Agreements, International Awards, the Decisions of Municipal Law, and the Writings of Jurists* (Government Printing Office 1906)

Morth TA, 'Considering Our Position: Viewing Information Warfare as a Use of Force Prohibited by Article 2(4) of the U.N. Charter' (1998) 30(2/3) Case W Res J Intl L 567

Mullerson R, 'The ABM Treaty: Changed Circumstances, Extraordinary Events, Supreme Interests and International Law' (2001) 50 ICLQ 509

Murphy SD, *Humanitarian Intervention: The United Nations in an Evolving World Order* (U Pen Press 1996)

Murphy SD, Snider TR, and Kidane W, *Litigating War: Mass Civil Injury and the Eritrea-Ethiopia Claims Commission* (OUP 2013)

Mus J, 'Conflicts between Treaties in International Law' (1998) 45 NILR 207

Neff SC, *War and the Law of Nations—A General History* (CUP 2005)

Neumayer E and Spess L, 'Do Bilateral Investment Treaties Increase Foreign Direct Investment to Developing Countries' in Sauvant K and Sachs L (eds), *The Effect of Treaties on Foreign Direct Investment* (OUP 2009)

Newcombe A, 'The Use of General Exceptions in IIAs: Increasing Legitimacy or Uncertainty' in De Mestral A and Celine Levesque C (eds), *Improving International Investment Agreements* (Routledge 2012)

Newcombe A and Paradell L, *Law and Practice of Investment Treaties* (Kluwer 2009)

Newton M, 'Reconsidering Reprisals' (2010) 20(361) Duke J Comp L 361

Newton M, 'Reframing the Proportionality Principle' (2018) 51(3) VJTL 867

O'Connell ME, 'Humanitarian Assistance in Non-International Armed Conflict, The Fourth Wave of Rights, Duties and Remedies' (2001) 31 Is Ybk on HR 183

O'Connell ME, 'Defining Armed Conflict' (2008) 13 JCSL 393

O'Connell DP, *International Law*, vol 1 (Stevens & Sons 1970)

O'Connell ME, 'Responsibility to Peace: A Critique of R2P' (2010) 4(1) J Interv Statebuilding 39

Oeter S, 'Methods and Means of Warfare' in Fleck D (ed), *The Handbook of International Humanitarian Law* (OUP 2013)

Oppenheim L, *International Law* (7th edn, Longmans 1952)

Orakhelashvili A, 'The Interaction between Human Rights and Humanitarian Law: Fragmentation, Conflict, Parallelism, or Convergence' (2008) 19 EJIL 161

Orford A, 'Moral Internationalism and the Responsibility to Protect' (2013) 24(1) EJIL 83

Orrego Vicuña F, 'Maintenance and Restoration of International Peace and Security through Arbitration and Judicial Settlement' in von Arnauld A et al (eds), *100 Years of Peace Through Law: Past and Future* (Duncker & Humblot 2015)

Österdahl I and van Zadel E, 'What Will Jus Post Bellum Mean? Of New Wines and Old Bottles' (2009) 14 JCSL 175

Ostřanský J, 'The Termination and Suspension of Bilateral Investment Treaties due to an Armed Conflict' (2015) 6 JIDS 136
Paddeu FI, 'A Genealogy of Force Majeure in International Law' (2012) 82(1) BYIL 381
Paparinskis M, 'Investment Arbitration and the Law of Countermeasures' (2008) 79 BYIL 264
Paparinskis M, 'Investment Treaty Arbitration and the (New) Law of State Responsibility (2013) 24(2) EJIL 617
Paparinskis M, *The International Minimum Standard and Fair and Equitable Treatment* (OUP 2013)
Paparinskis M, 'Circumstances Precluding Wrongfulness in International Investment Law' (2016) 31(2) ICSID Rev 484
Parkerson J, 'United States Compliance with Humanitarian Law Respecting Civilians during Operation Just Cause' (1991) 133 Mil L Rev 31
Parks WH, 'Air War and the Law of War' (1992) 32 Air Force L Rev 1
Parlett K, *The Individual in the International Legal System* (CUP 2011)
Pauwelyn J, *Conflict of Norms in Public International Law: How WTO Law Relates to Other Rules of International Law* (CUP 2003)
Pejić J, 'Conflict Classification and the Law Applicable to Detention and the Use of Force' in Wilmshurst E (ed), *International Law and the Classification of Conflicts* (OUP 2012)
Pellet A, 'Police Powers or the State's Right to Regulate' in Kinnear M et al (eds), *Building International Investment Law—The First 50 Years of ICSID* (Kluwer Law International 2016) 449
Peng BTZ, 'The International Law Commission's Draft Articles on the Effects of Armed Conflicts on Treaties: Evaluating the Applicability of Impossibility of Performance and Fundamental Change' (2013) 3 Asian J Intl L 51
Perez-Aznar F, 'Investment Protection in Exceptional Situations: Compensation-for-Losses Clauses in IIAs' (2017) 32(3) ICSID Review 696
Peterson T et al, *American Foreign Relations: A History Since 1895*, Vol 2 (7th edn, Wadsworth 2010)
Pissilo-Mazzeschi R, 'The Due Diligence Rule and the Nature of the International Responsibility of States' (1992) 35 German YB Intl L 9
Prescott MK, 'How War Affects Treaties between Belligerents: A Case Study of the Gulf War' (1993) 7(1) Emory Intl L Rev 197
Queguiner JF, 'Precautions under the Law Governing the Conduct of Hostilities (2006) 88(864) IRRC 793
Ralston J, *Venezuelan Arbitrations of 1903* (GPO 1904)
Ralston JH, *The Law and Procedure of International Tribunals* (Stanford University Press 1926)
Rank R, 'Modern War and the Validity of Treaties' (1952) 38(3) Corn L Q 321
Rasaratnam M, *Tamils and the Nation: India and Sri Lanka Compared* (OUP 2016)
Reinisch A, 'Necessity in International Investment Arbitration—An Unnecessary Split in Opinion in Recent ICSID Cases?' (2007) 8 JWIT 191
Ripinsky S with Williams K, *Damages in International Investment Law* (BIICL 2008)
Roberts A, 'Clash of Paradigms: Actors and Analogies Shaping the Investment Treaty System' (2013) 107 AJIL 45
Roberts A, 'State-to-State Investment Treaty Arbitration: A Hybrid Theory of Interdependent Rights and Shared Interpretive Authority' (2014) 55 HILJ 11
Roberts A, 'Triangular Treaties: the Nature and Limits of Investment Treaty Rights' (2015) 56(2) HILJ 353

Roberts G, 'The New Rules of Waging War: The Case against Ratification of Additional Protocol I' (1985–1986) 26 Va J Intl L 109

Rogers APV, *Law on the Battlefield* (Manchester University Press 1996)

Rogers APV, 'The Principle of Proportionality' in Hensel HM (ed), *The Legitimate Use of Military Force: The Just War Tradition and the Customary Law of Armed Conflict* (Ashgate 2008)

Ronen Y, 'Treaties and Armed Conflict' in Tams CJ, Tzanakopoulos A, and Zimmermann A (eds), *Research Handbook on the Law of Treaties* (Edward Elgar 2013)

Root E, 'Basis of Protection to Citizens Residing Abroad' (1910) 4 AJIL 517

Rosenrance R and Thompson P, 'Trade, Foreign Investment and Security' (2003) Annu Rev Polit Sci 377

Rossi CR, *Equity and International Law, A Legal Realist Approach to International Decisionmaking* (Transnational Publishers 1993)

Rubinstein A, 'The Soviet Union and Iran under Khomeini' (1981) 57(4) International Affairs 599

Ryk-Lakhman I, 'Foreign Investments as Non-Human Targets' in Baade B et al (eds), *International Humanitarian Law in Areas of Limited Statehood—Adaptable and Legitimate or Rigid and Unreasonable?* (Nomos 2018) 171

Sabahi B, *Compensation and Restitution in Investor-State Arbitration: Principles and Practice* (OUP 2011)

Salacuse J, *The Law of Investment Treaties* (2nd edn, OUP 2015)

Samaranayaka G, *Political Violence in Sri Lanka, 1971–1987* (Gyan Publishing House 2008)

Sands P, 'Treaty, Custom and the Cross-fertilization of International Law' (1998) 1(1) Yale HRDLJ 85

Sassoli M, 'Targeting: The Scope and Utility of the Concept of Military Objectives for the Protection of Civilians in Contemporary Armed Conflict' in Whippman D and Evangelista M (eds), *New Wars, New Laws? Applying the Laws of War in 21st-Century Conflicts* (Transnational Publishers 2005) 209

Scarfi JP, *The Hidden History of International Law in the Americas: Empire and Legal Networks* (OUP 2017).

Schill S, 'Do Investment Treaties Chill Unilateral State Regulation or Mitigate Climate Change?' (2009) 24(5) J Intl Arb 496

Schindler D, 'International Humanitarian Law: Its Remarkable Development and Its Persistent Violation' (2003) 5 J Hist Intl L 165, 167

Schmitt M, 'Computer Network Attack and the Use of Force in International Law: Thoughts on a Normative Framework' (1999) 37(3) Colum J Transl L 885

Schmitt MN, 'Military Necessity and Humanity in International Humanitarian Law: Preserving the Delicate Balance' (2010) 50 Va J Intl L 795

Schmitt MN, 'In Defense of Due Diligence in Cyberspace' (2015) 125 Yale LJ Forum 68

Schneiderman D, *Constitutionalizing Economic Globalization: Investment Rules and Democracy's Promise* (CUP 2008)

Schneiderman D, 'Investing in Democracy? Political Process and International Investment Law' (2010) 60(4) U Toronto L J 909

Schreuer C, 'Investment Protection and International Relations' in Reinisch A and Kriebaum U (eds), *The Law of International Relations, Liber Amicorum Hanspeter Neuhold* (Eleven 2007) 345

Schreuer C, 'Full Protection and Security' (2010) 1(2) JIDS 6

Schreuer C, 'The Protection of Investments in Armed Conflicts' in Baetens F (ed), *Investment Law within International Law: Integrationist Perspectives* (CUP 2013) 3

Schreuer C, 'Jurisdiction and Applicable Law Clause in Investment Treaties' (2014) 1(1) McGill J Disp Resol 1
Schreuer C and Kriebaum U, 'From Individual to Community Interest in International Investment Law' in Fastenrath U et al (eds), *From Bilateralism to Community Interest, Essays in Honour of Bruno Simma* (OUP 2011) 1079
Schwarzenberger G, *International Law and Order* (Praeger 1971) 172
Schwarzenberger G, 'Equity in International Law' (1972) 26 YB of World Aff 346
Seidl-Hohenveldern I, Reparations, in 4 Encyclopaedia of Public International Law 178 (Rudolf Bernhardt 2000)
Shalakany A, 'Arbitration and the Third World: A Plea for Reassessing Bias under the Specter of Neo-Liberalism' (2000) 41 HILJ 419
Shamash H, 'How Much is Too Much? An Examination of the Principle of Jus in Bello Proportionality' (2005–2006) 2 Israel Defense Forces L Rev 103
Shany Y, 'Human Rights and Humanitarian Law as Competing Legal Paradigms for Fighting Terror' in Ben-Naftali O (ed), *International Human Rights and International Humanitarian Law* (OUP 2011)
Sharpe JK, 'Iran-United States Claims Tribunal' in Giorgetti C (ed), *The Rules, Practice, and Jurisprudence of International Courts and Tribunals* (Nijhoff 2012)
Shea DR, *The Calvo Clause: A Problem of Inter-American and International Law and Diplomacy* (U Minnesota Press 1955)
Shihata I, 'Towards a Greater Depoliticization of Investment Disputes: The Role of ICSID and MIGA' (1986) 1 ICSID Rev-Foreign Inv L J 1
Siekmann RCR, 'Netherlands State Practice for the Parliamentary Year 1982–1983' (1984) 15 NYIL 321
Silvanie H, 'Responsibility of States for Acts of Insurgent Governments' (1939) 33(1) AJIL 78
Simma B, 'Universality of International Law from the Perspective of a Practitioner' (2009) 20 EJIL 265
Simma B and Pulkowski D, 'Of Planets and the Universe: Self-contained Regimes in International Law' (2003) 17(3) EJIL 484
Simms B and Trim DJB, *Humanitarian Intervention: A History* (CUP 2011)
Sinclair I, *The Vienna Convention on the Laws of Treaties* (2nd edn, MUP 1984)
Sivakumaran S, 'Re-envisaging the International Law of Internal Armed Conflict' (2011) 22(1) EJIL 219
Sloane RD, 'On the Use and Abuse of Necessity in the Law of State Responsibility' (2012) 106 AJIL 447
Solf WA, 'Article 52' in Bothe M et al (eds), *New Rules for Victims of Armed Conflict* (Brill 2013)
Sonnenfeld R, 'Succession and Continuation, A Study on Treaty Practice in Post-War Germany' (1976) 7 Nl Ybk of Intl L 91–130
Sornarajah M, *Resistance and Change in the International Law of Foreign Investment* (CUP 2015)
Sornarajah M, *The International Law on Foreign Investment* (4th edn, CUP 2017)
Soysa De I 'Paradise Is a Bazaar? Greed, Creed, and Governance in Civil War, 1989–1999' (2002) 39(4) J Peace Res 395
Stahn C, 'Jus ad bellum, jus in bello . . . jus post bellum?—Rethinking the Conception of the Law of Armed Force' (2006) 17 EJIL 921
Stahn C, 'Mapping the Discipline(s)' in Stahn C and Kleffner JK (eds), *Jus Post Bellum: Towards a Law of Transition From Conflict to Peace* (TMC Asser Press 2008) 105

Stahn C, Easterday JS, and Iverson J (eds), *Jus Post Bellum: Mapping the Normative Foundations* (OUP 2014)

Starke JG, *An Introduction to International Law* (5th edn, Butterworths 1963)

Stone R, 'Protecting Civilians During Operation Allied Force: The Enduring Importance of the Proportional Response and NATO's Use of Armed Force in Kosovo' (2001–2002) 50 Catholic Univ L Rev 501

Stone Sweet A and Mathews J, 'Proportionality Balancing and Global Constitutionalism' (2008) 47 Colum J Transnatl L 73

Stuyt AM, *Survey of International Arbitrations, 1794–1938* (Martinus Nijhoff 1939)

Sureda AR, *Investment Treaty Arbitration: Judging Under Uncertainty* (CUP 2012)

Szurek S, 'The Notion of Circumstances Precluding Wrongfulness' in Crawford J et al (eds), *The Law of International Responsibility* (OUP 2010) 475

Talmon S, 'The Constitutive versus the Declaratory Theory of Recognition: Tertium non Datur?' (2004) 75 BYIL 101

Tams C, *Enforcing Obligations Erga Omnes in International* Law (CUP 2010)

Tienhaara T, 'Regulatory Chill and the Threat of Arbitration: A View from Political Science' in Brown C and Miles K (eds), *Evolution in Investment Treaty Law and Arbitration* (CUP 2011) 606

Tilly C, *The Politics of Collective Violence* (CUP 2003)

Titi C, 'Police Powers Doctrine and International Investment Law' in Gattini A et al (eds), *General Principles of Law and International Investment Arbitration* (Brill 2018) 323

Tomuschat C, 'Individual Reparation Claims in Instances of Grave Human Rights Violations, The Position under General International Law' in Randelzhofer A and Tomuschat C (eds), *State Responsibility and the Individual, Reparation in Instances of Grave Violations of Human Rights* (Kluwer Law International 1999)

Townley S, 'The Rise of Risk in International Law' (2016) 18(2) Chicago J Intl L 594

Trapp KN, 'Great Resources Mean Great Responsibility: a Framework of Analysis For Assessing Compliance with API Obligations in the Information Age' in Saxon D (ed), *International Humanitarian Law and the Changing Technology of War* (Martinus Nijhoff 2013) 153

Tzevelekos V, 'Reconstructing the Effective Control Criterion in Extraterritorial Humans Rights Breaches: Direct Attribution of Wrongfulness, Due Diligence, and Concurrent Responsibility' (2014) 36(1) Michi L Intl L 129

Vamvoukos A, *Termination of Treaties in International Law: the Doctrine of Rebus Sic Stantibus and Desuetude* (OUP 1985)

Van Aaken A, 'International Investment Law and Decentralized Targeted Sanctions: an Uneasy Relationship' (2015) Columbia FDI Perspectives, No 164, 4 January 2015

Van Banning TRG, *The Human Right to Property* (Intersentia 2002)

Van Harten G, *Investment Treaty Arbitration and Public Law* (OUP 2007)

Van Houtte H, Das H, and Delmartino B, 'The United Nations Compensation Commission' in De Greiff P (ed), *The Handbook of Reparations* (OUP 2008)

Van Houtte H et al, *Post-War Restoration of Property Rights under International Law* (CUP 2008)

Vandevelde K, 'The Bilateral Investment Treaty Program of The United States' (1988) 21 Cornell Intl LJ 201

Vandevelde K, 'Of Politics and Markets: The Shifting Ideology of the BITs' (1993) 11 Intl Tax & Bus Law 159

Vandevelde K, *Bilateral Investment Treaties: History, Policy, and Interpretation* (OUP 2010)

Vandevelde K, *The First Bilateral Investment Treaties: U.S. Postwar Friendship, Commerce, and Navigation Treaties* (OUP 2017)
Vandevelde KJ, *United States Investment Treaties: Policy and Practice* (Kluwer Law and Taxation 1992)
Vandevelde KJ, 'The Economics of Bilateral Investment Treaties' (2000) 41 HILJ 46
Vasciannie SC, 'Bilateral Investment Treaties and Civil Strife: The AAPL/Sri Lanka Arbitration' (1992) 39(3) Nl ILR 332.
Vasquez J, *The War Puzzle* (CUP 1993)
Vattel de E, *The Law Of Nations or The Principles Of Natural* Law (1758), reprinted in *3 The Classics Of International Law 145* (James Brown Scott ed, Charles G Fenwick trans, 1916)
Villiger ME, *Commentary on the 1969 Vienna Convention on the Law of Treaties* (Martinus Nijhoff 2009)
Viñuales JE, 'Sovereignty in Foreign Investment Law' in Douglas Z et al (eds), *Foundations of International Investment Law* (OUP 2014) 329
Vité S, 'Typology of Armed Conflicts in International Humanitarian Law: Legal Concepts and Actual Situations' (2009) 91 IRRC 873
Volterra R, 'International Law Commission Articles on State Responsibility and Investor-State Arbitration: Do Investors Have Rights?' (2010) 25(1) ICSID Rev-FILJ 218
Waibel M, *Sovereign Defaults before International Courts and Tribunals* (CUP 2011)
Waibel M, 'Uniformity versus Specialisation (2): A Uniform Regime of Treaty Interpretation?' in Tams CJ et al (eds), *Research Handbook on the Law of Treaties* (Edgar Elgar 2014)
Waibel M, 'Interpretive Communities in International Law' in Bianchi A et al (eds), *Interpretation in International Law* (OUP 2015)
Waibel M et al (eds), *Backlash against Investment Arbitration* (Kluwer 2010)
Wälde TW and Sabahi B, 'Compensation, Damages, and Valuation in International Investment Law' in Muchlinski P, Ortino P, and Schreuer C (eds), *The Oxford Handbook of International Investment Law* (OUP 2008)
Watkin K, 'Assessing Proportionality: Moral Complexity and Legal Rules' (2005) 8 YIHL (2005) 4
Weiler T, *The Interpretation of International Investment Law* (Martinus Nijhoff 2013)
Weissbrodt D and de la Vega C, *International Human Rights Law: An Introduction* (University of Pennsylvania Press 2007)
Wells-Greco M, 'Operation "Cast Lead: Jus in Bello Proportionality"' (2010) 57 NILR 397
White N and Abass A, 'Countermeasures and Sanctions' in Evans M (ed), *International Law* (2nd edn, OUP 2006)
Wiesse C, *Reglas de Derecho Internacional Aplicables a las Guerras Civiles* (1893)
Wolff C, *Jus Gentium Methodo Scientifica Pertractatum* (1749), reprinted in *2 The Classics Of International Law 9* (James Brown Scott ed, Joseph H Drake trans, 1934) 536
Yackee J, 'Bilateral Investment Treaties, Credible Commitment, and the Rule of (International) Law: Do BITs Promote Foreign Direct Investment?' (2008) 42 L Soc Rev 805
Yacoub A, 'The Case of Ampal v Egypt: What Are the Parameters of the due Diligence Standard?' (*Cambridge International Law Journal*, 16 November 2018) <http://cilj.co.uk/2018/11/16/the-case-of-ampal-v-egypt-what-are-the-parameters-of-the-due-diligence-standard/> accessed 18 December 2018
Yates G, 'State Responsibility for Nonwealth Injuries to Aliens in the Postwar Era' in Lillich R (ed), *International Law of State Responsibility for Injuries to Aliens* (University Press of Virginia 1983) 213

Zegveld L, *Accountability and Armed Opposition Groups in International Law* (CUP 2002)
Zeiler T, *Free Trade, Free World, The Advent of GATT* (The University of North Carolina Press 1999)
Zeitler HE, 'Full Protection and Security' in Schill S (ed), *International Investment Law and Comparable Public Law* (OUP 2010) 184
Zrilič J, 'International Investment Law in the Context of Jus Post Bellum: Are Investment Treaties Likely to Facilitate or Hinder the Transition to Peace?' (2015) 16 JWIT 604
Zrilič J, 'Jurisprudential Interaction between ICSID Tribunals and the International Court of Justice' in Bjorklund AK (ed), *Yearbook on International Investment Law & Policy 2013–2014* (OUP 2015) 305
Zrilič J, 'Armed Conflict as Force Majeure in International Investment Law' (2019) 16(1) Manchester J Intl Econ L 28–56

Index

Tables and figures are indicated by an italic *t* and *f* following the paragraph number. BITs (bilateral investment treaties) are listed in the index under the name of the state party that is first alphabetically.

Note: *For the benefit of digital users, indexed terms that span two pages (e.g., 52–53) may, on occasion, appear on only one of those pages.*